PRESIDENTS and FOREIGN POLICY

SUNY Series on the Presidency:
Contemporary Issues
John Kenneth White, editor

and

SUNY Series in Leadership Studies
Barbara Kellerman, editor

PRESIDENTS and FOREIGN POLICY

Countdown to Ten Controversial Decisions

Edward R. Drachman
and
Alan Shank

with

Edward Kannyo
and
Steven R. Ligon

Foreword by Richard M. Pious

State University of New York Press

Published by
State University of New York Press, Albany

For information, address the State University of New York Press,
90 State Street, Suite 700, Albany, NY 12207

Production by Marilyn P. Semerad
Marketing by Theresa Abad Swierzowski

Library of Congress Cataloging-in-Publication Data

Drachman, Edward R., 1940–
    Presidents and foreign policy : countdown to ten controversial decisions / Edward R. Drachman and Alan Shank, with Edward Kannyo and Steven R. Ligon.
        p.   cm. — (SUNY series in leadership studies) (SUNY series on the presidency)
    Includes bibliographical references and index.
    ISBN 0-7914-3339-0 (hc : alk. paper). — ISBN 0-7914-3340-4 (pbk. : alk. paper)
        1. United States—Foreign relations—1945–1989—Case studies.
2. United States—Foreign relations—1989—Case studies.
3. Presidents—United States—Decision making—Case studies.
I. Shank, Alan, 1936– . II Title. III. Series. IV. Series:
SUNY series on the presidency.
E840.D73   1997
327.73—dc21   96-47514
                                                                                        CIP

10   9   8   7   6   5   4

Contents

Foreword

There is no aspect of American politics more important to understand than foreign policy. The most important decisions a president can make involve the use of our armed forces and other governmental agencies in deterrence or hostilities, humanitarian assistance and peacekeeping, and disaster relief and nation-building. Nothing about the post–Cold War period indicates a lessening of these presidential responsibilities. Though President Clinton may have wished to concentrate on domestic issues, though he campaigned with the strategic insight that "It's the Economy, stupid!," though voters chose him in 1992 over an incumbent president skilled in foreign affairs, foreign policy decision-making predominated in his first term, and his 1996 reelection campaign involved international issues from trade and immigration policies and their impact on the domestic economy, to interventions in Haiti and Bosnia and the issue of the U.S. role in international peacekeeping.

A citizenry informed about foreign affairs, and foreign policy decision-making, is vital in a democracy. It seems ironic that in a media age, with more information about world affairs available (and at lower cost) than ever before in our history, most Americans know and care little about world politics, and have only the foggiest idea of how American foreign policy is made. The lunatic fringe on the right embraces theories of a global conspiracy led by the United Nations, the International Monetary Fund, the Trilateral Commission, and Wall Street banking houses; in its view the U.S. government has become a tool of "one-world" conspirators about to impose its will by sending "black helicopters" down on an unsuspecting public. Radicals on the left see the hand of large corporate interests and the CIA in all foreign policy decisions. In the Hollywood version of presidential decision-making, corrupt and spineless politicians in the White House muzzle our military and intelligence officers and care more for their careers than for the country. Most Americans are too sensible to embrace conspiracy theories, but are nonetheless puzzled about the U.S. role in world affairs, and inclined to believe that presidents have neither been decisive nor effective enough in world affairs to defend the U.S. national interest. In this view, Uncle Sam too often becomes Uncle Sucker. Perhaps the problem is information overload; perhaps it is also a lack of good theory, clear analysis, and effective description of how foreign policy decisions are made.

How can we do better? Edward Drachman and Alan Shank have hit on the answer. They have created superb case studies of controversial presidential decisions. The case study approach is not new: what is exciting is the pedagogy they employ—the countdown approach. These cases are forward looking rather than retrospective: they describe each issue the president faced as it unfolded, and as it presented itself to the White House and the nation for decision. By using the concepts of forward planning (getting from here to there through a series of steps) and backward mapping (visualizing the desired outcome and working backwards to find the steps needed to achieve it), and by discussing the pitfalls of groupthink (the dysfunctions that occur within the presidential advisory system), Drachman and Shank offer the reader the tools needed to assess how influential presidential decision-making was to the ultimate outcome of each case study.

The advantages of presenting case studies through the viewpoint of the president—putting the reader in the Oval Office during the countdown to decision—are twofold. The cases become much more vivid to the reader because of the dramatic tension involved in unfolding events: even for seasoned scholars the method allows one to forget for a moment the historical outcome and immerse oneself in the choices a president and his advisers faced. The reader never analyzes the decisions with the benefit of hindsight, but always faces the decision *in the same way* that the U.S. government faced them. This "face forward" approach is the best antidote I know for the cynicism about the motives and capabilities for our government. Asking the reader, "What would you do *now*?" often gives a different answer than asking "What should the government have done *then*?"

The countdown approach to controversial presidential decisions is a major contribution to our understanding of presidential decision-making in foreign policy, not only for undergraduate and graduate students, but also for the general reader who wishes a better understanding of how presidents decide, and how their decisions affect our national interest. Drachman and Shank have produced a truly *propaedeutic* work: a study that ought to precede the reading of other analytical and theoretical approaches to presidential decision-making in foreign policy.

RICHARD M. PIOUS

Preface

The idea for this book originated with our determination that there was a need for alternative readings and teaching approaches in our courses on the presidency, U.S. foreign policy, and American pubic policy that would probe major issues and problems in a more in-depth manner than regularly used texts. We also believed that students would benefit greatly from an interactive approach to evaluating presidential decisions. Consequently, we decided to write case studies on controversial decisions and to design an evaluation scheme for student analysis.

We developed and field-tested our cases over a three-year period. In 1993, we presented a prototype case as members of a panel on presidential decision-making at the national meeting of the American Political Science Association in Washington, D.C. The next year, we asked Barbara Kellerman to comment on our work and provide suggestions when she came to Geneseo as our Pi Sigma Alpha guest lecturer. We then tested our cases in our classes and on panels of the New York State and Northeast Political Science Association meetings. Subsequently, we finalized our case study format and reader evaluation scheme.

Edward R. Drachman and Alan Shank wrote most of the cases and served as editors. Drachman received his Ph.D. in International Relations from the University of Pennsylvania, and is currently Associate Professor of Political Science at the State University of New York at Geneseo. He has specialized in U.S. foreign policy, comparative politics, and international relations. His publications include *United States Policy Toward Vietnam, 1940–1945* and *Challenging The Kremlin*. Drachman wrote the cases on Presidents Truman, Eisenhower, Nixon, Bush, and Clinton. He also developed the scheme for evaluation of controversial presidential decisions.

Shank received his Ph.D. in Political Science from Rutgers University, and is currently Professor and Chair of the Political Science Department at the State University of New York at Geneseo. He has specialized in Presidential Politics, American Public Policy, and Public

Administration. He has published *American Politics, Policies, and Priorities; Political Power and the Urban Crisis; Urban Perspectives; Presidential Policy Leadership: Kennedy and Social Welfare;* and *The Constitution and the American Presidency.* He has also been a Public Administration Fellow at the U.S. Department of Housing and Urban Development; a Guest Scholar at the Brookings Institution; and Director of the SUNY Urban Research Project. Shank wrote the introduction and the cases on Presidents Kennedy and Johnson.

We would like to thank Edward Kannyo and Steven R. Ligon for their contributions. Kannyo received his Ph.D. from Yale University, and is currently Associate Professor in the Political Science Department of the State University of New York at Geneseo. He has worked previously with the United Nations, the International League for Human Rights, the Lawyers Committee for Human Rights, and the U.S. Committee for Refugees. He has published articles in journals and chapters in books on African politics and human rights. Kannyo wrote the cases on Presidents Ford and Reagan.

Steven Ligon is a doctoral candidate in Political Science at the Catholic University of America, and is a retired U.S. naval intelligence officer. He currently teaches courses in Foreign Policy, Intelligence Analysis, and Latin America at the Joint Military Intelligence College of the Defense Intelligence Agency. Mr. Ligon wrote the case on President Carter.

We would also like to express our appreciation to Clay Morgan, our editor at SUNY Press, for his encouragement and support of our project; Richard Pious of Barnard College and Columbia University for many useful suggestions in his prepublication review of the manuscript; Barbara Kellerman and John F. Yaun for their review comments; Louis Ortmayer of Davidson College for ideas on teaching with the case study format; Liz Ancker, who did much of the typing; Geoff Maibohm, Susan Sablinski, and Jenny Moon, Drachman's students whose class research papers on President Bush's decision furnished helpful background material for this case; and the many students in our classes at Geneseo who made valuable comments on the evaluation scheme.

We offer special thanks to our families and our wives, Barbara Drachman and Bernice Shank; the Drachman children, Joy and Hayley and Dan Sherwood; the Shank children, Steven and his wife Anne, and Naomi; and grandchildren Daniel and David. Naomi suggested the "countdown" idea for the subtitle of the book.

Introduction

In the fifty years following World War II, American presidents have played a preeminent role in U.S. foreign policy. This book focuses on some of the most controversial foreign policy problems encountered by ten presidents during the Cold War and post–Cold War eras. Decisions made by the presidents in handling these problems caused considerable debate and disagreement in the domestic and international arenas. To more fully understand these decisions and their impact, we introduce them in the following context: First, we explain how ten selected foreign policy controversies are related to presidential diplomatic initiatives, approvals of covert operations, and deployments of U.S. troops in other countries. Next, we examine how controversial foreign policy decisions are affected by a "twilight zone" of executive-legislative relations. Presidential decisions may be challenged by Congress when the chief executive moves on a "fast track" of unilateral action. We conclude by offering several guidelines to analyze controversial presidential decisions and to assist readers in evaluating them.

Controversies in Presidential Foreign Policy Decisions

Presidential foreign policy decisions are controversial when arguments, debates, and disputes over opposing views occur before, during, and after the president decides what to do. Our ten presidential decisions include controversies over three types of issues: diplomatic initiatives, covert operations, and military deployments. Presidential decisions were debated in the domestic arena with Congress, among presidential advisers, in the media and by public opinion. They caused disputes in the international arena with allies and adversaries.

1

Diplomatic Initiatives: Truman, Eisenhower, Carter

Controversial presidential diplomatic initiatives included Truman's nonrecognition of China, Eisenhower's pressure on allies to end an invasion of Egypt and the Suez Canal, and Carter's decision to boycott the Olympic Games.

President Truman's decision not to recognize the People's Republic of China (PRC) resulted from domestic pressures to contain a militant communist regime. The decision produced controversy because conservatives argued that the Truman administration had "lost" China to the communists. Truman's decision no doubt led to Chinese Communist military intervention in the Korean War and subsequent isolation from the world community. The United States tried to keep China diplomatically isolated. Bowing to the inevitable, the PRC eventually won the coveted United Nations China seat in 1971. President Carter finally extended formal diplomatic recognition to the PRC in 1979.

President Eisenhower's decision to oppose the British-French-Israeli invasion of Suez occurred at the time of the 1956 presidential election campaign as well as the Soviet invasion of Hungary. It was most controversial in relations with close U.S. allies. Eisenhower believed the surprise attack was a blunder that threatened U.S. national security interests in the Middle East and world peace.

President Carter's decision to boycott the 1980 Summer Olympic Games in Moscow was a reaction to the Soviet invasion of Afghanistan. It caused heated domestic controversy between athletes, media commentators, and members of Congress. They argued that Carter's decision would not affect the Soviet Union's military activities, nor would it prevent the Olympic games from taking place. Instead, it would unfairly punish U.S. athletes who had trained for years to participate in international competition.

Covert Operations: Kennedy and Ford

Several presidents authorized the Central Intelligence Agency to sponsor covert military operations. When CIA plans resulted in a policy fiasco or were deliberately kept secret from Congress, the president's decision was strongly criticized.

The most compelling example of a CIA fiasco occurred when President Kennedy approved the Bay of Pigs invasion in 1961. The decision was controversial for several reasons: the president and his advisers never questioned the feasibility of the plan; there were no contingency or backup plans to deal with unanticipated problems; and the CIA seriously underestimated the strength of Cuba's military to repel an invasion. All of the invaders were captured or killed. Cuban leader Fidel Castro believed Kennedy was planning another attack. This led to the 1962 Cuban Missile Crisis, the most threatening military confrontation of the Cold War.

President Ford's approval in 1975 of CIA military aid to anticommunist factions in the Angolan civil war is a second example of a controversial covert operation. Ford was convinced by the CIA and Henry Kissinger, his national security adviser and secretary of state, that the Soviets and Cubans were fighting a "proxy war" in the African nation. The main controversy was between the Ford administration and Congress. Several senators opposed American involvement in a Vietnam-type quagmire. They were especially concerned about Ford's deception in failing to inform Congress about the sending of military aid. Congress voted to cut off appropriations and began a detailed investigation of CIA covert activities.

Five Controversial Military Deployments

Perhaps the most controversial type of presidential decision involves deployment of U.S. military forces into foreign combat situations. President Johnson's decision to reduce U.S. combat troops in the Vietnam War came in the aftermath of serious miscalculations concerning North Vietnamese military strength. Because Johnson and his advisers were overly optimistic that the United States was winning the war, they were caught by surprise when the North Vietnamese launched the vast military Tet Offensive against South Vietnam in early 1968. Johnson had to decide on changing war policy because the Tet Offensive was a tremendous political and psychological shock in the United States. Johnson had to choose between military demands for more U.S. troops, advice from some who urged unilateral steps to de-escalate the war, and recommendations from others who called for continuing military pressures together with demanding reciprocal de-escalation steps by the North Vietnamese.

President Nixon's Vietnamization strategy was also highly controversial. Although his decision to cut back U.S. ground troops was generally supported, Nixon's secret plan to expand the war by an "incursion" into Cambodia in the spring of 1970 provoked widespread domestic outrage. War critics felt deceived by Nixon's actions. Massive protests occurred with several students killed at Kent State University. Nixon reacted to domestic opposition by attacking critics and establishing a secret team of "plumbers" to plug intelligence leaks. Congress soon suspended appropriations for further military operations in Cambodia. Then, in 1973, with President Nixon severely weakened by the Watergate scandal, Congress approved the War Powers Resolution, an effort to check unilateral foreign military actions by the chief executive.

President Bush's decision to deploy 500,000 troops to Saudi Arabia after Iraqi President Saddam Hussein invaded Kuwait caused major controversy. Some critics pleaded "no blood for oil," while others feared massive U.S. casualties. Bush successfully used all the resources at his disposal to mobilize public opinion and Congress in support of his actions. He formed an international coalition and got the United Nations to approve resolutions opposing Iraq's invasion. Operation Desert Shield was a huge success for President Bush. The biggest controversy occurred during the last phase of Operation Desert Storm. Bush had to decide when to end the war. While the U.S.-led coalition was routing and slaughtering Iraqi troops, Bush and his advisers needed to decide whether the U.S. objectives had been achieved and when to declare victory.

The most recent example of a controversial presidential military deployment was President Clinton's Haiti decision of 1994. Clinton vacillated on a response to the refusal by Haiti's military regime to allow President Aristide's return. Clinton finally settled on dispatching U.S. troops. Congress demanded that Clinton follow the War Powers Act. Clinton disagreed by citing provisions of U.N. resolutions for his authority to act. U.S. public opinion overwhelmingly opposed Clinton's decision. The controversy was resolved at the last moment when Clinton dispatched a three-man negotiating team led by former President Carter, who convinced the military dictators to withdraw peacefully. Aristide returned to Haiti in October 1994 with great fanfare. Yet Haiti still faced daunting economic, political, and social problems.

There was generally widespread U.S. domestic support for President Reagan's decision to bomb Libya in 1986. The reasons for consensus were clear. This use of force was retaliation against a hostile foreign leader, Muammar Qadaffi, who was accused of training and sponsoring terrorist actions against U.S. civilians, including bombings, airplane hijackings, and the taking of hostages. Reagan's decision was much more controversial with U.S. European allies, who, except for Britain, opposed the attack against Libya.

Executive-Legislative Tensions
in Foreign Policy Controversies

The Constitution provides considerable authority to the president to deal with foreign policy problems. Under article II, the president is the commander in chief of the armed forces, the principal negotiator of treaties, and the chief diplomatic representative of the nation. In 1936, the Supreme Court defined the president's foreign policy powers as "plenary and exclusive," especially when Congress delegates broad authority for executive action. The Court's decision in *U.S. v. Curtiss-Wright Export Corporation*[1] established the subsequent legislative foundation for the president's strong foreign policy institutional and advisory system after World War II.

Under President Truman, the National Security Act of 1947 strengthened the chief executive's authority in dealing with the armed forces, intelligence activities, and overall coordination of national security policy. Up to this time, presidents relied upon the State and War Departments for foreign policy and military advice. Building upon the experiences of World War II and President Franklin D. Roosevelt's greatly expanded powers as commander-in-chief, the 1947 law created the Office of Secretary of Defense, the National Security Council, the Central Intelligence Agency, and the Joint Chiefs of Staff. A 1949 amendment established the Defense Department.

The president's formal constitutional powers coupled with the post–World War II institutional and advisory structure provided a powerful incentive for unilateral decision-making in foreign policy. According to presidency scholar Louis Koenig, presidents can operate on a "fast track" in conducting military deployments, negotiating and implementing executive agreements (rather than treaties), initiating diplomatic contacts, and approving covert operations.[2]

Executive-legislative tensions can occur in controversial foreign policy decisions when the two branches disagree over their constitutional authority. According to constitutional expert Louis Henkin, there is a "twilight zone" of concurring and overlapping powers which produces these tensions.[3]

Typically, presidents recognize that Congress has lawmaking, appropriations, war declaration, and Senate treaty ratification authority. Congress recognizes executive power to negotiate treaties, appoint ambassadors, establish and maintain diplomatic relations with foreign governments, and to conduct war after approval by Congress.

According to Henkin, a "twilight zone" of foreign policy authority is found when either the president or Congress claims to have power in less clearly defined policy actions. Generally, the "twilight zone" involves unilateral executive initiatives. Examples include Senate efforts to limit or challenge executive agreements; two-house efforts to control or hold the president accountable for deploying U.S. troops in combat situations short of a declaration of war; assertions of executive privilege to deny Congress documents or information on foreign, military, and national security policy decisions; and presidential impoundments of appropriated funds for defense or foreign policy purposes.[4]

Beginning with the military quagmire during the Vietnam War under President Johnson and the Watergate scandal under President Nixon, Congress began to reassert its foreign policy prerogatives. These included executive-legislative collaboration in declaring war, demands for executive accountability in deploying troops, and legislative appropriations rather than the use of secret or hidden executive funding of military, diplomatic, and covert initiatives. Congress was especially concerned about presidential abuses of power and claims of inherent authority without consulting Congress. President Johnson claimed, for example, that the 1964 Tonkin Gulf Resolution was a de facto declaration of war, permitting him to escalate the Vietnam conflict without consulting Congress. President Nixon asserted "executive privilege" in withholding taped conversations from Congress and the courts. Later, it was discovered that Nixon had ordered the CIA to stop the FBI from investigating the Watergate break-in. Arthur Schlesinger, Jr. characterized these unilateral presidential actions as evidence of an "imperial presidency" which ignored the Constitution and Congress in critical policy disputes.[5]

After President Nixon expanded the Vietnam War with a military "incursion" into Cambodia, Congress approved the 1973 War Powers Resolution. This was an attempt to regain legislative authority over the war-making power. However, every president from Nixon to Clinton claimed that the law represented an unconstitutional limitation on the executive's commander-in-chief powers. No president has willingly consulted with Congress under the War Powers Resolution prior to deploying U.S. troops in combat situations. Despite these objections, Congress insisted on debating President George Bush's decision to deploy ground troops in the Persian Gulf War and President Clinton's decision to use military force to restore President Aristide to office in Haiti.

Analysis of Presidential Decisions

According to presidency expert Richard Neustadt, presidential power is the power to persuade.[6] The ten presidents in this book (Truman to Clinton) tried to persuade domestic and international participants to accept controversial solutions to difficult foreign policy problems. Many of their decisions were made under severe time pressures. Presidents had to respond to deadlines, surprise military attacks, and unexpected actions by allies and adversaries.

Three guidelines are helpful in analyzing controversial presidential decisions: how well the president understands the historical context of the issue; how effectively the president applies his understanding of the controversy in the context of making a specific decision; and, how successful the president's decision is in both the short and long term.

Framework of Our Case Studies

The president needs knowledge of the historical background of the problem before making a decision. For example, was the controversy part of the Cold War competition between the United States and the Soviet Union? Did it threaten U.S. national security in Asia, Latin America, or the Middle East?

Presidential understanding of controversies is sharply defined in the immediate time pressures of the countdown to decision. Often he must also decide quickly how to respond to military attacks, national security threats, surprises, or other unexpected actions by allies or adversaries. The president needs to consider his foreign policy principles, worldview, national security strategy, and relations with allies and adversaries in making a decision. He needs to account for the domestic context of the decision in relations with Congress, the media, interest groups, and public opinion. The president's decision involves options considered and rejected. The president exercises leadership in persuading others to accept the decision. Finally, the president's decision has impacts and consequences in the short term and long run on other domestic and foreign policy participants.

Evaluation of Presidential Decisions

Evaluating the president's decision is the central theme of our ten case studies. We have developed an evaluation procedure found in appendix C. Five components of evaluating presidential decisions include

1. The nature of the controversy in domestic politics;
2. Controversy that arose among the president's advisers;
3. Degree of success by the president in achieving the major goals of the decision;
4. Assessment of the effectiveness of presidential leadership in the decision; and
5. Long-term assessment of the president's decision.

Evaluating the effectiveness or ineffectiveness of presidential decisions in controversial foreign policy issues can be assisted by applying Neustadt's concepts of backward mapping and forward planning; and Irving Janis' recommendations for avoiding groupthink.[7]

According to Neustadt, backward mapping involves the president's estimation of his decision choice on desired results. In other words, how will the decision affect the outcome? Presidents will make effective decisions when they can see what the outcome will be. They need to determine the steps needed to achieve the desired results.

In evaluating the ten decisions, the reader should consider whether any of the presidents used backward mapping. For example, did President Eisenhower anticipate that his decision to oppose the Suez invasion would so anger the British, French, and Israeli allies? How did President Johnson estimate the effects of a scaling back of U.S. troops and a limited bombing halt on getting the North Vietnamese to negotiate an end to the Vietnam War? What would have been the outcome of President Clinton's last-minute decision to send a negotiating team to Haiti if the negotiators had failed in their mission?

Forward planning involves the president's careful consideration of each step of a decision in achieving its goals. The president needs to be constantly aware of the impact of a decision, to consider any feedback or recommendations made by others to modify the decision, and to change the goals of the decision as assessment takes place.

Forward planning is especially difficult when the president faces immediate pressures to act. Several of our cases involve controversial presidential planning decisions. For example, why did President Kennedy not carefully consider any changes in the CIA plan to invade Cuba in 1961? Why did President Ford ignore negative congressional reaction to his plan for covert CIA military aid to Angola? Why did President Nixon agree to a plan for a secret military attack on Cambodia when his public policy was to deescalate the Vietnam War?

Groupthink, according to Janis, causes defective decision-making when groups are so cohesive and insulated that they resist a wide range of options leading to a false consensus or agreement in making a decision. Policy fiascoes result when the group moves quickly toward unanimous or uniform decisions rather than realistically appraising alternative courses of action. It includes poor information search, selective bias in processing existing information, and a failure to work out contingency or backup plans. Groupthink is especially a problem when policymakers are faced with an emergency or crisis. Real or perceived crisis may produce high stress within the group, causing it to act hastily without paying attention to the long-term consequences of the policy decision.

Several of the controversial presidential policy decisions involved the groupthink syndrome. For example, why did President Kennedy and his advisers willingly accept the CIA's secret plan to invade Cuba when there was a great possibility that the plan would fail? Why did President Johnson reject advice that would have led to a more successful resolution of the Vietnam conflict, and why did President Ford defer so much to Henry Kissinger and the CIA's definition of the U.S. role in the Angolan civil war?

You, the reader, are now ready to examine how and why presidents decided on solutions to ten controversial issues. You are also asked to be a participant with the presidents by evaluating their decisions. In this way, you will be directly involved in the cases. You can judge for yourself whether there were alternative solutions that might have dealt with these problems more effectively. You can also experience the challenge of making controversial foreign policy decisions.

Notes

1. 299 U.S. 204 (1936). Also, see the critique of Justice Sutherland's decision in Louis Fisher, *Presidential War* (Lawrence, Kan.: University Press of Kansas, 1995), pp. 57–61.
2. Louis Koenig, "The Modern Presidency and the Constitution: Foreign Policy," Chapter 9 in Martin Fausold and Alan Shank, eds., *The Constitution and the American Presidency* (Albany, N.Y.: SUNY Press, 1991).
3. Louis Henkin, "Foreign Affairs and The Constitution," *Foreign Affairs*, 66 (Winter 1987–88): 295–97. Henkin's "twilight zone" is adapted from Justice Robert Jackson's quote in the Supreme Court case of *Youngstown Sheet and Tube v. Sawyer* (1952), also known as the Steel Seizure decision.
4. Ibid., p. 296.
5. Arthur Schlesinger, Jr., *The Imperial Presidency* (Boston: Houghton Mifflin, 1973).
6. Richard E. Neustadt, *Presidential Power and the Modern Presidents* (New York: Free Press, 1980), p. 28 and chapter 3.
7. For a discussion of backward mapping and forward planning, see Neustadt, *Presidential Power and the Modern Presidents*, pp. 215, 293–94. Groupthink is found in Irving L. Janis, *Groupthink*, 2nd ed. (Boston: Houghton Mifflin, 1982). Figure 10–1 on page 244 is especially helpful.

Selected Bibliography

Briggs, Phillips J. *Making American Foreign Policy: Presidential-Congressional Relations From the Second World War to the Post–Cold War Era*, 2nd ed. Lanham, Md.: Rowman & Littlefield, 1994.

Corwin, Edward S. *The President: Office and Powers, 1787–1984*, 5th rev. ed. by Randall W. Bland, Theodore T. Hindson, and Jack W. Peltason. New York: New York University Press, 1984.

Fisher, Louis. *Presidential War*. Lawrence, Kan.: University Press of Kansas, 1995.

Koenig, Louis. "The Modern Presidency and the Constitution: Foreign Policy." In Martin Fausold and Alan Shank, eds., *The Constitution and the American Presidency*. Albany, N.Y.: SUNY Press, 1991.

Henkin, Louis. "Foreign Affairs and the Constitution." *Foreign Affairs*, 66.2 (Winter 1987–88): 284–310.

Janis, Irving L. *Groupthink*, 2nd ed. Boston: Houghton Mifflin, 1982.

Janis, Irving L. and Leon Mann. *Decision Making*. New York: Free Press, 1977.

Neustadt, Richard E. *Presidential Power and the Modern Presidents*. New York: Free Press, 1980.

Schlesinger, Arthur, Jr. *The Imperial Presidency*. Boston: Houghton Mifflin, 1973.

1

President Truman's Decision Not to Extend Diplomatic Recognition to the People's Republic of China

Setting and Overview of Truman's Decision

When the Chinese Communists marched into Peking in the fall of 1949 and established the People's Republic of China (PRC) on October 1, they established a dramatically new pattern of rule. It was to have tremendous repercussions not only for China, but for all of Asia and indeed the whole world.

On one issue the United States government officially was certain. The State Department's white paper released in the summer of 1949 maintained there was nothing the United States could have done to have avoided the "loss" of China to the Communists. The United States could not have sustained Nationalist rule under the corrupt and ineffectual leadership of Chiang Kai-shek.

Other issues seemed far less clear. The changing of the guard in China presented the United States with a number of thorny questions. Would the new Chinese regime be a likely satellite of the Soviet Union, its ally, or enemy? Would the Cold War now extend into East Asia, and with what consequences? Was Washington's Europe-focused containment strategy and assumptions applicable to Asia? Was Asia as important a theater for the Cold War as Europe? Should the United States continue to support Chiang Kai-shek and militarily defend the Nation-

13

alist regime on Formosa? And lastly, did the Chinese Communist victory necessarily mean the end of U.S. friendship with the Chinese people and the inevitability of serious conflict between the American and Chinese Communist governments?

Both before and after the Chinese Communist victory on the battlefield, there were opportunities for the United States to have dealt more cooperatively with the Communists. What difference these "lost" opportunities would have made in future U.S.-Chinese relations is highly debatable. Perhaps most controversial is the decision Truman made not to extend diplomatic recognition to the new Chinese Communist government. Would recognition have been the wiser policy? Would it have been politically feasible? Would it have significantly influenced developments inside China and future U.S.-Chinese relations? We will now examine why and how Truman made his decision and what its main consequences were.

President Truman's Decision

PRESIDENT TRUMAN DECIDED NOT TO EXTEND DIPLOMATIC RECOGNITION TO THE PEOPLE'S REPUBLIC OF CHINA. HE HAD NUMEROUS OPPORTUNITIES TO DO SO, BUT EACH TIME HE DECLINED.

Truman's decision was controversial for several main reasons:

1. It highlighted the question of what criteria the President should consider in extending diplomatic recognition beyond those established by international law.[1]
2. It was made at the beginning of another "Red Scare" soon to sweep the country.
3. It became enmeshed in an intensely partisan debated ignited by Republicans and the China lobby that criticized Truman, Acheson, and Far East experts in the State Department for "losing" China to the Communists.
4. The United States broke ranks with Great Britain, its main European ally, which extended diplomatic recognition almost immediately.
5. Truman was faced with the dilemma of a "two China policy." Particularly vexing was what to do about China's membership in the United Nations, especially China's permanent seat on the Security Council, and Chiang's newly established Nationalist government on Formosa.

6. There was serious doubt whether the Chinese Communists wanted U.S. recognition.
7. There was debate over whether the Chinese Communist Revolution was mainly an indigenous nationalist movement or part of an international Communist conspiracy directed by the Kremlin.
8. There was concern whether recognition was consonant with the Truman Doctrine of 1947.
9. There was anguish over how much damage the Chinese Communist Revolution had inflicted on America's "special relationship" with the Chinese people, developed over the years through a variety of missionary, cultural, and economic activities.

Background of the Decision

Historical Context

U.S. policy toward China, since Hay's Open Door, was forged by a combination of commercial, religious, cultural, humanitarian, and national security interests. Americans always considered themselves friends of the Chinese people, if not their government. When the Chinese Communists gained power in 1949, the United States had to decide how to relate to a Communist regime that viewed it as the center of world imperialism and exploitation and that was soon befriended by its major Cold War enemy, the Soviet Union.

Roosevelt's China Policy
President Roosevelt's main goals for postwar China were as follows:

1. Stave off resumption of the Civil War between Nationalist and Chinese Communist Party (CCP) armies. The war had begun in the late 1920s and was interrupted by Japanese military aggression in the 1930s and early 1940s.
2. Establish a strong, united, democratic, and pro-American China. Postwar China would be one of Roosevelt's "Four Policemen" to maintain the peace.
3. Prop up China to serve as a buffer against anticipated Soviet expansionism in Asia. China would also fill the power vacuum that would be left by Japan's defeat and the disintegration of the European colonial empires.

Roosevelt hoped that China would settle its civil war and take its rightful place among leading nations of the world. This should happen despite the fact that China was a weak ally during the world war and its ruling Nationalist government under Generalissimo Chiang Kai-shek was authoritarian, corrupt, manipulated by warlords, and very unpopular. Roosevelt expected China to be a continuing partner in postwar reconstruction and maintenance of world peace. He thus insisted on making her a permanent member of the United Nations Security Council and tried to raise Chiang to the status of world leader. Roosevelt supported Chiang while pressuring him to make political, economic, and social reforms.

Roosevelt's China policy failed on all accounts. The civil war resumed with new ferocity; China became even more unstable, disunited, and weak; Chiang proved incapable of democratic reform, could not win the support of the Chinese people, and lost the civil war; and the new Communist Chinese regime soon allied itself with the Soviet Union and threatened the security of both Asia and the United States. Once close friends, the United States and China became bitter enemies. Were all these developments inevitable? Or did the United States have any opportunities which, if she had chosen differently, could have significantly altered the course of history?

By 1944, with China's war against Japan stalling, Lieutenant General Joseph W. Stilwell ("Vinegar Joe"), commander of the China-Burma-India theater, pressured FDR to drop reliance on Chiang and let him control the war in China himself. This meant, among other things, using Communist armies which would be equipped with U.S. Lend-Lease weapons. U.S. leaders were at odds over the command issue and working with Chiang and the Communists. Vice President Henry Wallace, sent by Roosevelt to China in June 1944 to influence Chiang to work with the Communists, reported back that Chiang did not have "the intelligence or political strength to run postwar China." John Patton Davies, State Department adviser to Stilwell, noted the foolishness of continued U.S. support to Chiang. In a dispatch to Washington on November 7, 1944, he stated: "The Communists are in China to stay. . . . And China's destiny is not Chiang's but theirs."[2] This became the main thrust of advice from foreign service officers in China and in Washington. As events unfurled, it was repeatedly ignored or rejected outright, When the Communists won the civil war, opponents of this position vilified its advocates as Communist sympathizers or even traitors. During the "Red Scare" of the early fifties, they were driven from the government. Their expertise and advice would be sorely missed.

Initial U.S. Contacts with Chinese Communist Leaders

From the summer of 1944 through the summer of 1945, Chinese Communist leaders Mao Tse-tung and Chou En-lai sought aid, cooperation, and recognition from the United States. In China, they discussed possible cooperation with officers of the U.S. Foreign Service and Office of Strategic Services (OSS), the main U.S. war-time intelligence agency and precursor of the Central Intelligence Agency. The Chinese Communists had cooperated closely with the U.S. military and OSS, supplying vitally needed intelligence about the Japanese and rescuing downed U.S. flyers.

On July 22, 1944, a small U.S. Army observer group, known as "the Dixie Mission," landed in Yenan. Its main goal was to assess the potential of the Communists in allied resistance against the Japanese. CCP leaders were friendly to these Americans. Both publicly in their press and privately, they signaled their willingness to establish close postwar economic and political ties. They stressed that their armies were much more effective against the Japanese than those of the dying Nationalists. They also told U.S. Foreign Service Officer John Service that they hoped for a more democratic China, and that they sincerely looked forward to a positive relationship with the United States.[3]

Keenly aware of U.S. military power and economic might, which could be used for China's postwar reconstruction, and mindful of Roosevelt's strong stance against colonialism, Mao sent Roosevelt congratulations on his reelection in 1944. The president replied that he looked forward to "vigorous cooperation with all the Chinese forces" against Japan.

On January 9, 1945, Mao and Chou forwarded to Washington a secret message asking Roosevelt if they could fly to Washington to discuss prospects for U.S. aid and recognition. They sought an opportunity to tell Roosevelt personally that the Nationalists were corrupt and that the Communists deserved U.S. support. The Communists would accept partnership in a coalition government if they could receive U.S. military aid like that given Marshal Tito, the Communist leader who was leading the battle against Nazi forces in Yugoslavia. They insisted that this message remain secret, for if they did not see the president, its revelation would damage their relationship with Chiang.

Roosevelt never responded to this message. Major General Patrick J. Hurley, named ambassador to China on January 8, had blocked its transmission. He had cast his lot with Chiang and with the possibility of a coalition government under the Generalissimo. Earlier Hurley had agreed with the State Department's China experts, known as the old "China hands," that Mao and his followers were not true communists. In a visit to Moscow in August 1944 he had heard Soviet Foreign Minister Vyacheslav Molotov refer to Chinese Communists as "radish communists" (red on the outside only) who "had no relation whatever to Communism."[4] Perhaps, then, they should be considered "populists" or "agrarian reformers."

But soon Hurley changed his mind and began feuding with the "China hands." He believed they were deliberately exaggerating Communist strength and were trying to undercut his position by urging FDR to work with Mao. Moreover, he believed that Mao (whose name he pronounced as "Moose Dung") and his supporters were the main cause of China's problems. If they had not won the sympathy and even support of "traitorous" American foreign service officers who were conspiring against Chiang and Roosevelt, China's war against Japan would have been going much better. This blast became the basis of later charges by Senator Joseph McCarthy (R, Wisconsin) and others that China was not "lost" to the Communists by the inexorable march of historical events, but was handed over to them by disloyal Americans in the State Department.

Hurley prevailed in his struggle with the "China hands." He had influenced the president after his return from the Yalta Conference to give unqualified support to Chiang. Roosevelt eventually had learned of Mao's and Chou's request to visit him in Washington through a second telegram of February 7 (which arrived in Washington after the president left for Yalta). But by this time Roosevelt did not want to rock the China boat unnecessarily. At Yalta, Roosevelt thought he had won Stalin's support for the Nationalist government. The president anticipated this would force the Communists to join in a coalition under Chiang. Roosevelt, therefore, did not pay attention to those urging him to recognize the inevitablity of a Chinese Communist victory over the Nationalists.[5]

Roosevelt listened more to supporters of Chiang, who had influential friends inside and outside Washington. For several years the American media had built up Chiang's image and that of his attractive wife (the "Missimo"), a graduate of Wellesley College, as great leaders. In 1937, for example, Time magazine, published by Henry Luce who was the son of an American missionary in China, had named them "Man and Wife of the Year." The *Time* article presented a romanticized image of the ruling couple, who had converted to Christianity, as patriotic democratic leaders worthy of U.S. commitment and aid. This would be the prevailing view on Chinese leadership when Roosevelt died on April 12.

Truman's China Policy

When Truman became president, his main preoccupation was winning the war, first in Europe and then in Asia. Truman knew little about foreign affairs, and even less about Asia. When he became president, he believed Chiang "was on the road to real reform."[6] Truman relied on Roosevelt's key personal advisers on China (Hurley, General Albert C. Wedemeyer, and Fleet Admiral William D. Leahy), who were all strongly anti-Communist and committed to Chiang. Thus when the war ended Chiang had strong support both from the White House and the American people, whereas Mao had virtually none. Truman, wanting to win Congressional support for his own policies, went with the tide.

Initial U.S. Support for Chiang

After Japan's defeat, Truman's goals in China were to keep Soviet forces in Manchuria from helping the Chinese Communists, forestall serious fighting between Nationalist and Communist forces, and sustain U.S. influence. Truman took steps to support Chiang. For example, he ordered Japanese troops to surrender to the Nationalists. The president also used the U.S. military to pursue political objectives. He ordered the Marines to transport almost a half a million Nationalist troops to the north, where Chinese Communist military power was strongest. Ignoring Wedemeyer's advice, the Nationalists sent troops into Manchuria where they and U.S. Marine units reportedly fought the Chinese Communists. Truman did not start withdrawing the almost 100,000 U.S. military personnel until early 1947.

At the same time, Hurley became enraged when he concluded that certain U.S. State Department officials were plotting to support Mao. In September 1945, Service and several other foreign service officers sent a telegram to the State Department urging Truman to enlist the aid of the Chinese Communists before they sought Russian aid or intervention. When he saw this telegram, Hurley blew up: "I know who drafted that telegram: Service! Service! I'll get that S.O.B. if it's the last thing I do." Hurley then arranged for Service and the other signers to be recalled to the United States. Once again an opportunity to work with the Communists was lost. When Hurley returned to Washington on leave, he resigned as ambassador. His resignation was a political bombshell. In his letter of November 27, he loudly protested that "a considerable section of our State Department is endeavoring to support Communism generally as well as specifically in China."[7]

Hurley's outburst caused political sparks to fly in Congress. Republican critics of Truman's China policy, such as senators Robert Taft of Ohio and Styles Bridges of New Hampshire, damned U.S. policy as "soft" on Communism and too tolerant of "pinko" officers in the State Department. They also wanted Truman to disclose the entire Yalta agreement whereby, they claimed, the United States sold out not only Eastern Europe, but China as well. Although a Senate investigation in December found no substantiation for Hurley's accusations, the flurry of charges did find considerable sympathy in the media and the American public. To blunt this criticism, Truman decided to turn to General George C. Marshall for help. After the war, Marshall had retired to his home in Virginia. But when Truman called, once again the general would serve his country.

The Marshall Mission to China

At the end of 1945, Truman realized that civil war in China was about to resume and that his China policy was in disarray. On December 11, Marshall met at the White House with Truman, Secretary of State James F. Byrnes, and Leahy. All three agreed that U.S. desertion of Chiang would most likely result in a divided China and Soviet control of Manchuria.[8] At another meeting on December 14 to discuss Marshall's mission, Marshall, Truman, and Under Secretary of State Dean Acheson determined that even if Marshall could not win concessions from Chiang, the United States would still have to back the Nationalists.[9]

On December 15, 1945, Truman sent Marshall to China. His goals were incredibly difficult: to end Nationalist-Communist hostilities as fast as possible; to absorb Communist armies into the Chinese National Army; to establish a coalition government under control of the Nationalists; and to work for Nationalist supremacy in Manchuria, which meant withdrawal of Soviet troops by the February 1, 1946 deadline. When they finally pulled out in the spring, Marshall was to see they did not return. If both the Nationalists and Communists accepted Marshall's proposals, the United States would grant significant amounts of aid for economic reconstruction. If not, even though Truman had determined that the Nationalists would still receive aid, they would be told U.S. aid would end. That day Truman made his first public statement on China. He held that the Nationalists were "the only legal government in China" and that they were "the proper instrument to achieve a unified China."

Marshall almost miraculously arranged a truce between the warring Chinese sides in January, but it proved temporary. In the meantime, the American public became increasingly divided over U.S. China policy. A growing China lobby, backed by American and Chinese money and led by Representatives Walter Judd (R, Minn.), a former medical missionary to China, Clare Booth Luce (R, Conn.), wife of the publisher of *Time* and *Life* magazines, and Senator William F. Knowland (R, Calif.) urged increased support for Chiang. On May 15, 1946, these "Asia firsters," along with sixty-three other notable Americans, strongly criticized Roosevelt for selling China out to Russia at Yalta, and Truman for being soft on Communism. Opposing this group were those (mainly Democrats) who supported the Roosevelt-Truman China policy and who considered Chiang hopelessly corrupt, authoritarian , and consequently undeserving of U.S. aid. Partisan political considerations would continue to play an important role in determining Truman's China policy.

On August 10, 1946, frustrated by Chiang's actions, Truman sent him a message. It threatened a reexamination of U.S. China policy and curtailment of U.S. aid unless "convincing proof" was "shortly forthcoming that genuine progress is being made toward a peaceful solution of China's internal problems."[10] Truman was exasperated with Chiang. Then in a futile effort to look impartial and prod Chiang to cooperate with the Communists, he acceded to Marshall's request to place an embargo on the export of U.S. munitions to China. This lasted until May 1947. On December 18, 1946, Truman made another statement on China. He hoped for a peaceful solution" to the crisis, and "pledged not to interfere in the internal affairs of China."

During this period of publicly stated American neutrality, the United States continued to give Chiang significant economic and military aid. This emboldened the Nationalists to try to win a military victory over the Communists, while it infuriated the Communists. In late June 1946, the United States gave the Nationalists credit of $51.7 million in Lend-Lease supplies.[11] When the truce expired on June 30, the "third revolutionary civil war" began.

On January 7, 1947, Marshall returned to the United States. He had determined he could not deter China's opposing forces from engaging in a fight to the finish. His mission to end the civil war had failed, mainly, as Marshall said himself, because of the "complete, almost overwhelming suspicion with which the Chinese Communist Party and the Kuomintang [Nationalist Party] regard each other."

Despite Marshall's failure to arrange a lasting truce, Truman still held out some hope of stopping the war. In late winter of 1947, Congress accepted the Truman Doctrine. This called for containment of communism in Greece and Turkey and help for free people everywhere who were resisting outside pressures and aggression. Truman feared Republican opposition to the Marshall Plan for reconstruction of postwar Europe. He also responded to criticism by Judd and others of a double standard of U.S. opposition to communism in Europe but not in Asia. The president thus felt he had to demonstrate he was doing more for China.

The Wedemeyer Mission

In May, Truman ended the U.S. embargo on aid to Chiang. Then in July, almost as a last resort to learn whether there were any new reasons for increased U.S. aid to Chiang, Truman sent General Wedemeyer on a fact-finding mission to China. When this ended, in a public statement issued on August 24 before he left China, Wedemeyer saw little possibility that a coalition government could be established. "To gain and maintain the confidence of the people," Wedemeyer added, "the Central Government will have to effect immediately drastic, far-reaching political and economic reforms. Promises will no longer suffice. Performance is absolutely necessary. It should be accepted that military force in itself will not eliminate communism." Despite this pessimism, Wedemeyer recommended "moral, advisory, and material support to China and that Manchuria be placed under a Five Power Guardianship or under a United Nations Trusteeship." He then added that "the American mediation effort has been to the advantage of the Chinese Communists and conversely to the disadvantage of the Nationalist Government."[12]

Wedemeyer's report submitted to Truman on September 19, 1947, had no significant effect on American China policy. Marshall personally suppressed it.[13] He feared a backlash both from Chiang, who would not like the proposal on Manchuria, and from the Soviet Union, which might use the report to call for a trusteeship for Greece. Marshall was especially disturbed that "when his report came back, a great deal that was happening elsewhere in the world, particularly that part of the world dominated by the Soviets, was not considered."[14] The China Lobby called for its release, complaining that Truman did not want it known publicly that he favored more aid for Chiang. New York Governor Thomas Dewey, soon to be the Republican nominee for president in 1948, also began calling for more aid for Chiang.

Chiang supporters in the United States found some solace in the highly publicized "Report on China," by William Bullitt, former ambassador to the Soviet Union. Writing on October 13, 1947, in publisher Henry Luce's pro-Kuomintang *Life* magazine, Bullitt proposed a three-year U.S.-aid plan to save China under Chiang. He then warned ominously, in an early version of the domino theory: "If China falls into the hands of Stalin, all Asia, including Japan, sooner or later will fall into his hands. . . . The independence of the U.S. will not live a generation longer than the independence of China." Bullitt concluded by recommending that General Douglas MacArthur be appointed "Personal Representative of the President" in China to "prevent subjugation of China by the Soviet Union." Bullitt's article got widespread public attention, which caused concern in the Truman administration.

The China Aid Act

Truman was staying the course in his China policy, though he did bow somewhat to Republican criticism. On February 18, 1948, Truman asked Congress for a $570 million aid program for China. There was no recommendation for military aid, though the message stated that this aid would allow the Nationalist government "to devote its limited dollar resources to the most urgent of its other needs." Truman, who respected Marshall immensely, agreed with his conclusion that limited U.S. aid was necessary to help Chiang keep Soviet forces out of northern China. Too much aid though, especially of a military nature, would probably encourage Chiang to avoid making the political and economic reforms that Marshall and a growing number of critics in the United States considered necessary. On April 2, 1948, Congress passed the bill appropriating $338 million. But against Marshall's advice, it added $125 million for Chiang to use as he wanted, presumably for military purposes.

The State Department's China White Paper

When Truman surprisingly won reelection in 1948, he seemed bent on making no major shift in U.S. China policy. But events in China were moving fast. By early 1949, the Nationalists had lost the civil war.

Chiang resigned from the presidency on January 21, 1949, ironically the same day that Acheson was sworn in as secretary of state.

Both Acheson and Truman maintained that no amount of U.S. aid could have saved the Nationalists from defeat by the Chinese Communists. Their political, economic, and military weaknesses were far too serious. Finally, it seemed, U.S. support for Chiang and involvement in the Chinese civil war had ended. This was the major conclusion of the China white paper released by the State Department on August 5.

The Truman administration chose this approach as a giant public relations ploy to deflect criticism of its China policy. Yet as such it was not very successful. The report was criticized widely not only by the Republicans and China lobby, but by the Communist Chinese leadership. Among other things, Mao objected strongly to Acheson's contention in his letter of transmittal that the Communist leaders had "forsworn their Chinese heritage" and had "publicly announced their subservience to a foreign power, Russia, which during the last 50 years, under czars and Communists alike, had been most assiduous in its efforts to extend its control in the Far East." Mao was particularly offended by Acheson's assertion that "ultimately the profound civilization and the democratic individualism of China will reassert themselves and she will throw off the foreign yoke." Mao chafed at the charge his movement was not independent. Moreover, he inferred from this statement that the United States intended to foment fifth column (insurrectionist) action inside China to overthrow CCP leaders.

U.S. China policy had clearly failed, but why? Republicans and the China lobby had already begun leading the drumbeat attack against the Truman administration for "losing" China to the Communists. With this controversy swirling around him, Truman had to face the next very difficult choice in his China policy: whether to recognize the new Communist regime in China, officially established on October 1, 1949.

Countdown to the Decision

When the Manchu dynasty fell, the United States was the first treaty power to recognize the revolutionary republican government of 1912 and then the Nationalist regime established in Nanking in 1928. But the United States did not recognize the Chinese Communist regime until 1979, almost thirty years after it was established.

When support for Chiang seemed a lost cause, Acheson favored accommodation with the Chinese Communists. He believed recognition of the PRC was just a matter of time. Perhaps at first the United States would recognize the Communists on a *de facto* basis. This meant only acceptance of the fact that the Chinese Communists were in control of China. *De jure* recognition could come later, after the PRC had earned it by demonstrating acceptable behavior.

Overtures for Recognition by CCP Leaders

Beginning in the spring of 1949, the Communist Chinese made several bids for U.S recognition, all of which the United States rejected. In May and June, Huang Hua, director of the Chinese Communist Alien Affairs Office in Nanking, approached John Leighton Stuart, U.S. Ambassador in China. According to Stuart's telegram to Washington of May 14, the previous evening "Huang expressed much interest in recognition . . . on terms of equality and mutual benefit." Stuart responded that "it was customary to recognize whatever government clearly had support of people of country and was able and willing to perform its international obligations," but that U.S. recognition was premature because the Chinese Communists had not yet established a government.

Huang called on Stuart again on June 28. This time Huang invited Stuart, former president of Yenching University in Peking for almost thirty years and his former teacher, to return for a visit. There he could meet with Mao and Chou. But Truman seemed extrasensitive to likely Congressional charges of appeasement and softness on Communism. Just a few days earlier, on June 24, twenty-one senators (16 Republicans, 5 Democrats) had written him a letter opposing recognition and urging increased U.S. aid to the Nationalists. Truman, unwilling in effect to sign the death warrant for the Nationalists, decided that "under no circumstances" would Stuart be allowed to make this visit.

Between Huang's two meetings with Stuart, both Chou and Mao had made important overtures to establish good relations with the United States. On June 1, Chou reportedly sent a "top secret" message through Michael Keon, an Australian journalist, to O. Edmund Clubb, the American consul-general in Peking. It stated that the Communist Party leadership was divided into two major groups. The radicals wanted an alliance with the USSR. The liberals (Chou included), wanted to establish amicable relations with the United States. This meant U.S. trade and investment (for mutual benefit) that the USSR would be unable to provide. Indicating that Mao would make his decision on the basis of practicality, Chou hoped that "American authorities . . . would believe [that] there were genuine liberals in [the] party who are concerned with everything connected with [the] welfare [of the] Chinese people and peace in our times, rather than doctrinaire theories."[15] Chou wanted to establish de facto relations with the United States. Finally, Chou indicated that he and Mao would be receptive to a positive U.S. response, which might buoy the liberal wing of the party. But Truman, not wanting to appear soft toward the Communist Chinese, decided not to respond favorably to Chou's démarche. Instead, he approved the State Department's reply that the U.S. would judge the Communists' intentions by their actions.

On June 15, Mao announced he would establish diplomatic relations with any foreign government on "the basis of the principles of equality, mutual benefit, and mutual respect for territorial integrity and sovereignty, provided it is willing to sever relations with the Chinese reactionaries, stops conspiring with them or helping them and adopts an attitude of genuine, and not hypocritical, friendship toward People's China." Truman also ignored this initiative, in part because of Mao's condition of severing ties with Chiang.

On June 30, Mao made his soon to be famous "lean to one side" (i.e., toward the Soviet Union) speech. Mao and his colleagues may have feared U.S. military intervention in the Chinese Civil War on the side of the Nationalists, just as the U.S. and its allies had intervened militarily in Russia at the end of World War I to crush the Bolsheviks.[16] Truman, however, interpreted Mao's words as fresh evidence that the CCP leaders were closely tied to the Soviet Union.

In September, Secretary of State Acheson seemed ambivalent toward the Communist Chinese. On the one hand, he indicated that the United States might recognize the Communists on a Jeffersonian basis, stating: "We maintain diplomatic relations with other countries primarily because we are all on the same planet and must do business with each other. We do not establish an embassy in a foreign country to show approval of its Government." On the other hand, he was looking for ways to aid anti-Communist forces in those regions of China not yet under Communist control. He also still clung to his contention expressed in his letter of transmittal for the white paper that the Communist Chinese were controlled by Moscow.

Washington faced the issue of formal recognition when the PRC was officially established on October 1. Then Chou, the new premier and foreign minister, invited the United States and other countries to establish official diplomatic relations. This was yet another overture that the Chinese Communists made toward Washington.

The U.S. Hesitates to Extend Recognition

The Soviet Union recognized the PRC on October 2. The United States hesitated. On October 3, Truman's position was that the United States "should be in no hurry whatever to recognize this regime."[17] The president noted that the United States had waited to recognize the Soviet Union until 1933, sixteen years after the Bolshevik Revolution. The State Department announced that the United States would not recognize the PRC without consulting Congress and its allies. Moreover, it remained unconvinced the PRC would honor its international obligations.

From October 6 to 8, a special Round Table Conference of experts on China met to review U.S. East Asian policy. When the transcript of this meeting was published two years later, it was revealed that "a prevailing group" advocated withdrawal of recognition from the Nationalist government and recognition of the PRC "fairly soon." It argued "that a stabilization of relationships through quick recognition would be desirable from the viewpoint of commercial considerations, the ideological effect on the Chinese people, and to put the political orientation of the Communist leadership towards the Soviet Union under strain."[18]

At a news conference on October 12, Acheson reiterated three requirements for recognition: the PRC had to control the government; it should honor its international obligations; and it must rule with the consent of the governed. He doubted especially that the PRC met the second requirement.

At that time Truman seemed to oppose recognition. When asked off the record on October 19 under what circumstances he would recognize the PRC, Truman replied: "I hope we will not have to recognize it." Truman then also was privately pulling for the success of the newly established Nationalist blockade of mainland ports.[19]

Acheson, however, though still uncertain whether the Chinese Communist regime was independent of Soviet control, still leaned toward recognition. On October 12, for example, he testified before the Senate Foreign Relations Committee that the Chinese Communist government was "really a tool of Russian imperialism in China." By then, however, he had started to agree with the recommendation by the American Embassy in Moscow that the United States should recognize the PRC to facilitate a "Titoist"[20] communist regime, free from Moscow's control. This argument was consistent with that of the State Department's China specialists. They insisted that the Chinese Communists had come to power independently of Moscow, and possibly against its wishes. To maintain Communist Chinese independence,

Acheson wanted the United States to continue trade with Peking (in nonstrategic items) and stop aid to the Nationalists.[21]

Based on this assessment of the Communist Chinese, Acheson began paving the ground for U.S. recognition. On November 17, he presented Truman with two options. The first was "to oppose the Communist regime, harass it, needle it and if an opportunity appeared to overthrow it." The second, which he and his China specialists and consultants favored and which indicated recognition, was to try to unyoke the PRC "from subservience to Moscow and over a period of time encourage those vigorous influences which might modify it." Acheson then concluded: "The President thought that in the broad sense in which I was speaking that this was the correct analysis."[22]

Though Acheson was arguing for recognition, he also felt that the PRC had to demonstrate its willingness to get along with the United States. Opponents of recognition kept referring to Mao's "lean-to-one-side" speech. But it was the incident involving Angus Ward, the American Consul-General in Mukden, Manchuria, that placed a dark cloud over the prospect of early recognition.

On October 24, the Chinese Communists arrested Ward and several associates on charges of assault against a Chinese employee. The Communists had placed these Americans under house arrest for over a year, after accusing them of spying. After the Communists arrested Ward, they refused to let him communicate with Washington and disregarded all U.S. protests. One month later, the Communists deported Ward, who returned to the United States. But the damage was done, providing powerful ammunition to those who opposed recognition.

Truman was incensed over the Ward affair. Played up by the media, it stirred anti-Peking sentiment among Americans and caused further divisiveness in the Truman administration. Some policy advisers, like Soviet expert George Kennan, chief of the State Department's Policy Planning Staff, pushed for immediate U.S. recognition of the PRC. Kennan's view was that the Soviet Union, in retaliation for Washington's arrest of Soviet trade officials for spying and plotting to turn the United States and the PRC against each other, had prevailed upon the Chinese Communists to arrest Ward. Kennan told Acheson and other leading State Department officials that "the greatest single external threat to the complete Stalinization of China is that the U.S. should establish normal relations with the Chinese Communists and once more bring its influence to bear in that country, even if on a more restricted basis." Kennan maintained that the Communists would be "open to recognition," as Chou had indicated on October 1, 1949. Criticizing the anti-recognition position, Kennan argued that "if recognition had all the moral tones and implications of friendship which is being imputed to it in connection with the Chinese Communists, we could not possibly now be maintaining official relations with Tito, not to mention the Soviet and Satellite Governments."[23]

But Kennan soon became a minority voice. On November 22, James Reston of the *New York Times*, a columnist with close ties to "informed sources" in the government, reported that Senator Arthur Vandenberg (R, Michigan), chairman of the Senate Foreign Relations Committee and a champion of bipartisan foreign policy, was arguing that the United States should not recognize the PRC because it was not prepared to fulfill its basic obligations under international law. And on December 29, piqued by the Ward case, influential Senator Tom Connally (D, Texas) stated that he opposed recognition until the PRC gave satisfactory assurances of respect for international law.

By the end of 1949, Acheson started to pull back from his pro-recognition position. He concluded that the PRC might not want U.S. recognition. Writing in the *New York Times* on December 31, Reston reported that Truman, at a meeting with the National Security Council the day before, had found strong divisions among his defense and foreign affairs advisers. According to Reston, Acheson, concerned about congressional passage in January of the European Recovery Program and the next stage of the European Military Assistance Program, had shelved recognition for the time being at least. Reston concluded: "In short, while the air is now full of rumors about the formation of some new, clear and positive United States policy [toward China], the chances are that the Administration will change its policy very little."

Reston had reliable sources, for at the December 30 meeting Truman had approved National Security Council Document Number 48/2 (NSC 48/2). This held that the United States should use "covert, as well as overt means" . . . to "exploit . . . any rifts between the Chinese Communists and the USSR and between Stalinists and other elements in China, while scrupulously avoiding the appearance of intervention." Although it was decided that the United States would adopt a strategy of using Titoism to weaken Soviet influence in Communist countries, the United States would not recognize the PRC "until it is clearly in the interest of the United States to do so."[24]

The Formosa Issue

A series of events in late 1949 and the first half of 1950 solidified the anti-recognition view. In December, Chiang finally fled from his last base on the mainland to Formosa,[25] where he joined about 300,000 Nationalist troops. When Chiang announced he planned to attack the mainland and recover it by force, Truman faced the immediate problem of how to respond. To Democrats, still chafing from accusations of having "sold out" Eastern Europe to the Soviets at Yalta, it was one thing to "lose" the mainland. It would be another, especially in light of growing opposition of the Republicans and the increasingly shrill voice of the China lobby, to "lose" Formosa.

Some leading Republicans, such as former President Hoover and Senators H. Alexander Smith (R, New Jersey), Robert Taft (R, Ohio), and William Knowland (R, California), wanted Truman to defend Formosa and even establish a military base there. This would demonstrate that the United States would let communism go no farther in Asia. Truman's key foreign policy advisers were split over what to do. Deputy Under Secretary of State Rusk argued for establishment of a United Nations trusteeship over Formosa. Kennan had argued in a memorandum to Acheson in July 1949 that the U.S. should force Chiang and the Nationalists off Formosa, thereby removing even the possibility of rallying to the Generalissimo. But these proposals were never adopted.

The most serious conflict was between Secretary of Defense Louis Johnson and Acheson. Johnson, a strong supporter of Chiang, lobbied for U.S. military support to protect Formosa. But Acheson, though recognizing Formosa's strategic importance, strongly opposed Johnson's position. Acheson believed that forceful advocacy of political reform of the Nationalist government on Formosa, or lacking this, covert support for a native Taiwanese uprising against the Nationalists, would be more prudent options to keep the island out of Communist hands. Truman, relying more on Acheson's judgment, sided with his secretary of state.

On December 23, a State Department memorandum stated that Formosa held "no special military significance" for the United States. NSC 48/2 further signaled the end to U.S. support of Formosa. On January 3 the State Department informed all its posts that the public would soon learn that it expected Formosa to fall to the Communists but that this would not adversely affect U.S. security. Then at a press conference on January 5, Truman announced that the United States would supply economic assistance to the island, but would not seek to "establish military bases on Formosa at this time." Acheson later that day explained to the press that the phrase "at this time," inserted at the suggestion of Chairman of the Joint Chiefs of Staff General Omar Bradley, was "a recognition of the fact that, in the unlikely and unhappy event that our forces might be attacked in the Far East, the United States must be completely free to take whatever action in whatever area is necessary for its own security."[26]

Despite stiff pressure to the contrary, U.S. policy of not using military force to defend Formosa continued until the outbreak of the Korean War. In a speech before the National Press Club on January 12, Acheson repeated his argument that the United States must exploit the conflicting interests between the PRC and USSR. Yet his speech, understandably, would be remembered more for having placed Formosa (and Korea and Indo-China) outside the U.S. defense perimeter. But because of Formosa's strategic importance, and because of administration fears of appeasement, the United States continued to offer Formosa limited diplomatic and economic support. Although two days after the North Korean invasion of June 25 Truman ordered the Seventh Fleet to patrol the Formosa Straits, at that time the U.S. most likely would not have fought to protect the island from a Communist attack.

In his January 12 speech, Acheson also tried to soothe conflict in the administration over the China problem by proposing to "let the dust settle." But things were happening fast. On January 14, the Communist Chinese "requisitioned" the premises of the American Consulate General in Peking. Their motives were unclear. Perhaps the radical wing of the CCP wanted to demonstrate its anti-Americanism, or maybe some leaders wanted to use this incident to pressure the United States into offering recognition. Whatever the motive, Truman reacted angrily. He ordered the withdrawal of all American diplomats from China, which was completed by April. At a press conference on January 18, Acheson concluded that the seizure of the American consulate meant that Communist China did not want U.S. recognition.

The consulate incident also turned the minds of many China "moderates" in the State Department, such as Clubb and Davies, against the possibility of rapprochement with the Communist leadership. When Clubb left China, he concluded that the CCP leadership was "as perverted in some respects as that of Hitlerite Germany," and it had "attached China to the Soviet chariot, for better or worse." Davies then recommended sponsoring "counter-revolutionary movements in China and North Korea" to overthrow those Communist governments.[27] No doubt, both Clubb and Davies also had been influenced by the PRC's signing on February 14 of a thirty-year alliance with the Soviet Union. To Truman, Acheson, and most other China advisers in the government, this signaled a drawing of the battlelines between East and West. The next day, Acheson stated that the USSR would use this treaty to turn the PRC into a Soviet satellite.

The Korean War

What virtually sealed Truman's decision not to recognize the PRC was the outbreak of the Korean War in June 1950, especially the Chinese Communist military intervention in November. Whatever faint hope Truman and Acheson may have had that the PRC might demonstrate its independence of action from Moscow vanished. Though lacking hard evidence, the Truman administration assumed that the North Korean attack was orchestrated by Moscow and that Chinese military intervention, as stated by Acheson, was a clear and blatant act of aggression "directed by the Russians." Containment of communism on a a global basis had been the implied goal of the Truman Doctrine. With Korea, globalization of containment became reality.

The Korean War also eliminated any possibility that the United States might support the PRC's admission into the UN to take the "China" seat. Although the issues of diplomatic recognition and UN representation were legally separate, in reality they were very closely tied together. The Nationalist government's presence on the Security Council was necessary for continuation of the UN "police action" in Korea and official UN condemnation of the Chinese Communists as "aggressors." In addition, continued nonrecognition by the United States meant continued blockage of Communist China's admission to the UN. The U.S. "two China" policy would continue until 1971, when the PRC replaced the Nationalists in the UN and the United States began its move toward recognition of the PRC.

President Truman as Decision-Maker

Foreign Policy Context of Decision

When Truman suddenly became president after Roosevelt's death, he had virtually no preparation or experience in foreign affairs, and none at all regarding China. Indeed, in the classic sense, as vice president, Truman had been kept in the dark about almost all important issues, including the Manhattan Project. But Truman, the last president who was not a college graduate, was a voracious reader, especially of history and past presidents. Moreover, personal experiences had greatly affected him. He had fought in Europe during World War I. In addition, during the 1930s he had seen the forces of totalitarian aggression draw the world into World War II.

It was through his reading and personal experiences that Truman developed his main foreign policy principles:

1. Firm opposition to totalitarianism. By the end of World War II, this meant containment of Communism spearheaded by the Soviet Union.
2. No appeasement, such as at Munich, and no rewards for aggression.
3. Belief in the liberal vision that American democratic values and institutions had universal applicability. This especially applied to China with whom Americans had developed a special relationship.
4. Strong commitment to freedom for all people, both at home and abroad. Domestically, for example, Truman took a strong pro–civil rights stand in the 1948 election (which almost cost him victory, as Senator Strom Thurmond (D, South Carolina) led a "Dixiecrat Revolt"), and he desegregated the armed forces. In foreign policy, Truman stressed the indivisibility of world peace and freedom. In this regard, Truman focused on freedom from communism more than from European colonial rule or right-wing military dictatorships. In fact, Truman hesitated to drop support for corrupt, dictatorial rulers like Chiang because they resisted communism, which he considered an even greater evil. Until he realized by late 1949 that support of the Nationalists was futile and hopeless, he had continued Roosevelt's policy of supporting Chiang while urging him to carry out social and political reforms. This pattern of supporting anti-communist right-wing dictatorships would continue throughout the Cold War.
5. Elimination of poverty and want, reflected, for example, in the Marshall Plan, the Point Four program (aid to underdeveloped states), and the China Aid Act.
6. Belief in the UN and collective security to maintain world peace.

Context of Decision within Truman's
National Security Strategy
When the Communists won in China and established the PRC, Truman's national security strategy had two major components: Europe-first and containment of Soviet-led Communism. Truman saw

communism as the main threat to U.S. security, and dealing with the Soviet threat in Europe as his highest priority. As Roosevelt had considered Europe the most important theater of World War II, Truman
considered Europe the most important theater of the Cold War. Europe
was deemed more vital to U.S. security; the U.S. had troops stationed
there; its closest allies, Britain and France, were in Europe; Europe,
much more than Asia or elsewhere, had the technical base and human
wherewithal to absorb and effectively utilize American aid; and China
was embroiled in the chaos of civil war.

For all these reasons, Truman subordinated problems in Asia to
priorities in Europe. For example, in the fall of 1945, Truman reluctantly
decided to support France's reimposition of control in Indo-China because a strong postwar France was needed to fill the power vacuum left
in Europe by Germany's defeat. Later, the Europe-first strategy meant
paying insufficient attention to developments in China and subordinat-
ing decisions on China to policy needs in Europe. For example, in
1948–49 Truman hesitated to give Chiang more aid, or to take bold initiatives toward the Communist Chinese, for fear of congressional rejection of the Marshall Plan and NATO, his main priorities. Facing fiscally
tight Republicans, Truman had to choose carefully where to ask Congress for major funding. When Truman appointed Acheson secretary of
state, the secretary's anglophilism and Atlanticism reinforced this Europe-first strategy. Further indication of this strategy is that in Truman's
memoirs and books written about him, there is very little on China
compared to Europe.[28]

By the time of the Chinese Communist victory in late 1949 and
early 1950, Truman decided he needed a reevaluation of U.S. national
security strategy. After the USSR tested its first atomic bomb in September 1949, the United States could no longer rely on its atomic monopoly
to deter Soviet advances in Western Europe while maintaining drastic
cuts in its armed forces and defense budget. In addition, the Communist Chinese victory in October 1949 meant that communism was now
a major threat in Asia as well as Europe. This was especially so if the
PRC linked up with the USSR or were to become dominated by the
Kremlin. Moreover, Truman realized that British power was continuing
its slide and that the United States alone faced the burden of becoming
the leader of the "free world."

At first, Truman was reluctant to apply containment to China. He
and his foreign policy advisers perhaps feared that U.S. intervention in
the Chinese civil war might lead to a situation similar to the Spanish

civil war of the 1930s. The United States officially kept out of this war, but the USSR intervened as a counterweight to the involvement of Nazi Germany. If the United States kept its distance from China, perhaps the Soviet Union might do the same. But by late 1948, undoubtedly influenced by developing confrontation with the Soviet Union in Europe (e.g., the Soviet-engineered coup in Czechoslovakia in February and the Soviet-imposed Berlin Blockade in May), Truman toughened his stance against the Communist Chinese. With the formal establishment of the PRC in October, Truman worried more about the global and monolithic nature of the communist threat. The conclusion of the Sino-Soviet alliance in February 1950 further strengthened the president's view.

Sensing growing vulnerability of the U.S. and the West, Truman ordered the drafting of NSC 68. Completed in April 1950, this document sat on the president's desk until the Korean War. Its main points, however, were to dominate U.S. national security strategy for several years, including the early Eisenhower period. In essence, NSC 68 aimed to make containment effective during what was considered a dangerous period of U.S. vulnerability. Its basic premise was that world communism, led by the Soviet Union, was the main threat of the 1950s just as fascism had been in the thirties and forties, and that the U.S. had to spend what was needed to contain it. The Soviet Union was hesitant to engage the West in a general war, but it would find ways to spread communism through proxies.

The U.S., therefore, had to be able to respond to communist threats wherever they occurred, including Asia. It also had to be wary of a domino effect if communism won out anywhere. This point was in contrast with Kennan's early views on containment that stressed priorities of containment in Britain, Germany, and Japan. Also in contrast to Kennan's early views that containment should be implemented through a variety of political, diplomatic, economic, psychological, and military means, NSC 68 focused almost exclusively on the military.

NSC 68 also neglected another of Kennan's views that stressed a "divide and conquer" strategy within the communist world. No longer was "Titoism" seen as a viable alternative for U.S. strategy in China. Mao was seen as closely tied to and even subservient to Stalin. Dean Rusk, when he first took over as secretary of far eastern affairs in March 1950, at first pursued the strategy of pushing "Titoism" for Communist China. But the Korean War changed everything. In one of the clearest signs of this changed viewpoint, Rusk argued in 1951: " China has been driven by foreign masters into an adventure of foreign aggression. . . .

The Peiping regime may be a colonial Russian government. . . . It is not the government of China. . . . It is not Chinese."[29]

The adoption of NSC 68 after the outbreak of the Korean War thus had an important impact on Truman's China policy. Japan became the cornerstone of U.S. defense against communist advances in Asia. In addition, the United States beefed up noncommunist governments throughout Southeast Asia. Furthermore, defense of Asia became intertwined with that of Europe. According to Truman:

> From the very beginning of the Korean action I had always looked at it as a Russian maneuver, as part of the Kremlin's plan to destroy the unity of the free world. NATO, the Russians knew, would succeed only if the United States took part in the defense of Europe. The easiest way to keep us from doing our share in NATO was to draw us into military conflict in Asia. We could not deny military aid to a victim of Communist aggression in Asia unless we wanted other small nations to swing into the Soviet camp for fear of aggression which, alone, they could not resist. At the same time, it served to weaken us on a global plane and that, of course, was Russia's aim.[30]

Truman saw the Soviets behind the North Korean attack, and then behind Chinese Communist military intervention. The argument of Chinese Communist independence from the USSR, and the possibility of driving a wedge between the two communist giants, which Acheson and others had relied on in considering extension of recognition to the PRC, thus faded away. This view of the Chinese Communist regime was not shared by U.S. allies, particularly Britain, which had a different policy toward recognition of the PRC.

Context of Decision within President's Relations with Allies
U.S. allies had differing views toward the Communist Chinese, and consequently toward recognition. Some allies, including France, Italy, Canada, and Australia, did not offer recognition. For different reasons, each preferred to remain in concert with U.S. policy. France, for example, believed recognition might jeopardize U.S. aid for its war in Indo-China. Both the PRC and the USSR had been supporting Ho Chi Minh. In January 1950, both communist giants recognized Ho. The United States, accepting France's argument that it was fighting international communist aggression in Indo-China, recognized Bao Dai. France had

propped up this former emperor as a noncommunist nationalist alternative to Ho. In the spring, the United States set up a military advisory group in Vietnam and stepped up its economic and military aid to the French.

Great Britain took an entirely different approach to recognition of the PRC. On January 5, 1950, Britain withdrew recognition from the Nationalist government and the next day extended de jure recognition to the PRC. On January 9, Peking accepted recognition and intimated it would not move against Hong Kong.[31]

Protection of British economic and colonial interests in Asia was one of the main reasons for British recognition. As British Foreign Secretary Ernest Bevin explained to Acheson: "There are some factors which affect us specially, not only our interests in China but the position in Hong Kong, and also in Malaya and Singapore where there are vast Chinese communities. . . . [W]e have to be careful not to lose our grip of the situation on Asia."[32]

Almost from the outset, the United States tried to coordinate recognition policy with its allies, especially Britain. The United States sought to establish a united front toward Peking so that the West could utilize nonrecognition as a lever to influence the Chinese leadership. British cooperation was deemed essential, for unilateral British recognition would be seen by the USSR as an opportunity to split NATO and possibly influence Republicans in Congress to reduce Marshall Plan appropriations for Britain.

Britain's policy through the summer and early fall of 1949 was at first to delay recognition and adopt a unified policy with the U.S. But Britain changed course when the PRC was officially established in October and Chou invited foreign governments to establish official relations. Britain then, in effect, extended de facto recognition to the PRC. By January 1950, however, Britain had joined a number of other states in granting de jure recognition: the Soviet Union and its Eastern European satellites, Yugoslavia, India, Pakistan, Burma, Ceylon, Afghanistan, Norway, Denmark, Israel, Sweden, and Switzerland. The Netherlands extended recognition in March.

London reportedly gave Washington no official advance notice of its policy change, which upset Truman and angered the State Department. But Washington had seen the handwriting on the wall for some time, for there was no serious opposition to recognition in Britain as there was in the United States. Moreover, members of the British Commonwealth generally stood solidly behind the recognition decision.

Britain did not feel it was acting contrary to Washington's interests. It believed U.S. recognition was imminent, perhaps a few months away. In addition, Britain pointed out that its recognition of Peking did not connote approval. Rather, in Bevin's words, "there was no point not recognizing something that was there." But the lingering bad taste of the Ward affair and Peking's "requisitioning" of the American consulate in January forced Truman and Acheson to back off. Truman, though, still wanted to keep his options open. The president and Acheson still were considering using recognition to develop a "Titoist" alternative in China.

Britain's Prime Minister Clement Atlee and Bevin also sought a Titoist alternative, but their assumptions on dealing with China were quite different from those of Truman and Acheson. As already stated, Britain assumed the PRC was there to stay, so it might as well recognize what was a diplomatic fact of life. It also assumed that Chinese nationalism over time would prove more durable than communist ideological affiliation with the USSR. But unlike the United States, Britain decided that recognition was the best way to take advantage of eventual Sino-Soviet conflict and to encourage "Titoism." By keeping a diplomatic presence in China, Britain hoped to be in a better position to understand what was happening there, to communicate more easily with the Chinese leadership, and possibly to influence developments. Britain thus diverged from the United States on other issues, such as advocating the PRC's membership in the UN. Moreover, Britain feared that the U.S. policy of nonrecognition, accompanied by support of Chiang and blockage of Peking's UN membership, would drive Peking toward closer ties with Moscow and, in Bevin's words, result in "the permanent alienation of China from the West."

Why the divergence of British and U.S. policy? One view is that the level of British economic interests in China, about ten times that of the United States, and protection of Hong Kong were the key differences. But this does not explain why so many other states without economic or colonial interests in China recognized Peking.

Another view stresses Chinese Communist harassment of U.S. officials in the country. But Britain was also a victim of Chinese anti-Western hostility. For example, in the *Amethyst* incident of April 1949 Chinese forces fired on British warships, killing forty-two sailors and wounding fifty-three. Yet Britain did not let such incidents scuttle her decision to recognize the PRC.

A third explanation for this divergence of positions lies in the lack of conviction of Acheson and Truman regarding the advisability of recognizing the PRC. As Truman greatly respected Acheson and his ideas, he probably would have recognized the PRC if Acheson had pushed hard and convincingly for it. But Acheson himself, though seemingly favoring eventual recognition, wavered and remained indecisive. Moreover, there was a serious difference of views between the more moderate State Department, which looked for ways for accommodation with the PRC, and the Joint Chiefs of Staff and Defense Department, which pushed for increased support of Chiang.[33]

Still a fourth explanation lies in the opposition to accommodation with the PRC by domestic public opinion and Congress.

Domestic Context of Decision

The China issue was perhaps the most bedeviling and inflammable foreign policy issue Truman faced. In Europe, issues seemed clearer and public and congressional support for Truman's initiatives generally was favorable. But Truman's China policy, especially after the Chinese Communist victory, became a subject of intense controversy. Scholars, missionaries, businessmen, journalists, congresspersons, and much of the public as a whole took sides. There was significant opposition to recognition, yet there also was strong support.

Among the many groups urging cordial relations with the Chinese Communist regime, including recognition, were the Committee for a Democratic Far Eastern Policy and the Institute of Pacific Relations. Arrayed in opposition was the Asia-first wing of the Republican Party which joined forces with what came to be known as the China lobby. The major groups in this lobby were the American China Policy Association, the China Emergency Committee, The Committee to Defend America by Aiding Anti-Communist China, and the Committee on National Affairs.[34] By early 1950, the China issue had become one of the main rallying cries of McCarthyism. McCarthy claimed Communist sympathizers and traitors in the Truman administration had "lost" China to the Communists just like those in Roosevelt's administration, like Alger Hiss, had "lost" Eastern Europe and Manchuria to the Soviets at Yalta. On January 25, the conviction of Hiss on charges of perjury (and by implication espionage for the Soviet Union), lent further credence to McCarthyism and added a chill to the Cold War.

Truman and Acheson both were wary of the political power of the China lobby. Truman did not want to jeopardize his European economic and military programs. Nor did he take kindly to accusations of "losing" China to the Communists, or being labeled "soft" on communism. These concerns always loomed in the background, and surely influenced Truman's China decision not to recognize the Chinese Communist regime.

At the 1951 hearings on Truman's dismissal of General MacArthur for disobeying his orders in Korea, both Acheson and Ambassador-at-Large Philip Jessup testified that the United States never seriously considered recognition of the PRC. But as scholar Foster Rhea Dulles argues, these statements after the fact were "suspect." They were made at a time when both men were under attack for having been sympathetic toward the Chinese Communists and for wanting to abandon Chiang while he still might have been saved. What their hostile questioners were trying to establish was that both Acheson and Jessup had favored recognition, which encouraged the PRC to undertake an aggressive policy in East Asia. As Dulles concluded:

> In the prevailing climate of public opinion, the heyday of McCarthyism, Acheson and Jessup were very much on the defensive. In stressing their opposition to Peking's recognition at any time in the winter of 1949–50, they may well have felt driven in 1951 to go much further than their own thinking in the earlier period would really justify.[35]

Dulles was probably right, for U.S. domestic considerations did play a major role in Truman's nonrecognition decision. They also account, to a large extent, for the virtual absence of open and honest discussion of the pro-recognition position for many years. Truman tried to put off his recognition decision, preferably until after the Congressional elections of November 1950, but the Korean War changed everything.

Decision Options

After the Communist Chinese won the civil war, Truman faced several options. He could have listened to the counsel of "hawks" like Major General Claire Chennault and General MacArthur. They wanted to keep backing Chiang to the hilt and to fight a war on the mainland, if necessary, to overthrow the PRC and stamp out Chinese Communism. But Truman had already discarded this option, having accepted the warnings against such a folly from General Marshall and others.

Truman also could have committed the United States to military defense of Formosa, as advocated by the Pentagon, the Department of Defense, and anti–Truman administration supporters of Chiang both inside and outside of Washington. By early January 1950, the president had decided on a "hands-off" policy toward Formosa, as a first step toward complete U.S. disengagement and then recognition of the PRC. But when the Korean War broke out, as already noted, Truman decided to use the Seventh Fleet to prevent a Communist Chinese invasion of Formosa. Truman then rejected Chiang's offer to send 33,000 crack Nationalist troops to fight in Korea, but he had already put the United States on a course of support for Chiang and the Nationalists which would last for over two decades.

Truman's other main options revolved around recognition of the PRC. The pro-recognition proponents argued that early recognition would indicate American understanding of the forces of revolutionary nationalism in Asia; cause disunity in the Soviet bloc in Eastern Europe; encourage "Titoism" and thereby decrease Moscow's capability of making Peking an Asian satellite; accelerate Japan's postwar recovery through increased trade with China; help open China to added U.S. investment and trade, for mutual benefit; accept the reality of the PRC rather than launch a futile moral crusade to reform her; solidify relations with Great Britain and other allies that favored recognition, thereby taking away any Soviet attempt to exploit fissures in the Atlantic alliance; and help the West "moderate" extremist Chinese Communist behavior.

Opponents of recognition argued that U.S. recognition of the PRC, judging by its experience in recognizing the USSR, would not moderate Peking's behavior. Instead, recognition would give legal sanction to an outlaw state; support a government which had never held a free election; give up the possibility of using Chiang's military to drive the Chinese Communists out of power; reduce the credibility of U.S. support for an ally; destroy the will of Asian countries to resist future communist aggression; and make communism itself more respectable around the world.

By late 1949, Truman had leaned toward recognition. He would try, in Acheson's words, "to detach" the PRC "from subservience to Moscow and over a period of time encourage those vigorous influences which might modify it." But Truman decided to "wait and see" how the Communist Chinese leaders behaved, thereby keeping his options open and policies flexible. He was hoping, perhaps, that the natural course of events, that is, a Chinese Communist takeover of Formosa, would render U.S. support for Chiang moot and recognition far less controversial. He also was wavering because the CCP displayed anti-Americanism (especially in the Ward incident and requisitioning of the American consulate building in Peking); the PRC signed an alliance with the USSR; domestic critics had seized upon the China issue to weaken him politically; and he still was not convinced that recognition was the wisest course of action.

Truman's Leadership Role in the Decision

Truman was buffeted by criticism of his China policy and advice from all sides. Despite expected significant public and congressional opposition to recognition, Truman probably could have prevailed politically had he extended recognition before the Korean War. But to do so, first he had to be convinced that recognition was the best policy.

Realizing he had virtually no expertise on China, Truman let the State Department make China policy. The Joint Chiefs of Staff and Defense Department tried unsuccessfully to win Truman over to their generally pro-Chiang arguments. Instead, for policy advice Truman deferred to Acheson, whom he respected and admired greatly for his ability and intelligence. Acheson seemed to have accepted the inevitability of U.S recognition of the PRC, but he was uncertain as to its timing. In the short run, Acheson was not sure of either economic or political benefits, especially whether recognition was the best bet to foster "Titoism." One reason for uncertainty was the split in the CCP leadership between liberal and radical elements. Would recognition bolster the liberals or play into the hands of the radicals? Was the Chinese Communist government already a tool of Soviet imperialism? Nobody knew for sure.

Historian David McLean argues that Truman's hesitancy to extend recognition was mainly a reflection of Acheson's indecision. For sure, Truman, more so than Acheson, was concerned about criticism from Republicans and the China lobby; worried that recognition might jeopardize congressional support for his domestic programs and European policies; and outraged by anti-American acts by Chinese Communist leaders. But McLean argues that Truman still would have gone to bat for recognition if he was sure he was right.[36]

Truman was a president who weighed advice, sorted out nuances and complexities, then made a decision and stuck to it. As popular author David Halberstam noted, Truman "made his decisions quickly and cleanly by listening to the evidence and the best advice of those around him, and he did not look back."[37] Did Truman make the right decision on recognition or did he miss opportunities that might have positively changed the course of history? Although the long-term outcome of his decision is still being played out, short-term consequences are generally clearer.

Consequences of Truman's Decision for the United States and Other Countries Involved

The United States

The United States missed several opportunities to recognize the Chinese Communists, both before and after the official establishment of the PRC. It did not respond favorably, for example, to Mao's request in early 1945 to fly to Washington and meet Roosevelt, to Chou's démarche in June 1949 to establish amicable relations with the United States, to Mao's bid for diplomatic recognition in mid-June, or to Chou's open invitation after the establishment of the PRC for recognition from all countries of good will. It seemed there were always other issues and priorities that precluded U.S. acceptance. In 1945, Roosevelt was preparing for Yalta; and in 1949–50, the specter of "losing" China to the Communists was haunting Truman and his advisers. Thus what might have been diplomatically advisable at various times was not deemed politically feasible. It remains a subject of historical debate, however, whether favorable U.S. response to any of these initiatives would have made a significant difference in subsequent U.S.-Chinese relations.

Truman's policy of nonrecognition of the Communists had numerous important consequences, especially after the outbreak of the Korean War:

1. Truman ordered the Seventh Fleet to "prevent any attack on Formosa." Presaging the future American "two China policy," he declared that Formosa's future status "must await the restoration of security in the Pacific, a peace settlement with Japan, or consideration by the United Nations." This reversed an earlier decision to accept eventual PRC control of the island, and soon led to unintended

strong support for Chiang on Formosa. It also ignored the pleas of native Taiwanese for self-determination, and indeed overlooked reports that the Nationalists were terrorizing the Taiwanese into submission.

2. Japan replaced China as the focus of U.S. plans for postwar stability and security in Asia.

3. Truman stated that the United States would step up its military aid to the French in Indo-China and the Philippine government. He assumed that both were on the front lines in the fight against Soviet-directed communist guerrilla wars.

4. The United States abandoned the notion that the Communist Chinese Revolution was a "home grown" nationalist response to China's problems. Instead, it hardened its position that this revolution was part of a global communist threat directed by Moscow and that the Communist regime did not represent the will of the Chinese people.

5. Washington concluded that the PRC was driven more by communist ideology than practicality or national interest.

6. Washington steadfastly blocked the PRC's admission into the UN.

7. The China issue fueled the Red Scare of McCarthyism. This blamed the "loss" of China on subversion in the State Department and which, like Yalta, conjured up charges of appeasement, betrayal, and treason.

8. The United States developed prolonged hostility toward "Red China." This drove it deeper into the "Soviet camp" and complicated U.S.-Soviet relations. "Red China" became another Cold War adversary. In the 1970s, under Nixon and Carter, the United States played the "China card" to gain advantage in its relations with the Kremlin.

9. After the Korean War broke out, if Washington had recognized the PRC and established good communications links, the United States probably would have been much less likely to have crossed the 38th parallel into North Korea and misperceived PRC warnings on entering the war.

10. The United States lost an opportunity to align itself with the dynamic forces of Asian nationalism and anticolonialism, reflected in and inspired by the Chinese Communist Revolution.

11. U.S.-Chinese hostility confirmed the Chinese Communist view of the United States as an imperialist, exploitative, oppressive, and arrogant world power.

The People's Republic of China

To what extent did Chinese Communist leaders see conflict with the United States as inevitable? One position, taken by scholars like Warren Cohen, argues that the United States missed several opportunities to offer recognition that might have taken the United States and Communist China off a collision course.[38] According to Cohen, recognition was not only possible, but it could have made a significant difference in U.S.-Chinese relations. Truman, he argued, did not recognize Communist China because of his strong anti-Communism, McCarthyism, the China lobby, and the outbreak of the Korean War. Instead, Truman hesitated to dump Chiang, failed to respond to Communist Chinese "feelers," and took no initiatives of his own to establish friendly relations. These scholars also point out that Communist Chinese leaders were by no means in Stalin's hip pocket. For even though Mao signed a thirty-year treaty with Stalin, negotiations were prolonged and difficult because Stalin wanted to keep Mao in his place as a subordinate.

This view also criticizes Truman's "casual ascription" of the North Korean attack of South Korea to Soviet orchestration. Moreover, it faults Truman for branding the Communist Chinese "aggressors" in entering the Korean War. Instead, it holds that the United States misperceived China as a serious military threat in Korea, and ignored its warnings that it would enter the war if MacArthur's UN troops threatened its territorial integrity and sovereignty.

Finally, this position criticizes Truman for basing his nonrecognition decision in part on what he considered the PRC's oppressive domestic policies. The argument runs that if this criterion had been applied uniformly, the United States would not have maintained diplomatic relations with the Soviet Union, military juntas in Latin America, or authoritarian regimes anywhere else in the world.

An opposing position, held by scholars like Steven Goldstein,[39] holds that the Communist Chinese would have been implacably hostile to the United States whether or not it had offered recognition to the PRC. According to this view, recognition would not have led to mutual toleration and better understanding of each other's views, let alone amity. Instead, it would have led inexorably toward conflict and confrontation. According to Goldstein, by 1949 anti-Americanism was "rampant among the masses," and communist ideology was too strong among the Chinese Communist leadership. Moreover, CCP leaders believed U.S. support for the Nationalists both before and after they fled to Formosa was anathema; explanations of U.S. China policy offered by the white paper were "inflammatory"; advocacy of "Titoism" for China "was . . . an imperialist trick to win China over to the American side"; and neutralism was "at best unpatriotic, at worst treasonous." This view also points to the pro-Soviet aspect of Mao's "leaning to one side" speech; the "illusion" that the Communist Chinese were really "different" from the Soviet Communists; China's ignoring of international treaties and obligations as evidenced by the Ward affair and seizure of American governmental property in Peking; and finally Communist Chinese "aggression" in Korea. In short, argues Goldstein, previous U.S. policies, pressure by the Chinese people, and communist ideology meant there was no "lost chance" for the U.S. and China to develop peaceful relations.

No matter which view on "inevitability" of conflict is subscribed to, what is indisputable is that U.S. relations with the PRC became increasingly embittered. For many years, the United States vilified "Red China," and anti-Americanism became the core of Peking's foreign policy.[40]

Conclusion

Historians continue to debate the wisdom of Truman's decision not to recognize the PRC. Controversy swirls over the question of missed opportunities and misperceptions on the part of both the United States and the PRC. Truman was concerned about both the domestic and international political consequences of extending diplomatic recognition to the PRC. Strong opposition to recognition both inside and outside the Democratic Party surely influenced Truman and eventually won the day. There was widespread fixation in his administration on the threat of Soviet communism. Some, like Dean Rusk, believed Chinese Communist leaders were not only closely tied to Moscow, but even tools of the Kremlin. Severe critics of Truman's China policy outside the Democratic Party kept up a steady drumbeat. Pressure from Republican "Asia firsters" and the China lobby, soon intensified by the McCarthy-dominated "Red Scare," surely took their toll on the president. They argued that Truman and his State Department Asia experts had misjudged the Chinese Communist leaders as "agrarian reformers," had not done enough to counter the dangerous growth of communism in Asia, and had "lost" China. They wanted the United States to isolate and contain the Chinese Communist regime, work for its collapse, and thereby demonstrate to the rest of Asia that the United States would not accept further communist expansion.

The Chinese Communists, on their part, were divided over whether to seek recognition from the United States. Pragmatists tended to want U.S. recognition, whereas the more hardline ideologues tended toward rejectionism. The Formosa and the United Nations China seat issues decreased chances for U.S. recognition. Consequences of non-recognition were severe. In the short run, the most serious negative result was failure to keep the PRC out of the Korean War. In the long run, hostility between the United States and PRC grew during the fifties and sixties. Relations reached their low point, perhaps, during the Vietnam War. Looking for a way out of this war, President Richard Nixon played the first "China card" when he made his dramatic visit to the PRC in 1972. From the PRC viewpoint, the death of Mao and the seriousness of the Sino-Soviet split created the opportunity for closer relations with the United States. American diplomatic recognition finally came in January 1979 under President Jimmy Carter.

Questions for Discussion

1. Could the United States have done anything to prevent China from becoming communist?

2. Was U.S. recognition of the Nationalist government on Formosa inconsistent with its arguments against recognition of the PRC?

3. Why did the United States not agree with Britain's decision to recognize the PRC?

4. Was the proposed strategy of fostering "Titoism" in China through recognition realistic?

5. Was serious conflict between the United States and PRC inevitable regardless of U.S. recognition?

6. Should the United States have supported dictatorial regimes like Chiang's because they were anticommunist?

7. Did nonrecognition increase the likelihood of Communist Chinese military intervention in the Korean War ?

8. Should the United States recognize any regime which violates the human rights of its citizens?

9. If Acheson had advocated recognition of the PRC more forcefully and convincingly, would Truman have recognized the PRC?

10. How important was McCarthyism, the China lobby, and Republican Party criticism of Truman's China policy in keeping Truman from recognizing the PRC?

Notes

1. According to international law, the following are the major criteria for diplomatic recognition: the government seeking recognition must in fact govern without serious opposition to its rule; it must be reasonably stable and have staying power; it must declare its readiness to honor its international obligations to other states; and if UN membership is involved, presumably it must be a "peace-loving nation." For a discussion of these criteria and other matters related to Truman's diplomatic recognition decision, see Cecil V. Crabb, Jr., *American Foreign Policy In the Nuclear Age*, 5th ed. (New York: Harper & Row, 1988), pp. 60–62.

2. Quoted by Foster Rhea Dulles, *American Policy toward Communist China, 1949–1969* (New York: Thomas Y. Crowell, 1971), p. 27.

3. David D. Barrett, *Dixie Mission: The United States Observer Group in Yenan, 1944* (Berkeley: California Center for Chinese Studies, 1970); Barbara Tuchman, *Stilwell and the American Experience in China, 1941–45* (New York: Bantam, 1972), pp. 610–11; and Joseph W. Esherick (ed.), *Lost Chance in China: The World War II Dispatches of John S. Service* (New York: Random House, 1974), especially pp. 301–2.

4. Quoted by Russell D. Buhite, *Patrick J. Hurley and American Foreign Policy* (Ithaca, N.Y.: Cornell University Press, 1973), p. 152.

5. See Barbara Tuchman, "If Mao had Come to Washington," *Foreign Affairs*, 51 October 1972: 44–62.

6. Letter, Truman to Will Durant, November 7, 1951. Quoted by Robert J. Donovan, *Tumultuous Years: The Presidency of Harry S Truman, 1949–1953* (New York: W. W. Norton, 1982), p. 68.

7. Quoted in ibid., p. 71.

8. George C. Marshall, memorandum of conversation with President Truman, Secretary of State Byrnes, and Admiral Leahy, December 11, 1945, *Foreign Relations of the United States (FRUS)*, 1945, 7:767–69.

9. Marshall memorandum of conversation with the president and Dean Acheson, December 14, 1945, ibid., p. 770.

10. Quoted by Cabell Phillips, *The Truman Presidency* (New York: Macmillan, 1966), pp. 281–82.

11. The Truman administration gave the Nationalists more than $800 million in postwar Lend-Lease, which was more than it gave China during the war to fight Japan.

12. See Albert C. Wedemeyer, *Wedemeyer Reports!* (New York: Henry Holt, 1958).

13. Wedemeyer's Report was published for the first time as an annex to the white paper on China, released on August 5, 1949.

14. Senate Committee on Armed Services, *Hearings on the Nomination of General George C. Marshall as Secretary of State*, 81st Cong., 2d sess. (1950), p. 22

15. Clubb to Acheson, June 1, 1949, *FRUS*, 1949, 8:357–60.

16. For a good discussion of this interpretation of Mao's statement, see Jian Chen," The Sino-Soviet Alliance and China's Entry in the Korean War," Cold War International History Project, the Woodrow Wilson Center for Scholars, June 1992, pp. 1–4.

17. Memorandum from Under Secretary of State James Webb of his meeting with Truman, October 3, 1949, Executive Secretariat Records, box 3; cited by Wilson D. Miscamble, *George F. Kennan and the Making of American Foreign Policy, 1947–1950* (Princeton: Princeton University Press, 1992), p. 238.

18. Quoted in ibid., p. 239.

19. Donovan, p. 84.

20. Tito then was the communist ruler of Yugoslavia who broke with Stalin in 1948. Although he was dictatorial, the United States supported him because of his independence from Moscow.

21. See John Lewis Gaddis, *Strategies of Containment* (New York: Oxford University Press, 1982), pp. 68–69.

22. Acheson's memorandum of conversation with Truman, November 17, 1949, Executive Secretariat Records, box 3. Cited by ibid.

23. Miscamble, p. 240.

24. NSC 48/2, December 30, 1949. Collection of National Security Council Documents. Modern Military Branch, National Archives. See Gaddis, p. 69, and Donovan, p. 88.

25. Under the Truman administration, the island was commonly and officially called Formosa, the name given to it by Portugal when she "discovered" it in 1590. Japan seized Formosa in the Sino-Japanese War of 1894–95 and held it until the end of World War II. At the Cairo Conference of 1943, the Allies recognized Chinese *de facto* control of Formosa until the signing of a peace treaty with Japan. Taiwan is the island's Chinese name. Today, officially it is called the Republic of China.

26. Dean Acheson, *Present at the Creation* (New York: Signet, 1969), p. 460.

27. See Clubb's letter to Kennan, April 25, 1950 (top secret), and Davies' internal State Department memorandum, June 6, 1950 (secret), in Michael Schaller, "Consul General O. Edmund Clubb, John P. Davies, and the "Inevitability" of Conflict between the United States and China, 1949–50: A Comment and New Documentation," *Diplomatic History*, 9 (Spring 1985): 149–60.

28. See, for example, David McCullough, *Truman* (New York: Touchstone, 1992); and Clark Clifford, *Counsel to the President: A Memoir* (New York: Anchor, 1991).

29. Quoted by Michael Schaller, *The United States and China in the Twentieth Century* (New York: Oxford University Press, 1990), pp. 128–29. Schaller points out that Rusk, following U.S. government policy, never called the Communist Chinese capital by its original name, Peking (now Beijing), which means "northern capital." The Nationalists had made Nanking the capital and the old capital was renamed Peiping, or "northern peace." The United States continued this reference to Peiping until the late 1960s to indicate its refusal to recognize the legality of the PRC.

30. Harry S. Truman, *Memoirs* Vol. 2: *Years of Trial and Hope* (New York: Signet, 1956), p. 496.

31. Because Britain maintained a consulate on Formosa, Britain and the PRC did not exchange ambassadors until 1972.

32. Personal Message from Mr. Bevin to Mr. Acheson, December 16, 1949, *FRUS*, 1949, 9: 225–26.

33. For a good discussion of this view, see David McLean, "American Nationalism, the China Myth, and the Truman Doctrine: The Question of Accommodation with Peking, 1949–50," *Diplomatic History* 10 (Winter 1986): 25–42.

34. For details on these groups and others, see Congressional Quarterly, *China and U.S. Policy Since 1945* (Washington, D.C.: Congressional Quarterly, 1980), pp. 6–7.

35. Dulles, pp. 54–55.

36. McLean, pp. 30–31.

37. David Halberstam, *The Fifties* (New York: Villard Books, 1993), p. 23.

38. Warren Cohen, "Acheson's Search for Accommodation," in Thomas Patterson (ed.), *Major Problems in American Foreign Policy*, vol. 2: *Since 1914*, 3rd ed. (Lexington, Mass: D. C. Heath, 1989), pp. 371–81.

39. Steven M. Goldstein, "No Lost Chance: Chinese Anti-Americanism," ibid., pp. 390–96.

40. For a good discussion of this issue, see O. Edmund Clubb, "Sino-American Relations," *Diplomat*, 17 (September 1966): 59–67.

Selected Bibliography

Acheson, Dean, *Present at the Creation*. New York: Signet, 1969.

Donovan, Robert J. *Tumultuous Years, the Presidency of Harry S. Truman, 1949–1953*. New York: W. W. Norton, 1982.

Dulles, Foster Rhea. *American Policy toward Communist China, 1949–1969*. New York: Thomas Crowell, 1971.

McCullough, David. *Truman*. New York: Touchstone, 1992.

Miscamble, Wilson. *George F. Kennan and the Making of American Foreign Policy, 1947–1950*. Princeton: Princeton University Press, 1992.

Phillipps, Cabell. *The Truman Presidency*. New York: Macmillan, 1966.

Schaller, Michael. *The United States and China in the Twentieth Century*. New York: Oxford University Press, 1990.

Truman, Harry S. *Memoirs of Harry S. Truman*, vol. 2: *Years of Trial and Hope*. New York: Signet, 1956.

Tuchman, Barbara. *Stilwell and the American Experience in China, 1941–45*. New York: Bantam, 1972.

Wedemeyer, Albert C. *Wedemeyer Reports!* New York: Henry Holt, 1958.

2

President Eisenhower's Decision to Oppose the British-French-Israeli Invasion of Suez

Setting and Overview of Eisenhower's Decision

The Suez Canal, which linked the Mediterranean with the Red Sea, opened in 1869. It was conceived by French leaders and built by Egyptian labor. The Sultan of Turkey, who controlled Egypt until 1914, had given the Suez Canal Maritime Company responsibility to operate, maintain, administer, and finance the waterway. He had granted shareholders of this company a concession to own and run the canal for ninety-nine years after its opening. After World War I and the demise of the Ottoman Empire, England and France increasingly considered the canal a key to defense of their colonies in the Middle East and the flow of oil to fuel their economies, and as a critical strategic and commercial link to their interests in Southwest Asia and the Far East. As time passed, the canal grew as a symbol of their dominance in the Middle East and status as world powers. To Egypt, however, the canal became an irritating reminder of colonial subjugation and sparked nationalist resentment. In 1949, Egypt was granted a greater share of the profits and more of a say in running the canal. When Egyptian President Nasser nationalized the canal in July 1956, Egyptians rejoiced. England and France, however, felt compelled to resist Nasser's action by force. In the fall, they were joined by Israel in launching an invasion of Egypt. Israel had its own objectives,

53

particularly ending Egypt's blockade of Israeli shipping through the Gulf of Aqaba, ending terrorist raids from the Gaza Strip, and eliminating Egypt's military threat from the Sinai Peninsula.

The Anglo-French-Israeli invasion presented President Eisenhower with one of his most important, delicate, and controversial foreign policy problems. His decision to oppose the invasion was made within the context of numerous complicated issues and considerations: relations with the Soviet Union, decolonization, Arab nationalism, balance of power (regional and worldwide), oil, historical analogies, egos and prestige of world leaders, use of military force, diplomacy, the peacekeeping role of the United Nations, the cohesion of the NATO alliance, and the U.S. presidential election. The Suez War had strategic, economic, and political repercussions on the international, regional, and individual country levels that severely tested Eisenhower's diplomatic and leadership skills.

President Eisenhower's Decision

EISENHOWER OPPOSED THE ANGLO-FRENCH-ISRAELI INVASION OF EGYPT BY CALLING THROUGH THE UNITED NATIONS FOR AN IMMEDIATE CEASE-FIRE AND CESSATION OF THE USE OR THREAT OF FORCE IN THE AREA AND BY INVOKING LIMITED BUT SIGNIFICANT ECONOMIC SANCTIONS AGAINST THE INVADERS.

Eisenhower's decision was controversial for several major reasons:

1. It created serious friction in the Western alliance. This was the first time during the Cold War that the United States had sided diplomatically against her key NATO allies.
2. Eisenhower joined with the Soviet Union in denouncing the invasion of Egypt. Adding to the controversy was the fact that the president's decision occurred at the same time the Soviet Union was brutally suppressing the rebellion in Hungary, which Eisenhower strongly denounced.
3. Eisenhower castigated Israel for its "aggressive" action in Suez, causing severe strain in U.S.-Israel relations.
4. Eisenhower acted through the United Nations to effect a cease-fire and peaceful resolution of the Suez conflict.

5. It was made during the stretch-run of the U.S. presidential election campaign, and in the face of stinging criticism from Democratic Party candidate Adlai Stevenson, the media, and the Israeli lobby.

Background of the Decision

Historical Context

U.S. policy during the Suez Canal crisis of 1956 had roots in both the Truman administration and the early years of the Eisenhower administration. After Truman supported the creation of the State of Israel,[1] he put Israel and indeed the entire Middle East region on the backburner of U.S. foreign policy. His priority was containing the Soviet threat to Western Europe and prosecution of the Korean War.

Although generally sympathetic to Israel, Truman did not offer it arms either during or after the 1948 War. Early in 1950, American Jews and their supporters, distressed over reports of increased shipments of British arms to Arab states, began lobbying Washington to send arms to Israel. Instead, the United States joined Britain and France in issuing the Tripartite Declaration of May 25, 1950. Accordingly, the three signatories pledged to limit arms shipments and to take joint action, either inside or outside the United Nations, against any attempt to alter the 1949 armistice boundaries by force. In early 1952, the United States and Britain floated the idea of a Middle East Defense Organization (MEDO), which they hoped might turn out to be a mini NATO and an extension of the West's anti-communist defense line. Egypt would serve as an anchor to provide security to the canal area and attract membership of other Arab states. But early optimism that Egypt might join MEDO under General Muhammad Naguib, who emerged as that country's strongman after the overthrow of King Farouk on July 23, 1952, faded fast in early 1953. By this time, Great Britain's grip over the Suez Canal base, which Egyptian nationalists bitterly opposed, was slipping, and the United States was changing administrations. The MEDO idea finally died when the more independent-minded Gamal Abdel Nasser, who became prime minister of Egypt on April 18, 1954, and ousted Naguib from the presidency on November 14 of that year, considered it neocolonialist entrapment.[2]

After Eisenhower helped end the Korean War in July 1953, he paid increasing attention to the Middle East. He recognized the region's importance for both economic and geostrategic reasons. The area had vast oil reserves that were critical to the economies and military defense of Western Europe. Most of this oil flowed through the Suez Canal. Moreover, major fields were situated on the southwestern flank of the Soviet Union. Eisenhower feared that Soviet-sponsored communist subversion in neighboring states would foreshadow Soviet military penetration of the region. At first, Eisenhower continued U.S. policy of relying on Britain, as the dominant power in the Middle East, to contain communist expansionism. Soon, though, he realized that the United States would have to act decisively in the region to prevent the Soviets from filling a power vacuum created by declining British power. In search of a new strategy in the Middle East, Eisenhower faced conflicting policy requirements which he never successfully reconciled: opposing European imperialism while maintaining cooperation with America's main allies, Britain and France; identifying the United States with indigenous nationalist movements and recognizing Arab diversity and disunity while continuing friendship with Israel and trying to settle the Israeli-Arab conflict; and enlisting countries in a collective security arrangement to deter Soviet aggression while accepting their independence of action.

Eisenhower's first major Middle East challenge was in Iran. He operated regionally within a global strategy of preventing the Soviet Union from gaining a toehold in areas formerly under Western influence. In the summer of 1953, the CIA orchestrated with Britain the overthrow of Premier Mohammed Mossadegh and the return to power of the Shah. Eisenhower justified this covert action on grounds of U.S. national security. He believed that Mossadegh, an Iranian nationalist supported by the Communist Tudeh Party, was a puppet of Moscow who had to be removed. Mossadegh had already nationalized Iran's oil fields, and soon he might strike a deal with Moscow. The coup spelled temporary "success" for the West: British and American companies divided control over the oil, and the perceived communist threat was repulsed.

Eisenhower did not hesitate to act similarly in Guatemala in 1954. When Jacob Arbenz Guzman became president in 1951, he aligned himself with a wide assortment of nationalist/communist elements. Worried about expropriation of United Fruit Company holdings, concerned that the Arbenz government threatened continued U.S. control over the Panama Canal, and fearful of increased communist influence in Central

America exercised by Moscow, Eisenhower approved the CIA's plan to overthrow Arbenz. Eisenhower erroneously believed that the Arbenz nationalist reform movement, like that of Mossadegh, was controlled by world communism. The president would make the same mistake again in the Middle East, this time with Nasser.

The overthrow of Mossadegh was the high water mark of Eisenhower's collaboration with the British in the Middle East. In Iran, U.S. and British oil and geostrategic interests converged. Subsequently, however, the United States would distance itself from British policy. Eisenhower recognized that England's power in the region was slipping. Furthermore, he agreed with the admonition from senior American diplomats in the field, such as American ambassador to Egypt Jefferson Caffrey, that continued association with London's imperialist goals would damage opportunities for the United States to ally itself with the forces of Arab nationalism. Secretary of State John Foster Dulles, whose views on foreign policy Eisenhower greatly respected and who dominated his cabinet, drew similar conclusions after his trip to the Middle East in May 1953. In a memorandum to the president, Dulles wrote:

> British position rapidly deteriorating, probably to the point of non-repair . . . we find an intense distrust and dislike for the British . . . no respect for the French as a political force . . . United States position also not good. [This last was attributed to the American policy of friendly support for Israel, and to the tendency of the Arabs to associate the United States with British and French "colonial and imperialistic policies."][3]

This memorandum clearly shows the general direction that Eisenhower's policy would take, straight through the Suez crisis of 1956. Believing that the Truman administration's tilt toward Israel had hurt Washington's chances of shoring up its position with Arab states, Eisenhower decided to act "even-handedly" in the Arab-Israeli conflict. In effect, this policy shift meant a tougher stance toward Israel. The United States would continue denying Israel's requests for arms while supplying its Arab neighbors, oppose Israel's shift of its capital to Jerusalem, protest Israel's raids on Arab lands, and criticize Israel's policies of unlimited Jewish immigration and minimal compensation paid to Arab refugees. In addition, the United States would firm up feudal monarchies in Saudi Arabia and the Persian Gulf, serve as an active neutral in helping Britain resolve its quarrel with Nasser over maintaining military strength in the Suez Canal area, and work with France to compose its differences with the Egyptian leader over his support for Arab revolutionaries in Algeria.

After the plan to base a regional defense against Soviet aggression in Egypt floundered, the United States shifted to a "Northern Tier" strategy. This involved strengthening states on or near the USSR's border in Southwest Asia. But Eisenhower mistakenly assumed that the Soviet threat in the Middle East was the same as in Europe. Consequently, he misperceived the more serious challenges to his Middle East diplomacy from Arab nationalism. In late 1954, Eisenhower encouraged a British initiative for an anti-Soviet alliance. On February 24, 1955, the American president was pleased when Iraq and Turkey signed the Baghdad Pact. Britain joined on April 4, Pakistan on September 23, and Iran on November 23.

U.S. support for the pact still led to tension and conflict with Nasser. He was suspicious that the pact was a Western subterfuge to reimpose imperialism and split the Arab world. Moreover, he was angry that the pact struck a blow at his dream of leading the Arab world because it bolstered a rival Arab leader, the pro-British premier General Nuri es-Said of Iraq. He thus sought to destroy it. Moreover, Nasser was determined to remain officially neutral in the Cold War. He would not join any Cold War alliances, nor would he countenance any in the region. At the first conference of twenty-nine nonaligned African and Asian countries held in Bandung, Indonesia in April 1955, he met with important world figures. India's Prime Minister Jawaharlal Nehru and Yugoslavia's Marshal Tito were especially influential in reinforcing his neutralist posture, bolstering his leadership position in Egypt and the Arab world, and supporting his anti-Israel stance.

Nasser eagerly sought arms from any source. At first, he looked to the West. But what he received from Britain and France fell far short of his needs. He was irked by London's comparatively large arms shipments to Iraq, and he was perturbed by stepped-up French arms supplies to Israel, especially advanced Mystère jet planes which were superior to what Arab countries had. Moreover, he was shocked by the effectiveness of the February 28, 1955 Israeli raid on Egyptian army headquarters in the Gaza Strip. Prime Minister David Ben-Gurion, the Israeli leader who had taken over as Minister of Defense on February 20, claimed that this raid was retaliation for *fedayeen* (self-sacrifice) commando attacks launched from the Strip on Jewish territory. Angered and humiliated by Israel, Nasser felt he had to restore Egyptian pride and dignity. He was also bent on revenge. Increasing Egypt's military power to fight Israel now seemed more important to him than building Egypt's economy. Soon he became obsessed with obtaining arms.

Nasser hoped that Eisenhower's "even-handed" policy in the Middle East would lead to arms shipments from the United States. In April 1954, and again a year later, Washington sent arms to Iraq but not Egypt. In November, after the signing of the Suez Base agreement, Eisenhower promised Nasser about $27 million in arms, but only if Egypt joined in a Western defense system.[4] When Nasser balked at what he considered a crass infringement of Egyptian sovereignty, at the end of December Secretary Dulles decided not to sell Egypt arms.[5]

The Czech Arms Deal

Because Nasser was distressed that Washington was dragging its feet on arms shipments, he turned to communist countries. At the Bandung Conference, Nasser first approached Premier Chou En-Lai of the People's Republic of China (PRC). Chou replied that his country could not meet Nasser's arms needs because she herself relied on Soviet arms. But sympathetic to his position, Chou told Nasser he would pass on his request to Kremlin leaders. The USSR then seized an historic opportunity. During the summer of 1955, the USSR arranged for arms shipments through Czechoslovakia.

Eisenhower and Dulles had made a double miscalculation. They did not believe Nasser would ask the Soviet Union for arms. Nor did they expect Moscow was serious about offering arms, for never before had the Kremlin extended military aid to non-communist nationalist leaders. Once the president realized the arms deal was on track, he tried desperately to derail it. He sent three emissaries on futile missions to change Nasser's mind, including one by Kermit Roosevelt (Theodore Roosevelt's grandson, known as 'Kim'), the CIA's chief representative in the Middle East.[6] But all to no avail. For on September 27, even before Roosevelt arrived, Cairo announced the barter deal: Czechoslovakia would trade Egypt $200 million in arms for Egyptian cotton.[7]

The Czech arms deal signalled a defeat for Eisenhower's Middle East policy. It upset the balance of power in the region, broke the Western monopoly of arms to the region, and boosted Nasser's prestige in the Arab world. This was the first time an Arab leader had successfully defied Western governments, and the newly received arms could be used to destroy Israel. The arms deal also was a harbinger of a significant Soviet presence in the Middle East. It indicated a failure of the "Northern Tier" containment strategy and pushed the Middle East into the Cold War arena. In addition, prospects of a dreaded arms race in the region now became a reality. Israel especially was in shock, for the Czech arms deal portended a grave danger to her security. France, which had begun secret arms and military training agreements with Israel in the early 1950s, stepped up her military aid to the Jewish state. But when Israel pressured the United States for arms, Dulles demurred. Like before, he told Israel "not to worry," for the UN and the Tripartite Declaration would guarantee her security.

The Czech arms deal set off a chain of events that eventually led to the 1956 Suez War. In 1953 and 1954, Eisenhower had approved covert action to overthrow nationalist leaders in Iran and Guatemala whose anti-American policies were interpreted as furthering the cause of world communism. But in 1955, even after the Czech arms deal, Eisenhower chose not to punish Nasser but to woo him. He sought to convince the Egyptian leader that his country's interests would be served best through cooperation with the West. The main Western enticement was aid for building the Aswan High Dam. If Western arms could not bind Nasser to the Western camp, Western money might.

Cancellation of the West's Aswan Dam Offer
and Nasser's Nationalization of the Canal

Egyptian leaders since 1947 had envisioned the building of a huge dam on the Nile River that would mean great economic benefits through vastly increased hydroelectric power and irrigation. But only President Nasser took concrete steps to realize this dream. At first, Nasser looked to West for financing. In December 1955, the U.S. and British governments and the World Bank made a preliminary commitment to Egypt to finance the dam. At this point, British and American policy converged over the importance of the project. Both wanted to keep Nasser from again turning to the Soviet Union. Dulles and Eisenhower differed over the likelihood of a legitimate Soviet offer. Dulles did not believe Moscow had the capability to complete such a highly complex engineering feat nor the economic wherewithal to finance the dam. Eisenhower feared that Moscow would make a more attractive offer.[8] Eisenhower though, like Dulles, was determined to keep Russia out of the Middle East. The president also felt the United States was the country best positioned to effect an Egyptian-Israeli peace, which would allow Egypt to concentrate on economic development.

Meanwhile, Nasser's delay in accepting the U.S.–British–World Bank loan offer for building the dam irritated Eisenhower. He believed the Egyptian leader had decided to "play off East against West by black-mailing both."[9] The issue of Nasser's recognition of the PRC on May 16, 1956 further annoyed the Eisenhower administration, particularly Secretary Dulles. Britain had recognized the PRC in 1949, without adverse consequences to U.S.-British relations. Israel's recognition of the PRC in 1950 had caused barely a stir in the more politically sympathetic Truman administration. But Egypt's, coming on the heels of the Czech arms deal and Washington's serious conflict with the PRC over control of the off-shore islands of Quemoy and Matsu, raised a tremendous ruckus. Opposition to Congress's financing the dam now included both the Israel and China lobbies. They were joined by Cold War conservatives alarmed by Nasser's "pro-Soviet neutralism," fiscally conservative congressmen worried about large, risky financial expenditures, and southern senators concerned that Egyptian cotton would hurt domestic growers.

By summer 1956, the clash over the Aswan Dam financing climaxed. In the middle of June, new Soviet Foreign Minister Dmitri Shepilov visited Cairo and made Nasser a serious offer. Nasser also agreed to buy more arms from the Soviets, again to be paid for with Egyptian cotton. Eisenhower then felt Egypt would never be able to pay for Western and World Bank financing. On July 13, Dulles met with Eisenhower at his Gettysburg farm, where the president was recuperating from his operation in early June for ileitis. The two decided to take a firmer anti-Nasser stand. On July 19, the Egyptian ambassador to Washington, according to Eisenhower, "issued a new demand for a huge commitment over a period of ten years." Dulles then told the ambassador that the United States was withdrawing its offer in light of Egypt's delay in accepting U.S. terms and making "unacceptable counterpropoals."[10] Britain withdrew its offer the next day because of continued quarrels over her future in Suez. Feeling betrayed by the West that had reneged on promises to send arms and finance the dam, Nasser countered almost immediately. On July 24, he bitterly attacked the United States. On the 26th, he announced the nationalization of the Suez Canal, ostensibly to gain revenue for financing the Aswan Dam.[11]

Secret Plans for the Suez War

The resultant crisis led Britain, France, and Israel to plan an invasion of Egypt. At first, Eisenhower tried to forestall the use of military force. He did not rule out force completely, however, intending to use it as a lever in negotiations with Nasser. "My view," he wrote, "was that if Nasser was wholly arrogant, the United States would have to support any reasonable countermeasures. The fate of Western Europe must never be placed at the whim of a dictator and it was conceivable that the use of force under *extreme* circumstances might become necessary. In this unhappy event, quick military action must be so strong as to be completed successfully without delay—any other course would create new problems." Eisenhower suggested such circumstances would entail Nasser's closing the canal, refusing to allow free passage, and endangering lives of U.S. citizens in the Canal Zone.[12]

When his stipulated circumstances for using force never materialized, Eisenhower opted for a strategy of delay, cooling off, playing for time, diplomacy, and negotiations. He hoped to avert military action by England and France, which he considered unwise, by letting the crisis "wither on the vine."

Eisenhower wrote several times to British Prime Minister Anthony Eden, warning his World War II friend not to use military force. The president maintained that both U.S. and world public opinion surely would condemn such action. Eisenhower also sent Secretary Dulles to arrange a conference of eighteen maritime nations to put pressure on Nasser to internationalize the canal. Nasser, who was not invited to the London conference held in late August, summarily rejected its recommended formula for an international Suez Canal Board. Eisenhower then searched for other peaceful alternatives. His instincts told him that using force over Suez would be a grave mistake. "My conviction," he wrote in his memoirs, "was that the Western world had gotten into a lot of difficulty by selecting the wrong issue about which to be tough. To choose a situation in which Nasser had legal and sovereign rights and in which world opinion was largely on his side, was not . . . a good one on which to make a stand."[13]

Then on September 8, Eisenhower suggested the idea of a Suez Canal Users Association designed "to organize the using nations for collective bargaining with Nasser, for mobilization of world opinion, and for mutual assistance if the Canal and the Middle East pipeline should become wholly or partially blocked. In the event that such an interregnum developed, we hoped to avoid open hostilities by placing responsibility for the Canal's operation on technicians rather than politicians." Although the plan was discussed at a second conference of maritime powers at London that began on September 19, it never got off the ground because Nasser rejected it as a scheme for "aggression."[14]

Eisenhower faced the difficult task of articulating a clear and forceful policy to various audiences: the American people, who would be holding presidential and congressional elections in November; Egypt, where the Middle East crisis was centered; Britain and France, his two key European allies who claimed a vital interest in the canal; Israel, which was on the verge of war with Egypt; and the Soviet Union, which was exerting increasing influence both in the Middle East and the entire world. Within weeks the president had to act swiftly and decisively when first Israel and then Britain and France invaded Suez.

Countdown to the Decision

By the fall of 1956, developments regarding Suez had rapidly taken on a momentum of their own. What Eisenhower did not know was that during the summer Britain, France, and Israel, each with its own agenda, were plotting to invade Egypt and overthrow Nasser. On October 22–24, they drew up secret invasion plans at the Parisian suburb of Sèvres. On October 29, as arranged, Israel launched operation "Kadesh"[15] by attacking Egypt in the Sinai.

In Israel's eyes, this war was justified by repeated Egyptian aggression. Israel was angered by Egypt's continued blockade of the Suez Canal and the vitally important Straits of Tiran (the gateway to the Gulf of Aqaba and Israel's port of Eilat) to Israeli shipping, disturbed by Soviet arms shipments to Egypt and Washington's refusal to supply her arms, and incensed over Egyptian-sponsored *fedayeen* raids from Gaza.

Israel's officially declared tactical goal was destruction of the Egyptian Army so it could no longer support *fedayeen* bases. Her immediate objective was control of Sharm el Sheikh (located on the southern tip of the Sinai peninsula) and the Straits of Tiran. Israel also had broader strategic goals of pressuring Nasser to open the Suez Canal to Israeli shipping, thwarting Nasser's bid for leadership of a united Arab world, weakening Egypt as a military threat to her security, and eventually achieving at least de facto recognition by the Arab states.

Deceived as planned by the secret scheme hatched in Sèvres, Eisenhower at first anticipated Israeli military action in Jordan in retaliation for sponsoring terrorist raids against Israel. Although Eisenhower knew of Israeli troop movements in the Sinai through CIA intelligence and the first U-2 flights, he still was shocked when military action actually began. The president disregarded what he considered Ben-Gurion's ploy to preclude a negative response from the White House by relying on pro-Israel voter sympathy in the forthcoming U.S.

election. Moreover, Eisenhower was concerned that Israel, under the "aggressive" Ben-Gurion, sought permanent occupation of the Sinai, with its oil reserves. This would cause an uproar in Egypt and elsewhere in the Arab world and possibly lead to intervention by the USSR.[16] When officially informed of Israel's action, Eisenhower replied angrily to Secretary Dulles: "All right, Foster, you tell 'em that goddamn it, we're going to apply sanctions, we're going to the United Nations, we're going to do everything there is so we can stop this thing." The United States did employ limited sanctions that, in Dulles's words, amounted to "a slap on the wrist." These included such measures as holding up recommendation of a $75 million loan from the Export-Import Bank and suspending the small U.S. technical assistance program. At the same time, Eisenhower personally appealed to Ben-Gurion to halt Israeli military action.

On October 30, the President sent Eden a long cable wherein he reiterated U.S. support for the Tripartite Declaration.[17] When British planes bombed Cairo the next day, Eisenhower's temper flared again. He took matters directly to the UN Security Council. Ambassador Henry Cabot Lodge offered a resolution calling for an immediate ceasefire and requiring "all members" to "refrain from the use of force or threat of force in the area." Britain and France vetoed this resolution. In accordance with the Uniting-for-Peace Resolution,[18] the United States brought its resolution before the General Assembly. Then, after a British-French ultimatum to Egypt and Israel to halt hostilities and withdraw forces failed, as planned at Sèvres, on November 5 and 6 Britain and France invaded the canal area.

One reason that official British and French policy claimed the invasion was justified was that Egypt did not have the technical competence to run the canal. Eisenhower, having had experience with the Panama Canal, considered this charge frivolous.[19] Eden's real aim, as was Premier Guy Mollet's of France, was to get rid of Nasser and reassert dominance in Suez. Here is where historical analogies and egos of key diplomats came to the fore. Whereas Eden considered Nasser another Mussolini, Mollet considered him another Hitler and Nasser's *The Philosophy of the Revolution* another *Mein Kampf*. Both European statesmen were afraid of repeating the disastrous policy of "appeasement" of fascist dictators which led to World War II. Eden warned Eisenhower that Nasser's seizure of the canal was "the opening gambit in a planned campaign designed by Nasser to expel all Western influence and interests from Arab countries." If Nasser got away with this, Eden added, "his prestige in Arabia will be so great that he will be able to mount revolutions of young officers in Saudi Arabia, Jordan, Syria, and Iraq. . . . These new governments will in effect be Egyptian satellites, if not Russian ones. They will have to place their united oil resources under the control of a united Arabia led by Egypt and under Russian influence." Then Nasser could "deny oil to Western Europe and we here shall all be at his mercy." Eden was especially worried that Jordan, under pressure of pro-Nasserites, would cut itself off from British defense and link up in a joint command with Egypt. Eden, therefore, pointed out to Eisenhower that Nasser was even more dangerous to U.S. security than Mossadegh or Arbenz, whom the CIA had helped overthrow. Eden, therefore, argued that Eisenhower should support British attempts to reassert their military presence in Egypt and secure control over the canal. Mollet, while agreeing generally with Eden, was eager to destroy Nasser in order to weaken Egyptian support for the Algerian rebels who were fighting for their independence.

The president, while recognizing the potential damage to the U.S. relationship with key NATO allies, rejected their case for force. Although Eisenhower viewed Nasser as a troublesome leader who was a tool of Moscow, he felt it was not appropriate, at least at the time, to try to overthrow him by covert action or military invasion. The canal, in short, was the wrong issue to make war on—politically, militarily, legally, and morally. As there was no *casus belli*, an invasion would be a tragic folly with possible long-term disastrous consequences for the West. The best approach, at least for the time being, was to deal with Nasser through diplomacy, not force.

What complicated the crisis and made it more dangerous was that at the same time Britain and France were invading Suez, Soviet tanks were crushing the Hungarian rebellion against Soviet imperialism.[20] During the Suez and Hungarian crises, Soviet Communist Party leader Nikita Khrushchev threatened to rain rockets on Britain and France and to send "volunteers" to Egypt if the invasion did not stop. Moreover, Soviet Premier Nikolai Bulganin sent a very threatening note to Ben-Gurion. Bulganin also sent a message to Eisenhower proposing joint Soviet-American military action under the UN flag to "crush the aggressors and restore peace" in the Middle East. Eisenhower rejected this proposal as "unthinkable" and "an obvious attempt to divert world opinion from the Hungarian tragedy." There was no chance that the United States would team up with the USSR. As Eisenhower told journalists: "This is incredible! Can the Russians be serious? To think that we could join them against Britain, France, and Israel! It's inconceivable!"

Dealing with Israel, Britain, and France was far more complicated and difficult. Eisenhower unequivocally decided to take a strong stance against Israel, which he believed was acting as an aggressor and trying to interfere in his presidential election campaign. By late October, Eisenhower had made up his mind to abide by the Tripartite Declaration, which he would invoke against Israel. The president would honor the U.S. pledge "to assist the victim of any aggression in the Middle East," which in this case was Egypt. Furthermore, feeling betrayed because he was not even consulted before the military action, he excoriated Britain, France, and Israel for their secret plotting. He also condemned their use of military force as stupid politically and militarily. As he lamented to his speech writer and confidant Emmet John Hughes on October 31: "I just don't know what got into those people. It's the damnest business I ever saw supposedly intelligent governments get themselves into." Hughes then observed: "His passing remarks suggest that what really troubles him most is neither moral nor political—but *military* judgment. He suspects British don't know *technically* what they are doing. This kind of demurral is refreshing contrast to White House staff's political righteousness prevailing just outside his office door."[21]

Then on November 2, Eisenhower expressed similar dismay in a letter to his friend General Alfred Gruenther: "If one has to fight, then that is that. But I don't see the point in getting into a fight to which there can be no satisfactory end, and in which the whole world believes you are playing the part of the bully and you do not even have the firm backing of your entire people."[22]

That same day, Eisenhower again took action in the United Nations. He clearly wanted to avoid public vilification of Britain and France. Worried that a resolution from another country, particularly the USSR, might be "harshly worded" and thus "put us in an acutely embarrassing position," the president told Secretary Dulles that "at all costs the Soviets must be prevented from seizing the mantle of world leadership through a false but convincing exhibition of concern for smaller nations. Since Africa and Asia almost unanimously hate one of the three nations, Britain, France, and Israel, the Soviets need only to propose severe and immediate punishment of these three to have the whole of two continents on their side." He then ordered Dulles, in his speech to the UN, "to avoid condemning any nation, but to put his stress on the need for a quick cease-fire."[23] On November 2, the General

Assembly by a wide margin adopted a U.S.-sponsored resolution calling for cessation of hostilities and despatch of a UN peacekeeping force
to the battle area.

On November 3, Secretary Dulles entered the hospital, striken by
the cancer from which he would eventually die. Herbert Hoover, Jr. became acting secretary of state. But Hoover had neither Dulles' stature nor
influence with the president. Thus, for the next few days of the crisis,
Eisenhower stood largely alone in his foreign policy decision-making.

Eisenhower's consistently strong condemnation of the invasion
forced Britain, France, and Israel to end the war. Hostilities stopped on
midnight of election day, November 6. The president took additional
measures that also greatly influenced Britain's and France's decision.
Together with his close associate Treasury Secretary George Humphrey,
perhaps the strongest advocate of anti-British measures, Eisenhower
imposed economic sanctions against Britain. The U.S. Federal Reserve
sold significant amounts of sterling which forced down its price,
thwarted Britain's drawing rights from the International Monetary
Fund, and delayed U.S. oil supplies to Western Europe. These actions
had a major psychological impact, though some scholars also considered them decisive in the halt of military operations.[24]

On November 7, the UN General Assembly called on Britain,
France, and Israel to withdraw their forces and decided to send a peacekeeping force to the battle areas. It brought about an armistice and sent
a United Nations Emergency Force (UNEF) to the Sinai, to be inter-
spersed between Egyptian and Israeli forces. On December 3, the
British, French, and Israelis, weakened by outside pressure, agreed to
withdraw their forces from Egypt. On December 22, after weeks of
wrangling, Britain and France completed their unconditional, phased
withdrawal. Israel continued its occupation of the Sinai, but it then
withdrew in March 1957, largely as a result of strong U.S. pressure.
Thus ended the 1956 Suez War.

President Eisenhower as Decision-Maker

Foreign Policy Context of Decision

President Eisenhower's worldview was a set of traditional American values tempered by Cold War calculations. Like previous presidents, Eisenhower believed in the "exceptionalism" of the United States. That is, the

United States had a special mission and unique responsibility to stand as an example of democracy around the world. In the spirit of Woodrow Wilson, Eisenhower saw democracy at home tied inextricably to political developments abroad. And as the moral and military leader of the "free world," Eisenhower believed that the United States had the moral right and duty to resolutely oppose all tyranny and forms of oppression.

This moral rectitude often led to seemingly contradictory policies. Eisenhower considered a strong NATO indispensable to the security of Western Europe and the United States. He preferred to act in concert with key NATO allies, Britain and France, but he would "go it alone" and even oppose them in situations with overriding national interests, such as the Suez War. This case also exemplified the influence of Eisenhower's other foreign policy guideposts: attentiveness to domestic and world opinion, importance of international law, sanctity of diplomatic agreements, reluctance to involve the United States in military operations abroad and the related fear of escalation of hostilities to nuclear holocaust, and reliance on the potential of the United Nations as a peacekeeping body. Eisenhower also took a very strong stance against colonialism and for self-determination. Yet, he did not flinch at using covert action to topple leftist leaders and install pliant authoritarian regimes.

Eisenhower's main criterion for intervention was his perception of the danger from monolithic world communism, directed by the Soviet Union. Like Secretary Dulles, Eisenhower viewed the world in Manichean terms: the good forces of democracy were battling the evil forces of communism. There were no gray areas and few nuances. In addition, Eisenhower's view of the communist threat had a religious underpinning. He agreed with Secretary Dulles, though with less fanaticism, that "godless Communism" had to be contained if not destroyed.

Eisenhower's global and regional strategies thus developed within a dualism of utopianism and realpolitik: in the long run he aimed to make the world safe for democracy and capitalism, but in the short run he relied on military force, alliances, balance of power, and covert activities to thwart what he believed was an ideologically driven enemy determined to destroy freedom.

Context of Decision within Eisenhower's National Security Strategy

Eisenhower believed that the "free world" could not afford to lose any more ground (e.g., after the "loss" of China) to communism. The Soviet Union was targeting weak states with limited capability to resist propaganda and subversion. Thus the United States had to recognize and counter this worldwide communist offensive. Fixation on communism blurred Eisenhower's understanding of the dynamic forces of indigenous Arab nationalism and revolution. Like Secretary Dulles, he misread Nasser's standing up to the West and neutralism as a "tilt" toward the Soviet Union.[25]

The best way to oppose communism in the Third World, Eisenhower believed, was to bolster and win support of indigenous nationalist forces with economic and military aid, funnelled either directly from the United States or through security pacts. This explains Eisenhower's promise to finance the Aswan Dam, which he withdrew when Nasser seemed to side with the Soviet Union; his early advocacy of MEDO, which never materialized; and his subsequent support of the Baghdad Pact. This strategy backfired, however, because the main threat to the stability and security of the Middle East was not world communism but intra-Arab divisions, Arab nationalism, and the Israeli-Arab conflict.[26] Thus the Baghdad Pact alienated Nasser because of its close ties to the West, especially Britain, and made him more receptive to Soviet economic and military assistance.

Context of Decision within President's Relations with Allies

After Nasser seized the canal, the United States, Britain, and France consulted frequently and openly. Britain and France, counting on Eisenhower's fear of communism, fully expected the president to support them in whatever actions they would take, or at the least not stand in their way. At a meeting with congressional leaders in mid-August 1956, Eisenhower and Dulles, like Eden and Mollet, compared Nasser to Hitler, categorizing him as "an extremely dangerous fanatic." Eisenhower "wanted everyone to understand clearly that we do not intend to stand by helplessly and let this one man get away with what he is trying to do." Dulles then added that he had urged Britain and France to refrain from using immediate force because they "had not yet made their case." Subsequently, Eisenhower expressed his opposition to the use of military force. At the same time, Dulles was insisting that Nasser must be "compelled to disgorge" the canal. Both Eden and Mollet, receiving confusing and conflicting signals from the White House, at first erroneously concluded that Eisenhower would not oppose their use of military force if peaceful diplomacy failed.[27]

As weeks passed, however, Britain and France began to realize that they could not count on Eisenhower's support. In fact, the president might even oppose their developing plan for military action against Nasser. Gradually, therefore, along with Israel, they proceeded secretly with their own plan. Eisenhower seethed when he realized his closest NATO allies were freezing him out of their plans. The resultant frigidity "opened a breach in the Atlantic alliance that required patient effort to rebuild."[28]

Eden maintained respect for Eisenhower as a friend and diplomatic colleague. He believed that the president's condemnation of the Suez invasion, at least in part, stemmed from his lack of understanding and appreciation of Britain's strategic, economic, and political stakes in Suez. He also suspected, with some foundation, that the United States was making a disguised attempt to replace Britain as the main power in the region. Eden was especially distrustful of Dulles. He considered the secretary personally irritating and insincere in his affirmation of U.S. support for British policy. In reality, Eden thought Dulles was angling to weaken British power so the United States could act more independently in the Middle East.

Damage to the "special relationship" with the United States caused by Eden's deception of Eisenhower before the invasion, by the president's public upbraiding of Britain, and by Britain's suspicions of U.S. motives during the crisis, was not longlasting. On November 6, his spirits buoyed by a phone call from Eisenhower, Eden optimistically concluded in a cable to Mollet that there was "no doubt at all that the friendship between us all is restored and even strengthened."[29] But Eden then misinterpreted Eisenhower's opposition to military contributions to UNEF from any of the permanent members of the Security Council. Eden thought the president's main motive was to keep the Soviet Union out of the region, but instead it was to pressure Britain and France to withdraw their forces. On January 8, 1957, Eden resigned. He had succumbed to a barrage of left-wing criticism of his Suez folly, bowed to ill health, and recognized that Britain was becoming Washington's junior partner in the Middle East. Soon, though, U.S.-Britain relations warmed up considerably, especially after Eisenhower and Secretary Dulles met in Bermuda in March 1957 with new Prime Minister Harold Macmillan.

Mollet was upset that Eisenhower did not believe that the Kremlin was directing Nasser's anti-Western moves and failed to treat the Suez War like the Korean War and the Berlin Blockade. At first he felt the president had abandoned France. Like Eden, Mollet was piqued at Eisenhower's strong opposition to his country's participation in the

Suez War, even though he too by early October had cut off the president from secret war plans. But by early 1957, both Mollet and Eisenhower tried to put the Suez crisis behind them. In February, Eisenhower and Dulles met with Mollet and Foreign Minister Christian Pineau in Washington. The French leaders, who had complained during the Suez crisis that Eisenhower's policies were damaging NATO, then briefed the Americans on the Treaty of Rome, which would establish the Common Market in Europe. Eisenhower responded that this would prove to be more important than the Suez War.[30] France's friendship with the United States was restored, at least for the time being.

Domestic Context of Decision

Eisenhower was running for reelection on November 6 on a platform of peace. This would have made it hard for him to support the invasion, let alone become a co-belligerent. Furthermore, the president feared losing more of the Jewish vote if he took a strong stance against Israel. (In the 1952 election, Democratic Party candidate Adlai Stevenson received about 75 percent of the Jewish vote.) Throughout the deepening crisis in the fall, Eisenhower was pressured both by Ben-Gurion and Stevenson to shift to a more pro-Israel position in his Suez policy. Neither was successful.

For political reasons, Eisenhower took a much stronger stand against Israel's invasion privately than publicly. In a campaign speech the evening of October 29, Stevenson had sharply condemned U.S. policy in the Middle East as a failure and deception of the American people. At a National Security Council meeting on November 1, Eisenhower quoted a telegram from Stevenson. The governor, who previously had encouraged Eisenhower to send arms to Israel, now advised him not to rush into the use of armed force. Eisenhower brushed off Stevenson's criticism, commenting: "It would be a complete mistake for this country to continue with any kind of aid to Israel, which was an aggressor."[31] In a campaign speech on November 1, Eisenhower summed up his conflicting concerns about the Suez crisis:

> We cannot—in the world, any more than in our own nation, subscribe to one law for the weak, another law for the strong; . . .
> There can be only one law—or there will be no peace. . . .
> We value—deeply and lastingly—the bonds with those great nations [Britain and France], those great friends, with whom we

now so plainly disagree. And I, for one, am confident that those bonds will do more than survive. They can—my friends, they must—grow to new and greater strength.

But this we know above all: there are some firm principles that cannot bend—they can only break. And we shall not break ours.[32]

Then on November 2, he wrote to his good friend E. Everett "Swede" Hazlitt that the Israelis were making a mistake if they thought they could "take advantage" of the United States because of the election. He added that he had told Ben-Gurion that "we would handle our affairs exactly as though we didn't have a Jew in America."[33] Two weeks earlier, on October 15, Eisenhower had written similar thoughts on Israel's motives: "Ben-Gurion should not make any grave mistakes based upon his belief that winning a domestic election is as important to us as preserving the interests of the United Nations and other nations of the free world in that region."[34]

Eisenhower probably also smarted from Stevenson's hard-hitting charges made in a televised election speech on November 2 that sharply criticized his Middle East policy as inconsistent and weak:

The Administration first offered and then refused to help Egypt with the Aswan Dam. It refused to send Israel defense arms but then encouraged others to do so. It came forward with one proposal after another in the dispute over the Suez Canal but never really committed itself to stand firm on anything. And it acquired for itself . . . a reputation for unreliability which is about as damaging a reputation as a Great Power can have. . . . [O]ne question which arises irresistibly out of the Middle Eastern crisis is this: has the President of the United States really been in charge of our foreign policy?

Some participants in the Suez crisis, however, believed that the election campaign did influence Eisenhower's decision. Although Vice President Richard Nixon, at the time, supported Eisenhower's decision as a "second declaration of independence," in his memoirs he described it as "a serious mistake" which Eisenhower would not have made "if the Suez crisis had not arisen during the heat of a presidential campaign."[35]

Throughout the Suez crisis, Eisenhower faced no serious congressional opposition to his policy. One reason was that, unlike in Britain and France, Nasser's seizure of the canal was not perceived as a critically important problem, at least at the outset. The canal simply did not have the same significance for the United States as it did for its NATO allies. Nonetheless, Eisenhower tried to head off congressional opposition to his Suez policy through consultation with congressional leaders and their involvement in decision-making. For example, he sought representation of Democratic senator leaders at the eighteen nation conference held in London in late August. But those asked to attend, such as Lyndon Johnson, Mike Mansfield, and J. William Fulbright, declined. They felt their attention would be better spent on winning the forthcoming election. A key Republican senator, H. Alexander Smith, then also declined to go to San Francisco.[36] As the crisis deepened, Eisenhower continued consultation with key congressional leaders, who generally rallied support behind his decision.

Decision Options

Eisenhower's decision during the Suez War was one of the most important, delicate, and controversial of his presidency. In the weeks immediately after Nasser seized the canal, Eisenhower had considerable decision-making elbow room. The president went along with Eden's rejection of Pineau's recommendation to blockade Egyptian trade and boycott shipping through the canal. Britain felt that a blockade would have limited economic impact on Egypt, and she wanted to maintain the flow of oil through the canal. Eisenhower considered legal action against Nasser, perhaps submission of the dispute to the International Court of Justice. Such action, of course, would play well before world opinion. Another early possibility was that Eisenhower might play the role of mediator. The president could not act alone, though, because Nasser would not have considered him an honest broker. Thus Eisenhower's press secretary, James Hagerty, floated the idea of Eisenhower's mediation with India's Prime Minister Nehru, whose neutralist credentials, at least to Nasser, were impeccable. Dulles, however, sensing no support from Britain and France who were growing increasingly hawkish, argued convincingly against this approach. Eisenhower then decided to rely on time and multilateral diplomacy to defuse the crisis. But as Nasser held firm at Western attempts to nullify Egyptian control of the canal, these options faded.

When first Israel and then Britain and France invaded Suez, Eisenhower had to wrestle with a different set of options. At a White

House meeting of his closest security advisers immediately after Israel's attack on October 29, the president raised the possibility of using the U.S. Sixth Fleet to blockade the Jewish state. But he backed off when Admiral Arthur Radford, Chairman of the Joint Chiefs of Staff, argued that a blockade could not prevent Israeli forces from reaching the canal in two or three days. Moreover, Eisenhower still thought he might be able to deter British and French military action. He then determined to bring the Suez issue before the Security Council early the next morning. He wanted to act before the Soviet Union could put forth a proposal of her own which assuredly would have branded Britain and France as "aggressors."[37] Eisenhower then was exercising damage control for NATO.

After Britain and France invaded Suez, Eisenhower considered the possibility of using the Sixth Fleet to influence the outcome of their military action. The Sixth Fleet received orders "to make sure we knew where they [the British and French] were and what they were doing." But when Admiral Arleigh Burke, the Chief of Staff of the U.S. Navy, sent orders to Admiral "Cat" Brown to "go to sea with his bombs up, ready to fight anything," Brown retorted quizzically: "Who's the enemy?" And when asked by Dulles whether the Sixth Fleet could stop the Suez War, Burke replied that the only way was "to blast hell out of them." Clearly, this was not an acceptable option.[38]

On November 2, Eisenhower again considered playing the role of mediator with Nehru. Dulles was somewhat enthusiastic, arguing that this approach could allow the president to play a proactive role in the crisis. But Eisenhower was not keen on this idea, especially because of his distrust of India's Foreign Minister Krishna Menon, whom he felt was too closely connected with communists.

Eisenhower had other alternatives, all unappealing. There was no serious consideration during the crisis of trying covert action to overthrow Nasser. The United States had plotted with Britain to overthrow Mossadegh in Iran in 1953, but there was no chance of a repeat action in Egypt. If toppling Nasser failed, the Egyptian leader would become even a greater hero who might open the door wider for Soviet penetration of the Middle East. The idea of planning covert action with Israel during the invasion seemed equally implausible.

Eisenhower clearly and decisively rejected what influential American statesmen like Dean Acheson, secretary of state under Truman, and respected and influential columnists like Walter Lippmann advocated as his "must" choice: co-belligerency with Britain and France, or at least diplomatic support for their actions. Eisenhower fretted over the prospect that public condemnation of the invasion would seriously damage Washington's relationship with its major NATO allies. This, in turn, would hurt U.S. security interests in Europe and the rest of the world. Acheson deplored Eisenhower's decision. "There is hardly a more lethal blow to any alliance," he wrote, "than to have one ally join the enemies of other allies."[39] According to Lippmann: "The American interest is to refrain from moral judgment. . . . The Franco-British action will be judged by its outcome—in the first instance whether the military objectives are achieved in reasonable time and a not too great cost. . . . The American interest, though we have dissented from the decision itself, is that France and Britain should now succeed. However much we may wish they had not started, we cannot now wish that they should fail."[40]

In his memoirs, Nixon maintained that Eisenhower realized later that he had erred. He quoted Eisenhower, after he left the presidency, as having called his decision to oppose his European allies during the Suez War his "major foreign policy mistake."[41] Nixon pointed out the dangerous consequences of the decision: "Nasser became even more rash and aggressive than before, and the seeds of another Mideast War were planted. The most tragic result was that Britain and France were so humiliated and discouraged by the Suez crisis that they lost the will to play a major role on the world scene. From this time forward the United States would by necessity be forced to "go it alone" in the foreign policy leadership of the free world."[42] When Eisenhower made his decision, however, he seemed confident that strong opposition to the British-French-Israeli invasion of Suez was best for the U.S. national interest and the right thing to do.

Eisenhower's Leadership Role in the Decision

There is considerable controversy over Eisenhower's leadership role as president. Some scholars, like James David Barber, conclude that Eisenhower was a "passive-negative president" for whom "politics was a botheration."[43] For these pundits, Dulles was the predominant figure in foreign policy conceptualization and decision-making. Others, such as Fred Greenstein, reject the argument that Eisenhower was disengaged from foreign policy and left major decision-making to Dulles. Greenstein, believing that the president was the key decision-maker behind the scenes, maintains that Eisenhower "was politically astute and informed, actively engaged in putting his personal stamp on public policy, and applied a carefully thought-out conception of leadership to the conduct of his presidency."[44] The memoirs of Eisenhower's close aides and confidantes, such as Sherman Adams, James Hagerty, and Emmet John Hughes, confirm Greenstein's position.

During the Suez crisis, the evidence points overwhelmingly in favor of the position that Eisenhower was the key decision-maker and exercised effective leadership. Author Donald Neff concludes:

> A shibboleth about Eisenhower's presidency was that he allowed his secretary of state to run the nation's foreign affairs with almost total independence. Nothing could have been farther from the truth. Eisenhower kept Dulles on a short leash, though he did grant him considerable latitude in handling the department's day-to-day routine. But when it came to major issues or crises, it was Eisenhower who made the decision.[45]

Keith Kyle, perhaps the foremost scholar on the Suez War, concludes that the documents show that although Dulles played a major role in decision-making both "in conceptual formulation" and in "matters of detail," he always deferred to the president when there were differences of opinion and Eisenhower clearly was the decision-maker.[46] Perhaps Israeli Ambassador Abba Eban put it best: "Throughout the many years that I served in Washington during the Eisenhower years I never found the least evidence for the media contention that he was a figurehead president. . . . Eisenhower as a reality was better than his own image [as foreign policy leader]."[47] Thus what may continue to be debated is not whether Eisenhower was the U.S. decision-maker during the Suez War, but how good a decision-maker he was and how well his decision turned out.

Consequences of Eisenhower's Decision for the United States and Other Countries Involved

The United States

Eisenhower won great respect in the Arab world for his strong stance against Western colonialism and Israel. But he soon squandered this political capital by refusing to help Egypt with food, medicine, and fuel that were badly needed after the cease-fire. Eisenhower had decided to weaken Nasser after the Suez War. After considering his removal by coup or assassination, Eisenhower opted instead to bolster King Saud of Saudi Arabia. With quiet U.S. support, the King might supplant Nasser as the leader of the Arab world. This angle never materialized. King Saud, invited to Washington at the end of January 1957, was unresponsive to U.S. overtures. Eisenhower's policy of "even-handedness," therefore, did not pay the expected dividend of enhanced U.S. prestige and influence in the Arab world.

After the Suez War, the Cold War, more than ever before, became the main touchstone of U.S. policy in the Middle East. The president was convinced that communism was the main threat to the Middle East and was greatly disturbed that the USSR had become a force in the region. Thus only one day after the cease-fire in Suez, he drafted what was to become known as the Eisenhower Doctrine. On January 5, 1957, Eisenhower urged a joint session of Congress to support the Joint Resolution to Promote Peace and Stability in the Middle East. This declared that the president was "prepared to use armed forces to assist . . . any nation or groups of nations requesting assistance against armed aggression from any country controlled by international communism."

When the monarchy in Iraq was overthrown on July 14, 1958, Eisenhower applied his new doctrine in Lebanon. Responding to a request from pro-Western President Camille Chamoun, Eisenhower sent about 15,000 U.S. Marines to deter political upheaval being stirred up by Cairo Radio and pro-Nasser forces. Britain acted similarly in Jordan by sending troops to bolster King Hussein whose rule was also threatened by pro-Nasserites. In the Suez crisis, Eisenhower had strongly denounced the use of force, firmly insisted on the rule of law, and insisted on taking issues of conflict to the United Nations. But by sending Marines into Lebanon, he began to lose the moral high ground which Soviet expert George Kennan had argued was so important for the West's containment of communism. Soon, the president supported development of CIA plans to invade Cuba in the Bay of Pigs, with disastrous results for the United States similar to those suffered by Britain and France after their Suez invasion.

The Soviet Union

The Soviet Union gained immeasurably from the crisis. It posed as the anticolonialist champion of the Arab people and claimed that its strong opposition to the Suez invasion forced the cease-fire. It gained influence in Egypt, and soon in other Arab states such as Iraq and Syria, through increased economic and military aid.

Egypt

Although Nasser lost the Suez War militarily, he was a big winner politically. Nasser became a hero not only in Egypt and the Arab world, but also throughout much of Africa and Asia for standing up to Western colonialism and fighting Israel. Israel would never have had military success in the Suez War, he contended, without the backing of Britain and France. As Nasser's prestige soared, he felt confident to vitriolically attack the Eisenhower Doctrine. Moreover, Nasser was not content with Egypt's successful management of the Suez Canal and tending her own garden. Instead, he began a series of foreign ventures: he tried unsuccessfully to overthrow King Hussein of Jordan in April 1957 and again in early 1958; he arranged Egypt's union with Syria, forming the United Arab Republic on February 1, 1958; he tried to destabilize the government of Lebanon in the summer of 1958; he helped inspire the overthrow of the pro-Western monarchy in Iraq in July; and for several years in the early 1960s he fought a costly and fruitless war to control Yemen, where he tried to topple the feudal monarchy. These ventures frightened royal families in Saudi Arabia and the Gulf states which began to look more and more to the United States for arms and protection.

Israel

For Israel, the Suez War had mixed results. On the negative side, the Suez Canal remained closed to Israeli shipping, Nasser greatly strengthened his leadership position and prestige inside Egypt and the Arab world, Israel became more closely connected with Western imperialism, and the Soviet Union gained a foothold in Egypt and dramatically increased its influence in the Middle East. The war also caused a serious strain in Israel's relations with the United States. Israel believed it could no longer rely on American Jews to lobby Washington successfully. Perhaps even worse, she felt deserted by the United States, which seemed to have been bullied by Kremlin leaders. U.S.-Israeli tension, however, did not result in a rupture of relations. Soon they warmed and Israel began receiving U.S. economic aid.

On the positive side, with U.S. assistance, Israel won free passage through the Straits of Tiran, leaving the Gulf of Aqaba open to Israeli navigation. The United Nations Emergency Force (UNEF), put in place to prevent border clashes with Egypt, bought Israel about ten years of relative peace with Egypt. In addition, the West's added fear of the serious threat of Soviet penetration of the Middle East benefitted Israel. In April, Israel had won favor with the CIA when the Mossad (Israel's intelligence agency) supplied it with a copy of Khrushchev's secret de-Stalinization speech delivered in February 1956. In return, the Mossad struck a deal with the CIA to cooperate on intelligence concerning the Arab world: Israel would help the U.S. combat Soviet activities in the Middle East, and the U.S. would increase aid to Israel, including help for her nuclear weapons development program.[48] At the same time, France, angry over its setbacks in the Arab world, became Israel's largest supplier of arms and also aided her nuclear weapons development program. According to journalist Seymour Hersh, Israel had sought and received French help with building nuclear weapons as early as September 1956, six weeks before the Suez War began. In addition, Ben-Gurion supposedly had agreed to withdraw from Sinai and accept UNEF only when France agreed to help Israel build a nuclear reactor and chemical reprocessing plant.[49]

Britain

Britain lost the Suez War on many fronts. In the short run, both she and France were denied oil from Saudi Arabia. After a brief period of belt tightening, the shortfall was made up by U.S. oil companies through the Middle East Emergency Committee. This marked a reversal of Eisenhower's suspension of this committee's meetings in July 1956 to pressure Britain and France not to use force against Nasser after he nationalized the canal. Of more lasting importance was the fact that Britain's days as a world power and as colonial master in the Middle East were over. Like France, she could no longer exercise "gunboat diplomacy." Both would gamely try to hang on to their influence, but with limited success.

France

France also suffered a serious setback as a power in the Middle East. The Mollet government fell in May 1957 on the eve of Algeria's breakaway. But France would remember that the United States, which had not come to her aid during the decisive battle of Dien Bien

Phu in Indo-China in 1954, did not support her again at Suez. During the Suez invasion, when Khrushchev threatened France with rockets, she was not confident of U.S. protection. France drew two major conclusions: she needed her own nuclear weapons, and her economic and military security rested more in Europe than with the United States and Britain. Soon, Paris pushed harder for European integration and the primacy of France's power on the Continent. When De-Gaulle came to power in 1958, he vetoed Britain's attempt to gain entry into the newly formed Common Market. He argued that London was tied too closely to Washington's coat-tails. In 1960, France began nuclear testing. In 1966 DeGaulle subsequently withdrew France from the integrated military command structure of NATO and spurred development of the *force de frappe*, France's independent nuclear strike force. France also began shying away from its previously close contact with Israel and began seeking ways to mend its fences with Arab states.

Conclusion

The Suez Crisis was a very stressful time for President Eisenhower. He wanted to support Britain and France, his major NATO allies, and to maintain his "even-handed" policy in the Middle East. Yet he thought that Nasser's nationalization of the canal was not sufficient grounds for use of military force against him. Moreover, the president was miffed that Britain, France, and Israel had colluded to invade Egypt without at least keeping him informed of their plans. Eisenhower reacted immediately and decisively, virtually disregarding the possible negative impact of his stance on the forthcoming presidential election. He worked through the United Nations to effect a cease fire and withdrawal of British, French, and Israeli forces. During the crisis Eisenhower acted as a decisive leader. He was not averse to taking a strong stand against Britain, France, and Israel, even though this meant temporarily siding diplomatically with the Soviet Union. His decision caused only a temporary rift with these countries. The crisis resulted in a historic diminution of British and French power and the intensification of U.S.-Soviet competition in the Middle East. It also led to a dramatic rise in Nasser's power and prestige, and only a temporary easing or interruption of Israel's hostilities with Egypt and her other Arab neighbors.

Questions for Discussion

1. Did Eisenhower's Middle East policy, designed to contain Soviet penetration of the Middle East, actually drive Nasser to look for military and economic aid from the Soviet Union?

2. Was Eisenhower's policy until the Suez invasion truly "evenhanded" between Israel and the Arab states?

3. Evaluate U.S. strategy in the Middle East from 1953–1956. Do you agree with Adlai Stevenson's criticism of Eisenhower's Middle East policy prior to the Suez War?

4. What developments might have occurred if Eisenhower had diplomatically or militarily supported the British-French-Israeli invasion of Suez?

5. To what extent did Eisenhower's decision to renege on financing the Aswan Dam influence Nasser to seize the canal?

6. Did Nasser's seizure of the Suez Canal pose a threat to the vital interests of the United States?

7. Was Eisenhower's condemnation of the British-French-Israeli invasion of Suez worth risking the strength and cohesion of the NATO alliance?

8. How important was the U.S. election in Eisenhower's decision to oppose the Suez invasion?

9. Should the United States have tried covert operations to overthrow Nasser as it had done with Mossadegh in Iran and Arbenz in Guatemala?

10. What lessons do you think Eisenhower should have learned from the Suez invasion before approving development of plans for the Bay of Pigs invasion of Cuba?

Notes

1. The United States was the first state to recognize Israel de facto; it gave de jure recognition in early 1949 after the first Israeli elections. The Soviet Union was the first state to recognize Israel de jure.

2. Nasser officially became President of Egypt on June 23, 1956.

3. Quoted in Peter Lyon, *Eisenhower: Portrait of a Hero* (Boston: Little, Brown, and Company, 1974), p. 547.

4. Anthony Nutting, *Nasser* (New York: E. P. Dutton, 1972), pp. 97–98.

5. See Wilbur C. Eveland, *Ropes of Sand* (New York: W. W. Norton, 1980), pp. 90–92; and Miles Copeland, *The Game of Nations* (New York: Simon & Schuster, 1970), pp. 123–31. Eveland and Copeland were key CIA operatives in the Middle East. Cited by Barry Rubin, "America and the Egyptian Revolution, 1950–1957," *Political Science Quarterly*, 7 (Spring 1983): 83.

6. Roosevelt had played a major role in the 1953 CIA overthrow of Mossadegh in Iran. Reportedly, that same year he offered Nasser a bribe through the CIA to work with the United States. Nasser refused the bribe for himself, but he used the money for economic development projects in Egypt. See Donald Neff, *Warriors at Suez* (Brattleboro, Vt.: Amana Books, 1988), pp. 87–88.

7. Rubin, pp. 81–85.

8. Eisenhower to Dulles, White House telecommunications file, box 11, file 3, DDE library. Cited by ibid., p. 86.

9. Dwight D. Eisenhower, *Waging Peace, 1956–1961* (Garden City, N.Y.: Doubleday & Co., 1965), p. 31.

10. Ibid., p. 32.

11. In late 1958, the Soviets agreed to loan Egypt $100 million for the dam. In early 1960 construction began.

12. Eisenhower, pp. 43–44.

13. Ibid., p. 50.

14. Ibid., p. 51.

15. In the Bible, Kadesh was the final resting spot in the Sinai for the Israelites on their way to the Promised Land after they had escaped from Egypt.

16. See Abba Eban, *An Autobiography* (New York: Random House, 1977), p. 218.

17. Eisenhower, p. 75.

18. The UN adopted this U.S.-sponsored resolution in 1950, soon after the outbreak of the Korean War. It specified that when the Security Council was paralyzed by a veto on the issue of preserving peace, the General Assembly could act. At that time, the resolution was clearly directed against the USSR, which had exercised its veto power numerous times. Ironically, the first time the resolution was invoked was against Britain and France in the 1956 Suez crisis.

19. Eisenhower, pp. 39–40.

20. The USSR finally quashed the Hungarian uprising on November 9. It had erupted on October 23. The USSR also suppressed a weaker revolt that had broken out in Poland on October 19.

21. Emmet John Hughes, *The Ordeal of Power: A Political Memoir of the Eisenhower Years* (New York: Atheneum, 1963), p. 219.

22. Eisenhower, p. 85.

23. Memo, NSC Meeting, 11/1/56, NSC Series; DDE to Dulles, 11/1/56, D/H.

Quoted in Stephen Ambrose, *Eisenhower: The President*, volume 2 (New York: Simon & Schuster, 1984), p. 364.

24. See Ritchie Ovendale, *The Origins of the Arab-Israeli War*, 2nd ed. (London: Longman, 1992), p. 182.

25. Eisenhower did not go so far as Secretary Dulles in condemning Nasser's neutralism as "immoral."

26. For elaboration of this misperception, see Steven Spiegel, *The Other Arab-Israeli Conflict* (Chicago: University of Chicago Press, 1985), pp. 63–64.

27. Robert Bowie, Dulles Oral History Collection (DOHC), 35; Lyon, p. 703; Anthony Eden, *Full Circle* (London: Cassell, 1960), pp. 524–26. Cited by Spiegel, p. 72.

28. Robert Stookey, *America and the Arab States: An Uneasy Encounter* (New York: John Wiley, 1975), p. 147.

29. Keith Kyle, *Suez* (New York: St. Martin's, 1991), p. 480.

30. *Foreign Relations of the United States (FRUS)* 17, doc. 160, February 26, 1957, p. 296. Cited by ibid., p. 535.

31. Quoted in Ambrose, p. 365.

32. Eisenhower, p. 83.

33. Quoted in Ambrose, p. 365.

34. Robert H. Ferrell (ed.), *The Eisenhower Diaries* (New York: W. W. Norton & Co., 1981), p. 332.

35. Richard Nixon, *R.N.: The Memoirs of Richard Nixon* (New York: Touchstone, 1990), p. 179.

36. Eisenhower, p. 45.

37. *FRUS* 16, doc. 412, October 29, 1956, pp. 839–40.

38. See Kyle, p. 412.

39. Dean Acheson, *Power and Diplomacy* (Cambridge, Mass.: Harvard University Press, 1959), p. 109.

40. Quoted in Kyle, p. 426.

41. See Richard Nixon, "My Debt to Macmillan," *The Times*, January 28, 1987, quoted in Kyle, p. 612n1.

42. Nixon, *R.N.: The Memoirs of Richard Nixon*, p. 179.

43. See James David Barber, *The Presidential Character*, 4th ed. (Englewood Cliffs, N.J.: Prentice Hall, 1992).

44. See Fred I. Greenstein, *The Hidden Hand Presidency* (New York: Basic Books, 1982).

45. Neff, p. 38.

46. Kyle, pp. 45, 192.

47. Abba Eban, *Personal Witness: Israel through My Eyes* (New York: G. P. Putnam's Sons, 1992), pp. 281, 297.

48. For more on the secret association between the United States and Israel, see Andrew and Leslie Cockburn, *Dangerous Liaison: The Inside Story of the U.S.-Israeli Covert Relationship* (New York: HarperCollins, 1991).

49. Seymour Hersh, *The Samson Option* (London: Faber and Faber, 1991), pp. 40–44.

Selected Bibliography

Ambrose, Stephen. *Eisenhower: The President*, volume 2. New York: Simon & Schuster, 1984.

Eban, Abba. *Personal Witness: Israel Through My Eyes*. New York: G. P. Putnam's Sons, 1992.

Eden, Anthony. *Full Circle*. London: Cassell, 1960.

Eisenhower, Dwight D. *Waging Peace, 1956–1961*. Garden City, N.Y.: Doubleday & Co., 1965.

Ferrell, Robert H. (ed.) *The Eisenhower Diaries*. New York: W. W. Norton, 1981.

Greenstein, Fred I. *The Hidden Hand Presidency*. New York: Basic Books, 1982.

Kyle, Keith. *Suez*. New York: St. Martin's Press, 1991.

Lyon, Peter. *Eisenhower: Portrait of a Hero*. Boston: Little, Brown, and Co., 1974.

Neff, Donald. *Warriors at Suez*. Brattleboro, Vt.: Amana Books, 1988.

Nutting, Anthony. *Nasser*. New York: E. P. Dutton, 1972.

Ovendale, Ritchie. *The Origins of the Arab-Israeli War*, 2nd ed. London: Longman, 1992.

3

President Kennedy's Decision to Support the Bay of Pigs Invasion

Setting and Overview of Kennedy's Decision

President Kennedy's decision approving the Bay of Pigs invasion in April 1961 was aimed at removing Fidel Castro from power in Cuba and reestablishing a government friendly to the United States. The goal was to end Castro's ties to the Soviet Union since American foreign policy considered Cuba as part of its sphere of influence in the Western Hemisphere. Consequently, Kennedy and his advisers agreed to a covert operation planned and executed by the Central Intelligence Agency. The plan had developed during the last year of the Eisenhower administration after Cuba and the United States were ready to end all diplomatic ties. After taking office, Kennedy agreed to the plan but insisted that it must appear to be a completely anti-Castro operation without any participation or sponsorship by the United States.

When the invasion occurred, nearly everything went wrong. It turned out to be a total fiasco, a "perfect failure" of presidential conduct of United States foreign policy. All of the CIA assurances of success were erroneous. Kennedy's new administration appeared weak and unsure of itself. But Kennedy quickly took full responsibility for the disaster and made several changes to ensure it would not happen again. However, the key question remains: How could a newly elected and popular president have made such serious misjudgments in a plan doomed to fail?

President Kennedy's Decision

ON APRIL 4, 1961, PRESIDENT KENNEDY APPROVED THE FINAL PLAN TO SEND A BRIGADE OF ANTI-CASTRO CUBANS TO A LANDING SITE AT THE BAY OF PIGS, AFTER ALL MEMBERS OF THE NATIONAL SECURITY COUNCIL, EXCEPT ONE (SENATOR FULBRIGHT), STATED THEIR APPROVAL. THE GOAL WAS TO HAVE A COMMANDO FORCE ESTABLISH A BEACHHEAD, MOVE INLAND, AND BEGIN A REVOLUTION WITH OTHER CUBANS TO OVERTHROW FIDEL CASTRO, THE COMMUNIST DICTATOR.

President Kennedy's decision was controversial for several reasons, including:

1. Although Castro had established ties with the Soviet Union, there was no evidence that a majority of Cubans would support an overthrow of the Castro regime.
2. The CIA plan assumed that Castro would not know of any of the preparations for an invasion, when, in fact, Castro was fully prepared for it.
3. The CIA took the lead in developing and implementing all aspects of the invasion plan, but never questioned any possibilities that it would fail.
4. President Kennedy and his advisers never questioned the CIA's assumptions for the invasion plan.
5. President Kennedy did not effectively consult with the Joint Chiefs of Staff in assessing the feasibility of the CIA plan.
6. President Kennedy did not want the United States publicly connected with the invasion plan, when, in fact, the goal of deniability contributed to its failure.
7. The failed invasion convinced Castro that the United States would try again and Soviet leader Khrushchev that Kennedy lacked resolve in the Cold War. After the Bay of Pigs, Castro and Khrushchev agreed to a secret plan to install Soviet nuclear missiles in Cuba, thereby precipitating the October 1962 Cuban Missile Crisis.

BACKGROUND OF THE DECISION

Historical Context

When John F. Kennedy ran for president in 1960, the Cold War competition with the Soviet Union was intensifying on several fronts, including Latin American, Berlin, Laos, and Vietnam. Cuban leader Fidel Castro was viewed as a serious threat to United States interests because he had established close ties to the Soviet Union, which both Kennedy and Richard Nixon strongly opposed.

Kennedy initially did not believe Castro was a threat to United States interests. In a collection of speeches and essays published before the 1960 campaign, *The Strategy of Peace*, Kennedy had compared Castro with other Latin American revolutionary heroes such as Simon Bolivar. Kennedy viewed Castro as a Cuban nationalist struggling to depose a corrupt dictator, Fulgencio Batista, who had been supported by the United States "so long and so uncritically."[1]

Located ninety miles from Florida, Cuba had been dominated by American political, military, and business interests for more than sixty years when Castro took control in 1959. Castro overthrew Batista, who had permitted American organized crime to control casinos, hotels, and prostitution in Havana, a popular tourist spot in the Caribbean.

Cuba had been dominated by American political, military, and business interests since the Spanish-American War of 1898. The Platt Amendment (1903) establishing Cuban independence included a provision that the United States could intervene at any time in the future. American marines went to Cuba in 1906–9, 1912, and 1917–22. President Roosevelt's Good Neighbor Policy of the 1930s ended the Yankee imperialism of the Platt amendment, but the United States kept a naval base at Guantanamo Bay, which it retained indefinitely.[2]

Batista came to power in 1933 after organizing a military coup. He controlled five presidents until taking office in 1940. After World War II, Batista left office but returned to power in 1952 after another coup. He ruled by graft and violence, but maintained close economic ties with the United States. American corporations controlled 40 percent of the Cuban sugar industry, 80 percent of its utilities, and 90 percent of mining.[3]

Fidel Castro led a revolutionary band of guerrillas into Havana to overthrow Batista in 1959. Castro described his leadership qualities as "violent, given to tantrums, devious, manipulative, and defiant of all authority."[4] He grew up as the son of a landowner in Oriente province, an area dominated by the United Fruit Company, a United States corporation which owned most of the large sugar estates, Cuba's principal export crop. In his youth, Castro was attracted to the Cuban revolutionary hero José Marti, who had opposed United States dominance and was killed in 1895.

Castro became politically active when he attended the law school at the University of Havana in 1945. He began to oppose the Batista regime. In 1953, Castro was arrested and sent to prison. After his release, he went to Mexico and worked with other Cubans to build a small guerrilla force. In 1956, Castro joined eighty-one others and began a revolution in Cuba's Sierre Maestre mountains.

Castro's revolutionary force grew in size as it moved through the countryside. By 1958, professional, intellectuals, landowners, and businessmen joined the anti-Batista forces. They were concerned about the repression, corruption, and violence of the Batista regime. Also, the sugar industry was deteriorating, the educational system was decaying, and illiteracy was increasing.[5]

As Castro's revolutionary movement proceeded toward the capital, Batista realized he had lost support. Castro entered Havana at the end of 1958 with 2,000 men. On New Year's Day 1959, Batista and his family fled to the Dominican Republic. Castro was now in power.

At first, there was no public evidence that Castro was a Communist. He supported replacement of Batista's dictatorship with a pledge to return to constitutional rule, including free elections, civil liberties, and agrarian reform. As the guerrilla forces gathered strength, Communists began to influence Castro's thinking on how to implement the revolution. Castro legalized the Communist Party and postponed new elections for two years.

In the spring of 1959, Castro made his first visit to the United States. In Washington, he promised a free Cuban press in a speech to the American Society of Newspaper Editors. He told the Senate Foreign Relations Committee he would not seize United States property in Cuba. President Eisenhower refused to meet with Castro, but he did speak with Vice President Richard Nixon and Secretary of State Christian Herter, assuring them he could "handle" the Communists.[6]

After the meeting, Nixon wrote a long memo to Eisenhower in which he observed that Castro was "either incredibly naive about communism or under Communist discipline—my guess is the former." But

Castro's repressive actions after he returned to Cuba convinced Nixon that Castro "was indeed a Communist." Nixon endorsed the CIA's view to support "anti-Castro forces inside and outside Cuba."[7]

Castro also went to New York City and Harvard University, where he gave reassurances that he would not turn Cuba over to the Communists, even though his brother Raul and his colleague, Che Guevara, were Marxists. But after returning to Cuba, Castro decided "to cast the United States in the role of the enemy of the revolution."[8]

In October 1959, the Soviet Union began making contacts with Castro, who welcomed the opportunity to begin trade with them. Following the explosion of a French freighter in Havana harbor (possibly by the CIA), Castro requested Soviet military aid. He demanded that United States oil companies begin processing Soviet crude oil. After their refusal, Castro seized the American oil refineries.

The Eisenhower administration responded by suspending all Cuban sugar imports into the United States. Soviet Chairman Nikita Khrushchev then offered to purchase all 700,000 tons of the 1960 United States sugar quota. In return for Cuban sugar, the Soviet Union offered credits to Castro to purchase materials, machinery, equipment, and weapons. Subsequently, Castro nationalized all United States sugar mills, ranches, refineries, and utilities.

United States–Cuban relations were rapidly deteriorating and Soviet influence was becoming dominant. By the summer of 1960, Khrushchev declared that the Monroe Doctrine was dead. President Eisenhower responded that the United States would not "permit the establishment of a regime dominated by international communism in the Western hemisphere."[9] On January 3, 1961, the United States broke off diplomatic relations with Cuba after Castro demanded that the American embassy staff be reduced to eleven people in forty-eight hours.[10] Eisenhower declared that Castro was "the greatest demagogue to have appeared anywhere in Latin America."[11]

CIA Plans to Depose Castro

Concerned with growing Soviet influence, the Communist leanings of Castro, and fears of Castro-supported military actions against other Latin American countries (including the Dominican Republic, Haiti, and Nicaragua), the Eisenhower administration began planning to depose Castro. In February 1959, CIA Director Allen Dulles warned Eisenhower that "the Castro regime is moving toward a complete dictatorship. Communists are now operating openly and legally in Cuba."[12]

In March 1959, Dulles supported covert action against Castro at a meeting of the National Security Council. Eisenhower approved establishment of a Special Group of the NSC to meet with the CIA to organize a Cuban Task Force.

The CIA focused on organizing a small group of Cuban exiles, fewer than thirty, to join an anti-Castro underground and precipitate a "typical Latin political upheaval."[13] This plan was based upon an earlier CIA-sponsored coup in Guatemala which removed President Jacobo Arbenz Guzman from power.

Guzman had been elected in 1951 as the Communist-sponsored candidate. By 1954, the Communists were dominating Guatemalan politics and the economy. Arbenz had embarked on a program of agrarian reform and seized 225,000 acres owned by the American-based United Fruit Company. President Eisenhower and CIA Director Dulles wanted to prevent Communist expansion and Soviet influence in Central America.

The CIA developed a plan in 1953 called Operation Success to remove Arbenz from power. With a secret $20 million appropriation approved by Eisenhower, the CIA organized a small air force with American pilots in Nicaragua, gathered together a band of mercenaries in Honduras led by Col. Castillo Armas, and supported an invasion of Guatemala in June 1954. Although there were some minor military problems, the combined attack by CIA-piloted fighter planes, the invasion of 200 troops led by Armas, and a revolt by Guatemalan army leaders quickly resulted in the collapse of the Arbenz regime. The CIA considered the Guatemalan coup totally effective. Richard Bissell, the CIA Deputy Director of Plans, believed it greatly influenced CIA planning to remove Castro from power in Cuba.[14]

The CIA presented a program of covert action against the Castro regime, also known as Operation Pluto, to President Eisenhower on March 17, 1960. As developed by Bissell, it consisted of coordinated political and military elements. Politically, the United States would organize anti-Castro refugee factions into a unified Cuban government-in-exile. This would be accompanied by a powerful radio propaganda offensive.

Militarily, the CIA would recruit and train a Cuban paramilitary force in Guatemala to prepare for future guerrilla action in Cuba. As an indigenous anti-Castro brigade, they would enter Cuba in small groups and establish active pockets of resistance. It was assumed that many Cubans opposed Castro and would overthrow him if given the opportunity. After establishing bases of operation, the invaders would received arms and supplies, build popular support, and undermine Castro's regime.[15]

Dulles suggested that the military plan might be operational before the November 1960 election. However, according to Brigadier General Andrew Goodpaster, Eisenhower's staff secretary, the president approved only the training part of the military plan. The president wanted a more comprehensive proposal before approving an invasion plan. According to Goodpaster, training was approved "but explicitly without obligation to commit the unit. We were nowhere close to making that decision."[16] Eisenhower insisted that it was important to identify a Cuban exile leader who would organize a new government and direct the activities of the covert and paramilitary forces.[17]

In June, the CIA brought together five anti-Castro groups in Miami to form into a united opposition. President Miguel Ydigoras Fuentes of Guatemala, who had benefitted from Operation Success in 1954, was persuaded to permit the CIA establish training camps. In July, the first Cuban exiles arrived, recruited by the CIA from Florida and Central America.[18]

In August 1960, Eisenhower privately approved a $13 million budget for the CIA plan to authorize the use of Defense Department personnel to equip and train the anti-Castro guerrillas in Guatemala. He prohibited the use of United States military in any combat operations. Eisenhower was concerned that the CIA was having problems with organizing the Cuban government-in-exile. The CIA reported that the exiles were so factionalized that no leader had emerged. Eisenhower refused to approve any invasion plans unless a popular, genuine anti-Castro government-in-exile was established.[19]

By the November presidential election, the CIA plan was changing from guerrilla infiltration to a full-scale amphibious attack. According to Bissell, the CIA was having problems making contact with any organized underground in Cuba since Castro's secret police were arresting all suspected opponents. This made it difficult to bring in enough Cuban invaders to establish a resistance force. Consequently, the CIA was altering plans "to place main reliance on the landing force, and only minor reliance on any resistance force."[20]

The CIA, apparently operating on its own, was also involved in a deep cover plan to assassinate Fidel Castro. (CIA plots to assassinate foreign leaders were not ended until 1975 when President Ford directed the agency to stop such actions.) Before the November 1960 elections, an associate of Richard Bissell met with Robert Maheu, a former FBI agent who worked under contract with the CIA, and the industrialist Howard Hughes. In October, Maheu met in Miami Beach with Chicago gangster

Sam Giancana, his associate John Roselli, and Santos Trafficante, a Havana gangster who had been jailed by Castro in 1959. They agreed on a plot to poison Castro. Bissell thought hiring gangsters was "the ultimate cover" because there was "very little chance that anything the Syndicate tried to do would be traced back to the United States government."[21]

Historian Michael R. Beschloss suggests that Vice President Nixon may have known and approved of the failed plot to kill Castro before the November elections. In the 1970s, the CIA insisted in congressional hearings that a high-level political official in the Eisenhower administration approved assassination plots against Castro. Beschloss argues that Nixon knew Maheu through his former foreign policy aide, Robert King, who was Maheu's business partner. In 1991, King denied he ever informed Nixon of Maheu's involvement with the Mafia in plotting to kill Castro. But King said he didn't know if Nixon was in direct contact with Maheu.[22]

In any event, the CIA's assassination plots were suspended possibly for political reasons before the November 1960 elections, but were revived following the failure of the Bay of Pigs invasion.

Kennedy, Cuba, and the 1960 Campaign

Kennedy was sharply critical of the Eisenhower administration's action toward Castro and Cuba during the presidential campaign. He repeatedly challenged Vice President Nixon in a contest of toughness in Cold War anti-communist rhetoric. Both men tried to outdo each other in showing who was stronger in confronting what they considered the global communist threat. Standing up to Castro was a principal focus of their verbal exchanges.

The highlight to the campaign and its most innovative feature was the first series of televised "debates" between the two candidates. Just prior to the fourth debate on October 21, Kennedy's campaign headquarters released a tough statement on Cuba: "We must attempt to strengthen the non-Batista Democratic and anti-Castro forces. . . . Thus far these fighters have had virtually no support from our Government."[23]

Nixon responded harshly to Kennedy's statement at the fourth debate, characterizing it as one of the most "dangerous recommendations that he's made during this campaign."[24]

Nixon criticized Kennedy for proposing direct United States military intervention in Cuban affairs. In reality, Nixon was fully aware of the CIA's plans for invading Cuba. He was urging the CIA to carry out an invasion of Cuba before the election. Kennedy personally did not know of the CIA plans until shortly after the election when Dulles provided him with a full briefing.

However, a disclosure in 1993 by Governor John Patterson of Alabama suggests that Kennedy knew much more about CIA plans before the election. According to Patterson, he was approached by a CIA official in early 1960 for permission to recruit personnel from the Alabama National Guard "to form a nucleus for assembling and equipping for a Cuban invasion force."[25] Patterson asked if President Eisenhower knew of and approved the proposal. The CIA agent said he did. Patterson then provided 350 guardsmen who were sent to Guatemala to train the Cuban brigade. He was concerned the invasion would occur before the November election which would help Nixon win.

Patterson claims that he privately met with Kennedy before November, telling him "I want you to promise me you are never going to breathe a word about this to anybody if you know about it, because there are a lot of lives at stake."[26] Kennedy apparently took Patterson's advice by not revealing the CIA's training plans before the election. Instead, his campaign rhetoric attacked the Eisenhower administration for not doing enough to remove Castro from Cuba.

Following the election, Kennedy received two full intelligence briefings from Dulles and Bissell on the CIA plan to train the Cuban brigade in Guatemala. A guerrilla force of 600 to 750 men was being prepared to invade Cuba at Trinidad on the south coast. They would be assisted by CIA-operated air strikes against Castro's military forces, flown in from bases in Nicaragua. Massive propaganda and bombing would increase resistance to defections from Castro, causing him to be overthrown.

Dulles and Bissell pressured Kennedy to support the plan. It was becoming difficult to prevent Castro from knowing about the training of Cuban exiles. Soviet influence over Cuba was increasing. The longer the invasion was delayed, the more difficult it would be to implement. Kennedy was surprised by the scope of the CIA plans, but he was not ready to approve them.

Countdown to the Decision

In the early months of 1961, President Kennedy was caught up in the CIA planning to invade Cuba without ever considering the possible flaws of its design. Rather than making a single decision, Kennedy and his advisers reviewed the CIA plan, sought reassurances from the Joint Chiefs of Staff (JCS) that it would work, modified it, and insisted on covering up any direct United States military involvement with the Cuban brigade. President Kennedy and his advisers never questioned the underlying assumptions of the Bay of Pigs invasion in April 1961. Dissenting views were minimized as the invasion plan gained momentum. In fact, the CIA planners, Dulles and Bissell, kept pressuring Kennedy to act, which he eventually did with disastrous results.

The CIA Plan Gains Momentum

Soon after his inauguration, President Kennedy requested the JCS to review the feasibility of the proposed Trinidad invasion site and to assess the chances for its success. According to the CIA, Trinidad had a good harbor and a defensible beachhead, was remotely located from Castro's army, and close to the Escambray mountains.[27] At a meeting of the National Security Council on January 28, Kennedy asked the JCS to make an assessment of the military aspects of the Trinidad site, emphasizing that direct United States military involvement be excluded.

Kennedy was concerned about renewed charges of Yankee imperialism as he was preparing to send his "Alliance for Progress" initiative to Congress. This proposal, announced in his January inaugural speech, supported democratic and economic development in Latin America with long-term aid, support for land reform, encouragement of private investment, and expansion of technical assistance.[28]

Kennedy also worried that a United States–sponsored attack against Cuba might provoke Khrushchev to retaliate against Berlin. Kennedy told almost no one about this concern until later, although United States policymakers knew about Khrushchev's ultimatum of November 1958 when he demanded that the United States, Britain, and France leave Berlin or he would sign a peace treaty with East Germany, thereby allowing them to control the access routes to West Berlin.[29] To prevent Khrushchev from making new demands on Allied rights in West Berlin, Kennedy wanted the Cuban invasion to be perceived by Castro and the Soviets as an indigenous attack.

In early February, the JCS raised some concerns about the CIA's Trinidad plan. In a report to Kennedy, the JCS stated that the invasion's success depended on a popular uprising against Castro. There were no margins for miscalculation or unforeseen contingencies. At the same time, the JCS was optimistic that the invasion would succeed, stating that "timely execution of this plan has a fair chance of ultimate success, and even if it does not achieve immediately the full results desired, it could contribute to the eventual overthrow of the Castro regime."[30]

Kennedy approved the Trinidad plan but told Bissell, "I reserve the right to cancel this right to the end."[31] Subsequently, the JCS sent an inspection team to the training camps in Guatemala and Nicaragua. By this time, press reports by *Time* magazine and the *New York Times* had disclosed details of CIA support for the Cuban exiles and the training camps. The JCS reported back to Kennedy that the odds of a surprise attack against Castro were 85 to 15 against. A single Cuban plan with a .50 calibre machine gun could destroy most of the brigade's ships.[32]

At a meeting in the Cabinet room on March 11, Bissell again presented the Trinidad plan to Kennedy, the Secretaries of State and Defense, and the JCS. Based upon the reservations of the JCS from its inspection report of the training camps, Kennedy asked for a revised plan. In his view, the Trinidad site was "too spectacular . . . too much like a World War Two invasion."[33] He wanted a "quieter landing, preferably at night and without any overt United States military support.[34]

Also by mid-March, the CIA had told Kennedy that the morale of the Cuban brigade was peaking. The Guatemalan president wanted the exiles gone by the end of April. Castro was about to receive shipments of Soviet jet fighters which would make any small-scale invasion suicidal.[35] Kennedy believed the invasion plan was moving forward without being able to stop it. He said, "I don't know if we could go down there and take the guns away from them."[36]

On March 15, the CIA presented an alternative plan for a landing site at the Bay of Pigs, located one hundred miles west of Trinidad. Kennedy authorized the CIA to proceed with the new location, code named Zapata, but he reserved the final decision on the invasion until it was ready to occur. The CIA believed Kennedy would support air cover for the invasion. Also, Dulles and Bissell assumed that the invaders could easily hide in the mountains if there was no popular uprising against Castro. But no one took into account that eighty miles of roadless swamps surrounded the Bay of Pigs.[37]

The Crucial Decision: Kennedy Approves the Bay of Pigs Plan

At a secret meeting of the National Security Council on April 4, Kennedy brought together his top military and Latin American advisers to review the Zapata plan. The meeting included Secretary of Defense Robert McNamara and his assistant, Paul Nitze; Secretary of State Dean Rusk and Thomas Mann, assistant secretary for inter-American affairs; General Lyman Lemnitzer, chairman of the JCS; Adolph Berle,

Jr., chair of the Interdepartmental Task Force on Latin America; and Allen Dulles and Richard Bissell from the CIA. Kennedy also invited Senator J. William Fulbright, chair of the Senate Foreign Relations Committee, to attend the meeting.

Bissell and Dulles defended the plan, arguing that the brigade would establish a base near the beach, holding it until the Cuban government-in-exile declared itself in power and rallied internal support for itself in Cuba. The brigade's planes (actually, CIA piloted aircraft) from Nicaragua would attack and destroy Castro's air force before the invaders left their ships. Also, Dulles and Bissell reiterated the need for quick approval since Castro was about to receive a shipment of Soviet fighter jets, along with Czech-trained pilots to fly them.[38]

Senator Fulbright was the only participant to oppose the plan. He repeated the same warnings that he had given to Kennedy in a memo a few days earlier. Fulbright believed that United States support for an invasion of Cuba "constituted a policy of such cynical hypocrisy as to be worthy of the Soviet Union rather than the United States." Even if it was successful, the invasion would be "denounced from the Rio Grande to Patagonia as an example of imperialism."[39] Fulbright believed the whole idea was "absurdly disproportionate to the threat Castro currently represented."[40]

Fulbright was the lone dissenter at the meeting. Schlesinger, who later expressed misgivings about the plan in *A Thousand Days*, his chronicle of the Kennedy administration, neither volunteered any comments nor was asked for them. Undersecretary of State Chester Bowles was not invited to the meeting. He had informed Rusk of his objections but Rusk discouraged him from talking directly to Kennedy. Adlai Stevenson, the United Nations Ambassador, was not asked to attend the meeting nor to state his opinion. In fact, Stevenson was not informed until after the invasion occurred.

After Fulbright's highly negative comments, Kennedy proceeded to ask each of the other participants to state his views. Each gave approval. Rusk approved even though he had private misgivings about the plan as did Mann, who had opposed the Trinidad plan. McNamara reluctantly approved because he believed United States military support was needed. General Lemnitzer was less than enthusiastic, stating that if Dulles's assumptions were accurate, the plan was militarily feasible.[41] According to Schlesinger, Kennedy concluded that all of his senior political and military advisers approved the plan. The only outright opposition was from Fulbright. "Had one senior adviser opposed the adventure, I believe that Kennedy would have canceled it. No one spoke against it."[42]

Irving L. Janis characterized the crucial April 4th decision by Kennedy and the NSC as an example of groupthink, a process of flawed decision-making.[43] Janus identified six symptoms of groupthink, which prevented the decision-makers from carefully analyzing and evaluating the CIA's invasion plan. These included:

1. *An illusion of invulnerability.* The president and his advisers believed they were immune from dangers arising from a risky action because of their overconfidence and "buoyant optimism" at the outset of a new administration. Their euphoria prevented them from examining the dangers of the CIA plan while, at the same time, they underestimated Castro's military capabilities. As a cohesive group, they acceded to the CIA plan and the cover story because of wishful thinking that it would succeed.

2. *Illusion of unanimity.* Kennedy and each of his key advisers believed the CIA plan would work because all members except Senator Fulbright agreed to the plan. Except for Fulbright, who was an invited outsider, the April 4th meeting had an atmosphere of "assumed consensus."

3. *Suppression of Personal Doubts.* Some of Kennedy's advisers offered only quiet objections. For the most part, they censored themselves at the April 4th meeting even though some had strong personal doubts. Most remained silent because they feared disapproval from other members as each one agreed to the CIA plan when President Kennedy asked for their votes. For example, Arthur Schlesinger, Jr. admitted he had some doubts, but withheld expressing them at the April 4th meeting.

4. *Self-Appointed Mindguards.* Some of Kennedy's key advisers prevented critics from expressing disapproval of the CIA plan. Janis calls this "mindguarding," a technique by which group consensus is preserved by suppressing dissidents. Recall that Secretary of State Rusk discouraged his undersecretary from talking directly to the president and that U.N. Ambassador Stevenson was not even invited to the April 4th meeting.

5. *Group Passivity Promoted by the Leader.* Although Kennedy raised skeptical questions about the CIA's landing site for the invasion at earlier meetings, he did not encourage the NSC members to ask probing or challenging questions at the key April 4th meeting. For

example, Kennedy did not ask for a response or discussion of Senator Fulbright's objections. Consequently, group consensus remained
strongly in favor of proceeding with the CIA plan.

6. *Group Acceptance of CIA Lead Role.* President Kennedy and most of
his key advisers avoided criticizing Allen Dulles and Richard Bissell
of the CIA, who had the lead roles in planning and implementing the
invasion plan. Although both were holdovers from the Eisenhower
administration, they were immediately accepted as insiders on
covert operations and the intelligence network. Since Bissell's proposal was already underway, Kennedy and his advisers agreed there
was momentum and urgency to follow through. Consequently, they
deferred to CIA expertise without questioning any of the underlying
assumptions of the plan. Such deference contributed to maintaining
group cohesion and prevented any other alternatives, including
scrapping the plan, from being seriously considered.

The Military Operation: A Tragic Comedy of Errors

After the April 4th meeting, Kennedy was under maximum pressure to
finalize the Bay of Pigs invasion. Two developments brought the military
operation underway. On April 7, Tad Szulc was ready to report in *The
New York Times* that the CIA was training anti-Castro forces for an imminent invasion. Kennedy quickly called the *Times* owner and asked to have
the story modified. Second, Kennedy had a report from Guatemala that
the Cuban brigade had "a fanatical urge to begin battle."[44]

Publicly, Kennedy went on record at his April 12 news conference
to deny that any plan was underway by the United States to attack
Cuba. In responding to a question concerning whether a decision had
"been reached on how far this country will be willing to go in helping
an anti-Castro uprising or invasion of Cuba," Kennedy answered there
would not be "under any conditions an intervention in Cuba by the
United States Armed Forces."[45] No Americans would be "involved in
any actions in Cuba."[46] At the same time, it was clear that Kennedy
viewed Castro as hostile to United States interests because he was a
Communist sympathizer. In responding to another question, Kennedy
said that Castro had "indicated his admiration on many occasions for
the Communist revolution" and had "appointed a great many Communists to high positions."[47]

Kennedy called Bissell on April 14 and approved air strikes at
three Cuban airfields for April 15. The attack began with six B-26
bombers flown in from Nicaragua. The planes had Cuban markings

and the cover story was that the pilots were Cuban defectors, although none were. At the United Nations, Stevenson was preparing to respond to Cuban charges of aggressive actions by the United States. Uninformed of the CIA plan, Stevenson defended the cover story that the attack was by Castro defectors. After discovering that the full nature of the CIA plan, he threatened to resign, but did not.

The bombers returned to Nicaragua with claims of widespread damage to Castro's air force. These turned out to be highly optimistic. Most of Castro's air force survived the attack. However, Kennedy on April 16 refused to authorize a second air strike. He wanted the brigade to secure a beachhead. Then, further air attacks could be portrayed as launched from Cuban soil.

McGeorge Bundy, Kennedy's special assistant for national security affairs, relayed the president's decision to Bissell. Bissell pleaded for reconsideration since Castro's air force could easily attack the ships bringing in the invaders. Rusk refused, telling Bissell that "political requirements" were now most essential. Stevenson could not defend the United States position at the United Nations with Castro denouncing the military intervention.[48]

The next day, April 17, the 1,400 men of the Cuban brigade began landing at the Bay of Pigs. Castro's army and air force knew immediately that it was occurring because of Castro's effective intelligence network. To prevent any local uprisings, Cuban police had rounded up suspected opponents and detained 200,000 people in theaters and auditoriums in Havana. Kennedy said later that if any Cubans knew of the invasion, they were "working in Castro's office."[49]

The invaders ran into several obstacles. Coral reefs tore through many of the landing craft. The beach was brightly lit by Castro's militia. Tanks were stationed to meet the invaders. At dawn, Castro's air force attacked, sinking the ships carrying ammunition reserves and most of the communications equipment.

On April 18, Kennedy authorized a second air attack to protect the brigade and help to evacuate them from the beach. He permitted an overflight by six unmarked jet fighters from the *Essex* aircraft carrier. The jets were intended to support an attack from B-26 bombers, flown in from Nicaragua. However, the attack failed. Due to confusion over time zone differences between Nicaragua and Cuba, the slow flying bombers arrived an hour before the jets. Castro's small T-33 jet trainers, which had survived the first B-26 assault, attacked the bombers, shot down four of them, and killed four Americans.[50]

Khrushchev knew of the first air attack and the invasion as soon as it occurred. On the same day as the failed second air attack, Khrushchev broadcast a message on Radio Moscow and then gave it to the United States Embassy for delivery to Kennedy. He warned that the invasion was "fraught with danger to world peace." He criticized Kennedy for his pledge against United States military involvement in Cuba. It was an open secret that the United States was directly involved with training and arming the invaders. Khrushchev promised to "render the Cuban people and their government all necessary assistance in beating back the armed attack on Cuba."[51]

Kennedy's response to Khrushchev was unyielding and tough. He claimed that the uprising against Castro was by opponents to his dictatorship. Khrushchev was "under a serious misapprehension" about Cuba. The United States intended "no military intervention in Cuba," but did not "conceal . . . admiration for Cuban patriots who wish to see a democratic system in an independent Cuba." Kennedy ended by warning Khrushchev that "I trust that this does not mean that the Soviet government, using the situation in Cuba as a pretext, is planning to inflame other areas of the world."[52]

While Kennedy and Khrushchev were exchanging threats, Castro's army and air force were systematically destroying the Cuban brigade. By April 19, three days after the operation began, the invaders began surrendering. Of the 1,400 men involved, 114 were killed and nearly 1,200 surrendered.[53] The Bay of Pigs had ended in a total and humiliating failure.

The Aftermath of the Bay of Pigs

Kennedy, although angered and depressed by the total collapse of the Bay of Pigs invasion, responded immediately to it. Speaking to the American Society of Newspaper Editors in Washington, Kennedy took a tough stand, warning Khrushchev not to take advantage of the situation in Cuba. He reiterated United States sympathy for the attack, but stated that United States armed forces had not intervened unilaterally because that "would have been contrary to our traditions and to our international obligations." At the same time, he warned the Soviets that "our restraint is not inexhaustible. . . . I want it clearly understood that this government will not hesitate in meeting its primary obligations, which are to the security of our nation." In the future, the United States would not accept "the same outcome which this small band of Cuban refugees must have known that they were chancing . . . against heavy odds." The invasion had been a struggle of freedom over totalitarianism. In Kennedy's view, it was not "the final episode in the eternal struggle of liberty against tyranny."[54]

On April 21, Kennedy held a press conference. He refused further questions on Cuba, referring to his speech to the newspaper editors. Sander Vanocur of NBS pressed Kennedy to explain the "real facts" behind the invasion. Kennedy's answer denied further explanation because he was "the responsible officer of the government" and that "such a discussion" would not "benefit us during the present difficult situation."[55] In Kennedy's view, the Bay of Pigs was an illustration of "an old saying that victory has a hundred fathers and defeat is an orphan."[56]

On April 22, Kennedy met with Eisenhower at Camp David to assess the Bay of Pigs. The former president was highly critical of how the decisions were made and the lack of sufficient military support to make it succeed. He asked if Kennedy had called a full meeting of the NSC to "have everybody in front of you debating the thing so you got the pros and cons yourself" before making the decision.[57] Kennedy admitted not requesting such an evaluation of the invasion plan.

Second, Eisenhower was critical about the absence of air cover for the invaders. Kennedy relayed his fears of Soviet retaliation: "If it was learned that we were really doing this than these rebels themselves, the Soviets would be very apt to cause trouble in Berlin."[58] Eisenhower strongly disagreed. In his view, the Soviets respected United States strength and "if they see us show any weakness, then is when they press us hardest. . . . The failure of the Bay of Pigs will embolden the Soviets to do something they would not do otherwise."[59]

Kennedy reiterated that his advice was to keep United States support for the invasion a secret. Eisenhower disagreed. In his view, once it was known that the United States was directly involved, everything needed to be done to assure military success. Kennedy reassured Eisenhower that if the United States got involved with Cuba again, "it is going to be a success."[60]

President Kennedy as Decision-Maker

Foreign Policy Context of Decision

President Kennedy's final decision to approve the Bay of Pigs invasion occurred at the fateful April 4, 1961 secret meeting of the National Security Council when none of his advisers, except Senator Fulbright, spoke out against it. But the origins of Kennedy's decision can be traced to the first formal CIA briefings on the earlier Trinidad plan soon after the 1960 election. Kennedy never once objected to the covert plan to depose Castro. He accepted nearly all of the CIA's proposals to train a force of anti-Castro Cubans, and with CIA assistance, to invade Cuba. The only real question debated in 1961 was the appropriate landing site for the invaders.

Kennedy's public support for removing Castro originated in the foreign policy debates with Nixon in the 1960 campaign. Kennedy was highly critical of the Eisenhower administration's inability to contain the communist threat. Since Castro assumed power in 1959, Kennedy argued that not enough had been done to remove Castro, to end Cuba's growing ties with the Soviet Union, or to stop Castro from endangering other Latin American governments. Kennedy portrayed himself as a determined Cold Warrior who could deal more effectively with Castro than Nixon. In turn, Nixon attacked Kennedy for reckless rhetoric advocating direct United States military intervention in Cuba, although Nixon was pressuring the CIA to launch an invasion and possibly even to kill Castro before the November elections.

Although Kennedy may have known about the secret training of anti-Castro Cubans before the election, he never told anyone. Instead, Kennedy argued that Castro threatened United States interests in Latin America and the United States would never tolerate a Soviet base of influence ninety miles from Florida. Kennedy's strategic goal in Latin America was part of his overall worldview of anti-communism. The United States needed to do something quickly about Castro to prevent the Soviet Union from establishing influence in the Western Hemisphere. Therefore, it is not surprising that Kennedy did not object to the CIA's evolving plans which were already underway to train a force of Cuban exiles in Guatemala.

Context of Decision within Kennedy's National Security Strategy

By early 1961, soon after his inauguration, Kennedy was taking steps to implement the CIA's Trinidad plan. These included training the Cuban brigade in Guatemala, establishing a secret CIA airforce base in Nicaragua, and selecting the best invasion landing site in Cuba. Kennedy wanted to maintain the utmost secrecy concerning direct United States military involvement with the plan. Presumably, Kennedy believed that earlier secret efforts by the CIA to overthrow governments in Guatemala and Iran (July 1953) would also work in

Cuba. Also, he trusted the CIA insiders, Dulles and Bissell, and had confidence in their expertise over covert operations. Consequently, Kennedy was caught up in the momentum of the CIA's plans. Only a very few of his trusted military, intelligence, and Latin American advisers were aware of the invasion planning. The plan assumed that after an "indigenous" rebellion succeeded, the United States wold openly support the establishment of a pro–United States government in Cuba.

As Kennedy and his advisers considered the CIA plan in early 1961, the overall strategy to overthrow Castro remained intact, while tactical aspects of the invasion were modified. After Kennedy rejected the Trinidad location, the Bay of Pigs was identified as the more effective landing site for the brigade. Kennedy also found himself under great pressure to approve the invasion. The CIA, led by Dulles and Bissell, told him that he either had to decide by April or cancel the mission.

Another key factor was that nearly all of Kennedy's advisers supported the Bay of Pigs invasion. Although a few had private reservations, no one urged Kennedy to cancel the plan. Senator Fulbright was greatly distressed but no one responded to his concerns at the crucial meeting of April 4. Bowles wanted to tell Kennedy directly that the invasion was a terrible mistake, but Rusk prevented him from doing so. Stevenson lied publicly in the United Nations about the absence of United States involvement because he was never informed of the CIA plan. All of this resulted in a groupthink syndrome among Kennedy and his advisers, which prevented them from rationally assessing the feasibility of the CIA plans.

Domestic Context of Decision

Public opinion in the United States strongly supported Kennedy's opposition to Castro before the Bay of Pigs and rallied to the president's side with very strong approval after the failed effort. The public would probably have approved of a direct United States invasion of Cuba, given the context of Castro's harsh rhetoric, his growing ties with the Soviet Union, and the rapidly increasing number of anti-Castro Cubans streaming into Florida.

At the same time, Kennedy was a youthful, newly elected president who was in the process of organizing his new administration. He faced many challenges during the transition period from the Eisenhower administration. Kennedy had not yet gained full control over foreign policy and therefore accepted the evolving CIA plans without critically evaluating them. Dulles and Bissell were forceful advocates who assured Kennedy that the CIA was in full control of the plan and any contingencies associated with it. Kennedy was not aware that CIA analysts had not been asked for a critical evaluation of the invasion plan. The JCS did not forcefully offer any serious reservations, even though for military reasons they believed the plan had only modest chances for success.

Kennedy failed to consider that the secrecy of United States involvement was unravelling quickly since American journalists were reporting on the CIA's involvement with training of the Cuban brigade in Guatemala. Kennedy was successful in persuading *The New York Times* not to publish a story that an invasion of Cuba was imminent. But he did not take into account that Castro knew of the invasion and was doing everything possible to repel the invaders. Kennedy and the CIA seriously underestimated the strength of Castro's intelligence operatives, police, militia, and air force, particularly after the failed first air attack on Cuban air bases.

Decision Options

Given the momentum of CIA plans to invade Cuba, President Kennedy never considered canceling them. Kennedy publicly supported diplomatic, economic, and military pressure against Castro. The most important question is why Kennedy accepted the CIA's plan without ever considering other contingencies. The answer probably lies in a combination of Kennedy's inexperience, his confidence in CIA reassurances, and the structure of his national security process, where his close advisers were not encouraged to speak out more forcefully on their reservations and objections to the CIA's plans. Learning from these mistakes and inexperience, Kennedy was much better prepared to deal with the Cuban Missile Crisis in October 1962.

Kennedy's only major decision was to change the landing site in order to reinsure secrecy. This constrained his options after the invasion encountered severe resistance from Castro's forces. After approving the initial air strike on Castro's bases and the landing of the brigade, it quickly became clear that Castro was fully prepared to repel the attack. Kennedy could have approved a second air strike, but he hesitated until it was too late.

The most intriguing aspect of Kennedy's decision-making was his fear of Soviet retaliation against Berlin if the United States military openly assisted the brigade. According to Beschloss, Kennedy did not confide his fears to anyone before the invasion. He waited until afterward when he disclosed them to Eisenhower. If he had openly shared his concerns earlier, the invasion may have been canceled or at least drastically changed from what the CIA envisioned. Perhaps the JCS would have told Kennedy that the Bay of Pigs site was surrounded by swamps and therefore almost impossible to defend. The Trinidad site, with a much smaller force, might have given the invaders a better chance to proceed into the mountains and hide out until they moved inward. However, such guerrilla activities would have required support from a Cuban underground of anti-Castro advocates. And Castro already seemed to know exactly what the CIA was doing by April 1961.

Kennedy's Leadership Role in the Decision

Most scholars, including James David Barber, agree that John F. Kennedy was an "active-positive" president, displaying a great deal of energy with inspiring speeches and new approaches to public policy.[61] Kennedy's inaugural address of January 1961 had a great impact in raising public expectations about the challenges of a new generation of Americans, especially in world affairs. He pledged a "celebration of freedom" and announced to "every nation . . . whether it wishes us well or ill, that we shall pay any price, bear any burden, meet any hardship, support any friend, oppose any foe to assure the survival and success of liberty."

According to Carl M. Brauer, Kennedy was a highly inspirational president, a leader who articulated a great deal of confidence about the role of America in world affairs. According to Brauer, Kennedy "raised people's hopes . . . about peace, the promise of democratic government, social justice, economic progress, and the exploration of 'New Frontiers' on earth and in space. . . . [H]e inspired idealism about the importance of trying to achieve great things for society as a whole."[62]

Brauer's assessment of Kennedy's leadership style needs to be modified in the light of the Bay of Pigs fiasco. Instead of policy innovation or new approaches, Kennedy went ahead with an inherited CIA plan because he saw no alternatives to the reassurances given to him by Dulles and Bissell.

According to Richard E. Neustadt, Kennedy's problems in the Bay of Pigs can be explained by two serious flaws in his leadership style: ignorance and arrogance.[63] Neustadt argues that the newness of the Kennedy administration made it difficult in early 1961 for the president and his close advisers (McNamara, Rusk, and Bundy) to really know what the CIA was doing. Kennedy trusted Bissell to tell him about all aspects of the plan when in fact the CIA had a stake in promoting it without communicating possible problems. Kennedy was overly reliant on secrecy when in fact the CIA leaders did not even share all aspects of the plan with their own analysts.

Arrogance, according to Neustadt, was also evident during Kennedy's early months in office. Kennedy and his aides were new, brash, self-confident, and assured they could succeed even with a half-baked scheme like the Bay of Pigs. The reality of failure was simply not anticipated. When it occurred, Kennedy realized he needed to have more direct control over foreign policy and covert activities.

The most important lesson of Kennedy's leadership style in the Bay of Pigs is that he learned from the mistakes. There would be no greater contrast to the Bay of Pigs than when President Kennedy publicly rebuffed Khrushchev in October 1962, compelling the Soviet leader to remove the nuclear missiles being placed in Cuba. Kennedy displayed decisive and effective presidential leadership which was not evident in the 1961 Bay of Pigs debacle.

Consequences of Kennedy's Decision for the United States and Other Countries Involved

United States

Following the Bay of Pigs invasion of April 1961, President Kennedy took steps to find out what went wrong. He appointed an internal committee with General Maxwell Taylor as chair, along with Dulles, Admiral Arleigh Burke, Chief of Naval Operations, and Attorney General Robert Kennedy. Focusing principally on the military aspects of the invasion, the Taylor committee concluded that the CIA and the JCS shared the blame for failure. The committee found the whole operation plagued by inadequate resources for the brigade when it landed and faced serious opposition from Castro's militia and air force. The president should have been made more aware of the consequences of canceling the second air strike, since it put the brigade into great jeopardy. Only a full-scale, United States-supported military operation would have succeeded. The JCS should have made their preference clearer for the Trinidad plan. In the future, the Committee recommended that the

United States military should be responsible for paramilitary operations and the CIA should be confined to covert political activities.[64]

An interagency investigation led by CIA Inspector General Lyman Kirkpatrick was more critical of the CIA. The report concluded that the CIA had miscalculated the quantity of forces required. Richard Bissell had been overly optimistic in anticipating mass defections from Castro's military to join the invaders. Dulles and Bissell should have asked CIA analysts to review the plan. Kirkpatrick's report concluded that the operation was "too big to be a raid and too small to be an invasion."[65] A successful attack would have required 10,000 to 15,000 men with full and open support from the United States military.

Kennedy made several changes after receiving the Taylor report. In June 1961, he transferred responsibility for most paramilitary operations from the CIA to the Defense Department. Responding to criticism of the JCS failure to express stronger objections to the Bay of Pigs plan, McNamara subsequently combined the three separate military intelligence operations into the Defense Intelligence Agency.

Kennedy asked for the resignations of Dulles and Bissell. They were replaced by John McCone, who became CIA director, and Richard Helms, who was appointed deputy director of CIA plans. Kennedy was also concerned about the lack of effective advice from the State Department. McGeorge Bundy was moved into the basement of the White House to coordinate all national security policy. In effect, Kennedy became his own secretary of state and bypassed Dean Rusk on most important foreign policy decisions. In November 1961, he transferred Richard Goodwin to the position of deputy assistant secretary for Latin American affairs and appointed Walt Rostow as head of policy planning in the State Department. Chester Bowles was removed as undersecretary and eventually appointed ambassador to India.

Despite Kennedy's problems with the Bay of Pigs operation, public opinion supported his actions. In the following week, Kennedy's approval ratings increased from 78 to 83 percent in a "rally around the president" statement of support.[66] The reason for this was clear. An overwhelming majority supported continued pressure to remove the Castro regime in Cuba. This sentiment was strongest among the growing number of Cuban refugees flooding into Florida. Kennedy responded by persuading all members of the Organization of American States, except Mexico, to expel Cuba. Kennedy also placed an economic embargo on Cuba, which continued through the Clinton administration.

Covert activities against Cuba, including efforts to assassinate Castro, were revived by the CIA with the approval of Kennedy. He selected his brother, Attorney General Robert Kennedy, to oversee and report back on all covert activities. Known as Operation Mongoose, the plan had a target date of October 1962 to overthrow Castro. Mongoose included contaminating Cuban sugar exports, along with various sabotage, espionage, and guerrilla warfare plans.[67] One of the most bizarre plots was to poison Castro. In April 1962, William Harvey the CIA chief of Operation Mongoose, met with the gangster John Roselli in Miami and gave him poison pills to put in Castro's food or water. The plot failed when the pills did not dissolve properly.[68]

Cuba

Castro solidified his power as Cuban dictator following the victory at the Bay of Pigs in April 1961. Castro began moving Cuba into the Soviet orbit by shipping nearly all sugar exports to the USSR and receiving in return economic and military assistance. He knew of Kennedy's efforts to isolate Cuba diplomatically and to weaken the island's economy. Castro also maintained an effective intelligence source which made him aware of Operation Mongoose. He concluded that Kennedy's overt and covert activities after the Bay of Pigs were leading to a full scale United States military attack. In the spring of 1962, Castro informed the Soviet Union that "we were more concerned about a direct invasion of Cuba by the United States and that we were thinking about how to step up our country's ability to resist an attack."[69] In April, Khrushchev rejected Castro's request to join the Warsaw pact, but approved $750 million of increased Soviet economic aid to Cuba.[70]

The Soviet Union

Khrushchev also believed that U.S. actions following the Bay of Pigs were leading to a full-scale military invasion of Cuba. Unlike Kennedy's public reassurances that the United States would not intervene in Cuba before the April 1961 fiasco, Kennedy made no similar statements after the Bay of Pigs. Khrushchev concluded that such a United States attack would occur before the end of 1962, probably after the November congressional elections.[71]

Consequently, Khrushchev began making the same kind of miscalculations about United States intentions that Kennedy had a year earlier when he assumed that the CIA operation could be a completely covert operation. Khrushchev decided to ship missiles and Soviet combat troops to Cuba before the November congressional elections. He was overoptimistic in expecting that United States intelligence would not discover these shipments for eight weeks, even though the Soviet Union had never before undertaken such a large-scale covert military operation outside of its territory.[72]

Khrushchev's larger goals were to end the missile gap with the United States, to force new concessions on Berlin, and perhaps to convince the United States and NATO to dismantle military bases along the Soviet border.[73] After informing five Soviet advisers of his plan in a highly secret meeting in May 1962, Khrushchev offered the missile plan to Castro, who accepted it. In September 1962, the Soviet Union began missile shipments to Cuba.

Khrushchev's strategic and political errors in sending nuclear missiles to Cuba were monumental. Kennedy, upon discovering the shipments and construction of missile sites in Cuba in October 1962, reacted with a direct United States ultimatum to the Soviet Union. Kennedy's actions in the Cuban Missile Crisis forced Khrushchev to dismantle all the sites and included a full-scale United States naval "quarantine" to prevent further missile shipments from reaching Cuba.

Before the United States discovered the Soviet plan, Khrushchev mistakenly believed that Kennedy would accept Soviet missiles in Cuba as a *fait accompli* just as the Soviets had accepted United States missiles in Turkey. Also, he believed Kennedy would not risk nuclear war to remove the missiles. The American president would not consider Soviet missiles a direct threat to United States security and would probably be paralyzed by the fear of Soviet retaliation against Berlin just as he was in the Bay of Pigs.[74] All of Khrushchev's assumptions proved to be false.

Conclusion

In attempting to deal with Castro's growing belligerency against the United States, Kennedy clearly knew something had to be done about protecting United States interests in competition with the Soviet Union. Cuba was an urgent problem of United States foreign policy which was high on the new president's agenda during the early months of his administration.

It appears that Kennedy and his advisers relied too heavily on the CIA's plans for a covert invasion of Cuba. Other decision options were never considered, such as a total embargo of the island, open United States military maneuvers, or criticizing Soviet assistance to Castro. For example, the United Nations could have been used more effectively as a forum to attack Castro's human rights violations.

It turned out that the CIA's invasion plan was so flawed that Kennedy's relations with Cuba and the USSR became worse after the Bay of Pigs invasion. The October 1962 Cuban Missile Crisis was the most serious United States–Soviet nuclear confrontation of the Cold War. Certainly, Kennedy and his advisers could have asked for more time or delayed the Bay of Pigs invasion until more effective feasibility analysis was conducted.

The Bay of Pigs case is an example of why the president, in the early months of a new administration, needs to make a systematic review of all pending crisis matters before rushing to accept risky plans of the preceding presidency. Continuity is necessary in United States foreign policy, but presidents must avoid being pressured to act on crisis management issues. Their first priority should be to develop long-range plans to deal with crisis matters.

Kennedy, in retrospect, should not have deferred to the CIA. He needed to encourage a wide range of options to deal with Castro rather than acceding to an invasion plan that lacked any possibility of success. Yet Kennedy did learn from his mistakes. If presidents accept responsibility for flawed decisions, they, like Kennedy, may be more effective in dealing with subsequent crises.

Questions for Discussion

1. Why did Nixon criticize Kennedy's views on Cuba at the fourth debate of the 1960 campaign?

2. Why didn't Kennedy disclose the secret briefing from Alabama Gov. Patterson on the training of Cuban exiles before the 1960 election?

3. What were the goals of the covert CIA plans to depose Castro prior to the 1960 election? Why did Eisenhower not approve the invasion of Cuba before the November 1960 election?

4. How did the Joint Chiefs assess the CIA's Trinidad plan? Why did Kennedy first accept the Trinidad plan and then reject it?

5. What were the CIA assumptions about the probability of success for the Bay of Pigs plan?

6. At the crucial April 4 meeting, what kind of advice did Kennedy encourage on the Bay of Pigs plan? Why were Senator Fulbright's arguments against the plan ignored by Kennedy and the others present at the meeting? Does Janis' groupthink analysis effectively explain the flawed decision-making process?

7. Why did Kennedy continue to deny publicly United States military involvement in the Bay of Pigs plan?

8. Why did Kennedy refuse to authorize a second air strike after the first one failed to destroy Castro's air force?

9. Why did the CIA and JCS misjudge the chances of military success of the Bay of Pigs operation?

10. Following the Bay of Pigs invasion, how do you assess Kennedy's defense of what occurred?

NOTES

1. John F. Kennedy, *The Strategy of Peace* (New York: Popular Library, 1960), p. 168.
2. Trumbull Higgins, *The Perfect Failure: Kennedy, Eisenhower, and the CIA at the Bay of Pigs* (New York: W. W. Norton, 1987), p. 16.
3. Michael R. Beschloss, *The Crisis Years: Kennedy and Khrushchev, 1960–1963* (New York: HarperCollins, 1991), p. 91.
4. Tad Szulc, *Fidel: A Critical Portrait* (New York: Avon Books, 1986), p. 105.
5. Arthur M. Schlesinger, Jr., *A Thousand Days* (New York: Fawcett World Library, 1965, 1967), p. 204.
6. Beschloss, p. 96.
7. Richard Nixon, *RN: The Memoirs of Richard Nixon* (New York: Simon & Schuster, 1978), pp. 202–3.
8. Schlesinger, p. 208.
9. Beschloss, p. 98.
10. Schlesinger, p. 209.
11. Herbert S. Parmet, *JFK: The Presidency of John F. Kennedy* (New York: Penguin Books, 1983, 1984), p. 159.

12. Stephen E. Ambrose, *Eisenhower: The President*, volume 2 (New York: Simon & Schuster, 1983), p. 506.

13. Gregory F. Treverton, *Covert Action: The Limits of Intervention in the Postwar World* (New York: Basic Books, 1987), p. 86.

14. Higgins, p. 35.

15. Schlesinger, pp. 214–15.

16. Gerald S. and Deborah H. Strober, *Let Us Begin Anew: An Oral History of the Kennedy Presidency* (New York: HarperCollins, 1993), p. 325.

17. Ambrose, p. 557.

18. Treverton, p. 87

19. Ambrose, p. 584.

20. Treverton, p. 87.

21. Beschloss, p. 135.

22. Ibid., pp. 135–36.

23. Parmet, pp. 46–47.

24. Ibid., p. 47.

25. Strober, p. 325.

26. Ibid., p. 326.

27. Schlesinger, p. 223.

28. Barbara Kellerman and Ryan T. Barilleaux, *The President as World Leader* (New York: St. Martin's Press, 1991), pp. 85–86.

29. Ambrose, p. 502; Michael R. Beschloss, *Mayday: The U-2 Affair* (New York: Harper & Row, 1986), p. 162.

30. Treverton, p. 90.

31. Ibid.

32. Ibid., p. 93.

33. Beschloss, *The Crisis Years*, p. 92.

34. Ibid.; Schlesinger, p. 228.

35. Treverton, p. 92.

36. Kenneth P. O'Donnell and David F. Powers, *John, We Hardly Know Ye: Memories of John Fitzgerald Kennedy* (New York: Pocket Books, 1972, 1973), p. 312.

37. Higgins, p. 105.

38. Ibid., p. 110.

39. Ibid., p. 106.

40. Ibid., pp. 110–11.

41. Ibid., p. 112.

42. Schlesinger, p. 242.

43. The following discussion is adapted from pp. 19–27 of Irving L. Janis, *Groupthink*, 2nd ed. (Boston: Houghton Mifflin, 1982).

44. Beschloss, *The Crisis Years*, p. 114.

45. *Public Papers of the Presidents of the United States: John F. Kennedy, 1961.* (Washington, D.C.: U.S. Government Printing Office, 1962), pp. 258–59.

46. Ibid.
47. Ibid.
48. Beschloss, *The Crisis Years*, p. 116.
49. Treverton, pp. 97–98.
50. Schlesinger, p. 25.
51. Beschloss, *The Crisis Years*, p. 120.
52. *Public Papers of the Presidents of the United States: John F. Kennedy, 1961*, p. 286.
53. Treverton, p. 98.
54. *Public Papers of the Presidents of the United States: John F. Kennedy, 1961*, pp. 304–5.
55. Ibid., pp. 307–8.
56. Beschloss, *The Crisis Years*, p. 130.
57. Ambrose, p. 638.
58. Ibid.
59. Ibid.
60. Ibid., p. 639.
61. See James David Barber, *The President Character*, 4th ed. (Englewood Cliffs, N.J.: Prentice Hall, 1992), chapter 11.
62. Carl M. Brauer, "John F. Kennedy: The Endurance of Inspirational Leadership," in Fred I. Greenstein, (ed.), *Leadership in the Modern Presidency* (Cambridge, Mass.: Harvard University Press, 1988), p. 109.
63. Richard E. Neustadt, *Presidential Power and the Modern Presidents* (New York: Free Press, 1990), pp. 247–49.
64. Higgins, pp. 157–58.
65. Ibid., p. 166.
66. Larry Hugick and Alec M. Gallup, "Rally Events and Presidential Approval," *The Gallup Poll Monthly*, June 1991, pp. 15–27.
67. Beschloss, *The Crisis Years*, p. 376.
68. Parmet, p. 161.
69. Beschloss, *The Crisis Years*, p. 377.
70. Ibid.
71. Ibid., p. 378.
72. Ibid., p. 388.
73. Ibid., p. 382.
74. Ibid., p. 383.

Selected Bibliography

Andrew, Christopher. *For the President's Eyes Only: Secret Intelligence and the American Presidency From Washington to Bush.* New York: HarperCollins, 1995.

Beschloss, Michael R. *The Crisis Years: Kennedy and Khrushchev, 1960–1963.* New York: HarperCollins, 1991.

Brauer, Carl M. "John F. Kennedy: The Endurance of Inspirational Leadership." In Fred I. Greenstein (ed.) *Leadership in the Modern Presidency.* Cambridge, Mass.: Harvard University Press, 1988.

Giglio, James N. *The Presidency of John F. Kennedy.* Lawrence, Kan.: University Press of Kansas, 1991.

Higgins, Trumbull. *The Perfect Failure: Kennedy, Eisenhower, and the CIA at the Bay of Pigs.* New York: W. W. Norton, 1987.

Janis, Irving L. *Groupthink,* 2nd ed. Boston: Houghton Mifflin, 1982. (Chapter 2, "A Perfect Failure: The Bay of Pigs")

Parmet, Herbert S. *JFK: The Presidency of John F. Kennedy.* New York: Penguin, 1983.

Reeves, Richard. *President Kennedy: Profile of Power.* New York: Simon & Schuster, 1993.

Schlesinger, Arthur M., Jr. *A Thousand Days: John F. Kennedy in the White House.* Boston: Houghton Mifflin, 1965.

Strober, Gerald S. and Deborah H. *Let Us Begin Anew: An Oral History of the Kennedy Presidency.* New York: HarperCollins, 1993.

Treverton, Gregory F. *Covert Action: The Limits of Intervention.* New York: Basic Books, 1987.

Wyden, Peter. *Bay of Pigs: The Untold Story.* New York: Simon & Schuster, 1979.

4

President Johnson's Decision to End the U.S. Escalation of the Vietnam War

Setting and Overview of Johnson's Decision

President Lyndon Johnson's nationally televised speech from the Oval Office on March 31, 1968 marked a critical turning point in the Vietnam War. Instead of continuing the gradual, incremental military policy of bombing North Vietnam and deploying increasingly greater numbers of U.S. ground troops to South Vietnam, Johnson decided on a new path to end U.S. military escalation of the war. This involved limited bombing of North Vietnam, a ceiling on ground troops, and a new offer of open, unconditional peace negotiations with North Vietnam. Johnson also made a dramatic and unexpected announcement that he was withdrawing from the 1968 presidential campaign by stating he would not seek reelection.

Johnson's policy decision of March 1968 resulted from several negative trends in the Vietnam War. First, his bombing and U.S. troop escalation decisions of 1965 had, by 1968, achieved nothing more than a stalemate. While Johnson persisted in trying to convince North Vietnam to stop the war in South Vietnam, the Communist North was equally determined to match every U.S. escalation to win the war and achieve a coalition government in the South. Second, North Vietnam changed its strategy of protracted guerrilla warfare in 1967 in planning for the Tet Offensive of January 1968. North Vietnam wanted to show the United States and South Vietnam that no territory was safe from attack by launching a massive, coordinated assault on South Vietnamese population centers.

While the Tet Offensive failed militarily for North Vietnam, it had profound psychological and political consequences in the United States. Congressional critics and the media reacted negatively to Johnson's reassurances that the U.S. military had quickly repelled the North Vietnamese surprise attack. Instead, critics of Johnson's policies considered the Tet Offensive as further evidence that the Vietnam War was a stalemate with no end in sight. The Tet Offensive placed tremendous political pressure on Johnson and his advisers to change war policy from escalation to de-escalation. Moreover, 1968 was a presidential election year. The American public was increasingly polarized as protest demonstrations against the war increased and political opposition within the Democratic Party intensified. Johnson needed a policy decision to reverse these negative trends by restoring confidence in how his administration was conducting the war.

President Johnson's Decision

ON MARCH 31, 1968, PRESIDENT JOHNSON APPEARED ON NATIONAL TELEVISION TO ANNOUNCE HIS DECISION TO END U.S. ESCALATION OF THE VIETNAM WAR. CHANGES IN U.S. POLICY INCLUDED A NEW OFFER TO NEGOTIATE A PEACE SETTLEMENT WITH NORTH VIETNAM, A LIMITATION OF U.S. BOMBING OF NORTH VIETNAM, THE DESIGNATION OF AVERELL HARRIMAN AS HIS PERSONAL REPRESENTATIVE FOR THE PARIS PEACE TALKS AND THE ENCOURAGEMENT OF SOUTH VIETNAM TO ASSUME MORE RESPONSIBILITY FOR THE WAR. HE ALSO ANNOUNCED HIS WITHDRAWAL FROM THE 1968 PRESIDENTIAL CAMPAIGN.

President Johnson's decision was controversial for several reasons:

1. Although the United States would no longer pursue a policy of escalation in the war, Johnson and his advisers still hoped that South Vietnam could become strong enough to prevent a Communist victory. However, South Vietnam's government and military were weak, torn apart by corruption and low morale, while North Vietnam and the Vietcong remained confident they would win no matter what the cost.

2. The United States had no way of knowing how North Vietnam would respond to the peace talk overture, since North Vietnam had rejected every past offer unless the United States was willing to agree on a coalition government in South Vietnam that included representatives of the Communist National Liberation Front. Johnson gave no indications he would accept this as a precondition to the peace talks.
3. The United States proposed to limit the bombing of North Vietnam, but previous bombing halts had not discouraged North Vietnam from continuing to ship supplies and troops along the Ho Chi Minh Trail. There were no assurances that North Vietnam would match militarily any of the de-escalation steps proposed by President Johnson.
4. Johnson's speech indicated that U.S. troop levels would be maintained at present levels to assist South Vietnam. Yet, there were no guidelines for changing the ground war strategy from "search and destroy" tactics to protecting population centers, while South Vietnam took over more responsibility for the war. The only new goal was to reduce American casualties, which was causing intensified protests and demonstrations against the war in the United States.
5. Johnson had rejected the strongest possible recommendations from some of his closest advisers to halt the bombing unilaterally, to announce significant U.S. troop reductions, and to end U.S. involvement in a war that they believed could not be won either sooner or later.

Background of the Decision

Historical Context

Before President Johnson made the crucial decision to scale back U.S. troop involvement after the Tet Offensive, three presidents—Truman, Eisenhower, and Kennedy—made decisions that escalated American military involvement in Vietnam. Truman applied the containment policy to Southeast Asia and committed the United States to support the French against a Communist military victory in Indochina. Eisenhower refused to aid the French directly with U.S. military intervention, but saw Vietnam as essential to U.S. national security by establishing and protecting the government of President Diem in South Vietnam after the French defeat in 1954. Kennedy made key decisions to increase U.S. military advisers to assist South Vietnam in the ground war against the

Vietcong, but was indecisive in considering the consequences of a military coup which overthrew the increasingly repressive regime of President Diem in November 1963.

President Johnson's Escalation Decisions

Before President Johnson decided to end U.S. military escalation of the Vietnam War in 1968, he made a series of critical decisions to escalate U.S. involvement. Johnson's goal was to assure U.S. responsibility for the war against the Vietcong and North Vietnam when it became increasingly clear that South Vietnam's government and military were unable to deal with the situation. When President Kennedy was assassinated, there were about 16,000 U.S. military advisers in South Vietnam. By the spring of 1965, 53,000 troops were assigned to combat duty in strategic hamlets and coastal enclaves. B-52 bombers had started daily bombing over North Vietnam and the Ho Chi Minh Trail. By the summer of 1965, U.S. ground forces (principally Marines) had doubled to 125,000 to protect U.S. bases and were engaging the Vietcong in direct combat. By 1966, U.S. troops increased to 185,000 and by 1967, that number stood at 385,000.[1]

The key escalation decisions made by President Johnson occurred between August 1964 and July 1965. They involved support from Congress to use U.S. military force to repel attacks by North Vietnam in the Tonkin Gulf Resolution; the initiation of large-scale bombing attacks by B-52 bombers on North Vietnam to cut supplies to the South in Operation Rolling Thunder; and the vast increase of U.S. ground troops to protect U.S. bases and engage in "search and destroy" missions against Vietcong threats to U.S. military forces and bases.

Gulf of Tonkin Resolution

As South Vietnam's government remained unstable and Vietcong guerrilla attacks continued, the Johnson administration's goal in 1964 was to maintain and expand President Kennedy's policy of deploying U.S. miliary advisers in South Vietnam. By the summer, Johnson's advisers had developed a plan to escalate pressure against North Vietnam, which included air strikes against selected targets. Also, the National Security Council approved CIA support for South Vietnamese covert operations against North Vietnam, including intelligence gathering and hit-and-run attacks against North Vietnamese shore and island bases.[2] American destroyers with CIA electronic equipment were deployed in the Gulf of Tonkin, southeast of Hanoi, to chart the position of North

Vietnamese radar and radio facilities which were potential targets for U.S. bombing attacks.

On August 1, the *USS Maddox*, a destroyer deployed on a secret surveillance mission, was attacked by three North Vietnamese torpedo boats. No damage occurred as the *Maddox* quickly retaliated and sank one of the patrol boats, while damaging the other two. The Navy sent the *Maddox* back to the Tonkin Gulf along with another U.S. destroyer, the *USS C. Turner Joy*. On August 4, operating in bad weather, the *Maddox* reported it was again under attack by North Vietnamese patrol boats. There were no visual sightings of any enemy boats or torpedoes and the *Maddox's* radar and sonar contacts were unclear as to whether an attack had occurred. Secretary of Defense McNamara contacted Admiral U.S. Grant Sharp, Commander-in-Chief of the Pacific Fleet in Honolulu, to verify the attack. Sharp initially reported an ambush attempt but was ambiguous on whether an actual attack had occurred. Later, he changed his mind and told McNamara he was certain an attack took place.

President Johnson immediately convened the National Security Council, where all members agreed that the United States must retaliate. Johnson ordered sixty-four air sorties against the patrol boat bases and nearby oil storage dumps, which resulted in damaging or destroying twenty-five North Vietnamese boats and 90 percent of its oil facilities.[3]

Johnson also reported the U.S. actions to Congress by drafting a resolution giving him authority to repel future attacks by military force against North Vietnam. The Tonkin Gulf Resolution stated that Congress "supports the determination of the President, as Commander-in-Chief, to take all necessary measure to repel any armed attack against the United States and to prevent further aggression."[4] In testimony before the Senate Foreign Relations Committee, Secretary of State Dean Rusk stated that the Tonkin Gulf Resolution could not anticipate "what [further] steps may in the future be required." But "if it develops in ways we cannot now anticipate, of course there will be close and continuous consultation between the President and Congress."[5] The Senate then approved the Resolution by a vote of 88–2 and the House voted for it unanimously (416–0).[6]

The Tonkin Gulf Resolution provided three short-term goals for President Johnson. First, the United States reaffirmed its military commitment to South Vietnam. Second, the president gained overwhelming public support for the U.S. presence in Vietnam. After the Tonkin Gulf incidents, Johnson's popular support in the Louis Harris poll soared from 42 percent to 73 percent.[7] Third, Johnson had the nearly unanimous support from Congress for his Vietnam policy, thereby diminishing the radical war escalation advocated by Senator Barry Goldwater, who was Johnson's presidential opponent in 1964.

However, the Tonkin Gulf Resolution had ominous long-term implications. Johnson had not explained to Congress or the public anything about increasing U.S. covert activities in the war. He had misled Congress on whether the second attacks on the *Maddox* had actually occurred. The stage was set for Johnson's future deception and credibility on Vietnam policy decisions. Throughout 1965 to 1967, Johnson and his military and civilian advisers used the Tonkin Gulf Resolution as a de facto declaration of war by the United States in Vietnam. Secretary Rusk's assurances of future consultation with Congress were forgotten. Johnson and his advisers made significant escalation decisions in 1965 without consulting Congress or informing the American public.

Operation Rolling Thunder

Following the Tonkin Gulf attacks, President Johnson did not order more bombing reprisals against North Vietnam because he wanted to wait until after the November elections. At the same time, the political and military situation in South Vietnam continued to deteriorate. In September, Johnson approved preparations for additional tit-for-tat retaliatory air strikes against North Vietnam if they continued to attack U.S. forces or military installations in the south. By the end of November, Johnson's advisers, particularly Ambassador Taylor and Secretary McNamara, agreed that the United States should develop a policy of "carefully orchestrated bombing attacks against North Vietnam.[8] On December 1, a working group recommended a two-phase bombing strategy to Johnson. Phase I would continue the tit-for-tat bombing reprisals against North Vietnam. Phase II would involve a series of graduated air attacks against North Vietnam to convince it to stop the war in the South and negotiate a peace settlement.[9] Johnson approved both parts of the plan.

By January 1965, South Vietnam's political situation was in a shambles. Vice Marshal Nguyen Cao Ky and General Nguyen Van Thieu had seized power from a weak civilian government and were establishing a military dictatorship. Ambassador Taylor pressured Ky and Thieu to form a new government, but Buddhist leaders refused to participate. Anti-American protests occurred in Saigon.

On the battlefield, the Vietcong gained military victories by destroying two South Vietnamese battalions at Binh Gia. Most seriously, Vietcong units attacked U.S. Army barracks and a nearby helicopter base at Pleiku, killing nine U.S. troops and destroying five aircraft, the heaviest losses suffered by Americans at that point in the war.[10]

President Johnson immediately ordered a series of reprisal air strikes against North Vietnam military bases located across the 17th parallel (the DMZ or demilitarized zone between North and South Vietnam). These air strikes represented an important change in U.S. policy. By attacking North Vietnam, the U.S. role in the war increased substantially. The February 7 raids were the opening move of sustained air power which would continue until 1968.

On February 13 Johnson approved Operation Rolling Thunder, which was a "measured and limited" air action by the United States against selected military targets in North Vietnam. Beginning on March 2, the United States began a series of spaced air attacks about once a week against North Vietnam. The goal was to determine North Vietnam's reaction in sending troops and supplies to the south. McNamara and Taylor complained to Johnson that this strategy was ineffective. By spring, U.S. air strikes had increased from one a week to about twelve per week and the number of sorties were 900 per week.[11] Air missions and targets were chosen directly from Washington. Only fighter-bombers were deployed rather than B-52 heavy bombers and population centers were avoided.

Operation Rolling Thunder caused massive damage in North Vietnam, but had virtually no effect in persuading Ho Chi Minh and the North Vietnamese military from stopping the war in the south. They rejected Johnson's peace proposals in a speech at Johns Hopkins University on April 7. There was no response to a week-long bombing pause in May.[12] And there was growing criticism of the massive bombing at home as Congress, the press, and college students began opposing Johnson's escalation policies in Vietnam.

U.S. Takeover of the Ground War

President Johnson's most important escalation decision occurred in July 1965, following repeated requests by General William Westmoreland, Commander of the U.S. Military Assistance Command in Vietnam. Westmoreland wanted ground forces to protect U.S. bases in South Vietnam from which the Operation Rolling Thunder planes were being launched. In February and March, Johnson approved the dispatch of two marine battalions to Da Nang for base security. By April, U.S. combat forces had increased to 75,000 personnel, deployed principally at Da Nang and other U.S. airfields. The Vietcong began attacking U.S. military installations. Consequently, on June 7, Westmoreland asked for a massive increase of U.S. troop strength up to 175,000 for further protection and aggressive "search and destroy" missions against the Vietcong. Approval of Westmoreland's request would mean a takeover of the ground war in South Vietnam, because it was an admission that neither air strikes nor assisting the South Vietnamese army was stopping the war.

Westmoreland's request set off intensive policy debate among Johnson's civilian and military advisers. The Joint Chiefs of Staff and Defense Secretary McNamara supported Westmoreland's request. McNamara visited South Vietnam in July and found the situation ominous. After his return to Washington, he argued for a short-term increase of combat troop strength to 200,000, activation of reserve units, and additional congressional appropriations. In contrast, Undersecretary of State George Ball argued for a withdrawal option, since he believed that no amount of U.S. troops could win the ground war. The French were unable to defeat the Vietminh in 1954 with 250,000 troops. More U.S. troops would only extend the war and postpone the defeat of South Vietnam, but only if the United States was willing to fight indefinitely with a massive commitment. Therefore, Ball argued for U.S. withdrawal and a negotiated settlement with North Vietnam.

On July 27, Johnson met with the National Security Council for a final decision on Westmoreland's request for U.S. combat forces. The President presented five options: (1) Increased bombing of North Vietnam; (2) Ball's withdrawal option; (3) maintenance of present U.S. force levels; (4) McNamara's and the JCS request for a larger increase in U.S. combat forces; and (5) a smaller escalation which would double U.S. troop strength, but without mobilizing the reserves or asking for additional congressional budget increases.[13] Johnson emphasized his preference for the fifth option as the least provocative to the Soviets and the Chinese. After urging all his advisers to "get on board" to support his Vietnam policy, Johnson then asked each of them for concurrence. Not surprisingly, they all agreed.

When Johnson announced his decision on July 28, he downplayed its significance. His statement made it appear that the United States was merely deciding to increase combat forces incrementally, rather than assuming a new, massive takeover of the ground war. He did not order mobilizing the reserves or ask for congressional support. Instead, Johnson stated that he would meet Westmoreland's requested needs by ordering an increase in "our fighting strength from 75,000 to 125,000 men almost immediately. Additional forces will be needed later, and they will be sent as requested."[14]

Johnson's decision, although not communicated dramatically to the press, Congress, or the public, was the critical turning point in escalating the Vietnam War. According to Secretary McNamara, it was Johnson's most important choice "that locked the United States onto a path of massive military intervention in Vietnam, an intervention that ultimately destroyed his presidency and polarized America like nothing since the Civil War."[15]

Countdown to the Decision: The Tet Offensive

By 1967, the Vietnam War was reaching a stalemate condition. Operation Rolling Thunder inflicted massive damage on North Vietnam, but Vietcong infiltration and shipment of supplies along the Ho Chi Minh Trail continued unabated. U.S. ground troops were generally successful when confronting Vietcong forces directly in battle, but hit-and-run guerrilla attacks by the Vietcong in rural areas continued to inflict serious damage. U.S. forces established military enclaves in the cities, particularly Saigon, but the Vietcong continued to control most of the villages and countryside.

Johnson's advisers in 1967 predicted a "light at the end of the tunnel." They argued that additional U.S. ground forces might convince North Vietnam to stop the war. Only Secretary McNamara was deeply pessimistic. In a memo to President Johnson on May 19, 1967, McNamara argued that more escalation was causing unpopularity in the U.S. as casualties increased; that the Vietcong remained strong while the South Vietnam government was weak and corrupt; and that North Vietnam was not interested in a political settlement, but was "determined to match U.S. military expansion of the conflict."[16] McNamara believed that General Westmoreland's request for 200,000 additional troops would cause bitter debate in Congress and threaten "to spin the war utterly out of control."[17] General Westmoreland disagreed with McNamara. He argued that "During 1967, the enemy has lost control of large sectors of the population. . . . In many areas the enemy has been driven away from the population centers; in others, he has been compelled to disperse and evade contact, thus nullifying much of his potential."[18]

North Vietnam's political and military leaders perceived that the war was not progressing in their favor. They had not won a major battle in two years because massive increases in U.S. troop strength had defeated them at every confrontation. In July 1967, the North Vietnamese Politburo met in Hanoi and developed a secret plan to change military strategy. Instead of continuing "protracted war" and guerrilla tactics in South Vietnam, which North Vietnam hoped would make the United States tired of fighting much the same as the French had in 1954, the Politburo decided to organize a large-scale coordinated attack on urban centers, designed to destroy the South Vietnam government. The plan was to combine conventional military attacks in the cities with calls for a general uprising in the population to overthrow the civilian government. Responsibility for carrying out the attack was given to General Giap.

The North Vietnamese military plan, which became known as the Tet Offensive, began in September 1967 with a series of attacks on U.S. bases in the Central Highlands and along the Laotian and Cambodian borders. This phase was designed to draw U.S. forces away from population centers. General Westmoreland assumed that North Vietnam was engaging U.S. forces for a final decisive battle at Khe Sanh, located near the demilitarized zone border between North and South Vietnam. This involved the largest U.S. troop engagement of the war, 6,000 men, and included massive B-52 bombings over a five-square mile battlefield.[19] Despite heavy North Vietnamese losses, the first phase of their plan succeeded. General Westmoreland believed that subsequent attacks on the cities were designed to draw U.S. troop strength away from Khe Sanh, when, in fact, North Vietnam's goal was precisely the opposite.[20]

The next phase of the military strategy was the major, coordinated attack on South Vietnam cities. This was designed as a surprise assault, but on January 5, 1968, the U.S. mission in Saigon released a captured secret North Vietnamese document. It outlined the North Vietnamese military strategy of coordinating a surprise attack with "uprisings of the local population to take over towns and cities."[21] No date was set for the attacks. The U.S. military and the press dismissed the document as deliberate, false propaganda, arguing it was too bold and risky for North Vietnam.[22] Instead, General Westmoreland cabled Washington that North Vietnam was changing its strategy to launch attacks in the countryside. He believed the odds were in favor of such attacks by late January. This would coincide with the Tet religious holiday of the lunar New Year, a traditional Vietnamese celebration where previous cease-fires had been honored by both North and South Vietnam military forces.

Consequently, when North Vietnam launched its general offensive on January 30, 1968, the U.S. military and South Vietnam were taken by a complete surprise. The Tet Offensive began with a full-scale assault on 36 of 44 South Vietnamese provincial capitals, five of its six major cities, 64 district capitals, and 50 hamlets.[23] The most spectacular attacks were raids on the U.S. Embassy in Saigon, the Tan Son Hut airport, the presidential palace, and the headquarters of South Vietnam's general staff.

U.S. forces quickly recovered from the surprise of the Tet Offensive, and, together with the South Vietnamese military, repelled the Vietcong and removed them from Saigon. However, a bloody battle raged on for three weeks in Hué, the ancient imperial capital, during which the United States and South Vietnam lost 500 troops to North Vietnam's 5,000 killed. During the eight weeks of the Tet Offensive, the U.S. and South Vietnam suffered 9,000 troops killed, while the Vietcong lost an estimated 58,000 men.[24] Militarily, the Tet Offensive was the worst defeat of North Vietnam in the long war. North Vietnam achieved none of its military goals: the South Vietnam government did not collapse, there were no takeovers of urban areas, and Vietcong units were severely decimated.

Nonetheless, the Tet Offensive was a huge psychological and political defeat for U.S. policy in Vietnam. Despite their crushing losses, North Vietnam had severely shaken U.S. confidence that its military strategy was effective. Press and television reports highlighted Vietcong attacks in Saigon, particularly the battle at the U.S. Embassy, which shocked the American public. President Johnson tried to reassure the public at a press conference on February 2 that the North Vietnamese had not achieved their military goals. Other Johnson administration officials, including Secretaries Rusk and McNamara, also made television appearances, but they could not restore public confidence. A major reappraisal of President Johnson's Vietnam War policy was needed.

Johnson Agonizes over Escalation and De-escalation

Johnson's military advisers saw the Tet Offensive as an opportunity to reinforce and expand U.S. forces in Vietnam. They wanted more troops and supplies to escalate the war further in order to defeat North Vietnam on the battlefield. President Johnson initially agreed "to hold the line at any cost" by protecting Khe Sanh and dispatching 10,500 additional troops.[25] He also wanted a complete assessment of the situation from General Westmoreland. General Earle Wheeler, chairman of the Joint Chiefs, was sent to Vietnam in February.

Wheeler returned with a gloomy evaluation, reporting that the Tet Offensive had nearly succeeded. He recommended that 206,000 more U.S. troops were needed to take advantage of Vietcong losses in the Tet Offensive and to prepare for a new strategy of attacking enemy sanctuaries in Cambodia, Laos, and across the DMZ.[26]

Wheeler's escalation request shocked Johnson's advisers. Pressures were building in Congress, the press, public opinion, and the Democratic Party to scale down U.S. involvement and reduce casualties. There was an urgent need to evaluate Wheeler's proposal and decide how to proceed. Johnson decided to appoint Clark Clifford, the incoming secretary of defense replacing McNamara, to lead an interagency group and report back in five days on Wheeler's request.

Clifford met with Defense Department civilians, many of whom shared McNamara's opposition to further escalation. They opposed existing policy and argued that additional troops would not end the war soon or erode North Vietnam's will to fight. Total Americanization of the war should be avoided.

Clifford presented his report to Johnson on March 4. Arguing that "[w]e seem to have gotten caught in a sinkhole,"[27] Clifford recommended no more than a token troop increase to meet "any exigencies in the next three or four months" because "We are not sure that a conventional military victory, as commonly defined, can be achieved."[28] The report also recommended shifting more responsibility to South Vietnam for the war, urging an end to government corruption, and developing a more efficient and effective military force. The report concluded with a recommendation for further study of other alternatives to Vietnam policy.

Johnson responded to Clifford's report by meeting with his advisers at the Tuesday lunch group on March 5. He expressed interest in pursuing a bombing halt as a way of getting negotiations started with North Vietnam. McNamara had proposed a full bombing halt in November 1967 but it had never been seriously discussed. Secretary Rusk proposed a limited bombing halt "during the period of bad weather coming up, when our bombing is limited in any case."[29] But Rusk was pessimistic on whether North Vietnam would respond positively to the U.S. initiative.

Over the next two weeks, Johnson met continuously with his advisers, attempting to develop a position on the military's request for more troops, Clifford's proposals for only token increases, and Rusk's limited bombing halt to encourage negotiations with North Vietnam. He made a key decision on March 22 by formally rejecting the Westmoreland-Wheeler proposals for a huge troop increase. Instead, Johnson accepted the Clifford recommendations by deploying only 13,500 support troops to augment the emergency reinforcements of February. More significantly, Johnson recalled Westmoreland from Vietnam by promoting him to Army chief of staff. General Creighton Abrams was appointed as Westmoreland's replacement.[30]

The most important meeting for Johnson took place on March 26 with the so-called Wise Men, a group of senior policy advisers who had served Johnson and other presidents in high-level military and national security positions. Throughout Johnson's conduct of the Vietnam War, he had frequently consulted with this group. They had supported all of his earlier escalation decisions. The goal of the March 26 meeting was to help Johnson decide how to resolve the contradictory advice he was getting from his civilian and military advisers.

McGeorge Bundy, Johnson's former national security adviser, led off the discussion by stating that Vietnam policies must be changed because the war was becoming "a bottomless pit."[31] This was a startling admission since Bundy had been one of the strongest advocates of Operation Rolling Thunder in 1965. Now he argued for a complete bombing halt and no more troops sent to Vietnam.

Johnson asked the other participants to state their views. Douglas Dillon, Kennedy's secretary of the treasury, agreed with Bundy. Henry Cabot Lodge, the former ambassador to Vietnam, urged a shift from Westmoreland's "search and destroy missions" to a defensive strategy to protect South Vietnamese populations centers. Former Secretary of State Dean Acheson and George Ball, who had left the State Department in 1966, both agreed that the bombing should end since U.S. objectives in Vietnam were "not attainable."[32] General Matthew Ridgeway urged that U.S. troops be withdrawn from Vietnam within two years. While other members, including Supreme Court Justice Abe Fortas, former Ambassador Robert Murphy, and retired General Omar Bradley, disagreed and backed the military, the consensus appeared to convince Johnson that he needed to make a break from past Vietnam policies and move toward de-escalation of U.S. involvement.

Clifford reinforced the de-escalation strategy in an emotional appeal to Johnson at a meeting of March 28. He proposed a "winching down" strategy of step-by-step de-escalation by maintaining U.S. forces at existing levels and deploying them to protect South Vietnam from another enemy offensive. Clifford proposed the U.S. should make major concessions to secure a negotiated settlement with North Vietnam.[33]

The March 31 Speech

Johnson put all of these suggestions together in a dramatic nationwide television speech from the White House Oval Office on March 31, 1968.[34] Johnson's goals were to review recent events from the Tet Offensive and to develop new policy initiatives on the future conduct of the Vietnam War.

He began by emphasizing that his consistent objective in Vietnam was a peaceful settlement of the conflict. He stated that at San Antonio, Texas in September 1967 he had proposed a halt in the bombing of North Vietnam when "that would lead promptly to productive discussions" and "that North Vietnam would not take military advantage of our restraint." Instead, North Vietnam had denounced the offer and planned the Tet Offensive, which "failed to achieve its principal objectives."

Johnson then stated he was renewing his previous offer "to stop the bombardment of North Vietnam. We ask that talks begin promptly, that they be serious talks on the substance of peace." Consequently, Johnson announced an immediate and unilateral bombing halt "except in the area north of the demilitarized zone where the continuing enemy buildup directly threatens allied forward positions and where the movements of their troops and supplies are clearly related to that threat." Here, Johnson had accepted Rusk's earlier proposal for a limited bombing halt and rejected Clifford and the Wise Men's arguments for a complete stoppage.

Johnson stated that limited bombing would end "if our restraint is matched by restraint in Hanoi." This appeared to be Johnson's acceptance of Clifford's and the Wise Men's recommendations.

He went on to announce that Ambassador Averell Harriman would be his personal representative for the peace talks. Also, Johnson urged the South Vietnamese to assume more responsibility for the war effort and announced that the United States would assist them with more supplies and equipment. This represented a shift from the "Americanization" of the war to a policy of "Vietnamization," which President Nixon pursued in 1969.

Johnson ended the speech with a totally unexpected and dramatic statement concerning his political future. Admitting that the war was causing division and polarization in the United States, Johnson said he should not "permit the presidency to become involved in the partisan divisions that are developing in this political year. Accordingly, I shall not seek, nor will I accept, the nomination of my party for another term as your President."

Johnson's March 31 speech was a significant turning point in the Vietnam War. U.S. policy was now moving toward de-escalation of military involvement and a peace initiative with North Vietnam. However, Johnson's policy decisions had several very serious problems. They did not promise an early end to the war. Instead, Johnson had shifted back to the pre-1965 period when both he and President Kennedy had anticipated U.S. support for South Vietnam would prevent a Communist victory. Johnson believed North Vietnam was sufficiently weakened by the defeats in the Tet Offensive that it would be willing to negotiate a settlement to end the war. In fact, there was no evidence that North Vietnam was prepared to do so. The proposed bombing halt offered no assurance that North Vietnam would end infiltration and support of the Vietcong. Johnson did not know if diplomacy would be effective. The March 31 speech gave no indication of what concessions either side would be willing to make. All it promised was U.S. commitment to the stalemate without further U.S. escalation. The only important change was Johnson's acknowledgement that further U.S. casualties should be reduced because of increasing domestic protests and partisan opposition to his previous escalation policies.

President Johnson as Decision-Maker

Foreign Policy Context of Decision

Prior to the Tet Offensive, President Johnson and his advisers were concerned about bombing North Vietnam targets that might hit Soviet supply ships in the port city of Haiphong. They did not want the Soviets to get directly involved in the war. More importantly, Johnson wanted to avoid China's entry into Vietnam. In September 1965, Chinese Defense Minister Lin Piao had declared support for Third World revolutions by "encircling" the world's industrial powers. However, that statement was modified by Mao's comment that Chinese armies would not be sent outside the country. Unlike the Korean War, China was not going to become directly involved in national wars of liberation.[35]

After the Tet Offensive, Johnson's focus was consistent with earlier objectives. His March 31 speech reflected determination to oppose a Communist takeover of South Vietnam, a position endorsed by Truman, Eisenhower, and Kennedy. Containment of communism and prevention of the domino effect predominated Johnson's policy decisions both before and after the Tet Offensive.

Context of the Decision within Johnson's National Security Strategy

Johnson's speech of March 31, 1968 represented an effort to strike a balance between the "hawks," military and civilian advisers who wanted to hold the line and continue further escalation, and "doves," who favored a unilateral halt of the bombing and significant concessions to North Vietnam in peace negotiations. Both sides were responding to the Tet Offensive, North Vietnam's major military effort to win the Vietnam War. All of Johnson's advisers agreed that the Tet Offensive had failed and that North Vietnam had suffered huge casualties.

Before the Tet Offensive, Johnson's earlier escalation decisions reflected a strategic objective of limited war in Vietnam. Limited war, according to Robert Osgood and others, involved the use of conventional military forces whose principal object "would be not to destroy opponents but to persuade them to break off the conflict short of achieving their goals and without resorting to nuclear war."[36] Leaders needed to communicate their objectives to the enemy and keep diplomatic channels open to end the war through negotiations on the basis of limited objectives. Consequently, the limited war theory was a bargaining process through which force was employed "to persuade enemies that persisting in what they were doing was too expensive to continue."[37]

As applied to Vietnam, the limited war approach was used by the Johnson administration to persuade North Vietnam to stop supporting the Vietcong guerrillas in the South. This would be achieved by the gradual escalation of air power (Operation Rolling Thunder) and U.S. ground forces (deployed on search and destroy missions) without invading and threatening to destroy North Vietnam.

The problem with the limited war strategy was that the North Vietnamese, despite suffering enormous losses from continual bombing and battlefield casualties, were focused on a powerful strategy: a protracted war of attrition with the United States and South Vietnam. No matter what level of force was applied, North Vietnam would fight until the United States grew weary and eventually decided it could not afford the costs of continuation. North Vietnam believed it had succeeded with this strategy in the nine-year war with the French (1945–54), and was prepared to continue it indefinitely against the United States.

When Johnson announced his de-escalation strategy in March 1968, the North Vietnamese, although seriously damaged by the failures of the Tet Offensive, moved toward the "talking while fighting" strategy. Johnson wanted mutual concessions from North Vietnam to get the peace talks underway, but Hanoi remained intransigent until Johnson stopped all the bombing. Johnson's deescalation proposals lacked an implementation strategy on how to proceed in negotiations with North Vietnam. The United States and North Vietnam became locked in a stalemate over both the objectives of the war and the negotiations. The period following the Tet Offensive and Johnson's deescalation speech included 3,700 U.S. troops killed, and 8,000 seriously wounded, while Vietcong losses were estimated at 43,000.[38]

Domestic Context of Decision

The Tet Offensive had a profound impact on American public opinion, the media, and the 1968 presidential primaries. Before Tet, most of the public supported Johnson's policies in Vietnam. A Gallup poll of November 1967 agreed with the administration's optimistic assessments of the war, with 50 percent stating that the United States was making progress. A minority of 41 percent believed the United States was standing still (33%) or losing (8%). After the Tet Offensive, these figures changed dramatically. Public opinion now included 23 percent who believed the United States was losing the war; another 33 percent responded that the war was at standstill; while only 33 percent believed progress was being made.[39] Johnson's personal approval ratings paralleled this decline in war support, dropping from 40 percent before Tet to 26 percent afterward.[40]

Decline of public support for the war was most likely a reflection of dismay over the Johnson administration's optimistic assessments at the end of 1967. Here, the media, especially television coverage played a major role. Before Tet, most television coverage of the war was neutral or favorable to administration policies. During Tet, television news emphasized the Vietcong attacks in Saigon, particularly at the U.S. Embassy. The violent responses were also presented, especially when General Nguyen Ngoc Loan, chief of the South Vietnam national police, was shown killing a Vietcong captive with a shot to the head.

Walter Cronkite, anchorperson of the *CBS Evening News* and arguably the most respected and reliable reporter of the 1960s, had perhaps the most startling impact. Cronkite went to Vietnam during the Tet Offensive and returned with a half-hour news special, *Report from Vietnam*, shown on February 27th. Cronkite ended the program with his own personal assessment, stating that he believed the United States was not "close to victory" or "on the edge of defeat." Instead, he concluded that it was "increasingly clear to this reporter that the only rational way out then will be to negotiate."[41]

Public opinion and critical news coverage of the war during the Tet Offensive had a profound impact on the Democratic Party, which was preparing for the 1968 presidential campaign. Antiwar liberals were increasingly upset with Johnson's credibility gap. They believed that stalemate was becoming the reality and they disagreed with the optimistic progress expressed by the administration. Eugene McCarthy, a relatively unknown U.S. Senator with no nationwide standing, decided to enter the presidential race by opposing Johnson in the New Hampshire primaries. McCarthy's goal was to bring together youthful antiwar protesters and other Democrats by offering an alternative to the radical opponents of the war. McCarthy urged an end to the bombing, an immediate cease fire, and a negotiated settlement giving the Vietcong a role in a coalition government in South Vietnam.[42] Johnson discounted McCarthy's challenge and believed that Robert Kennedy, U.S. senator from New York, would be a more serious threat.

In the March 12 New Hampshire primary, Johnson had not formally entered the race but local Democrats had organized a write-in campaign for him. Johnson was shocked by the outcome. Although he received 49 percent of the votes, McCarthy won 42 percent. The vote was interpreted as a defeat for Johnson. Four days later, Robert Kennedy declared his candidacy for the presidential nomination.

Johnson's March 31 de-scalation speech could be interpreted as a public relations response to the growing domestic discord over his Vietnam policies. He needed a new initiative to regain public support, counter media criticism, and check political opposition. His speech tried to achieve these goals, especially his withdrawal from the presidential campaign. However, Johnson was unable to change perceptions that the war was stalemated, because his speech offered no concessions or changes from previous policy on how to reach a negotiated settlement with North Vietnam.

Decision Options

In developing his response to the Tet Offensive, President Johnson rejected two major options presented to him by his advisers:

1. *Further escalation of U.S. involvement in the war.*

General Wheeler, in consultation with General Westmoreland, proposed that 206,000 additional U.S. troops be sent to Vietnam to provide reinforcements and deal a final blow to the Vietcong on the battlefield. Domestic pressures against further U.S. casualties and conflicting advice from Johnson's military and civilian advisers convinced Johnson to rule out this option.

2. *A complete bombing halt, no more U.S. troops sent to Vietnam, a shift away from "search and destroy" missions to a defensive strategy of protecting South Vietnamese population centers, and major concessions to secure a negotiated settlement with North Vietnam.*

These unilateral deescalation options were strongly recommended by a majority of the "Wise Men," Johnson's senior foreign policy advisers, and Secretary Clifford at meetings with Johnson on March 26 and March 28. They were a recognition that only bold and new presidential initiatives could change an increasingly stalemated war, evidenced by the Tet Offensive. If accepted, these deescalation steps would have ended U.S. participation in the war within a year or two. They would have provided a platform for Johnson to run for reelection by countering opposition to his war policies in the Democratic Party, the media, and public opinion. However, Johnson was intransigent on making major concessions to North Vietnam. He preferred reciprocity, that is, demonstrable deescalation moves by North Vietnam leading to a negotiated settlement.

Consequently, instead of either radical escalation or significant deescalation, Johnson chose a middle course proposed in Clifford's March 4 report and the Tuesday lunch group meeting of March 5. These decisions options, eventually implemented and announced in the March 31 speech, included:

1. A token increase in U.S. troop reinforcements, together with replacing General Westmoreland as the U.S. commander in Vietnam with General Creighton Abrams.

2. A limited bombing halt, as recommended by Secretary of State Dean Rusk.
3. Shifting more responsibility for the war to South Vietnam, the so-called "Vietnamization" of the war effort, also proposed by the March 4 Clifford report.
4. A restatement of the September 1967 San Antonio peace formula, which required reciprocity from North Vietnam as a precondition for negotiations when the U.S. implemented a limited bombing halt.

In selecting these options, Johnson hoped to salvage his Vietnam policies by not losing the war or agreeing to North Vietnam's demands for NLF (Vietcong) participation in a coalition government in South Vietnam.

Johnson's Leadership Role in the Decision

President Johnson's leadership role before and after the Tet Offensive revealed many weaknesses in convincing Congress, the media, and public opinion that he was changing the course of the Vietnam War. Unlike his leadership in domestic policy, Johnson failed to lead, persuade, or develop a consensus in support of his war policy.

Between 1964 and 1965, Johnson had demonstrated enormous creative leadership skills with Congress and the public in achieving nearly all of his legislative goals—civil rights, voting rights, and the Great Society programs of the war against poverty, medical care for the elderly, education, and many others. During these years, Johnson used the skills he had acquired as Senate majority leader in the 1950s to build legislative coalitions and lead Congress more successfully than any president since Franklin Roosevelt.

In the 1964 presidential campaign, Johnson had promised not to send any American troops to fight a ground war in Vietnam. His emphasis on coalition-building and consensus served him well in winning a landslide victory over Barry Goldwater, the advocate of radical escalation in the war. Johnson had been careful in informing Congress and getting support for the Tonkin Gulf Resolution prior to the election.

However, Johnson's strategies of open consultation and educating the public on his domestic policy goals were never applied to the war escalation decisions. Beginning in 1965, he began to withdraw into the

White House, meeting with his closest military and civilian advisers in an atmosphere of tightly controlled secrecy. Not wanting to jeopardize his legislative programs in Congress, Johnson chose to understate the bombing decision (Operation Rolling Thunder) and the troops escalation decision of July 1965.

Johnson's closed approach to the gradual escalation decisions left him without a base of political or public support. From 1965 to 1967, he needed to demonstrate progress in the war and generally succeeded as public opinion remained favorable. However, by 1967, the media began portraying the war as a stalemate. The increased deployment of U.S. troops, which had reached 525,000, did not appear to change the course of the war.

Johnson's response was extreme sensitivity to criticism, a need to control information, and a preoccupation with secrecy.[43] Instead of leading public opinion, he became withdrawn, reclusive, and ineffective in presenting his views on national television. Optimistic reports were issued by General Westmoreland and others, but press reports contradicted them. Johnson faced a growing credibility gap on how well the war was proceeding. Consequently, when the Tet Offensive occurred, Johnson was blamed personally for misleading statements that the United States was moving toward victory.

Johnson was torn by indecision and uncertainty after the Tet Offensive. He could not choose quickly between the escalation advocated by the military or the unilateral de-escalation proposed by Clifford and the Wise Men. Instead, he portrayed Tet as a military failure of North Vietnam and spent over a month agonizing on what direction to take.

Lacking a sense of direction, an inability to define a precise mission, and explicit limits to the war,[44] Johnson decided on a middle-of-the-road approach in his March 31 speech. He spliced together parts of the advice given to him: a limited bombing halt, willingness to negotiate, urging South Vietnam to take more responsibility, and threatening to reescalate if North Vietnam did not reciprocate. These choices gave all of his advisers some of what they wanted, but did not spell out a new direction on the war. None of these choices were convincing to critics who wanted major changes in war policy, since the perception of bloody, ceaseless stalemate was no longer acceptable. Johnson failed to make new choices, thereby demonstrating the failures of his leadership in resolving the polarization over the war in American society and politics.

Consequences of Johnson's Decision for the
United States and Other Countries Involved

United States

The aftermath of Johnson's de-escalation speech included more turmoil, discord, and polarization in American society and politics than at any time since the Civil War. America was seriously divided over the Vietnam War. Terrible violence and civil disorder erupted across the country. Campus protests grew in intensity, breaking out with more than 200 demonstrations after the Tet offensive. The most violent was at Columbia University, where 1,000 police broke up a mass sit-in.[45]

In April, Martin Luther King, the articulate and charismatic black leader of the civil rights movement, was assassinated by a rifle shot, after leading a march in Memphis, Tennessee. King had begun opposing the Vietnam War and was considered a symbol of interracial harmony. His death precipitated violence and riots in more than 100 cities. Federal troops had to be mobilized in Washington, D.C. as fires burned out of control.

Within the Democratic Party, Vice President Hubert Humphrey declared his presidential candidacy in later April, pledging to support Johnson's war policies. Humphrey was supported by centrists and pro-war Democrats in contrast to the antiwar liberals, Robert Kennedy and Eugene McCarthy. Humphrey declared he would not campaign in any of the primaries except as a write-in candidate.

Kennedy and McCarthy battled each other in the early primaries, with Kennedy winning in Indiana, the District of Columbia, and Nebraska. McCarthy won in Oregon in late May. Kennedy turned his campaign around with a victory in the June 3 California primary. That evening he was assassinated at a victory celebration in Los Angeles.

Richard Nixon avoided criticizing Johnson on the peace negotiations with North Vietnam. Instead, he gained the Republican nomination and competed with Governor George Wallace on domestic issues, focusing on "law and order."

The most disruptive political events of 1968 occurred at the Democratic Party national convention in August. Inside the convention, pro-war and antiwar Democrats angrily debated each other, while outside thousands of demonstrators and police battled in the streets. National television coverage clearly showed the severe strains among the Democrats as they nominated Humphrey for president.

Nixon, pledging that he had a secret plan "to end the war and win the peace," won a very close victory over Humphrey in the November elections. Humphrey nearly closed the gap in the last few days of the campaign after he had pledged to stop the bombing of North Vietnam "as an acceptable risk for peace."[46] Nonetheless, Nixon became president with 43.4 percent of the popular vote to Humphrey's 42.7 percent, and 302 electoral college votes to Humphrey's 191.[47]

Vietnam

Johnson changed his tone toward war policy in the March 31 speech, but not his overall objectives. He remained insistent that he would not accept a Communist takeover of South Vietnam. Consequently, it was not surprising that the peace talks with North Vietnam produced stalemate. North Vietnam's strategy was to continue fighting while negotiating a demand for a coalition government with the NLF in South Vietnam. Johnson, in turn, demanded reciprocity from North Vietnam to match U.S. de-escalation steps. As the peace talks continued in Paris during May and June, Averell Harriman urged Johnson to compromise. North Vietnam troops had been withdrawn from the South and Vietcong rocket attacks had subsided. Johnson wanted North Vietnam to acknowledge publicly its de-escalation steps. When it refused, Johnson ignored Harriman's proposal and resumed the bombing. The air war intensified in South Vietnam. B-52 missions tripled in 1968 and the bombs dropped on South Vietnam exceeded one million tons.[48]

Johnson also continued to pursue the "search and destroy" strategy. In March and April, the United States and South Vietnam deployed 100,000 troops against enemy forces in provinces near Saigon.[49] Vietnamization of the war was implemented, but resisted by South Vietnam, which continued to want strong U.S. fighting forces in the war. The military performance of South Vietnam's government improved after Tet, but General Thieu resisted having more civilians to broaden its base.

Johnson ignored an indication by Soviet premier Alexei Kosygin that North Vietnam would negotiate if the United States stopped all bombing. Johnson rejected the proposal, along with the military's request to resume it above the DMZ. He wanted a concession from North Vietnam before agreeing to resume the peace talks.[50]

On October 12, the Soviet Union again informed Johnson that a bombing halt would lead to North Vietnam's participation in substantive talks. Johnson was suspicious, believing a halt would endanger U.S.

forces in Vietnam. He also faced opposition from Generals Thieu and Ky of South Vietnam, who believed that peace talks would lead to a sell-out to the Communists. Thieu had established secret contacts with Nixon's campaign. Johnson suspected Nixon was encouraging Thieu to delay South Vietnamese participation until after the November elections.

Johnson finally decided on October 31 to stop the bombing and restart the peace negotiations. However, he remained opposed to any concessions. Clifford saw the negotiations as a way for the United States to get out of Vietnam, while Rusk wanted an independent South Vietnam, free of Communist control. The indecision among Johnson's advisers meant that the United States had no "clear sense of what it wanted or was prepare to accept" at the negotiations.[51]

After Nixon's victory on November 5, the Paris peace talks began the next day. Weeks of indecisive haggling ensued between representatives of North and South Vietnam over the shape of the conference table. South Vietnam objected to a round table suggested by the United States, because it implied recognition of the NLF (and Vietcong) as a separate and equal party to the negotiations. It took two months to agree on two rectangular tables placed at opposite ends of a round table.[52] This ludicrous debate ended any prospects of serious negotiations before President Johnson ended his term of office.

Conclusion

The indecisive outcome of Johnson's March 31 peace offer to North Vietnam demonstrated the overall weakness of U.S. policy. Johnson's efforts to salvage his Vietnam policy were recognized by North Vietnam from the outset. Hanoi had every reason to believe that it could force Johnson toward a complete bombing halt before any serious talks would begin because they had rejected every previous U.S. offer (sixteen as reported by Johnson in his memoirs). Consequently, Johnson left the presidency with his Vietnamese policy locked into a bloody, indecisive stalemate. After his de-escalation initiatives, the war continued and peace negotiations with North Vietnam were stalled. Protest demonstrations against the war became increasingly hostile and angry toward President Johnson. The Democratic Party was torn apart by hawks and doves arguing over which course to take. The United States appeared to be on the edge of a civil war as police and protesters battled in Chicago during the Democratic Party convention. Without any progress on the Paris peace talks, further efforts to de-escalate the war were left to Johnson's successor, Richard Nixon, who defeated Hubert Humphrey in the 1968 presidential election. Nixon's Vietnamization policy is discussed in the next chapter.

Questions for Discussion

1. How did President Johnson's escalation decisions of 1964 and 1965 affect the U.S. commitment in the Vietnam War?

2. Why were President Johnson's military advisers optimistic about the progress of the Vietnam War in 1967, while Defense Secretary McNamara was pessimistic?

3. Why did North Vietnam change its military strategy in 1967? What were the goals and objectives of the Tet Offensive?

4. Why was the Tet Offensive a military disaster for North Vietnam but a psychological defeat for the United States?

5. How did President Johnson's advisers respond to the Tet Offensive? What was the conflicting advice given to President Johnson?

6. What were the recommendations of the Clifford report and how did the Tuesday lunch group respond to them?

7. Why was the advice given to Johnson by the Wise Men significant in influencing his subsequent deescalation decision?

8. What were Johnson's policy decisions announced in the March 31, 1968 television speech? What were the potential risks and problems with Johnson's proposed policy initiatives?

9. How did the Tet Offensive affect American public opinion, the media, and the 1968 presidential campaign?

10. What were the consequences of Johnson's March 31 speech in the United States and Vietnam?

Notes

1. Haynes Johnson, *Sleepwalking through History: America in the Reagan Years* (New York: Anchor Books, 1992), p. 77.

2. Robert S. McNamara, *In Retrospect: The Tragedy and Lessons of Vietnam* (New York: Times Books, 1995), p. 129.

3. George C. Herring, *America's Longest War: The United States and Vietnam, 1950–1975*, 2nd ed. (New York: Alfred A. Knopf, 1986), p. 27; and McNamara, p. 135.

4. *Department of State Bulletin*, August 24, 1964, p. 268.

5. McNamara, p. 138.

6. Ibid., p. 139.

7. Herring, p. 123.

8. Ibid., p. 124.

9. Herbert Y. Schandler, *The Unmaking of a President: Lyndon Johnson and Vietnam* (Princeton, N.J.: Princeton University Press, 1977), p. 8.

10. Ibid., pp. 11–12.

11. Ibid., pp. 17–18.

12. Ibid., pp. 18–19.

13. Robert A. Strong, *Decisions and Dilemmas: Case Studies in Presidential Foreign Policy Making* (Englewood Cliffs, N.J.: Prentice Hall, 1992), pp. 95–96.

14. David M. Barrett, *Uncertain Warriors: Lyndon Johnson and His Vietnam Advisers* (Lawrence, Kan.: University Press of Kansas, 1993), p. 59.

15. McNamara, p. 169.

16. Ibid., p. 267.

17. Ibid., p. 269.

18. Marvin E. Gettleman, Jane Franklin, Marilyn Young, and H. Bruce Franklin, *Vietnam and America: A Documented History* (New York: Grove Press, 1985), p. 335.

19. Herring, p. 188.

20. Stanley Karnow, *Vietnam: A History* (New York: Penguin Books, 1984), p. 542.

21. Schandler, p. 70.

22. Don Oberdorfer, *Tet! The Turning Point in the Vietnam War* (New York: DaCapo Press, 1971), pp. 117–21.

23. Herring, p. 189.

24. Clark Clifford, *Counsel to the President* (New York: Random House, 1991), p. 473.

25. Herring, p. 192.

26. Lyndon Baines Johnson, *The Vantage Point: Perspectives on the Presidency, 1963–1969* (New York: Holt, Rinehart and Winston, 1971), p. 389.

27. Clifford, p. 495.

28. Ibid.

29. Ibid., p. 496.

30. Herring, pp. 203–4.

31. Barrett, p. 149.

32. Ibid., pp. 149–50.

33. Herring, p. 205.
34. All of the quotes from Johnson's speech are from "Peace in Vietnam and Southeast Asia: Address to the Nation," March 31, 1968, from *Public Papers of the Presidents of the United States, 1968–1969* (Washington, D.C.: U.S. Government Printing Office, 1970), pp. 468–76.
35. Henry Kissinger, *Diplomacy* (New York: Simon & Schuster, 1994), pp. 644–45.
36. George C. Herring, *LBJ and Vietnam: A Different Kind of War* (Austin, Tex.: University of Texas Press, 1994), p. 4.
37. Ibid., p. 5.
38. Ronald H. Spector, *After Tet: The Bloodiest Year in Vietnam* (New York: The Free Press, 1993), p. 25.
39. Oberdorfer, p. 246.
40. Herring, *America's Longest War*, pp. 201–2.
41. Oberdorfer, p. 251.
42. John Morton Blum, *Years of Discord: American Politics and Society, 1961–1974* (New York: W. W. Norton, 1991), p. 290.
43. Larry Berman, "Lyndon B. Johnson: Paths Chosen and Opportunities Lost," in Fred I. Greenstein (ed.), *Leadership in the Modern Presidency* (Cambridge, Mass.: Harvard University Press, 1988), p. 137.
44. Herring, *LBJ and Vietnam*, p. 181.
45. Herring, *America's Longest War*, p. 215.
46. Blum, p. 315.
47. Ibid.
48. Herring, *America's Longest War*, p. 215.
49. Ibid.
50. Herring, *LBJ and Vietnam*, p. 174.
51. Ibid.
52. Spector, pp. 305–6.

Selected Bibliography

Berman, Larry. "Lyndon B. Johnson: Paths Chosen and Opportunities Lost." In Fred I. Greenstein (ed.), *Leadership in the Modern Presidency*. Cambridge, Mass.: Harvard University Press, 1988.

Barrett, David M. *Uncertain Warriors: Lyndon Johnson and His Vietnam Advisers*. Lawrence, Kan.: University Press of Kansas, 1993.

Blum, John M. *Years of Discord: American Politics and Society, 1961–1974*. New York: W. W. Norton, 1991.

Clifford, Clark. *Counsel to the President*. New York: Random House, 1991.

Herring, George C. *America's Longest War: The United States and Vietnam, 1950–1975*, 2nd ed. New York: Alfred A. Knopf, 1986.

Herring, George C. *LBJ and Vietnam: A Different Kind of War*. Austin, Tex.: University of Texas Press, 1994.

Karnow, Stanley. *Vietnam: A History*. New York: Penguin, 1984.

McNamara, Robert S. *In Retrospect: The Tragedy and Lessons of Vietnam*. New York: Times Books, 1995.

Oberdorfer, Don. *Tet! The Turning Point in the Vietnam War*. New York: DaCapo Press, 1971.

Schandler, Herbert Y. *The Unmaking of a President: Lyndon Johnson and Vietnam*. Princeton, N.J.: Princeton University Press, 1977.

Spector, Ronald H. *After Tet: The Bloodiest Year in Vietnam*. New York: The Free Press, 1993.

Strong, Robert A. *Decisions and Dilemmas: Case Studies in Presidential Foreign Policy Making*. Englewood Cliffs, N.J.: Prentice Hall, 1992.

5

President Nixon's Decision to Order an Incursion into Cambodia

Setting and Overview of Nixon's Decision

President Nixon's announcement on November 3, 1969 that U.S. forces, in conjunction with South Vietnamese troops, were launching an incursion into Cambodia was a pivotal moment in the Vietnam War. Nixon hoped this incursion would shorten the war through locating and destroying North Vietnamese sanctuaries and COSVN (Central Office for South Vietnam), the elusive headquarters of enemy military activity. Nixon expected that the incursion would lead to more meaningful negotiations with North Vietnam and bring about his version of an honorable peace, for he would be demonstrating to Communist leaders that they were not dealing with a "pitiful giant." Moreover, Nixon anticipated that his decision would quicken the pace of "Vietnamization" of the war: South Vietnamese troops would be able to assume an increasing share of the military burden, which would allow the president to withdraw more and more American soldiers. Thus, Nixon believed, he could continue to defuse the antiwar movement in the United States and escape history's tagging the Vietnam War as "Nixon's War."

Nixon claimed success for his decision. Critics, however, pointed out that little damage was inflicted on North Vietnamese sanctuaries; U.S. troops never found COSVN; the incursion into Cambodia foolishly widened the war, with horrific short-term and long-term results; antiwar protests erupted throughout the United States, especially on

143

college campuses, resulting in the killing of four students at Kent State University; and the war hardly ended on favorable or honorable terms for the United States. Controversy continues to linger over Nixon's decision. What led to his decision, and how should you judge it?

President Nixon's Decision

ON APRIL 29, 1970, PRESIDENT NIXON SENT SOUTH VIETNAMESE FORCES INTO THE PARROT'S BEAK AREA OF CAMBODIA (A SLIVER OF LAND THAT JUTTED INTO SOUTH VIETNAM AND REACHED JUST THIRTY-THREE MILES FROM SAIGON) AND A JOINT U.S.–SOUTH VIETNAMESE FORCE INTO THE FISHHOOK REGION OF THAT COUNTRY (A SLICE THAT EXTENDED INTO THE MIDDLE OF SOUTH VIETNAM, ABOUT FIFTY MILES NORTHWEST OF SAIGON). ABOUT 31,000 U.S. AND 43,000 SOUTH VIETNAMESE TROOPS PARTICIPATED IN THIS "INCURSION." ACCORDING TO NIXON, THEIR GOALS WERE TO DESTROY ENEMY SUPPLIES, SANCTUARIES, AND HEADQUARTERS.

Nixon's decision was controversial because this incursion:

1. Widened the war in Indo-China, creating more "killing fields" in Cambodia.
2. Violated Cambodia's neutrality.
3. Infuriated the antiwar movement, which led to student protests all over the country.
4. Influenced Congressional critics to push for "end-to-the-war" resolutions and amendments.
5. Led to charges of continued abuse of presidential power.
6. Caused serious divisions within the Nixon administration, causing many to quit in protest.
7. Threatened progress of U.S.-Soviet détente and improved U.S. relations with the People's Republic of China (PRC).

Background of the Decision

Historical Context

When Richard Nixon ran for president in 1968, he maintained that U.S. military efforts in Vietnam were essential for national security. Like former Presidents Eisenhower, Kennedy, and Johnson, Nixon saw a Communist victory in Vietnam as damaging to U.S. strategic interests and leading to Communist aggression elsewhere in Southeast Asia and other areas of the "free world." Henry Kissinger, President Nixon's national security advisor, also defended the U.S. military presence in Vietnam as necessary for maintaining "confidence in America's promises."[1]

During the election campaign, Nixon claimed that he had a secret plan "to end the war and win the peace." Once elected, it became apparent Nixon had no such plan. But he was seriously considering an "approach" similar to Eisenhower's in ending the Korean War in 1953. Before the election, Nixon said he had no intention of seeking a military victory in Vietnam. He saw how "Johnson's war" had so severely wounded his predecessor. He did not want Vietnam to become "Nixon's war," especially if he wanted to be reelected and secure his place in history as a great president. He also did not want to become the first American president to lose a war. Years earlier, Nixon had criticized President Truman for "losing" China to the Communists. Similarly, he did not want to be accused of "losing" South Vietnam. So, remembering that Eisenhower had threatened the PRC and North Korea with atomic weapons unless they negotiated seriously, Nixon believed he might be able to frighten North Vietnam to the bargaining table by hinting he might use nuclear weapons.

Nixon called this approach to ending the Vietnam War his "madman theory." As he told his chief-of-staff H. R. Haldeman: "I want North Vietnam to believe that I've reached the point where I might do anything to stop the war. We'll just slip the word to them that, 'for God's sake, you know Nixon is obsessed about Communists. We can't restrain him when he's angry—and he has his hand on the nuclear button'—and Ho Chi Minh himself will be in Paris in two days begging for peace."[2]

The "madman theory" aside, Nixon's main preoccupation was to gain "peace with honor" as fast as possible, or to "end the war without losing it." His main strategy was Vietnamization.[3] This called for the gradual replacement of U.S. soldiers by South Vietnamese forces. The goal was to destroy or severely weaken enemy resistance. In reality, then, Vietnamization meant steady withdrawal of U.S. combat troops, but escalation of the overall military effort while pressing the enemy to negotiate an "honorable end to the war," that is, honorable to the United States. After a "decent interval," it would be South Vietnam's war to win or lose. If South Vietnam lost the war, the United States still could be seen as having stood by its allies and up to the Communists, criticism from Congress and the antiwar movement would be deflated, and Nixon could blame South Vietnam for the loss.

President Nixon's first speech on the Vietnam War was on May 14, 1969. The president called for an international body to monitor mutual withdrawal of U.S. and North Vietnamese troops over a one-year period and to supervise the subsequent holding of free elections in South Vietnam. Nixon also asked all parties to abide by the Geneva Accords of 1954 regarding South Vietnam and Cambodia and the Laos Accords of 1962, and to arrange for the earliest possible release of prisoners of war on both sides. But Nixon warned Hanoi, as he wrote in his memoirs, "not to confuse our flexibility with weakness." According to the president, Hanoi made "no serious response" to his request.[4]

Three weeks later, on June 8, Nixon and Kissinger flew to Midway Island to meet South Vietnam's President Nguyen Van Thieu. On the way, Nixon's party stopped in Hawaii to inform General Creighton Abrams, the new commander of U.S. forces in Vietnam, of the extent of the Vietnamization plan. Nixon would announce withdrawal of 25,000 U.S. combat troops, from a total of about a half million. Abrams and his Joint Chiefs of Staff (JCS) colleagues opposed this plan. Abrams wanted the United States to pull out some supply troops rather than all combat troops. Evidently, in Nixon's eyes, Abrams did not appreciate the *political* aspect of Vietnamization. Despite added opposition from Thieu, whose idea of Vietnamization was to rely more on U.S. aid and less on South Vietnam's own resources, Nixon announced his Vietnamization plan on Midway. He wanted to send a signal to Ho Chi Minh that the United States was reducing its war-making capabilities in Vietnam. The main goal of this troop withdrawal was to encourage Ho to pursue peace through negotiations.

Nixon's ploy did not work. Hanoi continued to reject his proposal for mutual withdrawal, and the Paris peace talks, begun in May 1968, went nowhere. In the meantime, the antiwar movement in the U.S. was gaining momentum as frustration grew with continued U.S. prosecution of the war.

In a *Look* magazine interview in the summer of 1969, Kissinger criticized student dissenters and conscientious objectors. "Conscientious objection must be reserved for only the great moral issues," Kissinger maintained, "and Vietnam is not of this magnitude." According to reporter Seymour Hersh, Kissinger then became an increasingly enthusiastic supporter of Nixon's "get tough" attitude toward Hanoi. On July 15, Nixon wrote to Ho reiterating his offer to end the war through negotiations. Nixon sent this letter through a personal acquaintance of Kissinger, Jean Sainteny, a French diplomat who had served in Hanoi during France's Indo-China War. Nixon asked Sainteny to tell Ho that unless Hanoi made some serious response to his negotiations overture by November 1 (the first anniversary of Johnson's bombing halt), the United States regretfully would have to resort "to measures of great consequence and force."[5]

Though Nixon's initiative did lead to a secret meeting on August 4 between Kissinger and Xuan Thuy (head of North Vietnam's delegation in Paris), which would be the first of many between Kissinger and North Vietnamese delegates over the net three years, there was no breakthrough. Ho rejected Nixon's proposal in a letter of August 25. He told the president that there would be no peace until the United States stopped "the war of aggression," withdrew its troops, and left the Vietnamese to settle their affairs "without foreign interference." Nixon considered this response a "cold rebuff." Ho's death on September 3 held out some hope to Washington for drawing the war to a close. According to Hersh, however, by the time Nixon had written his July 15 letter, he and Kissinger had already decided to "go for broke" and "attempt to end the war one way or the other—either by negotiated agreement or by an increased use of force."[6]

On July 20, Nixon received a top secret study from the military liaison office in the national Security Council that he had ordered earlier that summer. Under the code name "Duck Hook," plans were drawn for the escalation of the war in North Vietnam. These plans had been completed by the Office of the Chief of Naval Operations without Secretary Laird's knowledge.[7] "Duck Hook" called for massive bombing of Hanoi, Haiphong, and other major targets in North Vietnam; the mining of harbors and rivers; bombing of dikes; a ground invasion of North Vietnam; destruction of main North-south passes of the Ho Chi Minh Trail (the principal land supply route from North to south Vietnam); and bombing of North Vietnam's main railroad links with the PRC. The United States would destroy twenty-nine targets in North Vietnam by bombing raids over four days, to be renewed if necessary. These were clearly designed to force Hanoi to surrender.[8]

The Nixon Doctrine
Five days later, on July 25, at a talk with U.S. reporters in Guam where Nixon went to watch the splashdown of American astronauts (the first men on the moon), the president announced the "Nixon Doctrine."

From then on, Nixon stated, international security and military defense problems would be "handled by, and the responsibility for it taken by, the Asian countries themselves." On September 16, Nixon announced that he would withdraw 35,000 more U.S. troops by December 15, 1969. He then said on radio and television: "The time has come to end this war. The time for meaningful negotiations has . . . arrived."

By the fall of 1969, there was a growing contradiction between Nixon's publicly stated policy of Vietnamization and his privately conceived plan for escalation of the war. As Hersh points out, neither the public, the media, Congress, nor most government officials knew about this secret plan that was already under way. Nixon had actually begun the secret bombing of Cambodia as early as March 1969, just two months after taking office.

While Nixon was publicly talking "peace with honor," privately he was exerting intense pressure on North Vietnam to make peace. Kissinger, at his secret meeting with Xuan Thuy on August 4, reminded the North Vietnamese representative that November 1 would be the first anniversary of the U.S. bombing halt of North Vietnam. Kissinger also reminded Xuan that despite the fact that the United States had withdrawn 25,000 combat troops and had stated it would accept the results of free elections, North Vietnam had not reciprocated. Kissinger then laid down this threat: "I have been asked to tell you in all solemnity, that if by November 1 no major progress has been made toward a solution, we will be compelled—with great reluctance—to take measures of the greatest consequences." Kissinger mentioned that North Vietnamese propaganda was trying to portray the war as "Mr. Nixon's war." Kissinger then commented: "We do not believe that this is in your interest, because if it is Mr. Nixon's war, then he cannot afford not to win it." Xuan restated North Vietnam's demand for complete withdrawal of all U.S. forces and observance of the ten points issued by the National Liberation Front (the political arm of the Viet Cong, which was the main force opposing the South Vietnamese government). But acceptance of North Vietnam's demands meant, in Nixon's words, "total Communist domination over South Vietnam."[9]

Nixon mentioned in his memoirs that by October 14 he "knew for sure" that his ultimatum to Hanoi had failed. Nixon did not want to appear weak to the North Vietnamese, for this would lead to their contempt and make negotiations more difficult. He thus reconsidered his response to operation "Duck Hook." In late September, Nixon gathered a group of Republican senators and let them know he was considering part of this plan: blockade of Haiphong and invasion of North Vietnam. Though he eventually decided not to escalate the war at that time, Nixon did send a signal to Moscow that there could be serious consequences for U.S.-Soviet relations if the Kremlin did not use its influence with Hanoi to negotiate an end to the war. The president secretly ordered the Strategic Air Command (SAC) to place its nuclear-armored B-52 bombers on "combat ready status." It was the first time since the Cuban missile crisis that Washington had put SAC on full alert. It lasted twenty-nine days.

Nixon, meanwhile, had to concern himself with the growing strength of the country's antiwar movement. In his eyes, this included three main groups: sincere opponents of the war, such as followers of Senator Eugene McCarthy who ran for president in 1968; political activists, who misread the antiwar opposition as a majority view; and, in speechwriter William Safire's words, "the nuts and kooks—the anarchists and yippies, deadbeats and acidheads, haters and burners to whom Vietnam was nothing more than a handy issue to help infuriate the Establishment, trigger right-wing repression, and pick up the marbles in the ensuing chaos."[10] On October 15, the antiwar movement organized a "Moratorium" (Nixon's own word in 1968 that referred to avoidance of public comment on Vietnam) in Washington, D.C. with about 250,000 demonstrators. This demonstration, for the most part, was peaceful.

Nixon believed that the Moratorium raised "a basic question about the nature of leadership in a democracy." Nixon raised the question whether the president or Congress or any other responsible elected officials should let public demonstrations influence their decision. Replying to a letter from a Georgetown University student, Nixon wrote:

> If a President—any President—allowed his course to be set by those who demonstrate, he would betray the trust of all the rest. Whatever the issue, to allow government policy to be made in the streets would destroy the democratic process. It would give the decision, not to the majority, and not to those with the strongest arguments, but to those with the loudest voices. . . . It would allow every group to test its strength not at the ballot box but through confrontation in the streets.[11]

On the night of the Moratorium, Nixon jotted down on top of the page of his preliminary notes to a major speech he was preparing for November 3: "Don't get rattled—don't waver—don't react."[12]

Nixon's Speech on November 3

In his speech to the American people on the war, the president referred to "the great silent majority of Americans—good people with good judgment who stand ready to do whatever they believe to be right." He estimated that this "silent majority" that supported his Vietnam policy would prevail over the antiwar protesters and take the steam out of criticism from Congress and the media. His main point was that the United States would keep its commitment in Vietnam. The United States would continue fighting "until the Communists agreed to negotiate a fair and honorable peace or until the South Vietnamese were able to defend themselves on their own—whichever came first." Concurrently, the United States would continue withdrawal based on principles of the Nixon Doctrine. In no way, Nixon asserted, would U.S. policy be influenced by antiwar demonstrations.

Nixon held that his speech changed "the course of history. . . . Now . . . the enemy could no longer count on dissent in America to give them the victory they could not win on the battlefield."[13] The speech was generally well received. A Gallup Poll showed 77 percent of those who heard it supported Nixon. Buoyed by such polls, Nixon decided to try to "take on" the news media for what he considered their distortions and "instant analysis." In the next few weeks, Nixon and Kissinger stepped up their rhetoric against the antiwar movement.

The November 15 Moratorium was less effective than October's, with less media coverage and the appearance of fewer leading Congressional critics. It seemed that the Nixon administration was successful, for the time being at least, in getting American people to believe Vietnamization would soon end the war.

In an added measure to weaken the antiwar movement, Nixon stopped the draft. This had been a major target of antiwar demonstrators, largely because of its inequities. More and more, it seemed, the draft had been "selecting" a disproportionate number of poor and racial minority youths to fight in Vietnam, while well-to-do white college students were receiving deferments or conscientious objector status, or were fleeing to other countries such as Canada and Sweden. On November 16, moreover, the media broke the story that one year earlier the U.S. Army had massacred more than 350 South Vietnamese in the hamlet of My Lai. Outraged by this "leak," Nixon ordered the military to spy on the soldier who had revealed this incident. The same month, he ordered the FBI and CIA to exercise surveillance on newspersons.

The antiwar movement received an unexpected shot in the arm when Nixon decided to launch an "incursion" into Cambodia in the spring of 1970. It would have been reinvigorated earlier had the public known about the secret bombing of Cambodia.

The Secret Bombing of Cambodia

From the middle of March through early April 1970, while Kissinger was conducting secret negotiations in a villa outside Paris with North Vietnam's envoy and Politburo member Le Duc Tho, the U.S. secret bombing war in Cambodia was in full force.

Cambodia had fallen under French rule in 1864. In 1953, it won its independence under Prince Norodom Sihanouk. In 1954, the Geneva Conference on Indo-China recognized Cambodia's neutrality. As South Vietnam drifted toward war in the early 1960s, Sihanouk adroitly preserved his country's neutrality on three fronts: between the United States and North Vietnam, between Communist China and the Soviet Union, and between North and South Vietnam. On May 3, 1965, as the U.S. stepped up its military involvement in Vietnam, Sihanouk broke diplomatic relations with Washington. At the same time, he allowed North Vietnam to establish bases in his country, especially along border areas adjoining South Vietnam. There the North Vietnamese and Viet Cong could launch raids into South Vietnam and then retreat to sanctuaries.[14] Yet, Sihanouk did not like the fact that North Vietnam was encouraging Khmer Rouge (Cambodian Communists) guerrillas. He began sentencing their leaders to death in absentia.

In the meantime, the United States continued sending "Daniel Boone squads" into Cambodia. These were covert Green Beret teams dressed as peasants that sought to gather intelligence or sabotage enemy operations. In so doing, some of these teams enlisted the aid of Khmer Serei. These were anti-Communist Cambodians based in Thailand whose goal was to overthrow Sihanouk. Official U.S. policy, however, denied the Green Berets the use of ethnic Cambodians inside Cambodia, so most operations were conducted with Vietnamese and Thai soldiers.[15]

About one week after President Nixon's inauguration, the Joint Chiefs of Staff (JCS) resumed its efforts, begun in the Johnson administration, to press for American bombing of North Vietnamese and Viet Cong sanctuaries in Cambodia. The main arguments against this bombing were that it would violate Cambodia's neutrality, widen the war, increase casualties, and if made public, enrage antiwar demonstrators. In February, the Pentagon told the White House that it had received intelligence information from a North Vietnamese defector regarding the exact location of the Central Office for South Vietnam (COSVN), the elusive enemy headquarters. General Abrams also urged the use of B-52 raids to destroy COSVN. Because U.S. intelligence reported no Cambodian civilians lived in the area where COSVN was supposed to be located, presumably Sihanouk would not object to U.S. raids there. Ellsworth Bunker, U.S. ambassador to South Vietnam, agreed with Abrams and General Earl Wheeler, Chairman of JCS, that a North Vietnamese offensive was imminent, so he approved the bombing raids.

The State Department and CIA were hesitant to support bombing raids in Cambodia. They believed that the Ho Chi Minh Trail in Laos was a more important supply route to South Vietnam. Among those who opposed the raids was Richard Sneider, Kissinger's National Security aide on East Asia. He argued that raids would not wipe out COSVN and made no "military sense." Secretary of State William Rogers also feared the negative effect the raids would have on peace talks. Secretary of Defense Melvin Laird supported the bombing itself, but not its secrecy, which he feared would have negative effects on Congress and public opinion.

But hardliners, such as Colonel Alexander Haig, Kissinger's new military aide, prevailed. When Hanoi launched an offensive in South Vietnam on February 22, Nixon felt compelled to retaliate to avoid humiliation.[16] On March 16, at a meeting with Kissinger, Rogers, Laird, and Wheeler in Washington, Nixon argued that the "only way" to get the enemy to negotiate was "to do something on the military front, . . . something they will understand." The bombing decision thus was made essentially on both military and political grounds. Apparently there was no serious discussion of legal, diplomatic, or ethical ramifications.[17]

The bombing raids on Cambodia, dubbed "Operation Menu" by the Pentagon, began the next day. According to Nixon, the first attack ("Operation Breakfast") "was the first turning point in my administration's conduct of the Vietnam War." Nixon took "maximum precautions" to keep the bombing secret. The United States, Nixon believed, would not want to embarrass Sihanouk, who publicly guarded Cambodia's neutrality. If the bombing were made public, Sihanouk would be forced to protest publicly. Nixon also sensed that the North Vietnamese would not publicly object if the bombings were secret, for to do so would be to admit their military presence in Cambodia. A third reason for secrecy was not to let the antiwar movement seize upon the issue. Nixon also kept the bombing secret from Congress. He informed only supporters Senators Richard Russell (D, Georgia) and John Stennis

(D, Miss.), the chairman and ranking member of the Senate Armed Services Committee.[18] The only person outside the government whom Nixon told was former President Eisenhower, who, according to Nixon, "strongly endorsed the decision."[19]

The secret bombing, intended originally to be of "short duration," lasted fourteen months. The Pentagon devised elaborate cover stories and false reporting schemes designed to keep the bombing secret both inside and outside the government. But on May 9, *New York Times* reporter William Beecher revealed the secret bombing of Cambodia and North Vietnam, which clearly violated President Johnson's bombing halt announced on March 31, 1968. This assumed "leak" (Beecher's article was actually based on a story from a British reporter in Cambodia) angered Nixon and Kissinger. Nixon directed FBI chief J. Edgar Hoover to place wiretaps on the phones of four journalists and thirteen government officials, many of whom were Kissinger's aides. The main suspect was Morton Halperin, Kissinger's former colleague at Harvard University. Hoover felt Halperin was one of those "arrogant Harvard-type Kennedy men"; Kissinger believed Halperin was "philosophically in disagreement" with the president; and Nixon himself disliked Halperin for supposedly being part of a traitorous "Eastern Jewish Establishment."[20] No leaks on the bombing were found, because there were none.

The bombing in Cambodia was having mixed results. On the positive side, on June 11, 1969, Sihanouk announced that Cambodia would restore diplomatic relations with the United States. In his memoirs, Nixon points to the "steady decline in American casualties in South Vietnam" and to the successful use of the bombing as a lever to force the North Vietnamese to bargain more seriously.[21] On the negative side, the secret bombing infringed on Cambodia's neutrality (though Nixon claimed that his action was legal under international law because North Vietnam was using Cambodia "as a staging ground for its aggression"); did not destroy COSVN; failed to deter the North Vietnamese or Viet Cong from war-making; widened the war; and created greater casualties among Cambodians.

On March 18, 1970, the secret bombing also paved the way for General Lon Nol, the Cambodian prime minister, to overthrow Sihanouk. The next day, Washington extended de jure recognition to the Lon Nol government. The United States officially denied any prior support for this coup. Yet it clearly was pleased with a strongly anti-communist leader who would be more sympathetic to its efforts to wipe out North Vietnamese sanctuaries. In early 1969, Sihanouk had given quiet assent to U.S. bombing of these sanctuaries. The North Vietnamese, expecting him to back U.S. war efforts in his country, then began stepping up their arming and training of Khmer Rouge guerrillas in North Vietnam. Hanoi, in turn, began infiltrating several thousand Khmer Rouge units into Cambodia, thereby incurring the wrath of Sihanouk and sparking a bloody civil war there. At first, Lon Nol denounced all invasion forces and underlined Cambodia's "strict neutrality." But on April 14, encouraged by the U.S., he appealed for foreign help. Supposedly, Nixon "from day one" had decided to help Lon Nol even before he deposed Sihanouk.[22]

The Secret War in Laos

While the secret bombing of Cambodia continued after the overthrow of Sihanouk, Nixon faced another challenge in Laos. The United States had been waging a secret war there since the early 1960s when the CIA began financing Meo tribesmen to fight the Pathet Lao (Communist) forces. Laos had been neutralized by an international agreement in 1962 that prohibited the stationing of foreign troops on its soil or its involvement in neighboring wars. But this agreement fell apart in April 1963. The U.S. goal then was to support neutralist Souvana Phouma and gain his acquiescence to U.S. efforts to stop supplies coming down from North Vietnam along the Ho Chi Minh Trail. Hanoi, in the eyes of the United States, was fighting in northern Laos to help the Pathet Lao, and in southern Laos to send supplies to the Viet Cong in Vietnam.

When Nixon became president, he ordered the bombing of the Ho Chi Minh Trail. Nixon's main goal was to stop the supplies from North to South Vietnam, which he believed would also improve chances for success of Vietnamization.

When Hanoi sent 13,000 troops to help the Pathet Lao in January 1970, Nixon believed this posed a serious threat to Souvana Phouma. The war in Laos also threatened Thailand. If the Communists gained a foothold in northeast Thailand where their guerrilla forces were operating, the United States might be denied the use of Thai air bases. These were considered necessary for air operations in Vietnam.

On February 12, the North Vietnamese offensive began on the Laotian Plain of Jars. The next day, Souvana Phouma requested B-52 strikes, which Nixon ordered. On February 19, the *New York Times* reported U.S. air strikes against North Vietnam and Pathet Lao troops in Laos. Immediately there was a public outcry and criticism from Congress. The Nixon administration faced the problem of how to handle the secrecy of the U.S. operation. According to Kissinger, "to spell out the limits publicly was as dangerous . . . as to spell out the extent of our involvement. We were being pressed to do both."[23]

After much reflection and discussion, Nixon decided that the United States should issue a public statement on March 6. It would describe and explain U.S. involvement in Laos and the reasons for secrecy stemming from the days of the Kennedy administration. Nixon's statement justified the secret war in Laos on the basis of Vietnamization. It stirred great controversy, largely because it inadvertently (according to Kissinger) claimed that "no American stationed in Laos has ever been killed in ground combat operations." But on March 8, the *Los Angeles Times* revealed that an American captain had been killed in Laos the previous year. Kissinger tried to wiggle out of this public relations mess by claiming these soldiers technically were not "stationed" in Vietnam. But in the public eye, the Nixon administration was clearly caught in a lie. Increasingly it was criticized for what became known as the "credibility gap": discrepancies between official versions of events and realities.

Not wanting to elicit further criticism, Nixon decided against further U.S. military commitment in Laos. He seemed satisfied that the Laotian government army, with the aid of Thai volunteers, could hold off further Communist advances.[24] The president then turned his attention to Cambodia. In contrast to the situation in Laos, he decided to act there more boldly.

The president was convinced that success of his Vietnamization policy depended on eliminating North Vietnam's sanctuaries and supply centers both in Cambodia and Laos, and on demonstrating his toughness to the enemy. So, while he was fulfilling his pledge to withdraw U.S. combat troops from Vietnam, he was secretly escalating the war in northern Laos and Cambodia. Thus Nixon could publicly honor his policy of Vietnamization, yet privately signal the North Vietnamese and Viet Cong that he was hard-nosed and prepared to use force. It was within the context of the widening secret wars in Laos and Cambodia that in April 1970 Nixon made his decision to send U.S. forces into Cambodia.

Countdown to the Decision

President Nixon explained that he made his decision because "events beyond our control had forced our hand."[25] As Nixon explained, North Vietnam had "rebuffed" his initiative to restore the neutrality of Cambodia and through the end of March had "geared up for an attack on Cambodia."[26] When on April 14 Lon Nol appealed for "unconditional foreign aid from all sources" to drive out the North Vietnamese, Nixon thought "North Vietnam was threatening to convert all of eastern Cambodia into one huge base area . . . that would enable its forces to strike at both Phnom Penh [the Cambodian capital] and South Vietnam at will."[27]

April of 1970 was a particularly tough month for Nixon. Kissinger's secret negotiations with Le Duc Tho in Paris had been suspended; the North Vietnamese were mounting another offensive in Cambodia and expanding their bases there; Kissinger was unable to arrange a U.S.-Soviet summit in Moscow; the Senate had rejected Nixon's Supreme Court nominee, Harrold Carswell; concern for antiwar demonstrations had influenced Nixon not to attend his daughter Julie's graduation at Smith College; and the Apollo 13 astronauts, after a serious scare, had finally landed safely.

Nixon flew to Hawaii to greet the astronauts. On April 18, he met with Admiral John McCain who urged him to wipe out North Vietnam's sanctuaries in Cambodia. Two days later, at the Western White House in San Clemente, California, Nixon announced his fourth U.S. troop withdrawal: 150,000 troops were to leave South Vietnam by May 1, 1971. He had increased this number to appease antiwar critics, but he also had extended the timetable to ease General Abrams's worry over the potential danger of pulling out too fast. In his announcement, Nixon added this warning to North Vietnam: "If increased enemy action jeopardizes our remaining forces in Vietnam, I shall not hesitate to take strong and effective measures to deal with that situation."[28] He then left for Washington.

On the morning of April 21, Nixon met with Kissinger and CIA Director Richard Helms. Helms warned that North Vietnam was surrounding Phnom Penh. Kissinger asserted that Helms's report lent "new poignancy" to Lon Nol's appeals for aid. That afternoon, Nixon met with Kissinger and Laird to discuss North Vietnam's "new aggressiveness." Their major concern was its effect on Vietnamization.

On April 22, before he started his official work day, Nixon wrote a memorandum to Kissinger explaining why the United States needed "a bold move in Cambodia." Nixon then met with Helms. Later that morning, Kissinger met with Ray Cline, director of intelligence and research for the State Department, and Lieutenant General John Vogt, director of operations for the JCS, to learn whether they had any new information or ideas. They did not.

That afternoon, Nixon met with the full National Security Council (NSC) in the Cabinet room. Present were Vice President Spiro Agnew, Secretaries Laird and Rogers, Brigadier General George Lincoln, director of the Office of Emergency Preparedness, Admiral Thomas Moorer, acting chairman of the JCS, Attorney General John Mitchell, Helms, and Kissinger. Kissinger gave a detailed report on the increasingly dangerous situation in Cambodia. He stressed that enlarged sanctuaries gave North Vietnam greater capability of endangering U.S. troops and thereby the Vietnamization process.

The NSC discussed three main options: watching and waiting; attacking the sanctuaries inside Cambodia with South Vietnamese troops, aided by U.S. air support; and sending in U.S. troops with the South Vietnamese. What transpired subsequently was a classic example of "groupthink."[29] According to reporters Marvin and Bernard Kalb: "Kissinger's presentation was meticulous; no one in the room questioned its facts or assumptions. A consensus seemed to emerge: in order to protect American lives in South Vietnam, the U.S. should take some sort of military action to prevent a Communist victory in Cambodia."[30]

Nixon decided on the second option. He would send South Vietnamese troops into the Parrot's Beak, with small-scale U.S. air cover. Agnew then criticized Nixon for "pussyfooting." The vice president argued that the United States should attack and clean out not only the Parrot's Beak, but also the Fish Hook region which had been the main target of secret U.S. bombing. Perhaps then, as the military had argued, the United States could finally destroy COSVN. Nixon was flustered, for he always wanted to appear tougher than his advisers.

On April 23, Nixon believed that U.S. arms to Lon Nol would not be enough to prevent North Vietnam from taking over Cambodia. Kissinger then asked for a meeting of his executive committee called the Washington Special Action Group (WSAG). This group recommended an invasion of South Vietnamese forces into the Parrot's Beak. Present were U. Alexis Johnson, under secretary of state for political affairs, David Packard, deputy secretary of defense, Admiral Moorer, Helms, and Marshall Green, assistant secretary of state.

That evening, according to the president's log, Nixon telephoned Senator J. William Fulbright, dovish chairman of the Senate Foreign Relations Committee, and then Kissinger. Safire points out that Nixon made ten calls to Kissinger between 6:30 and 11 P.M.[31] In one call, Nixon said: "The liberals are waiting to see Nixon let Cambodia go down the drain the way Eisenhower let Cuba go down the drain."[32]

According to Kissinger, Nixon was in a "monumental rage" because his order to open a CIA station in Cambodia, issued three weeks earlier, still had not been carried out.[33] By the time of Nixon's last call to Kissinger after midnight, Kissinger was convinced that Nixon had decided to toughen his stance and send U.S. troops into Cambodia.

On the morning of April 24, Nixon met with Helms and his deputy, Lieutenant General Robert Cushman (a former commander of the I Corps in Vietnam), Moorer, and Kissinger. He sought plans for a joint U.S.-South Vietnamese invasion of the Fish Hook area, where the U.S. military believed COSVN was located, and for a South Vietnamese solo invasion of the Parrot's Beak. Laird and Rogers were not invited because they would not have supported this option. Kissinger did present the president's decision to Laird by phone, who as expected expressed his dissent. Later, Nixon told a group of advisers: "If we were going to take the flak for doing it at all, we might as well do it right."[34]

On April 26, Nixon made his final decision to "go for broke."[35] He put aside concerns both about antiwar demonstrations that surely would grow, and divisions among his foreign policy advisers. He would do what he felt was right and had to be done.[36]

Nixon's Announcement of the Cambodian "Incursion"

Nixon explained his decision for an "incursion" into Cambodia in a televised speech on April 30. The president wrote most of this tough-sounding speech himself. It was strident, combative, and jingoistic. Nixon defied his critics at home, and he challenged the North Vietnamese to negotiate. At first, he ruled out the options "to do nothing" or "to provide massive military assistance to Cambodia." Instead, Nixon concluded, the U.S. choice was "to go to the heart of the trouble."

Nixon's main points were these:

1. The "incursion" was a response to North Vietnam's "aggression."
2. The main U.S. target was COSVN.
3. The United States had to avoid acting like a "pitiful, helpless giant" when "the forces of totalitarianism and anarchy" threatened "free nations and free institutions around the world."
4. The credibility of the United States as a dependable ally was at stake if it did not respond forcefully to the challenge of North Vietnam's aggression.
5. He would follow his conscience rather than "be a two-term president at the cost of seeing America become a second-rate power."

Nixon's staff thought that in general the public had favorably received his speech. But critics like independent journalist I. F. Stone pointed again to the "credibility gap." They lambasted the speech for its lies, deceit, and distortions. Among the examples Stone cited were Nixon's statements that U.S. policy since the Geneva Conference of 1954 "has been to scrupulously respect the neutrality of the Cambodian people;" that "for the past 5 years we have provided no military assistance and no economic assistance whatever to Cambodia"; and "for five years, neither the U.S. nor South Vietnam [has] moved against enemy sanctuaries because we did not wish to violate the territory of a neutral nation."[37] In his memoirs, Kissinger described this speech as "divisive . . . , apocalyptic in its claim, excessive in his pretension." Moreover, he noted, "no doubt" Nixon "personalized the issue excessively."[38]

Nixon followed up his April 30 speech by going to the Pentagon the next day for a briefing. After being told of the initial success of the "incursion," he asked: "Could we take out *all* the sanctuaries?" Pentagon officials responded it was feasible, but they had not presented this option because they anticipated criticism by the media and Congress. Nixon responded: "Let me be the judge as far as the political reactions are concerned. The fact is that we have already taken the political heat for this particular operation. If we can substantially reduce the threat to our forces by wiping out the rest of the sanctuaries, now is the time to do it."

Nixon then made an on-the-spot decision to take out all the sanctuaries. "Make whatever plans are necessary, and then just do it," he told the Pentagon officials. "Knock them all out so that they can't be used against us again, ever." Nixon described this encounter as a "textbook case" of "the tendency of our armed forces to confuse *military* analysis with *political* analysis. Given the political restrictions imposed on the military during the early years of the war, and given the abuses heaped on them by the antiwar movement and the media, I could understand why they were so tentative by the time I came into office. I could sense that they were surprised and pleased when I directed them to take out all the sanctuaries."[39] At a press conference afterward, Nixon praised the "kids" fighting in Vietnam as "the greatest," but he called student demonstrators "bums." This reference was to haunt Nixon for months to come.

On May 3, Beecher reported that the United States had secretly renewed bombing of North Vietnam. According to Hersh, Nixon and Kissinger had ordered these attacks through Admiral Moorer, bypassing Laird. Kissinger tried to prevent publication of Beecher's story, even though its substance had been announced by Hanoi Radio. When Kissinger failed, Nixon asked the FBI for more wiretapping.[40]

On May 8, Nixon announced at a news conference that "the great majority" of the U.S. forces in Cambodia would leave by the second week of June, that all U.S. soldiers would leave by July 1, and that no U.S. soldiers could go farther than twenty-one miles inside Cambodia. This decision seemingly was influenced by public pressure. On the whole, however, the president made decisions seemingly unruffled by growing criticism at home and abroad.

President Nixon as Decision-Maker

Foreign Policy Context of Decision

Unlike Truman, Nixon considered himself an expert on foreign policy. His specialty was relations with the communist world. Indeed, Nixon had built his career on anti-communism. As a congressman from California in the late 1940s and early 1950s, as mentioned previously, he had led the Republican attack on Truman for "losing" China to the communists and for being "soft" on communism.

Nixon believed strongly in using force to achieve foreign policy goals and in standing firm in the face of aggression or a test of will with the enemy. For example, in 1954 he had favored the use of American bombers to save the French at Dien Bien Phu, the battle loss that marked the end of French control of Indo-china. He even considered then the use of tactical nuclear weapons, arguing that "tactical atomic explosives are now conventional and will be used against the targets of any aggressive forces."[41] Nixon also had seriously contemplated the possibility of fighting a limited nuclear war. Interestingly, this was a central theme in Kissinger's 1957 book, *Nuclear Weapons and Foreign Policy*.

Like Kissinger, Nixon considered himself a practitioner of realpolitik. Nixon stressed balance of power, pragmatism, and secrecy over idealism, morality, legality, and openness. Thus, in the Cambodian decision, one finds little personal soul-searching or encouragement of debate over morality with policy advisers or in public.

Nixon also believed strongly in preserving and solidifying the U.S. place as leader of the "free world." The United States must not be a "pitiful giant" (noted in his April 30 speech), must stand by its allies, which included South Vietnam, and must reassure states in the "free world" of a strong anti-communist stance. Nixon felt he had to appear and act strong, lest foreign enemies (particularly the Soviet Union, the PRC, and North Vietnam) try to take advantage of any perceived weakness.

Context of Decision within Nixon's National Security Strategy

A decade after the Vietnam War, Nixon wrote that his goal in Vietnam "was not to conquer North Vietnam but to prevent North Vietnam from conquering South Vietnam." Accordingly, he had developed a five point strategy "to win the war—or more precisely, to end the war and win the peace":

1. *Vietnamization,* which the State Department officially defined as "a military-economic program of South Vietnamese development which will permit rapid but phased withdrawal of the U.S. forces without radically upsetting the power balance in Southeast Asia." This meant, in effect, bankrolling the South Vietnamese government and Army of the Republic of Vietnam (ARVN) to fight the war as the U.S. withdrew its troops.
2. *Pacification,* which replaced the strategy of attrition and involved trying to extend South Vietnamese government control over the countryside. This would be achieved through trying to win the hearts and minds of the peasants through such inducements as land reform and added protection from the Viet Cong and North Vietnamese troops.
3. *Peace negotiations,* which meant forgoing a quick military victory but using "irresistible military pressure" to end the war on "honorable" terms. Nixon wrote that negotiations had to satisfy only two conditions: return of all U.S. prisoners of war and protection of the right of self-determination of the South Vietnamese people.
4. *Gradual withdrawal of U.S. combat troops,* which "was to be made from strength, not weakness." The pace of U.S. withdrawal would be linked to success of Vietnamization and the enemy's response on the battlefield and at the bargaining table in Paris.
5. *Diplomatic isolation,* which called for enlisting the cooperation of the Soviet Union and Communist China to stop sending North Vietnam military supplies and to pressure Hanoi to negotiate an end to the war. According to Nixon: "At worst, Hanoi was bound to feel less confident if Washington was dealing with Moscow and Peking. At best, if the two major communist powers decided that they had big-

ger fish to fry, Hanoi would be pressured into negotiating a settlement we could accept."[42]

Diplomatic isolation was a key part of Nixon's overall national security strategy. One important tactic was playing the first "China card." In 1971, Nixon directed Kissinger to secretly open up a channel of communication with the country it had long treated as an international outlaw and pariah. One of his main goals was to enlist Peking's support in ending the Vietnam War. This démarche (change of diplomatic policy) turned out to be the first step toward normalization of U.S. relations with the PRC which was to culminate in official U.S. diplomatic recognition under President Carter on January 1, 1979. Nixon also was using the prospect of better relations with the PRC to pressure the Kremlin into closer cooperation with the United States. Indeed, détente (reduction of tension) with the Soviet Union would become the cornerstone of Nixon's national security strategy.

Soviet President Leonid Brezhnev was also committed to détente. He sought U.S. trade, credits, technology, and a strategic arms agreement to escape growing Soviet economic problems and avert the disaster of nuclear war. He was also worried about a hostile PRC on his border. The Sino-Soviet dispute had deepened and had become much more serious during the late 1960s. In 1969, Soviet and Chinese Communist forces clashed at the Ussuri River in Manchuria, an ominous indication of the level of hostility between the two communist giants. Warming of U.S.-Chinese relations would be a setback for Brezhnev. Perhaps then, Nixon hoped, Brezhnev would see the benefits of helping out the United States by exerting more pressure on Hanoi to negotiate an end to the Vietnam War.

To Nixon and Kissinger, the key element of the détente strategy with the Soviet union was "linkage." This "integrating conceptual framework," developed by Kissinger, held that rational policy in a thermonuclear age was to be based on relative rather than absolute security. According to Kissinger, the two superpowers must balance rather than impose rival claims, interests, and problems, all of which were "linked" to one another.

Nixon believed that the road to peace in Vietnam (as well as in the Middle East and other regions) ran through the Kremlin. Instead of confrontation, Nixon offered Brezhnev cooperation, arms agreements, and economic carrots—provided the Soviet leader helped the United States get out of Vietnam. Moreover, Nixon and Kissinger believed, linkage diplomacy should be conducted secretly, far from the glare of the media and public debate. Furthermore, it should try to influence only Soviet foreign policy, not domestic policy.

Nixon tried repeatedly to link the Vietnam War with the broad spectrum of U.S.-Soviet problems. Kissinger told Anatoly Dobrynin, Soviet ambassador to Washington, that the U.S. could not meet the Kremlin's needs until it helped end the Vietnam War. So that the United States would not appear weak in its relations with the Soviet Union or in the eyes of the rest of the world, the United States, in Kissinger's eyes, was "determined that our withdrawal from Vietnam occur not as a collapse but as an American strategy."[43] Moreover, for linkage to work, there had to be reduced tension between the superpowers. But this could not occur until Moscow stopped its support for North Vietnam. Thus, Kissinger concluded: "We saw linkage, in short, as synonymous with an overall strategy and geopolitical view. To ignore the interconnection of events was to undermine the coherence of *all* policy."[44]

Nixon's and Kissinger's persistent attempts to link the end of the Vietnam War with other U.S.-Soviet problems met with failure. The Soviet Union feared loss of stature as champion of nationalism and anti-Western imperialism in the Third World. Moreover, it did not want to appear less supportive than Communist China of "wars of national liberation." Thus the Kremlin was unresponsive to American pressure and "signals" of strength to stay the course in Vietnam, such as Nixon's decision for an "incursion" into Cambodia. Moreover, it is doubtful whether any pressure that Moscow brought to bear on Hanoi would have made any difference, given North Vietnam's determination to end the war on its own terms.

The American public and Congress generally were aware of all the elements of Nixon's strategy on Indo-China. Kept secret though, throughout the time of Nixon's Cambodian incursion decision and not revealed until "leaks" and antiwar protests forced them into the open, were other elements of Nixon's strategy: the Daniel Boone raids in Cambodia, the bombing of Cambodia, the U.S. war in Laos, and the Phoenix program. Under this program, planned and instituted by the CIA in 1967 under President Johnson, South Vietnam's government officials, military, police, and civilians trained by the CIA infiltrated South Vietnamese peasant villages in order to destroy the Viet Cong infrastructure. This meant "neutralizing" (assassinating or maiming) Viet Cong operatives including organizers and tax collectors. Not surprisingly, neither Nixon nor Kissinger mentioned the Phoenix program in their memoirs.

Context of Decision within President's Relations with Allies
Consultation with key NATO allies, Britain and France, was not a factor in Nixon's Cambodia decision. To its allies, the United States appeared foolishly obsessed with the Vietnam War. They considered the war unnecessary, economically wasteful, and politically debilitating because it caused such serious domestic divisions and unrest. To some leaders, such as France's Charles DeGaulle, the United States had lost its sense of priorities. DeGaulle, who remembered how France had been kicked out of Indo-China and who oversaw France's withdrawal from a painful war in Algeria, thought that the United States had not learned its lessons from history. Nixon and Kissinger, however, believed the United States could win in Vietnam because it had more firepower than the French had there, particularly high-tech weapons. Moreover, the United States was fighting for different purposes from the French. They had struggled to hang on to their colonial empire. The United States, in contrast, "was fighting to get out."[45] To its allies, however, Nixon's arguments seemed shallow and unconvincing.

Although détente did not work in helping end the Vietnam War, it nevertheless became the overarching strategy of the Nixon presidency. Following West German leader Willy Brandt's *ostpolitik* (his new policy of easing the West's relations with Eastern Europe and the Soviet Union), Nixon established the foundation of détente strategy that yielded such achievements as the Strategic Arms Limitation Treaty (SALT I) and the Four Power Berlin Accord. Both Presidents Ford and Carter followed this strategy, until it collapsed in the aftermath of the Soviet invasion of Afghanistan in December 1979.

Domestic Context of Decision

Many Americans rallied around the president after he announced the incursion into Cambodia. Yet his decision also reinvigorated the antiwar movement. It had been losing steam because of phased U.S. troop withdrawals under Vietnamization. As noted previously, antiwar protests swept the colleges, with the deaths of students at Kent State University shocking the nation as never before. Nixon appointed a commission, headed by William Scranton (former Republican governor of Pennsylvania), to study the unrest on college college campuses. It concluded that divisions in the country were "as deep as any since the Civil War" and argued that "nothing is more important than an end to the war in Vietnam."

Nixon's decision also led to a wave of protests, resignations, and firings in his administration. For example, over 200 State Department employees protested in a public petition; several NSC staff members resigned; and Secretary of the Interior Walter Hickel was fired after he publicly criticized the president. Nixon tended to take criticism personally, attributing it either to the protesters' ignorance, unsophistication in international affairs, or ill-will against him. Perhaps this was exemplified most clearly in his relations with Congress.

Struggling with Nixon all the way, Congress tried to limit his actions in Indo-China. Although public protests began to diminish when Nixon promised to remove U.S. troops by the end of June, Congressional antiwar maneuvers increased. On June 24, the Senate voted by a large margin to rescind the Gulf of Tonkin Resolution. This resolution had given the president essentially a blank check to repel armed attack on U.S. forces. It was passed in August 1964 after President Johnson charged that North Vietnamese torpedo boats had attacked U.S. destroyers off the coast of North Vietnam on two occasions for no valid reason. Later, it was learned that Johnson had misled both Congress and the American people in his account of the alleged attacks: U.S. ships may not have been in international waters; they were providing communications assistance for South Vietnamese raids on the North; and at least on the second occasion, there was doubt whether attacks on U.S. ships had actually occurred.

The Senate Foreign Relations Committee accused Nixon of usurping Congress's war-making powers by failing to consult with it before ordering the incursion into Cambodia. It concluded that Nixon was "conducting a constitutionally unauthorized war in Indo-China." On June 30, the Senate approved an amendment sponsored by Senator Frank Church (D, Idaho) and John Sherman Cooper (R, Ky.) to terminate all funds for U.S. military operations in Cambodia after that date. This was the first time that Congress had ever acted to restrict presidential military actions during a war, albeit undeclared. The Senate narrowly defeated a proposal by Senator George McGovern (D, S.D.) and Mark Hatfield (D, Oreg.) to withdraw U.S. soldiers from Indo-China by June 30, 1971. Finally in 1973, Congress passed the War Powers Resolution over Nixon's veto. This resolution, in essence, stated that the president could not send U.S. troops into combat without congressional authorization.

Nixon fought back. He told his staff: "Don't worry about divisiveness. Having drawn the sword, don't take it out—stick it in hard."[46] He then warned that Congress would have to face the consequences if any restrictions it put on him cost American lives.

Rejecting congressional criticism that his decision was an illegal use of presidential power, he called the Cooper-Church and McGovern-Hatfield amendments unconstitutional. The president maintained that as commander-in-chief he had the constitutional authority to order the Cambodian operation to protect U.S. troops. Thus, he did not have to consult Congress first. He argued he was acting just like President Kennedy had when he made secret moves in the Cuban Missile Crisis. Nixon also denied that his decision violated international law. U.S. troops were not *invading* Cambodia, but were participating with ARVN troops in an *incursion*. Moreover, this incursion was justified because Cambodia had failed in its responsibility as an independent state to prevent foreign troops on its territory from supplying a combatant in a neighboring state.

Nixon also decided to spy further on his critics. On June 5, he approved the Huston Plan.[47] This authorized intelligence agencies to find security risks by spying on individual Americans suspected of being a "threat to the internal security," reading their mail, and intercepting and transcribing their communication. Huston recognized the illegality of the president's orders and their abuse of civil liberties, but he agreed with Nixon that the ends justified the means. Senator Sam Ervin (D, N.C.) called this plan evidence of a "Gestapo mentality." Nixon later told interviewer David Frost that "when the president does it, that means it is not illegal." This hubris was indicative of the president's hard-headed, combative leadership style.[48]

Decision Options

President Nixon rejected a number of options before deciding on the incursion into Cambodia:

1. *Unilateral U.S. withdrawal from Indo-China*
   To Nixon, this option was out of the question because it would have meant defeat and humiliation. Senator George Aiken (R, Vermont) had proposed an interesting variation of this option: the United States should leave Indo-China and declare victory. This would have gotten Nixon off the hook of becoming the first president to lose a war. But a U.S. declara-

tion of victory would not have been credible, so this proposal was rejected. Another related option was a variant on Nixon's Vietnamization policy: acceptance of Hanoi's demand for a fixed timetable for withdrawal of all U.S. forces, not just combat troops. But Nixon wanted to withdraw at his own pace. He also believed that acceptance of this demand would have removed any incentive for North Vietnam to negotiate an end to the war.

2. *Use of nuclear weapons*

U.S. policy was not to use nuclear weapons. Nixon maintained that he "gave no serious consideration to the nuclear option."[49] A variant of this option, which Nixon did consider and at least partially exercised, was the "madman strategy" of threatening the use of nuclear weapons to force North Vietnam to negotiate more on his terms. One problem in this regard was credibility: how could Nixon demonstrate he was *seriously* considering use of nuclear weapons? The more direct question, however, was whether using nuclear weapons was necessary for U.S. national security. The clear answer was no.

3. *Nonnuclear escalation of the war*

Nixon did consider recommendations by the military for escalation, which included blockading Haiphong, bombing dikes in the North, and invading North Vietnam. But the president rejected these plans mainly, perhaps, because of his fear of the response of the antiwar movement.

4. *Declaration of war against North Vietnam*

On May 6, 1970, several days after Nixon announced the incursion into Cambodia, Senator Jacob Javits (R, N.Y.) asked him how Congress could "properly manifest our will." Nixon replied: "The cleanest way is to declare war, but that would be a great mistake." He added that Congress, through the appropriate power, could control the president's action, but "I don't see what purpose another declaration or resolution would serve."[50] Nixon realized that Congress was increasingly in an antiwar mood, so it was hardly likely to declare war. A related problem was deciding against whom war could be declared. Certainly not the Soviet Union or Communist China or both countries, even though Nixon believed aid from them was essential for North Vietnam's prosecution of the war. Should Congress declare war on the Viet Cong? To do this would contradict Nixon's position that the United States was intervening in a war of aggression launched by North Vietnam, not in a civil war in South Vietnam.

5. *Calling for another international conference on Indo-China*

France was the leading proponent of this proposal. Nixon never seriously considered it, however, because he was determined to demonstrate his firmness to Hanoi. Perhaps Nixon would have considered this option later on.

6. *Bring back Sihanouk to rule Cambodia and restore its limited but acceptable neutrality.* But Nixon preferred to rely on supporting Lon Nol, who was more receptive to U.S. aid. To Nixon, moreover, the fact that Sihanouk then was residing in Peking also seemed to rule out his further usefulness.

7. *Strengthen the Lon Nol government*

The argument of this option was that a stronger Cambodia could better resist North Vietnam's use of its territory for sanctuaries and bases. To strengthen Cambodia, Washington could have pressured Thailand and South Vietnam to drop their border claims against Cambodia, or have asked Australia to send Lon Nol significant amounts of military advisers and economic aid. But this option would have complicated Vietnamization and probably have widened the war even more.

Nixon decided to focus on eliminating COSVN, which he considered necessary for success of Vietnamization. Once Nixon decided to respond to North Vietnam's use of sanctuaries and base areas in Cambodia with a show of force, he had to decide how to use force. In early April 1970, in addition to presenting Nixon with three military alternatives discussed previously, General Abrams asked Nixon to send Daniel Boone teams deeper into Cambodia, to be followed by a month of tactical air strikes that would be kept secret "to preclude compromise." The president was not yet sure what to do.

Nixon decided not to use force to block North Vietnam's escape route westward into the heart of Cambodia. Nor would he authorize blockading Cambodian ports and airports in order to interdict North Vietnam's supplies to South Vietnam. These two options would take more time than Nixon wanted, which would open him up for more criticism from Congress and the antiwar movement. Nixon's goal, moreover, was to push North Vietnam's troops away from South Vietnam and reduce U.S. casualties rather than to protect Cambodian civilians. The president thus boxed himself into choosing which military operation he would order in eastern Cambodia, and whether the United States should use its own troops.

In late April, Secretary Laird, once he realized Nixon had decided to make an "incursion" into Cambodia, tried to limit the military action. Laird favored an attack on the Parrot's Beak by South Vietnamese forces, aided by U.S. advisers. Nixon called Laird "the most pusillani-

mous little nit-picker I ever saw."[51] Nixon had already decided on a
"big play philosophy" meant to "go for all the marbles." When Nixon
mentioned to Kissinger that he wanted not only to send U.S. forces with
the ARVN into both the Parrot's Beak and Fish Hook areas, but also to
mine Haiphong and bomb Hanoi, Kissinger restrained him, telling the
president they already had "enough on their plates."

Several of Nixon's foreign policy advisers on the NSC argued
against an invasion of eastern Cambodia to destroy North Vietnam's
sanctuaries. Lawrence Lynn, for example, maintained that a U.S. invasion with ARVN troops would drive North Vietnam deeper into Cambodia, leaving South Vietnam more open and vulnerable to a Viet Cong
offensive.[52] Then, using a cost-benefit analysis, he contended that the
"same resources could more effectively be used in South Vietnam." He
added that "the costs on the ground—mainly human costs [on the civilian population] were going to be devastating."[53] Lynn thus was also
making a *moral* case against the invasion. Roger Morris warned
Kissinger about the domestic consequences of an invasion, which
would surely fire up the waning antiwar movement. Anthony Lake[54]
argued that "you don't invade a sovereign country." Lake, Morris, and
Winston Lord argued that the U.S. goal should be a neutral Cambodia,
albeit one that might allow some "cross-border skirmishes." William
Watts was opposed because he believed the incursion into Cambodia
would lead to unending escalation, which soon would include an invasion of Laos and a blockade of Haiphong. Lynn, Morris, Lake, Watts,
and other advisers soon resigned in protest over Nixon's decision. They
were worried not only about its dubious wisdom , but also about
Nixon's excessive drinking, wiretapping, and paranoia.

Nixon's Leadership Role in the Decision

Nixon made his decision mainly to demonstrate to Hanoi, Moscow, and
Peking that he had the resolve to stand strong against any test of U.S. will
and character. As Nixon himself put it: "If we fail to meet this challenge,
all other nations will be on notice that despite its overwhelming power
the United States, when a real crisis comes, will be found wanting."

Nixon believed in resolute decision-making. He would not be
swayed by public protests or criticism from Congress or the media. It
was necessary to stand strong for principle and against his enemies,
both at home and abroad. Officially, he tried to ignore antiwar critics or
mute their criticism. Sometimes he denounced them as "bums," and

sometimes he courted them by letter writing or meetings. As regards public opinion in general, Nixon felt it should follow the president, not lead him.

Nixon repeatedly watched the movie *Patton*, and at times asked Kissinger and other foreign policy aides to watch it with him. Nixon admired Patton's defiant and independent will, which held fast no matter the odds or opposition. Ambrose describes Nixon's attraction to Patton in these words:

> To millions of American males of all ages, George S. Patton, Jr., is the essence of maleness. Tough, decisive, self-confident, willing to take great risks for great gains, trusting in his intuition, impatient of restraint, a student and practioner of the art of leadership, bold and brave in his actions, often vulgar in his language, contemptuous of his critics, Patton was the model for innumerable American men and boys, including Richard Nixon.[55]

Pointing to another dimension of Nixon the leader, Morris observed that memoranda from Nixon to Kissinger showed Nixon as "a man angry and obsessed with the idea that the other side was trying to push him around" in Cambodia.[56] Nixon was always suspicious that critics inside the government were trying to sabotage his decisions, such as the secret bombing and incursion into Cambodia. As noted previously, he thus ordered the FBI and CIA to wiretap phones of certain advisers as well as journalists, ostensibly to find out who was "leaking" information.

Nixon desperately wanted to maintain the secrecy of numerous operations in the Indo-China war such as the bombing of Cambodia, Daniel Boone squads operating inside Cambodia, and support for Meo tribesmen in Laos. He also was obsessed with secret decision-making, which led to falsification of Pentagon records (e.g., the number of battlefield deaths and North Vietnamese troop strength) and outright lies. Supposedly, this was necessary to maintain secrecy and forestall congressional and antiwar criticism.

Officially, Nixon made foreign policy decisions through the NSC. By the time he made his decision for an incursion into Cambodia, Kissinger had acquired exceptional power in foreign policy decision-making. He had done so through his personal access to the president, his screening of ideas and persons, and his controlling what the bureaucracy examined.

As Kissinger gained more influence with Nixon, Secretaries Laird and Rogers lost influence. Kissinger centralized decision-making in the White House and avoided other possible advisory channels such as the Pentagon and State Department. To ensure secrecy, Nixon set up dual systems of communication ("back channels") to transmit and receive messages from Indo-China. This was designed also to bypass critics of his decisions. Nixon would communicate through "back channels" to General Abrams in Saigon or through the sympathetic JCS, thereby by-passing Laird and Rogers. Kissinger had his own power rivalry with Rogers, whom he increasingly kept in the dark.

When Nixon made his decision for the incursion into Cambodia, he relied on a small group of supporters to advise him. This included Kissinger, Agnew, Haig, Bunker, Admiral Moorer, Helms, Haldeman, Mitchell, selected members of Congress such as Senators Russell and Stennis, and close friend Charles "Bebe" Rebozo.

When Nixon felt that Kissinger may have been having second thoughts about the incursion decision a few days after it began, Nixon told him: "Remember Lot's wife—don't look back." In his memoirs, Kissinger wrote not only about Nixon's resoluteness, but also his lone-liness and failure to solicit criticism which he always took personally, not constructively. According to Kissinger, Nixon

> was prepared to make decisions without illusion. Once convinced, he went ruthlessly and courageously to the heart of the matter; but each controversial decision drove him deeper into his all-encompassing solitude. He was almost physically unable to con-front people who disagreed with him; and he shunned persuading or inspiring his subordinates. He would decide from inside his self-imposed cocoon, but he was unwilling to commu-nicate with those who disagreed. It was the paradox of a President strong in his decision but inconclusive in his leadership. Making and enforcing decision left so many scars on him and others that it sacrificed administrative cohesion on the altar of executive discre-tion; it perversely created the maximum incentive for strong-willed subordinates to evade his directives. Since Nixon disavowed any effort to instill a team spirit and usually kept his designs to himself, his Cabinet was tempted to exaggerate its au-tonomy. This in turn reinforced his conviction that the bureau-cracy did not support him; it surely went out of its way to carry out the spirit of his orders. All this became a vicious circle in

which the President withdrew even more into his isolation and pulled the central decisions increasingly into the White House, in turn heightening the resentment and defiant mood of his appointees.[57]

Although Nixon considered his decision to make an incursion into Cambodia just and justifiable, controversy lingers over its wisdom. Safire's view is representative of those who praised Nixon's decision. He called it "the turning point of the war in Vietnam, making possible "peace with honor," not an altogether unworthy goal." Safire then added this lofty praise:

> Contrary to the fears of many doves, this move was part of the steady Vietnamization of the war—not an escalation of the war. Given his long-range plan, Nixon made his best decision at the crucial moment; the "incursion" was daring, surprising, successful in the short run and successful in the long run.[58]

Representatives of the severe critics of Nixon's decision is Clark Clifford, presidential adviser under Truman and secretary of defense under Johnson. Clifford called it "reckless," "foolhardy," and "an infinitely greater mistake" than Kennedy's Bay of Pigs decision.[59]

The debate over Nixon's decision continues. What is clear, however, is that it lends credence to a major conclusion of *The Pentagon Papers*, released publicly in 1971 over Nixon's opposition, that rejected the "quagmire theory." This theory held that the United States got caught in a web of events and circumstances largely beyond its control that sucked it deeper and deeper into the Indo-China War. Instead, as Nixon's Cambodia decision indicates, the United States escalated this war consciously and willingly, with far-reaching consequences at home and abroad.

Consequences of Nixon's Decision for the United States and Other Countries Involved

The United States

Nixon's decision had a profound affect on U.S. domestic politics. Student demonstrations and protests swept college campuses. Most shocking was the killing of four students and the wounding of eleven others at Kent State University by Ohio's National Guard. There were calls for Nixon's impeachment and for Kissinger's resignation. Kissinger was pilloried by many of his former colleagues from Harvard University and others in the academic community who were exasperated by his complicity in Nixon's decision.

Nixon claimed military success. In late May he called the operation "the most successful operation of this long and difficult war." Nixon took pride in commenting how U.S. troops went into and out of Cambodia "on schedule," leaving by June 30. Moreover, according to the president, the incursion supposedly "dealt a crushing blow to North Vietnam's military campaign in the Mekong Delta region"; it "saved Lon Nol's government and thereby ensured that the port of Sihanoukville would remain closed to Communist arms shipments"; it effected a significant drop in U.S. casualties in Vietnam; and most "most important, . . . it achieved the Operation's 2 main goals: prevention of the fall of Cambodia and relief of pressure on Phnom Penh."[60]

Critics, however, argued that the Cambodian operation:

1. Added Cambodia as another U.S. client state in Indo-China. The United States was supporting the corrupt Lon Nol government in Cambodia just as it was supporting the corrupt Thieu government in South Vietnam.
2. Enlarged the war when the United States was trying to de-escalate. When the Cambodian operation failed to convince Hanoi to negotiate an "honorable" end to the war, Nixon escalated further. In early 1971, ARVN forces invaded Laos. This was to be a "test" of Vietnamization, but the invasion failed and was over in five weeks. Later, when North Vietnam launched an offensive in the spring of 1972, Nixon escalated further by bombing North Vietnam and blockading and mining Haiphong.
3. Hurt rather than helped chances for serious negotiations to end the war.
4. Led Nixon to stress alleged military success of the operation even though COSVN, the main military target, was never located and North Vietnamese sanctuaries were neither wiped out nor seriously weakened. But, like official U.S. reaction to the Tet Offensive in 1968, Nixon seriously underestimated the *political* consequences of his decision.

The Cambodian operation, like Tet, proved to be a great political victory for North Vietnam. General Giap's strategy, following Mao

Tse-tung's, aimed at protracted conflict that would wear down the enemy over a period of time and erode his will to fight. But unlike Mao, Giap also stressed the international political context of the war: whenever public opinion inside and outside the United States seriously criticized Washington's war effort, this would be a victory for North Vietnam and the Viet Cong. The Cambodian operation led to severe criticism of Nixon's war policy, which shortened the war to Hanoi's advantage.

Nixon's Cambodian decision contributed to what pundits called the "Vietnam syndrome:" Presidents would be reluctant to send troops abroad for fear of becoming drawn into another "quagmire." This was seen, for example, in President Gerald Ford's and Jimmy Carter's reluctance to send U.S. forces into such troublespots as the civil war in Angola and guerrilla wars in Central America . Only years later, after the Persian Gulf War, did President Bush claim that the United States had finally "kicked" the "Vietnam syndrome."

Cambodia

The Cambodian operation clearly widened the Indo-China War by exposing Cambodia's territory and civilian population to massive bombing and fighting. As in South Vietnam, this ruined the lush countryside and caused despair among the people. It also forced North Vietnam to move outside its sanctuaries in Cambodia into the heartland, spreading from about one quarter of the country to over half. Soon Cambodia was fully involved in the war. To counter beefed-up U.S. support for Lon Nol and his army, Hanoi stepped up its arming and training of the Khmer Rouge. A terrible civil war ensued.

After the Peace Accord of January 1973, despite Hanoi's pressure, the Khmer Rouge refused to negotiate a peace. Lon Nol's regime finally fell in 1975. The Khmer Rouge, led by the fanatical communist Pol Pol, then went on one of the bloodiest campaigns in history. His radical, maniacal policies, designed to eradicate all vestiges of capitalism, led to the sickening "killing fields." About 1.5 million Cambodians (some say up to 3 million, out of a population of about 7 million) died from famine, forced labor, disease, and brutal execution.[61]

Sihanouk placed the blame for Cambodia's tragedy squarely on Nixon and Kissinger: "There are only 2 men responsible for the tragedy in Cambodia," the Prince lamented, "Mr. Nixon and Dr. Kissinger. Lon Nol was nothing without them, and the Khmer Rouge were nothing without Lon Nol. They demoralized America. They lost all of Indo-China to the communists, and they created the Khmer Rouge."[62]

Would the communists, if not for the Cambodian incursion, have forcefully taken over Cambodia "years earlier" as Kissinger claims? This is now a moot point. What clearly did occur, however, was one of history's greatest horrors, tragedies, and catastrophes.

Conclusion

Before Nixon became president, he announced that he had a secret plan to end the Vietnam War. He was determined that the war would end according to his concept of honor and justice. To achieve this goal, he believed he had to demonstrate strength and resoluteness of purpose. Like his predecessors in the Oval Office, the president viewed the Vietnam War as part of a worldwide struggle against international communism directed by the Soviet Union. His main strategy, based largely on the *realpolitik* advice of Henry Kissinger, his most influential adviser on national security, was "linkage." Holding up détente as an inducement to the Kremlin, he unsuccessfully pressed Moscow to influence Hanoi to agree to a peaceful settlement of the war. In pursuit of the same elusive goal, he also opened up U.S. relations with the PRC and tried to derive benefits from the Sino-Soviet rift.

Nixon was cognizant of growing domestic criticism. Although he always insisted he would not be influenced by the antiwar movement, he realized that politically he had to end the Vietnam War as soon as possible. His dilemma was how to do this without appearing weak and without the United States being seen as a "pitiful giant." Relying on support from the "silent majority" of Americans, the president utilized a variety of measures to end the war: "Vietnamization" of the war effort; increased military pressure on Hanoi (such as stepped up bombing of the Ho Chi Minh Trail); continuation of the secret war in neighboring Laos; initiation of secret bombing of Cambodia; and his eventual decision to launch an "incursion" into Cambodia. This was done mainly to cut off the enemy's use of that country as a sanctuary and to locate and destroy COSVN, the supposed enemy headquarters. Because of the frequent disparity between official pronouncements about the war and realities, Nixon became plagued by a "credibility gap." To eliminate this gap, Nixon became obsessed with secrecy. He took all sorts of measures, many of questionable legality, to prevent "leaks" from his advisers and journalists.

Sending troops into Cambodia was one of the most controversial presidential decisions of the Vietnam War. It injected renewed anger and fury into the domestic antiwar movement, especially on college campuses. Its impact on the war itself remains a matter of debate. Nixon claimed the incursion was a great success, as it sent an important message of strength to the enemy. Critics, however, pointed to a widenening and prolongation of the war that led to the horror of Pol Pot's "killing fields."

Questions for Discussion

1. Do you agree more with William Safire's or Clark Clifford's assessment of Nixon's decision?

2. Did Nixon's decision contravene the "Nixon Doctrine" as charged?

3. Do you think it was permissible for Nixon to lie and deceive Congress and the American public over secret operations in Cambodia? Do covert operations sometimes require government lies to protect them?

4. Why did Nixon secretly bomb Cambodia? Do you agree with his reasons for this?

5. Do you think Nixon was right to order wiretaps on government aides and journalists to detect information leaks?

6. Did Nixon have the constitutional authority he claimed to order U.S. troops into Cambodia?

7. Was the "incursion" into Cambodia in reality an "invasion" of that country?

8. Could Nixon have prevented the "fall" of Cambodia to the Khmer Rouge?

9. Should Nixon shoulder any blame, as charged, for Pol Pot's "killing fields" in Cambodia?

10. If you were a college student at the time of Nixon's decision, how would you have reacted to Nixon's decision? Would you have supported the president? Demonstrated against the decision? Burned your draft card? Fled to Canada? Done nothing at all?

Notes

1. Henry Kissinger, "The Vietnam Negotiations," *Foreign Affairs*, 47 (January 1969): 219.
2. Quoted in Stanley Karnow, *Vietnam: A History* (New York: Penguin, 1983), p. 582.
3. "Vietnamization" was a term decided by Melvin Laird, Nixon's secretary of defense, who thought it sounded better than "de-Americanization." This strategy was reluctantly initiated by Johnson at the end of his presidency.
4. Richard Nixon, *RN: The Memoirs of Richard Nixon* (New York: Touchstone, 1990), p. 391.
5. Ibid., pp. 393–94.
6. Ibid., p. 393; and Seymour Hersh, *The Price of Power: Kissinger in the Nixon White House* (New York: Summit, 1983), p. 120.
7. Hersh, ibid.
8. Ibid., p. 121.
9. Nixon, p. 396.
10. William Safire, *Before the Fall: An Inside View of the Pre-Watergate White House* (New York: Ballantine, 1977), p. 217.
11. Nixon, p. 403.
12. Ibid.
13. Ibid., p. 410.
14. According to Kissinger, Sihanouk gave his permission reluctantly. See Kissinger, *White House Years* (Boston: Little, Brown and Co., 1979), p. 250.
15. These Daniel Boone teams operated throughout the sixties, without the knowledge of Congress. Originally institutionalized under the name Salem House, these teams were authorized to go thirty kilometers inside Cambodia and to plant "sanitized self-destruct antipersonnel" land mines. Their main goal was intelligence gathering. See William Shawcross, *Sideshow: Kissinger, Nixon and the Destruction of Cambodia* (New York: Simon & Schuster, 1979), p. 31.
16. Hersh, p. 58.
17. Nixon, p. 380.
18. Ibid., p. 382.
19. Nixon, *No More Vietnams* (New York: Arbor House, 1985), p. 110.
20. See Stephen Ambrose, *Nixon: The Triumph of a Politician 1962–1972* (New York: Simon & Schuster, 1989), pp. 272–73. Ambrose quoted Nixon aide John Erlichman who recalled that Nixon used to use the Jewish traitor issue to play off Kissinger, who also was Jewish. Kissinger supposedly replied: "Well, Mr. President, there are Jews and Jews." Halperin later sued Kissinger on the wiretapping and years later won his case.
21. Nixon, *RN: The Memoirs of Richard Nixon*, p. 382.
22. Walter Isaacson, *Kissinger: A Biography* (New York: Simon & Schuster, 1992), p. 258; Karnow, p. 606.
23. Kissinger, *White House Years*, p. 453.

24. Because the bombing never succeeded in significant interdiction of supplies, in the summer of 1970 Nixon planned for the Army of the Republic of South Vietnam (ARVN) forces to invade Laos. The ARVN began its invasion in January 1971. Though this invasion ended in failure after forty-four days, the officially announced boast, in Premier Nguyen Van Thieu's words, was that it was ARVN's "biggest victory ever."

25. Nixon, *No More Vietnams*, p. 116.

26. Ibid., p. 118.

27. Ibid., p. 119.

28. Marvin Kalb and Bernard Kalb, *Kissinger* (New York: Dell, 1975), p. 181.

29. According to the hypothesis of Irving L. Janis, individual members of a decision-making group tend to try to avoid friction that would result from strong presentation of differing positions and to seek conformity and consensus instead. This phenomenon, according to Janis, resulted in several costly errors of group decisions such as the Bay of Pigs invasion and escalation of the Korean War across the 38th parallel. See Janis, *Victims of Groupthink* (Boston: Houghton-Mifflin, 1972).

30. Kalb and Kalb, p. 182.

31. Safire, p. 232.

32. Quoted in Ambrose, p. 341.

33. Isaacson, p. 261.

34. Safire, p. 232.

35. Nixon, *RN: The Memoirs of Richard Nixon*, p. 450.

36. Ibid., pp. 449–50.

37. I. F. Stone, *Polemics and Prophecies, 1967–1970* (New York: Random House, 1970), pp. 402–3. Isaacson called the last example cited by Stone "an outright lie." See Isaacson, p. 268.

38. Kissinger, *White House Years*, pp. 504–5.

39. Nixon, *No More Vietnams*, p. 120.

40. Hersh, pp. 193–94.

41. Quoted in Shawcross, p. 76.

42. Nixon, *No More Vietnams*, pp. 104–6.

43. Kissinger, *White House Years*, p. 129.

44. Ibid.

45. Nixon, *No More Vietnams*, p. 106.

46. Safire, p. 242.

47. This plan was named after Tom Huston, a former Army intelligence officer who served on the White House's Internal Security Committee.

48. Shawcross, pp. 157–60.

49. Nixon, *No More Vietnams*, p. 101.

50. Safire, p. 247.

51. Karnow, p. 608.

52. Hersh, p. 188.

53. Isaacson, p. 264.

54. Lake served later as President Clinton's national security adviser.
55. Ambrose, p. 322.
56. Hersh, p. 189.
57. Kissinger, *White House Years*, pp. 482–83.
58. Safire, p. 239.
59. See Clark Clifford, *Counsel to the President* (New York: Anchor, 1992), pp. 609–11.
60. Nixon, *No More Vietnams*, pp. 121–22.
61. See Neil Sheehan, *A Bright, Shining Light* (New York: Vintage, 1988), pp. 745–47.
62. Quoted by Isaacson, p. 273.

Selected Bibliography

Ambrose, Stephen. *Nixon: The Triumph of a Politician, 1962–1972*. New York: Simon & Schuster, 1989.

Clifford, Clark. *Counsel to the President*. New York: Anchor, 1992.

Gettleman, Marvin, Jane Franklin, Marilyn Young, and H. Bruce Franklin (eds.). *Vietnam and America: A Documentary History*. New York: Grove Press, 1985.

Hersh, Seymour. *The Price of Power: Kissinger in the Nixon White House*. New York: Summit, 1993.

Isaacson, Walter. *Kissinger: A Biography*. New York: Simon & Schuster, 1992.

Kalb, Marvin and Bernard Kalb. *Kissinger*. New York: Dell, 1975.

Karnow, Stanley. *Vietnam: A History*. New York: Penguin, 1983.

Kissinger, Henry. *White House Years*. Boston: Little, Brown and Co., 1979.

Nixon, Richard. *No More Vietnams*. New York: Arbor House, 1985.

———. *RN: The Memoirs of Richard Nixon*. New York: Touchstone, 1990.

Safire, William. *Before the Fall: An Inside View of the Pre-Watergate White House*. New York: Ballantine, 1977.

Shawcross, William. *Sideshow: Kissinger, Nixon, and the Destruction of Cambodia*. New York: Simon & Schuster, 1979.

Sheehan, Neil. *A Bright, Shining Light*. New York: Vintage, 1988.

6

President Ford's Decision to Intervene in the Angolan Civil War

Setting and Overview of Ford's Decision

In early 1975, a full-scale civil war broke out in Angola, a Central African state, as it moved toward formal political independence from Portuguese colonial rule. The conflict involved the struggle between the MPLA (the Popular Movement for the Liberation of Angola) and two allied rival organizations: UNITA (the Union for the Total Independence of Angola) and the FNLA (the National Front for the Liberation of Angola).

The Angolan civil war had significant implications for U.S. foreign policy. The Marxist-oriented MPLA was receiving political and military support from the Soviet Union, Cuba, and other communist countries. UNITA and the FNLA were supported by the United States and other Western countries, China and other Soviet-dominated countries.

By the middle of 1975, it appeared that the MPLA was on the verge of defeating its rivals and was gaining momentum to formally take over control of the country from the Portuguese colonial regime on November 11, 1975. From the perspective of the Cold War, this would be regarded as a "gain" for the Soviet Union and its allies and a setback for the United States and the West.

In July 1975, President Ford authorized the CIA to secretly intervene against the MPLA and support its opponents. This intervention involved the provision of financial and military resources to defeat the MPLA and its Soviet, Cuban, and other supporters.

The covert intervention caused dissension in the executive branch, Congress, and the foreign policy establishment. In the end, Congress defeated President Ford's efforts to prevent Soviet and Cuban gains in Angola through covert political and military means.

President Ford's Decision

ON JULY 18, 1975, PRESIDENT GERALD FORD SENT CONGRESS A SECRET "FINDING" FORMALLY COMMUNICATING HIS DECISION TO INITIATE COVERT ACTIVITIES IN ANGOLA IN SUPPORT OF TWO FACTIONS INVOLVED IN THE ONGOING AND ESCALATING ANGOLAN CIVIL WAR. THE FINDING DID NOT SPECIFY THE COUNTRY OR THE EXACT NATURE OF THE ACTIVITIES TO BE UNDERTAKEN. ON THE SAME DAY, HE AUTHORIZED THE RELEASE OF $6 MILLION FOR THE OPERATION TO BE UNDERTAKEN BY THE CIA.

President Ford's decision was controversial because:

1. If U.S. national interests were considered important enough to justify intervention, the aid to the two factions in Angola should have been overt and publicly debated, rather than clandestine.
2. The use of covert means meant that Congress and the public could not easily debate the merits of the policy decision.
3. The necessarily limited nature of the covert operation limited its effectiveness. To succeed, the initiative would have had to be broadened. This threatened to lead the United States into a Third World civil war and possibly another Vietnam.
4. A violent test of wills with the Soviets and Cubans, using surrogates, would intensify deaths and suffering among the Angolan people.
5. Diplomacy coordinated with African and European states and international organizations should have been given a chance to resolve the Angolan civil war.
6. The South African apartheid (segregationist) government was already involved in the civil war on the side of the MPLA's opponents. U.S. intervention on the same side would taint its image in Africa and elsewhere.
7. The Angolan operation was another instance of secret foreign policy making which in the past had resulted in failure and embarrassment.

Background of the Decision

Historical Context

The emergence of the Cold War thrust the United States into a global role as the spearhead of resistance to the spread of Soviet and communist power. This role involved United States military, political, and economic activities in virtually every part of the world.

Until the 1970s, Africa was of limited strategic and political concern. Until the late 1950s and early 1960s, with the exception of South Africa, Liberia, and Ethiopia, Africa was under the colonial domination of West European powers allied with the United States. The colonial status of these territories ensured that communism had limited opportunities to penetrate the continent.

All of the three independent African states had close political, economic, and military relations with the United States. Throughout most of the period of the Cold War, they were all firmly within the Western camp.

Internal political developments in Africa during the 1960s and 1970s created situations which intensified U.S. involvement in the region. Anticolonial nationalism and violent resistance against the apartheid regime in Southern Africa, and irredentist nationalism and revolution in the northeastern part of the continent—the "Horn of Africa"—turned large parts of the continent into global crisis regions.[1] American policy attempted to counter perceived communist political inroads resulting from these crises.

The Problem of Southern Africa

The southern region of Africa includes Angola, Zambia, Mozambique, Zimbabwe (formerly Rhodesia), Swaziland, Botswana, Lesotho, South Africa, and Namibia (formerly Southwest Africa). This area posed special and complex problems for the United States and other Western countries in the context of the Cold War.

By the mid-1970s, European colonial powers had withdrawn from most of Africa. Nevertheless, in Southern Africa the European colonial regime continued in the form of Portuguese imperialism in Angola and Mozambique. In South Africa, under the apartheid regime, millions of nonwhites, constituting the majority of the population, were subjected to political, economic, and social segregation and domination.[2] And in neighboring Rhodesia, the minority White population had seized power in 1965 and continued to dominate the African majority.

Southern Africa was also one of the few areas in Africa where there were substantial U.S. investments, particularly in the mineral industry. American corporations had significant investments in the diamonds, copper, iron ore, gold, uranium, and other subterranean resources of Angola, Rhodesia, South Africa, and Southwest Africa.

The conflict between African anticolonial nationalism and the Portuguese and white regimes had led to violent confrontation and brutal repression. The Portuguese in Angola and Mozambique and the Rhodesian regime were fighting active insurgencies in the 1970s.

The United States and other Western countries faced a dilemma in attempting to reconcile the demands of their global Cold War strategy with the protection of their economic and political interests in the region. Portugal was an ally in the anti-communist North Atlantic Treaty Organization (NATO) and the white regimes of Southern Africa were militantly anti-communist. African nationalists increasingly sought political and military assistance from the Cold War adversaries of the Western countries, namely the Soviet Union, China, and other communist countries.

Pragmatic considerations compelled the U.S. and Western leaders to resist the temptation to give open political support to the Portuguese and the white regimes. In the context of the East-West struggle, the continued existence of the colonial and minority white regimes was the chink in the Western ideological armor. Overt support for them would alienate the Africans and other Third World people and drive them into the Soviet and Chinese embrace.

U.S. Policy toward Angola before the Ford Administration

In the late 1950s and early 1960s, the main policy issue for the United States in Angola was the conflict between African anticolonial nationalism and the recalcitrant Portuguese colonial regime. Unlike other Western colonial powers, Portugal regarded its colonies as "overseas provinces" which could not be separated through a grant of independence.

In the 1950s, the Eisenhower administration refrained from criticizing Portugal for its refusal to accept decolonization of its African and Asian territories. The main considerations were Portugal's membership in NATO and the fear of losing access to the important U.S. military base on the Azores islands which the U.S. leased from Portugal. Shortly before President Eisenhower left office, the United States abstained in a December 1960 United Nations vote in favor of self-determination for the Portuguese colonies.[3]

President John Kennedy had a more sympathetic view of African anticolonial nationalism. Nevertheless, he did not ignore the Cold War dimensions of the decolonization movement.

The first test of Kennedy's convictions came in Angola. In March 1961, there was an uprising against the Portuguese colonial regime in the north of the country, organized by the Uniao das Populacaoes de Angola (Angolan Peoples Union—UPA), a forerunner of the FNLA. It was brutally suppressed by the colonial authorities at a cost of thousands of Angolan lives. When the issue was discussed in the United Nations Security Council, Kennedy instructed Ambassador Adlai Stevenson to vote against Portugal. Rhetorically at least, this action gave the impression of placing the United States for the first time on the side of the nationalists.[4]

During the Kennedy administration, U.S. policy began to support United Nations resolutions condemning Portuguese colonialism in the United Nations while resisting more forceful measures, such as arms embargoes or economic sanctions. This was a tactical stance. The calculation was that since the communist bloc also supported the anticolonial movements, U.S. support, even if largely rhetorical, would prevent the complete alignment of African anticolonial nationalism with communism. At the same time, U.S. and Western economic and political interests in Southern Africa would be protected.

Following the 1961 armed revolt against the Portuguese, the United States began to supply UPA with nonmilitary supplies. Its leader, Holden Roberto, was put on the CIA payroll. From 1969, he was reportedly receiving a yearly stipend of $10,000 for "intelligence gathering."[5] American officials accompanied their covert support of Roberto with rhetorical support for Angolan independence.[6]

In 1962, President Kennedy ordered the U.S. ambassador to Portugal to offer up to $70 million in direct aid in exchange for negotiating the eventual independence of its colonies. The offer was rejected.[7] Portugal still clung to its colonial possessions.

In the end, Cold War strategic considerations prevented President Kennedy from going beyond rhetorical support for Angolan self-determination. By the time Kennedy was assassinated in November 1963, the pro-NATO and "anti-Angolan nationalist" elements within the government had gained the upper hand on the issue.[8]

The Johnson administration continued the policy of giving verbal support to the principle of Angolan self-determination while maintaining political and strategic cooperation with the Portuguese colonial regime. However, Johnson's policy tilted towards Portugal. In 1965, the CIA began to deliver to Portugal military aircraft equipped for jungle warfare. This support was important for Portugal's antiguerrilla campaigns in the African colonies.[9]

Between 1962 and 1968, the United States provided Portugal with $39 million in military and $124 million in economic assistance. Hundreds of Portuguese troops received military training from U.S. instructors in Portugal or at bases in the United States.[10]

The Nixon-Kissinger Approach to Southern Africa

Prior to the 1968 presidential election, Richard Nixon had established a reputation as a staunch anti-communist. It was expected that he would enthusiastically support all anti-communist regimes. However, in Southern Africa at least, the situation was too complex for such a simple ideological option. Support for anti-communist regimes could actually increase the prospects for the spread of communist ideas or at least sympathy for the Soviet Union and China.

Shortly after President Nixon came into office, the National Security Council Interdepartmental Group for Africa (involving representatives from the CIA, and the Departments of Defense and State) prepared a comprehensive review of U.S. Southern Africa policy under the direction and guidance of National Security Adviser Henry Kissinger. The result was the National Security Study Memorandum 39 (NSSM 39) originally a secret document which laid out the various policy options required to deal with the contradictory goals of U.S. foreign policy in the region.

NSSN 39 defined U.S. interests in Southern Africa, reviewed past policies, projected future trends, and recommended future policies. The analysis was framed in the context of the Cold War as it affected Africa and the Third World.

The study concluded that U.S. interests in the white-dominated region were "important but not vital." However, in the context of white-black conflict, which was likely to get increasingly violent, protection of these interests associated the United States with the white political regimes and gave the impression of "at least tacit acceptance of racism."

Past U.S. policy had opposed African and Asian demands for stronger international measures, including economic sanctions, against the white regimes. On the other hand, the Soviet Union and China had taken firm positions supporting African independence movements and had made some gains in Africa and the United Nations.[11]

The study identified five broad policy objectives for Southern Africa:

1. Improving the U.S. standing in black Africa and internationally on the race issue.
2. Minimizing the likelihood of escalation of violence in the area and the risk of American involvement.
3. Minimizing the opportunities for the Soviet Union and China to "exploit" the racial issue in the region for propaganda advantage and gain political influence among the black governments and liberation movements.
4. Encouraging "moderation" of the rigid racial and colonial policies of the white regimes.
5. Protecting U.S. economic, scientific, and strategic interests in the region, including the "orderly" marketing of South Africa's gold production.

Five alternative policy options were recommended:

1. Closer association with the white regimes to protect and enhance U.S. economic, strategic, and scientific interests.
2. Broader association with both black and white states in an effort to encourage "moderation" in the white states, enlist cooperation of the black states in reducing tensions and violence, and encourage improved relations among the states of the region.
3. Limited association with the white states and continuing association with the Africans. The aim would be to protect U.S. interests in the white states while supporting the political aspirations of the Africans but attempting to moderate them.
4. Dissociation with the white regimes and seeking closer links with the African states. This would be the opposite of option 1.
5. Dissociation form both black and white states and limited involvement in the region, in effect "walking away" from the problems.

The Nixon administration decided to choose Option 2. This decision was based on the assumption that the white regimes were strong enough to resist African nationalist pressures and that the **status quo** would continue indefinitely. It confidently stated that the African majority could not gain political rights through violence. Change could only come about through the acquiescence of the white regimes.[12]

The new policy involved substantial changes of emphasis, including: the muting of criticism of the white regimes; establishing high-level contacts; protecting them against severe measures in the United Nations; encouraging increased U.S. investments in South Africa; relaxing the UN-mandated arms embargo against the regime and improving relations with Portugal.

In 1969, President Nixon stopped CIA assistance to African anti-colonial movements.[13] In December 1971, he signed an executive agreement with Portugal permitting continued U.S. access to the Azores military facilities in exchange for a credit-loan from the U.S. government Export-Import Bank worth $436 million. Between 1969 and 1972, $108 million worth of American aircraft and helicopters was exported to Portugal, Mozambique, and Angola.[14] American training of Portuguese military personnel and other forms of assistance reflected a more tolerant attitude toward the Portuguese colonial regime.[15]

On April 24, 1974, a group of military officers calling themselves the Armed Forces Movement overthrew the Portuguese government. The new government, which enjoyed support from the Portuguese Communist and Socialist parties, soon recognized the right of the "Overseas Territories" to self-determination, including complete independence.

The military coup in Portugal created a fundamentally novel situation for the white regimes in South Africa and Rhodesia and U.S. foreign policy. For South Africa and Rhodesia, there was danger in the sudden collapse of the buffer which the Portuguese colonies of Angola and Mozambique had provided. Black African regimes were going to rise in those countries.

The military coup in Portugal and the attitude of the new regime toward colonialism undermined one of the basic assumptions of the Kissinger study, namely, the expectation of the indefinite perpetuation of the status quo in Southern Africa. An even more worrying prospect was that African nationalist political movements, which were poised to take over in the region, all had Marxist inclinations or at least received Soviet and Chinese military and political support. Through its close association with the white regimes, U.S. foreign policy appeared to have backed the losing horse.

In Mozambique, there was one dominant political movement which had led the military challenge to Portuguese colonial rule, that is, the Marxist-oriented Frente da Libertacao de Mocambique (FRELIMO—Mozambique Liberation Front). It was the obvious successor to the colonial regime. However, in Angola, the situation was much more complicated.

Background to the Angolan Civil War

The Angolan civil war is directly traceable to the nature of the Portuguese colonial regime. By refusing to consider the legitimacy of African self-determination and independence, Portugal made it inevitable that military force would be the principal instrument to establish an independent Angolan state.[16]

Armed resistance to the Portuguese colonial regime broke out in the early 1960s at a time when most of the rest of the continent was achieving independence from Britain, France, Belgium, and Italy. Three major independent movements based on three distinct regions of Angola waged low-level guerrilla warfare against Portuguese control until the 1974 coup, namely: the MPLA, UNITA, and the FNLA.

The MPLA was formed in 1956 by Marxist and other left-wing Portuguese, mulattoes (Afro-Portuguese), and black Angolans. It was led by Dr. Agostinho Neto and drew most of its support from intellectuals, urbanized Angolans, the mulattoes, and the 1.3 million members of the Mbundu ethnic group of the north-central region.

UNITA, led by Jonas Savimbi, drew most of its support from the 2 million Ovimbundu of the south-central region and related ethnic groups in the south and east of Angola. The FNLA, led by Holden Roberto, was predominantly supported by the 1 million Bakongo ethnic group, which occupied the northern part of the country. Thus, from the beginning, Angolan nationalism was deeply divided by ideological and ethnic conflicts.

By the mid-1970s, the three Angolan independence movements were involved with regional and international sponsors and supporters linked to the Cold War and Chinese-Soviet global rivalry. The MPLA received support from the Soviet Union, Cuba, the East European states aligned with the USSR, and other African and Third World states which were generally opposed to the United States and the West on major international issues. The FNLA initially received backing from radical African and Third World states, such as Guinea and Algeria. Later, it was aided by the United States, China, and Zaire, Angola's neighbor to the north.

Savimbi, UNITA's leader, initially adopted a revolutionary Marxist stance and received Chinese support. Later, he adopted a more eclectic ideological position and received support from a motley collection of states, including Tanzania and Zambia.

The Alvor Accords and the Aftermath

Between April 1974 and January 1975, the Portuguese Armed Forces Movement sought a formula for the decolonization of Angola. As part of this process, it established a provisional administration under a Portuguese high commissioner.

In January 1975, talks between the leaders of all three Angolan movements and Portugal took place in the Portuguese town of Alvor. This led to a set of agreements known as the "Alvor Accords." They stipulated the creation of a transitional government, formed by the three movements. It would make arrangements to write a constitution, organize elections, and create a national army out of their guerrilla forces. Independence would be formally granted by Portugal on November 11, 1975.

In spite of the Alvor Accords, there was a lot of pessimism about the prospects for a peaceful transition to independence. There was already a history of bitter rivalry between the three movements even as they struggled against Portuguese rule. In some cases, there had been armed clashes between the MPLA and the FNLA.[17] To complicate matters further, the Armed Forces Movement generally sympathized with the MPLA, which made it harder for the Portuguese to play a moderating role in the conflict.

Shortly after the military coup in Portugal, each of the liberation movements ended hostilities against the colonial forces. However, they then embarked on vigorous campaigns to recruit soldiers and acquire arms in preparation for what appeared to be an inevitable military contest for power.

Although the transitional coalition government established under the Alvor Accords limped on for some time, no effective cooperation between the independence movements was ever established.

In February, the FNLA moved large numbers of troops into northern Angola and Luanda, the capital and an MPLA political stronghold. Within a short time, armed clashes broke out between the FLNA and the MPLA civilian and military supporters. From that time, the contest for power in postcolonial Angola was transformed into a race for control of Luanda before November 11, the date set for the formal end of Portuguese colonial rule. Throughout most of 1975, prospects for victory seesawed between the MPLA and its allied FNLA and UNITA opponents as a direct result of the nature and level of external involvement.

By July, the MPLA had evicted the FNLA military from Luanda. This led to the flight of most its civilian operatives. Later, UNITA also abandoned the capital. The MPLA military forces pushed out in all directions until, by the end of August they controlled most of the country's provinces and major cities.

Between September and November, the tide shifted against the MPLA. From the north, the FNLA, reinforced by regular Zairian troops and mercenaries recruited by the CIA, were driving toward the capital. From the south, regular South African troops, accompanied by UNITA forces, were rolling up the coast and threatening to seize the capital from that direction. At this time, the MPLA leadership began to give serious consideration to a possible sea evacuation to the Cabinda enclave, which was one of their political strongholds.

Only the timely and massive intervention of 3,000–5,000 well-armed Cuban combat units saved the MPLA from destruction. They mauled the FNLA-Zairian-mercenary units which had reached the northern outskirts of Luanda on the eve of independence day. They also quickly established defense lines against the South African forces in the south and enabled Dr. Neto to declare the formation of the Peoples Republic of Angola in Luanda on independence day. The FNLA and UNITA made their own declarations of independence in their respective strongholds in the north and the center of Angola.

International and regional powers had different but complementary motives for assisting the warring factions. The Soviet Union and Cuba had supported the MPLA even before the coup in Portugal, which had opened the door to decolonization. Their support was based on the Marxist credentials of the MPLA leadership. The degree and scope of Cuban intervention on behalf of the MPLA is explicable by the nature of Cuban postrevolutionary foreign policy. Until the end of the Soviet Union and the collapse of communist regimes in Eastern Europe, President Fidel Castro and his colleagues in the Cuban leadership had been willing to commit men and resources in support of anti-imperialist and revolutionary movements in Latin America and even Africa. Between March and December 1975, the Soviet Union and Cuba are estimated to have shipped some $200 million in arms and other military assistance to the MPLA.[18]

The United States, through the CIA, had been giving limited support to Holden Roberto, leader of the FNLA, as a kind of insurance for the future when Portugal would leave Angola. Roberto was anticommunist and was close to Mobutu Sese Seko, the U.S.-supported president of Zaire. As the struggle for Angola intensified in the wake of the Portuguese coup, the choice of Roberto and the FNLA as the principal client to back seemed obvious.

The Chinese government began providing arms and training to the FNLA as early as 1973. In May 1974, it sent over 100 military advisers and 450 tons of weapons. The primary Chinese motive at that time was to support practically anyone or any regime that opposed the Soviet Union. They had also established close relations with President Mobutu who shared their anti-Soviet views.

South Africa had been shocked by the collapse of Portuguese colonialism in Angola and Mozambique because this had suddenly removed the buffer against hostile black African states. The change increased the threat to the apartheid regime. In the calculation of South African leaders, if they had to coexist with black African governments on their borders, they would prefer and actively support the moderates, such as the FNLA and UNITA, and oppose the militant nationalists, especially if they were also Marxist, such as the MPLA.

Zairian involvement was motivated by political as well as ideological factors. Mobutu was a strong anti-communist ruler who had faced communist-supported rebellions in his own country in the 1960s. He was close to the United States and had cultivated ties with the anti-Soviet Chinese. He was also related to Roberto through marriage. He could expect to exercise influence if his protégé seized power in Angola.

Throughout 1975, the Organization of African Unity (OAU), the principal regional organization in Africa, unsuccessfully tried to mediate between the Angolans. The OAU itself was divided ideologically between the radicals, who supported the MPLA, and conservatives, who supported UNITA and the FNLA. These divisions were increased when news of the covert involvement of the CIA and the direct intervention of South African military forces against the MPLA came out in the middle of the year.

The extent of the split within the OAU was revealed during an emergency meeting called to deal with the Angolan crisis on January 10–13, 1976. The delegations split down the middle, with twenty-two of them voting to recognize the MPLA, which held the capital and the surrounding regions, as the official government of Angola. In opposition, twenty-two voted against the MPLA and two delegations abstained.

Countdown to the Decision

In 1974, the CIA began to get indirectly involved in the incipient struggle for control of postcolonial Angola by providing funds to Roberto without the approval of the "40 Committee."[19] This was a subsidiary body of the National Security Council which had responsibility for authorizing and overseeing the covert activities of the CIA.

By the beginning of 1975, the contest for control of Angola among the three independence movements had moved into high gear. In September 1974, President Mobutu secretly met General Antonio Spinola, the head of the Portuguese military government, to lobby on behalf of Roberto. On January 22, 1975, the "40 Committee" met in Washington and approved a CIA request for providing an additional $300,000 to Roberto to support his efforts to gain control of Angola.[20]

On April 19 and 20, President Kenneth Kaunda of Zambia, Angola's eastern neighbor, visited Washington and lobbied for U.S. support for the FNLA and UNITA in order to counter Soviet support for the MPLA. Kaunda was a strong advocate of African nonalignment in the Cold War.

The Africa Bureau of the State Department was wary of the growing U.S. covert involvement in Angola. Nathaniel Davis, assistant secretary of state for African affairs, had been criticized for his suspected role in the 1973 overthrow of President Salvador Allende of Chile, where he had been the U.S. ambassador. This experience had made him sensitive about association with official covert activities. Davis was especially concerned about the likely impact of South Africa's involvement with the FNLA-UNITA military coalition.

In May 1975, he was asked by Henry Kissinger to head an interagency task force of the National Security Council which included members of the State Department's Intelligence and Research, Policy Planning, and Africa bureaus, and representatives of the Defense Department and the CIA. The goal of the task force was to develop policy options on the civil war in Angola.

The task force gave its report to Kissinger on June 13, 1975. Most members favored a peaceful resolution of the Angolan civil war through diplomatic and political means. These would involve encouraging Portugal, still the formal power in Angola, to play a less passive role in the unfolding events; pressing the Soviets to reduce their support for the MPLA; and promoting and supporting mediation by the United Nations and the Organization of African Unity.

The task force recommended that such efforts would move the civil war from the battlefield to electoral competition among the three factions. This, they argued, would favor the anti-MPLA forces and would reduce the danger of superpower confrontation.

It argued against covert intervention through the CIA because of the danger of committing U.S. resources and prestige in a situation whose outcome was uncertain. There was also the risk of provoking greater Soviet and other foreign involvement. Furthermore, covert aid would compromise U.S. relations with the MPLA, which was bound to play a major role in Angola's future, most African states, Portugal, other Third World states, and large segments of the U.S. public and Congress.[21]

On July 12, Davis sent a letter to Joseph Sisco, under-secretary of state, outlining the reasons behind the opposition of the Africa Bureau to proposed covert intervention. These included: the difficulty of keeping the operation secret; the absence of an irrevocable U.S. commitment in power or prestige; and the fact that providing arms and other military support would only lead to general escalation of the war.[22]

Davis sent two other memoranda to Kissinger and Sisco on July 14 and July 17. Both memos reiterated the Africa Bureau's opposition to the proposed covert CIA intervention.

Kissinger was not happy with the recommendations of the task force and directed that other options be added for consideration. The two added were: no involvement and substantial military involvement. At a meeting of the "40 Committee" on July 14, Kissinger asked the CIA to provide a covert plan for intervention in Angola.[23]

The plan, code-named "IA Feature," was drafted by the Africa Division of the CIA and submitted on July 16. The initial phase involved $14 million to be spent on arms for the FNLA and UNITA. It was approved by President Ford on July 18. Soon after, a frustrated Davis resigned his post as assistant secretary of state for African affairs.[24]

The mandate of the CIA in Angola was to prevent the MPLA from seizing power when Portugal withdrew in November 1975. It tried to accomplish its mission by supplying arms and other logistical equipment, training FNLA officers, and later recruiting and dispatching American and European mercenaries to fight for the FNLA and UNITA. The agency also generated and disseminated propaganda against the MPLA and its Cuban and other allies.

President Ford as Decision-Maker

Foreign Policy Context of Decision

In the course of his long career in Congress, beginning in 1949, Gerald Ford had become exposed to some aspects of international affairs. During his first term in the House, he became a member of the House Appropriations Committee and shortly after reelection in 1952, he was appointed chairman of the Army subcommittee of the Appropriations Committee In that capacity, he visited South Korea, Vietnam, Taiwan, and Japan. Later, he visited Western Europe as well as Poland and the Soviet Union.

In 1956, Ford joined the Intelligence subcommittee of the Appropriations Committee and served on it for eight years. In that capacity, he became privy to CIA and other intelligence briefings. His period of service coincided with the height of the Cold War and the crises it provoked in Europe as well as the Third World.

In 1965, Ford was elected House Minority Leader by the Republicans. As the leader of the opposition, he criticized President Johnson's conduct of the Vietnam War. In a one-on-one meeting, he urged Johnson to bomb Hanoi "with everything short of nuclear weapons."[25]

In 1972, Ford visited China in the company of House Majority leader Hale Boggs. They met Prime Minister Chou En-lai and discussed international affairs. As Nixon's vice-president from October 1973 to August 1974, Ford was a member of the National Security Council. He was regularly briefed by Secretary of State and National Security Adviser Kissinger on international matters relevant to the United States.

Ford's involvement in foreign affairs was indirect and limited in scope. His primary political interest was in domestic matters, particularly his responsibilities as the Republican leader in the House. His major ambition was to become Speaker if and when the Republicans managed to become the majority party.

Nixon's major foreign policy achievement had been the initiation of détente with the Soviet Union and rapprochement with China. He had worked closely with Henry Kissinger in the formulation and pursuit of these policies. When he became president on August 9, 1974, Gerald Ford decided to continue them.

Under Nixon, Kissinger had moved from the post of national security adviser to secretary of state, while retaining both posts. President Ford retained him in both positions until November 1975, when he appointed a new national security adviser. Kissinger remained secretary of state.

President Ford was deferential toward Kissinger and came to rely on him for foreign policy decisions.[26] Ford's foreign policy during his brief tenure can therefore best be understood in terms of Kissinger's worldview and the strategies he had laid out under the Nixon presidency.

The efforts of the Ford administration to prevent the MPLA from seizing power in Angola reflected several aspects of Kissinger's global views. As a "realist," Kissinger believed that global powers had legitimate national interests which they were entitled to defend. He also believed that global peace depended on an equilibrium of power which was based on mutual respect of those interests. In his memoirs, Kissinger stated: "If history teaches us anything it is that there can be no peace without equilibrium and no justice without restraint."[27]

In Kissinger's view, the United States had been gripped by a sense of self-doubt about its past actions, especially during the Vietnam War. He believed that the Ford administration

> confronted a world of turbulence and complexity, which would require of us qualities that had no precedence in American experience. Simultaneously we had to end a war, manage global rivalry with the Soviet Union in the shadow of nuclear weapons, reinvigorate our alliance with the industrial democracies, and integrate the new nations into a new world equilibrium that would last only if it was compatible with the aspirations of all nations . . . we had to find within ourselves the moral stamina to persevere while our society was assailed by doubt.[28]

Kissinger and Nixon were the architects of the policy of **détente** between the United States and the Soviet Union. Both countries agreed that this strategy involved reducing tensions in their mutual relations, expanding economic relations, negotiating arms control agreements, and avoiding direct military confrontation through diffusion of local conflicts in different parts of the world.

There was, however, no U.S.-Soviet consensus with regard to the implications of détente for mutual policies toward the Third World. Kissinger believed détente entailed maintaining spheres of influence and the global status quo. The sphere of U.S. influence included North and South America, Western Europe, and Southeast Asia and Japan. The Soviet Union's sphere of influence was restricted to Eastern Europe. Africa and the Middle East were considered to be outside the Soviet sphere.

By contrast, the Soviet Union took the position that while it was important to avoid direct U.S.-Soviet clashes, global revolutionary changes were not incompatible with détente. Wars of "national liberation" could be expected to continue to break out. These were wars waged against recalcitrant colonial regimes such as the Portuguese;

racist regimes such as South Africa; or class-oppressive and exploitative regimes such as the Somozista dictatorship in Nicaragua. Détente and peaceful coexistence with the United States did not mean any lessening of the global "class struggle" or of Soviet support for progressive historical change.[29]

Kissinger believed that such armed conflicts disrupted "order," which he regarded as even more important than justice.[30] Moreover, since they occurred in areas in which the Soviet Union had no historic interests, and were therefore outside its legitimate sphere of influence, Soviet support for the insurgents was unacceptable meddling.

Kissinger was not too interested in Angola, or Africa in general. He regarded these areas as marginal to the great power chess game. Kissinger hoped that African conflicts could be isolated from the East-West competition. However, the United States had supported Zaire's President Mobutu on the grounds that the country was strategically located in the heart of Central Africa; and Mobutu was deeply involved in the Angolan civil war.[31]

Kissinger had hoped that the initial limited U.S. involvement would bring success to U.S. clients without turning the conflict into a test of strength with the Soviets. Until 1975, it was believed by some in the Ford administration that the FLNA was strong enough to defeat the MPLA. It was only later, when poor military and political performance by the U.S. allies was compounded by massive Cuban and Soviet support for the MPLA, that the Ford administration related the civil war to the broader American-Soviet relationship.[32]

After the covert intervention became public knowledge and the debate about the merits of the intervention began, President Ford and Kissinger explained the reasoning behind the policy. At a news conference on January 14, 1976, Kissinger described Soviet support of the MPLA as incompatible with a "genuine reduction of tensions." Soviet actions were against "crucial principles of avoidance of unilateral advantage and scrupulous concern for the interests of others which we have jointly enunciated."[33] In a letter to House Speaker Carl Albert, on January 27, 1976, President Ford argued that "resistance to Soviet expansion by military means must be a fundamental element of U.S. foreign policy. There must be no question in Angola or elsewhere in the world of American resolve in this regard."[34]

In a statement to the Subcommittee on African Affairs of the Senate Committee on Foreign Relations on January 29, Kissinger again cast the Angolan civil war in the framework of U.S.-Soviet relations and détente policy. He argued that détente depended on the maintenance of an "equilibrium" in relations between the two superpowers. This equilibrium could not be sustained unless the United States remained "strong and determined to use its strength when required."[35]

Kissinger was also concerned about the impact on the United States' international image of the failure to check the Soviet-Cuban side: "If the United States is seen to emasculate itself in the face of massive, unprecedented Soviet and Cuban intervention, what will be the perception of leaders around the world as they make decisions concerning their future security?"[36]

These concerns were heightened by the dramatic setbacks for U.S. foreign policy in Southeast Asia in 1975, especially the humiliatingly hasty withdrawal of American civilian and military personnel from Vietnam and the seizure of Cambodia by the Khmer Rouge Communist forces. Kissinger and Ford wanted to use American resources in the Angolan imbroglio to show the world and Congress that the Ford administration was still in command of its foreign policy.[37]

Domestic Context of Decision

On December 6, 1973, Gerald Ford was sworn in as vice president, following the resignation of Spiro Agnew who had faced corruption charges. On August 9, 1974, he acceded to the presidency, taking over from Nixon, who had resigned over the Watergate affair. President Ford had thus moved into the two most important political positions in the country without the benefit of a national electoral mandate.

The November 1974 elections, held just three months after Ford's accession to the presidency, resulted in the Democrats winning majorities in both Houses of Congress. These two factors made Ford's presidency unusually weak.

Another handicap which President Ford faced stemmed from shifts in attitudes toward the goals and means of U.S. foreign policy as well as the balance of power between the executive branch and Congress which had occurred in the course of the early 1970s. By the mid-1970s, U.S. foreign policy was clouded by the effects of the Vietnam fiasco and the deep moral reexamination of the country's global role which had accompanied it. One of the consequences of this reexamination was the determination of Congress to assert its role in foreign policy and seek ways to counterbalance the president's prerogatives in this sphere.

In 1973, Congress had passed the War Powers Resolution which directed the president to consult with the legislative branch "in every instance" before committing U.S. troops to military combat and required congressional approval for such commitment for any period longer than sixty-four days. This measure was a direct reflection of the frustration which congressional critics of the Vietnam War had experienced in trying to wind down the conflict in the late 1960s and early 1970s.

There was also increased skepticism concerning executive secrecy in domestic and foreign policy matters, partly arising out of the events surrounding the Watergate scandal. In 1974, Congress passed the Hughes-Ryan Amendment to the National Assistance Act requiring that no funds would be authorized for CIA operations going beyond intelligence gathering unless the president made a "finding" that such operations were important to the national security of the United States. These operations had to be reported to the relevant congressional committees.

Reports and rumors of CIA involvement in illegal or morally questionable activities at home and abroad resulted in a congressional investigation of the agency in 1975. The investigation revealed, among other things, that the CIA had been involved in attempts to assassinate President Rafael Trujillo of the Dominican Republic and Prime Minister Patrice Lumumba of the Begian Congo (Zaire). Although both met violent deaths, the investigation concluded that the CIA was not responsible. It was also revealed that attempts were made by the CIA to murder Fidel Castro.

These reports tarnished the image of the CIA. As former Director William Colby stated: "Secrecy was perceived to cover error and wrongdoing. The once dashing James Bond image of the agent was seen as a disguise for an immoral, cynical assassin."[38]

Congressional investigations of the CIA led to the establishment of a formal congressional review of intelligence matters by eight separate oversight committees, including a permanent Select Committee on Intelligence in the House and Senate. Before this development, the agency had been answerable only to the Armed Services Committees of the two Houses, where it was treated with deference and a high degree of confidentiality. The president and the director of the CIA were able to work on intelligence operations insulated from the glare of the media and the scrutiny of Congress.[39]

Congressional Opposition to the Covert Angolan Operation

Growing congressional opposition and the successful intervention of Cuban combat units which had saved the MPLA from destruction by its domestic and foreign enemies presented the Ford administration with a set of difficult policy choices. One possible option was abandonment of the policy and cutting losses. This option had the disadvantage of implying admission of defeat in the domestic and foreign policy contexts. Another possibility was continuation of the policy of covert intervention. However, this required the injection of more resources.

In response to a request from the National Security Council to outline a program which could reverse the defeats suffered by U.S. allies, the CIA considered a set of possible measures which would have involved both escalation of the nature of the conflict and much more money than had been budgeted. These included introduction of Redeye ground-to-air missiles, antitank missiles, heavy artillery, tactical air support, and C-47 gunplatforms. The financial cost of such an expanded effort was estimated in the range of $30–100 million.[40]

The $31.7 million which was initially budgeted for the covert CIA operations was drawn from the CIA Contingency Reserve Fund for the current fiscal year. By the end of November 1975, the funds were exhausted. President Ford had authorized the expenditure of $6 million dollars on July 6 when he approved the program. On July 27, he authorized an additional $8 million and $10.7 million on August 20. On November 27, he authorized expenditure of the remaining $7 million. The funds had been primarily used for the purchase of arms, aircraft, hiring of mercenaries and other related expenses. Thus, at the time consideration was being given to a more costly escalation of the CIA Angolan intervention in order to reverse the successes of the MPLA-Cuban alliance, there was no more money to sustain even the limited ongoing operation.

Congressional opposition to the Ford administration's Angola policy was intensified by the gradual realization that the administration had not been fully candid in its communications to the various committees which had to be informed about CIA covert operations. The deception had begun with the July "finding" which President Ford had communicated to Congress. It did not specify that Angola was the country concerned. It only mentioned the African continent. The operation was described as "the provision of material, support, and advice to moderate nationalist movements for their use in creating a stable climate to allow genuine self-determination in newly emerging African states."[41]

Reports of U.S. covert involvement began to circulate in April 1975. Dr. Neto, the MPLA leader, charged that Angola was being subjected to a "silent invasion" from Zaire backed by the United States and

South Africa.[42] This was a reference to the entry of FNLA and Zairian military units from the north. In August, the U.S. Army denied MPLA accusations that its planes had been transporting military supplies to the FNLA from bases in West Germany.[43] And in September, the *New York Times* reported that the CIA was aiding MPLA opponents through Zaire.[44]

In briefings before congressional committees throughout 1975, William Colby, the director of the CIA, denied that the United States was directly involved in the civil war in Angola. Toward the end of 1975, congressional critics of the intervention began to question the veracity of the Ford administration's protestations.

In August, Senator Dick Clark (D, Iowa), chairman of the Subcommittee on Africa of the Senate Foreign Affairs Committee and one of the strongest critics of the Angolan intervention, undertook a visit to Southern Africa, including Angola. He came back from his African trip with the strong conviction that the Senate and the public had been misled by the Ford administration about the extent of direct U.S. involvement in the Angolan civil war.[45]

It was the financial crisis of the Angolan covert operation which provided congressional critics with an opening. They moved to stop the policy on two fronts: to prevent replenishment of funds for the operation and to bar any other forms of U.S. involvement in the Angolan civil war.

On December 5, 1975, Senator Clark successfully moved an amendment in the Senate Foreign Relations Committee to a draft bill which later became the International Security Assistance and Arms Control Act of 1976. The amendment prohibited military or other forms of U.S. assistance (excluding humanitarian aid) to any group in Angola.

The determination to terminate the program had been increased by an inadvertent admission of the administration's deception when Bill Nelson, the CIA deputy director of operations, and Ed Mulcahy, the deputy assistant secretary of state for African affairs, contradicted each other before the committee. Nelson admitted that the agency was directly involved in the Angolan civil war, while Mulcahy, who came in later, denied it. He was later compelled to reverse himself and concede the truth about the covert operation.[46] It was the first time that the Senate had cut a "covert" program with an open vote.[47]

Twelve days later, Senator John Tunney (D, California) introduced an amendment to the draft of what became the 1976 Defense Appropriations Bill which sought to cut $33 million from the proposed budget. This was the estimated amount sought by the CIA to continue covert military activities in Angola. It also sought to ban use of any additional funds for activities directly or indirectly involving Angola. This proviso was an effort to prevent the indirect supply of the anti-MPLA forces through the replenishment of Zairian arms stocks which would be used to arm the factions in Angola.

The ensuing debate was passionate. The Ford administration argued that aid to the anti-MPLA forces was needed to counter the Soviet Union and Cuba in Angola. More generally, it was important to maintain executive prerogatives in U.S. foreign policy. They pointed to the strategic significance of Angola in Central Africa, and its geographical proximity to the Southern African sea lanes. There would be a negative impact on American prestige among allies in Africa and elsewhere if U.S. policy failed in Angola.

Opponents of continued covert involvement in Angola argued about the danger of a gradual and escalating U.S. involvement similar to the Vietnam War. Regardless of which faction won the civil war, U.S. military involvement would inevitably escalate as Cuban combat units and shipments of more sophisticated weapons assisted the MPLA.

Critics also responded to the administration's arguments about the need to thwart Soviet influence in Angola and elsewhere in Africa. They suggested that any Soviet and Cuban influence would eventually be overwhelmed by the forces of nationalism. This had occurred, for example, in Egypt where, after years of Soviet assistance, close ties had been terminated by President Sadat when he succeeded President Nasser in 1970.

Congressional opponents also criticized the covert nature of U.S. intervention in Angola. Senator Alan Cranston (D, Calif.), for example, argued that:

> In refusing to vote more money for the covert funding of paramilitary activities in Angola and environs, we have rejected the road to another Vietnam. Further, we have rejected insofar as Angola is concerned the closed system under which so many fateful foreign and defense policy decisions have been made by a few men in the executive branch and even fewer men in Congress. This is an important precedent.[48]

The first version of the International Assistance and Arms Control bill was approved by Congress in April 1976 but was vetoed by President Ford. He objected to a number of aspects of the bill, particularly what he regarded as congressional invasion of the executive's prerogatives in foreign policy.

The bill was revised by the House and Senate and approved by both Houses in June 1976 with the Clark Amendment still incorporated. President Ford later signed it into law.

The Tunney Amendment was approved in the Senate on December 19, 1975 and in the House on January 27, 1976. On February 9, 1976, President Ford signed the act into law. With the passage of these two measures, President Ford's covert intervention in the Angolan civil war was over.

Decision Options

President Ford had main three options on the civil war in Angola: (1) Do nothing and allow events to take run their course; (2) use American political and military resources to bring about a resolution of the conflict among the three warring factions through United Nations or other multilateral mediation resulting in elections or some other peaceful settlement; and (3) directly intervene with U.S. political and military resources.

The first option was clearly excluded by the context of the Cold War. Moreover, the United States was already indirectly involved in the civil war on a limited scale, through its earlier support for Roberto, and his political patron, President Mobutu.

Administration officials argued that covert CIA intervention was initially intended to achieve the goals of the second option. On February 6, 1976, William Shauffele, assistant secretary of state for African affairs, argued that the initial grant of money to the FNLA in January 1975 had been for political activities to enable it to compete in Luanda, the capital, which was an MPLA stronghold. Even when military support was provided later, such aid was intended to preserve a military balance between the MPLA and its opponents. This would encourage the establishment of a coalition government.[49]

One of the major problems with covert CIA aid was that due to the Cold War context, it provoked escalation of the level of external involvement in the conflict. As the impact of U.S. aid changed the military and political situation in favor of its clients, the Soviets, Cubans, and their allies countered with greater assistance to the MPLA.

Moreover, given the history of bitter hostility among the liberation movements, there was little likelihood that the contest would be decided through the ballot box. If the initial aim of President Ford was to pursue the second option, the reality was that it escalated into the third option, namely, more direct intervention.

The second option might have been successful if the Ford administration had divorced the Angolan conflict from the Cold War context. This might have been achieved through a multinational peaceful solution involving United Nations–supervised elections, an arms embargo, and political and humanitarian intervention to address the immediate needs of those affected by the war and defuse tensions. There is no evidence that President Ford ever considered this approach.

The Ford administration settled on option 3. However, by adopting covert, rather than overt means of intervention, it chose a risky approach. Why did Kissinger and Ford decide to intervene in the Angolan civil war secretly rather than openly?

First, an overt policy would have immediately roused the ghosts of Vietnam. Angola was another distant, Third World country. It was hard to demonstrate that whoever controlled it could possibly threaten U.S. national interests.

Second, the United States had previously aided the Portuguese colonial regime and given only rhetorical support to the Angolan nationalists. This history had weakened the U.S. moral stance in Angola and Southern African. Overt intervention against one of the nationalist movements at the time of decolonization would have provoked strong domestic and international opposition.

Third, a covert intervention was tempting because, if it succeeded without use of U.S. troops or domestic and international acrimony, it would be a cheap victory for American foreign policy in the region. It was a tempting but very tricky gamble.

Ford's Leadership Role in the Decision

With every crisis, Ford's first instinct was to listen, ask questions, and to hear the facts from those who knew about the situation. Then he made his decision without delay.[50] There is little doubt that on the Angolan problem, Kissinger was the one taking the lead in decision-making.[51]

Like Kissinger, President Ford looked at the Angolan civil war through the prism of the Soviet-American Cold War rivalry. He regarded the role of the Cubans in giving military support to the MPLA as an indirect expression of Soviet policy. He regarded them as "proxies" for the Soviets.

As the situation deteriorated for the anti-MPLA factions, he called in Soviet Ambassador Anatoly Dobrynin and told him that Soviet policies in Angola were "very damaging" to mutual relations.[52] He also wrote to House Speaker Albert seeking support for continuation of the covert operation. Ford believed that the Democratic House leaders wanted to help him, but liberal Democrats were greatly worried about the danger of Angola becoming another Vietnam and refused to go along with his policy.[53]

Consequences of Ford's Decision for the United States and Other Countries Involved

United States

A major immediate foreign policy consequence of the cut-off of U.S. aid for the anti-MPLA factions in Angola was Secretary Kissinger's decision to give more attention to Southern African affairs. He was responding to the fact that the continent had not figured prominently in his Cold War strategy and especially the perception, reflected in his 1969 study, that the United States was more sympathetic to the white colonial and settler regimes than African nationalists. This perception had encouraged African nationalists to seek support from the Soviet Union and other countries.

In April 1976, Kissinger went to Africa, where he visited Kenya, Tanzania, Zaire, Liberia, and Senegal. The highlight of his trip was a speech in Lusaka, Zambia. Kissinger asserted that the United States supported the right to African self-determination, majority (nonracial) rule, and equal rights, and human dignity "for all the peoples of Southern Africa."[54]

Subsequently, with the active participation of the United States under Presidents Carter and Reagan, Rhodesia became independent in 1980 and the Republic of Zimbabwe and Namibia followed suit in 1990. In 1994, the system of apartheid was abolished in South Africa and Nelson Mandela became the first black African to be elected president of the country.

On the domestic front, the Clark Amendment prompted President Ford to propose reform of the White House mechanism for dealing with intelligence gathering and oversight. Among other things, this involved the establishment of the Committee on Foreign Intelligence and the Operations Advisory Group to serve as checks on the autonomy of the CIA from the executive office. Another oversight body, the Oversight Board, made up of three private citizens, would receive reports from the intelligence community at least once each quarter.[55]

Angola

By December 1975, U.S. covert intervention in Angola had failed. The MPLA had expelled UNITA and the FNLA from the capital, proclaimed the "Peoples' Republic of Angola" on November 11, and controlled most of the country. South African and Zairian troops had been withdrawn and Cuban military and civilian personnel were firmly entrenched in the country.

The South Africans later claimed that their withdrawal was not motivated by military setbacks. To the contrary, they had reportedly mauled the MPLA and Cuban troops. They simply did not want to end up bogged down in Angola without U.S. and other Western support. Yet, given the widespread domestic and international abhorrence of apartheid, the Ford administration would have found it difficult to openly support South Africa's intervention, even if it had been willing to soldier on alone after the congressional termination of the covert operation.

The MPLA retained control of Angola and was eventually recognized by most countries as the legitimate authority. However, the civil war continued.

President Reagan focused on Angola as one of the targets of the "Reagan Doctrine." This sought to undermine and overthrow Third World governments which were aligned with the Soviet Union and Cuba. In 1985, with a more conservative congress, the Clark Amendment was repealed and the CIA resumed covert assistance, this time primarily channelled to UNITA. By then, using classical guerrilla tactics, it had become the only effective armed opposition to the MPLA government.

As the civil war intensified, Cuban combat troops increased to 50,000. South African troops regularly crossed over and engaged Angolan and Cuban troops. The Angolans and Cubans provided military support and shelter to Namibian guerrillas who challenged South African colonial control of their country.

Under a 1988 accord brokered by the United States, the Soviet Union, Cuba, Portugal, and African states, Cuban forces withdrew from Angola. South Africa granted independence to Namibia two years later.

The MPLA won in United Nations–supervised elections held in 1992. However, UNITA rejected the results and restarted the civil war.

In 1993, the Clinton administration gave recognition to the MPLA government. By the middle of 1995, UNITA appeared to have once more given up fighting. It was involved in negotiations designed to establish a power-sharing arrangement with the MPLA. However, prospects for the eventual establishment of peace remained uncertain.

The Soviet Union

The rise to power of Mikhail Gorbachev in the Soviet Union in 1985 eventually led to fundamental domestic and foreign policy changes. The Soviet communist state collapsed in 1991. In foreign policy, Gorbachev had already withdrawn from prior commitments in Third World conflicts. His government cooperated with the United States, Portugal, South Africa, and the United Nations to bring about the 1988 accords which had led to the withdrawal of Cuban troops from Angola and Namibian independence.

Cuba

The effort to sustain the MPLA against the guerrilla insurgency in Angola was costly for Cuba. Thousands of Cubans were killed in combat, accidents, or by disease. One estimate suggests that 10,000 died.[56] By 1988, President Castro wanted a settlement of Angolan and Namibian issues which did not humiliate his African allies as he withdrew from the region.[57]

Conclusion

In the 1970s, the processes of African political emancipation from colonial and segregationist regimes in Southern Africa got entangled in the U.S.-Soviet global rivalry. In 1975, Angola became a flash point in this global contest.

President Ford's decision to intervene covertly in the Angolan civil war was designed to check perceived Soviet gains in Africa. But Congress prevented the escalation of CIA-sponsored military support for U.S. allies. The CIA had just been investigated by Congress. Reports of morally and politically questionable covert actions had damaged the reputation of the agency. The fact that it was the designated tool of the clandestine policy added to the controversy and opposition.

Why did President Ford encounter such great difficulty in achieving his policy goals in Angola? First, the failure of U.S. policy in the Vietnam War made it difficult to get congressional support for major military or paramilitary involvement in a Third World civil war. The "Vietnam syndrome" caused Congress to reject the continuation of CIA covert involvement.

Second, the Ford administration's policy options were constrained because previous U.S. policies toward Africa had cast it in the position of a tacit ally of the colonial and apartheid regimes. By 1975, antiracist and anticolonial sentiments were sufficiently strong in Congress and among critics of U.S. foreign policy to prevent cooperation with South Africa. Such cooperation might have enhanced the military and political effects of the CIA covert intervention.

Third, Angola was a remote and underdeveloped African country. There were some U.S. economic interests in the country's oil and coffee production and exports but these were relatively minor in the context of American global strategic considerations. It was located in a part of the world where U.S. national interests were not central. The Ford administration had difficulty making a case that any particular faction in Angola would threaten U.S. national security.

Finally, President Ford was handicapped by political weakness. As an unelected president, he lacked the kind of strong mandate which would have fortified him for controversial foreign policy initiatives such as covert intervention in Angola. He faced a Democratic-controlled Congress which had asserted control in foreign policymaking after the defeat in Vietnam. By contrast, President Reagan, who came into office in 1981 with a strong mandate, was able to get the Clark Amendment repealed and resume U.S. covert intervention in the Angolan civil war.

Questions for Discussion

1. How did Portuguese colonial attitudes toward the principle of self-determination differ from those of other European colonial powers?

2. Why did the conflict between colonial and white settler regimes and resurgent African nationalism pose acute problems for U.S. foreign policy in the 1950s and 1960s?

3. How did the United States seek to deal with the dilemmas of Southern Africa before the Ford administration?

4. What did the choice of option 2 of NSSM 39 constrain U.S. policies toward Angola in the wake of the 1974 Portuguese coup?

5. What were U.S. national interests in Angola?

6. Why did the Ford administration work to support the FNLA and UNITA against the MPLA?

7. Why did Ford choose covert rather than overt means of intervention? $\sqrt{} \, 204$

8. Why did the choice of this particular mode of intervention complicate the problem of defending the policy?

9. Why did Kissinger and Ford fail to persuade Congress to support their Angola policy?

10. Would an overt approach have had more success? If you were Ford, what approach would you have adopted?

Notes

1. Gerald J. Bender, James S. Coleman, and Richard L. Sklar (eds.), *African Crisis Areas* (Berkeley: University of California Press, 1985).

2. In 1980, some 4.5 million people of European origin forcibly dominated some 19.8 million indigenous Africans, 2.6 million mixed race (Coloreds), and 800,00 people who traced their origins on the Indian subcontinent (Indians) through the segregationist system known as apartheid. On South Africa and apartheid, see Foreign Policy Study Foundation, *South Africa: Time Running Out* (Berkeley: University of California Press, 1986). South Africa also ruled its neighbor Southwest Africa (Namibia) as a colony. Rhodesia (Southern Rhodesia / Zimbabwe) had been a British colony until 1965 when the white settlers declared their independence and created a minority regime which dominated the African majority.

3. Gerald J. Bender, "American Policy toward Angola: A History of Linkage," in Bender et al., p. 111.

4. Daniel Spikes, *Angola and the Politics of Intervention* (Jefferson, N.C., and London: McFarland & Company, 1993), p. 36.

5. Gregory F. Treverton, *Covert Action*, (New York: Basic Books, 1987), p. 151.

6. Thomas Noer, "New Frontiers and Old Priorities in Africa," in Thomas G.

Paterson, (ed.), *Kennedy's Quest for Victory: American Foreign Policy, 1961–63* (New York: Oxford University Press, 1989), p. 271.

7. Ibid, pp. 273–74.

8. Bender, p. 112.

9. Ibid.

10. Ernest Harsch and Tony Thomas, *Angola: The Hidden History of Washington's War* (New York: Pathfinder Press, 1976), p. 17.

11. Mohamed A. Al-Khawas and Barry Cohen, *The Kissinger Study of Southern Africa*. (Westport, Conn.: Lawrence Hill and Company, 1976), p. 82.

12. Ibid., p. 84; Jennifer S. Whitaker, "Introduction: Africa and US Interests," in Jennifer S. Whitaker (ed.), *Africa and the United States: Vital Interests* (New York: Council on Foreign Relations and New York University Press, 1978).

13. Harsch and Thomas, p. 22.

14. Ibid., p. 23.

15. El-Khawas and Cohen, pp. 45–52.

16. Douglas L. Wheeler and René Pélissier, *Angola* (New York: Praeger, 1971).

17. Charles K. Ebinger, "External Intervention in Internal War: The Politics and Diplomacy of the Angolan Civil War," *Orbis* 20.3 (Fall 1976): 671–87; and John A. Marcum, "The Lessons of Angola," *Foreign Affairs*, 54.3 (April 1976): 409–13.

18. See "The Situation in Angola: The President's Letter to the Speaker of the House of Representatives" (January 27, 1976) in, *Weekly Compilation of Presidential Documents* 12.5 (February 2, 1976): 89.

19. John Stockwell, *In Search of Enemies, A CIA Story* (New York: W. W. Norton, 1978), p. 67.

20. Spikes, pp. 130–31.

21. Nathaniel Davis, "The Angola Decision of 1975: A Personal Memoir," *Foreign Affairs*, 57.1 (Fall 1978): pp. 112–13.

22. Ibid., pp. 115–16.

23. Raymond L. Garthoff, *Détente and Confrontation* (Washington, D.C.: Brookings Institution, 1985), p. 509.

24. Davis, p. 117.

25. James Cannon, *Time and Chance* (New York: HarperCollins, 1994), p. 88.

26. See Joseph J. Sisco, "Ford, Kissinger and the Nixon-Ford Foreign Policy," in Kenneth W. Thompson (ed.), *The Ford Presidency* (Lanham, Md.: University Press of America, 1988), pp. 319–32.

27. Henry Kissinger, *White House Years* (Boston and Toronto: Little, Brown and Company, 1979), p. 55.

28. Ibid., pp. 69–70.

29. Garthoff, p. 530.

30. Walter LaFeber, *The American Age* (New York: W. W. Norton, 1989), p. 603.

31. Spikes, pp. 156–57.

32. Garthoff, p. 520.

33. *Department of State Bulletin*, 74. 1910 (February 2, 1976): 125.

34. "The Situation in Angola: The President's Letter to the Speaker of the House of Representatives": 90.

35. *Department of State Bulletin*, 74. 1912 (February 16, 1976): 174–75.

36. Ibid., p. 175.

37. John Robert Greene, *The Presidency of Gerald Ford* (Lawrence, Kan.: University Press of Kansas, 1995), p. 114.

38. William Colby and Peter Forbath, *Honorable Men: My Life in the CIA* (New York: Simon & Schuster, 1978), p. 20.

39. Greene, p. 102.

40. Stockwell, p. 216.

41. Ibid., p. 47.

42. *Africa Research Bulletin (Political, Social and Cultural Series)*, 12.4 (May 15, 1975): 3601a–b.

43. Ibid., 12.8 (September 1975).

44. *New York Times*, September 25, 1975.

45. Stockwell, p. 229.

46. Ibid., p. 230.

47. Treverton, pp. 158–59.

48. *Congressional Record*, vol. 121, part 32: 42225.

49. *Department of State Bulletin*, 74. 1914 (March 1, 1976): 280.

50. Cannon, p. 394.

51. See the account in Stockwell.

52. Gerald R. Ford, *A Time to Heal* (New York: Harper & Row, and the Reader's Digest Association, 1979), p. 358.

53. Ibid., pp. 358–59.

54. *Africa Research Bulletin (Political, Social and Cultural Series)*, 13.4 (May 15, 1976): 4004a–4004c.

55. Greene, p. 115.

56. Spikes, p. 323.

57. See Chester A. Crocker, *High Noon in Southern Africa* (New York: W. W. Norton, 1992).

Selected Bibliography

Al-Khawas, Mohamed A., and Barry Cohen. *The Kissinger Study of Southern Africa*. Westport, Conn.: Lawrence Hill and Company, 1976.

Bender, Gerald J., James S. Coleman, and Richard L. Sklar (eds.). *African Crisis Areas*. Berkeley: University of California Press, 1985.

Cannon, James. *Time and Chance*. New York: HarperCollins, 1994.

Ford, Gerald R.. *A Time to Heal*. New York: Harper & Row and the Reader's Digest Association, 1979.

Greene, John, R. *The Presidency of Gerald Ford*. Lawrence, Kan.: University Press of Kansas, 1995.

Harsch, Ernest, and Tony Thomas. *Angola: The Hidden History of Washington's War*. New York: Pathfinder Press, 1976.

Kissinger, Henry. *White House Years*. Boston and Toronto: Little, Brown and Company, 1989.

Spikes, Daniel. *Angola and the Politics of Intervention*. Jefferson, N.C. and London: McFarland & Company, 1993.

Stockwell, John. *In Search of Enemies: A CIA Story*. New York: W. W. Norton, 1978.

Treverton, Gregory F. *Covert Action*. New York: Basic Books, 1987.

7

President Carter's Decision to Boycott the 1980 Summer Olympic Games in Moscow

Setting and Overview of Carter's Decision

The Carter administration train sped quickly from inauguration station through its first year in office. Despite the president's foreign policy inexperience, early actions yielded impressive results: the Panama Canal treaties; improved Third World relationships in Africa and Latin America; Andrew Young's[1] leadership in the United Nations; the Camp David peace accords between Israel and Egypt; and establishment of official diplomatic relations with the People's Republic of China (PRC). President James E. "Jimmy" Carter, elected largely in protest against traditional Washington politics, Richard Nixon, and the Watergate scandal, set ambitious foreign and domestic policy agendas. Carter sought a moral foreign policy that would harmonize American strategic objectives with professed beliefs in justice, peace, protection of human rights, and nuclear arms control. Domestically, the president took immediate actions to strengthen energy and environmental policy and to more effectively address social issues such as housing and equal employment opportunity.[2]

By 1978, however, the Carter administration was sending mixed signals at home and abroad. Carter's moral-based foreign policy at times conflicted with U.S. economic interests such as extension of most-favored-nation (MFN) trading status to the Soviet Union.[3] The administration's indecisiveness on such issues created an international perception of weakness. Christmas-time 1979 presented Carter with one of his most challenging dilemmas, the Soviet invasion of Afghanistan. In the face of upcoming 1980 elections, and with critics attacking his weakness as evidenced, for example, by perceived disproportionate U.S. concessions in Strategic Arms Limitation Treaty II (SALT II) talks, Carter needed the opportunity to appear strong and decisively respond to yet another Soviet advance. Carter hoped to accomplish this by boycotting the 1980 Summer Olympics scheduled for Moscow. In the end, most Western allies failed to see the importance of the linkage between the Olympic boycott and the Soviet invasion of Afghanistan; the Soviets would leave Afghanistan in their own time; and the 1980 Moscow and 1984 Los Angeles Olympics (which Soviet bloc countries boycotted) faded into history as comparatively meaningless world competitions.

President Carter's Decision

ON JANUARY 4, 1980, PRESIDENT CARTER MET WITH HIS ADVISERS TO REVIEW FORTY PROPOSED SANCTIONS AGAINST THE SOVIET UNION IN RESPONSE TO ITS ATTACK ON AFGHANISTAN.[4] HE DECIDED TO PURSUE MULTIPLE RESPONSES INCLUDING ECONOMIC, CULTURAL, AND DIPLOMATIC INITIATIVES. OF THE SEVEN RESPONSES HE SELECTED, PERHAPS THE MOST CONTROVERSIAL WAS THE BOYCOTT OF THE 1980 SUMMER OLYMPIC GAMES SCHEDULED FOR MOSCOW.

Carter's decision was controversial for several major reasons:

1. It forced a national debate over U.S. security interests in Afghanistan.
2. It led to reexamination of U.S. linkage policy by asking whether the Soviets would recognize the relationship between the boycott and their invasion.
3. Carter made the announcement without meaningful prior consultation with NATO allies, who for the most part did not join the boycott.
4. Forcing athletes who had trained their entire lives for the Olympics to this level of sacrifice questioned federal power over the citizenry.
5. It raised the question of separation of the Olympics and politics.

6. There would be a possible negative impact on other ongoing initiatives such as the Middle East peace talks, Salt II, and the Iranian hostage negotiations.
7. It placed in jeopardy continuation of détente with the Soviet Union.

Background of the Decision

Historical Context:

The Soviet Perspective of the Invasion of Afghanistan
Afghanistan, a predominantly Muslim country of about 16 million people, was traditionally contested by both Great Britain and Russia in what historians call the Great Game. Great Britain gained control of Afghanistan in 1857, but could never bring it completely under colonial control. Russian-Afghan relations began in the 1830s when local leaders turned to the Tsar for help in expelling the British. After World War I, the newly established Bolshevik government in Russia, calling for self-determination of all people under Western imperialism, signed a treaty of friendship with Afghanistan in 1921 and a nonaggression pact in 1926. World War II severely weakened British power around the world. When Britain was forced to relinquish control of India in 1947 and withdraw from the Asian subcontinent, in effect the Great Game was over.

It seemed that the Soviet Union would now have a relatively free hand to try to fulfill the tsarist dream of influence in Afghanistan. Wary of its colossus to the north, Afghanistan at first looked to establish economic, political, and military ties with the United States. But by the mid-1950s, the United States was supporting Pakistan, which was in conflict with Afghanistan over rights of territory and self-determination for national minorities. Moreover, the Eisenhower administration had disdain for the principle of neutralism. It believed all countries should take a stand for freedom and democracy, so it tried hard to win over neutral countries to its side in the Cold War. During this early Cold War period, Afghanistan, unlike its neighbor Pakistan, refused to accept requests by the United States to join anti-communist pacts, such as the Southeast Asia Treaty Organization (SEATO) that was founded in September 1954 after the French defeat in Indo-China. Afghanistan soon turned to the Soviet Union for aid. The new Soviet leadership of the post-Stalin era accepted the principle of neutralism. Seeking an opportunity to woo Afghanistan, the USSR extended both economic and military aid.

But Soviet-Afghan relations were never particularly smooth. The closeness desired by the Soviets was not achieved until July 1973 when Prince Mohammed Daoud Khan toppled the monarchy and took power in a bloodless coup. At first, the West dubbed Daoud "the Red premier" because he allowed the Soviet Union considerable influence in the country, especially the economy. But by the mid-1970s, Daoud began to reduce ties with the Soviet Union and exhibit Afghanistan's independence as a member of the Non-Aligned Movement. To consolidate his power, Daoud dispersed into the hinterlands potential rival members of the two small Afghan Marxist groups, Khalq (Masses) and Parcham (Banner). Khalq was the more radical group and had closer ties to Moscow. Daoud also purged Marxists from military leadership positions. Soon Daoud began to criticize Soviet foreign policy, particularly Soviet support of Cuban troops fighting in Angola. He also sought improved relations with Iran (then ruled by the Western-oriented Shah) and the People's Republic of China (PRC), its hostile Communist rival. When it looked like Daoud was planning to bring into the government conservative leaders not friendly toward communism, the Soviet Union was even further perturbed.

On April 27, 1978, Daoud was killed in a military coup that brought to power the small (about 6,000 members) Soviet-influenced People's Democratic Party (PDP). Although the Soviets were pleased with this turn of events, there is no evidence of their complicity in the coup. Hard-line Marxists of Khalq, led by Nur Mohammed Taraki, got the upper hand in the new government. One important sign of the new power equation was the sending off of Barbak Karmal, the Parcham leader, as ambassador to Prague.

Taraki tried to adopt socialist reforms without real knowledge and consideration of Afghan traditions. Forces of Muslim-led resistance fought back. In February 1979, the murder in the Afghan capital Kabul of the U.S. ambassador, Adolph Dubs, caused considerable friction in U.S.-Soviet relations. Although Moscow expressed its regrets, the United States suspected Soviet complicity. By this time, the Afghan government was losing control of the country which had slipped into civil war.

In September 1979, a counter-coup brought to power Hafizullah Amin. On his orders, Taraki was killed on October 8. But Amin's dictatorial regime was very unpopular. Civil unrest continued, much to the exasperation of Soviet leaders. Soon, the Soviets began to believe Amin could not keep order in the country. Moreover, they concluded he was not a reliable ally. They feared he might expel Soviet advisers, like President Anwar Sadat did in Egypt. He might even take Soviet nationals as hostages, as Iran did with Americans. In addition, the Soviets were upset that in November and December, Amin sought to establish contact with President Zia of Pakistan. They were worried that Amin might try to break away from Soviet influence and establish closer ties also with the PRC and the United States. According to Anatoly Dobrynin, at the time Soviet ambassador to the United States, the KGB distrusted Amin and even considered him a CIA agent.[5]

The Soviet Union thus desperately tried to stabilize Afghanistan and keep it within its sphere of influence. Foreign policy experts such as Raymond Garthoff, Henry Bradsher, and Thomas Hammond all chronicled the Soviet search for a sympathetic leader during 1978 and 1979.[6] Several significant points deserve special attention:

- Each succeeding Afghan leader strove for independence from Soviet domination. Their continual attempts to establish closer ties with the West and PRC irritated Soviet leaders.
- One particularly bloody uprising at Herat greatly embarrassed and infuriated the Soviet leadership. Soviet advisers and their families were hunted down, murdered, and their heads paraded through the streets.
- Afghanistan's position to the south of the Soviet Islamic republics, coupled with the surge in fundamentalist Islamic militancy in Iran after the Shah was deposed in 1979, presented the Soviets with a serious security dilemma that they believed necessitated control of Afghanistan.
- The Afghans ignored a special Soviet adviser sent to aid in the stabilization of their country. Nothing the Soviet leadership attempted seemed to yield success.

Exacerbating the growing problems on the USSR's southern doorstep were disturbing U.S. gains in the Middle East. Improving Egyptian-U.S. relations, apparent success in the Camp David peace process, and rapidly building U.S. military presence in the region in response to the Iranian hostage situation, presented an ever-increasing threat to the Soviets. Five U.S. carrier battle groups with 350 aircraft moved within striking distance of Iran. This signaled to the Soviets that the United States was about to reassert itself in the Middle East.[7]

About 100,000 Soviet troops invaded Afghanistan on December 27, 1979. At the same time, KGB operatives, working with the Afghan secret police, engineered a coup against Amin that resulted in his death.

To blunt charges of aggression, the Soviets claimed that the Afghan government had invited them into the country to help keep order.

The Soviet decision to intervene with great military force in Afghanistan would have a disastrous effect on U.S.-Soviet relations for almost a decade. The Kremlin contended that its main goal was to stabilize Afghanistan and maintain it as a buffer. According to Dobrynin, the decision was not an outgrowth of a "grand strategic plan by Moscow to seize a new footing on the way to the oil riches of the Middle East and thus gain global superiority over the United States." Dobrynin concluded: "It can be unambiguously stated that the appearance of Soviet troops in Afghanistan was not the result of a conscious choice between expansionism and détente made by the Kremlin leadership. To my knowledge, the Kremlin was not even considering this kind of choice in any discussion."[8] The Carter administration, however, thought otherwise. The perception of Soviet aggressive expansionism became the foundation of the president's decision to order the boycott of the 1980 Olympic Games in Moscow.

Jimmy Carter ran for president because of his disagreement with many of the policies pursued by his two predecessors, Richard Nixon and Gerald Ford. In Carter's view, the United States was too dependent on foreign oil, increasingly vulnerable to terrorist attacks against American citizens, beset with corruption in Washington, and faltering in the eyes of its allies. Carter believed that U.S. foreign policy required more attention to moral principles and respect for human rights. By 1979, Carter's reelection prospects were threatened by serious domestic economic problems. Inflation had risen into the double-digit range, launching long-term loan rates to near 20 percent. Investment slowed as scarcity was replaced by inability to obtain credit. Economic sluggishness fostered criticism of Carter's policies. Presidential hopefuls such as California Governor Ronald Reagan and Senators Robert Dole (R, Kan.) and Edward Kennedy (D, Mass.) attacked Carter's indecisiveness on the economy, claiming it sent the wrong signal to America's adversaries.

By July 1979, Pat Cadell, Carter's pollster, indicated that a repetition of the president's earlier themes "would either put the public to sleep or arouse in them a greater level of alienation and rejection."[9] Consulting with Chief of Staff Hamilton Jordan, Vice President Walter Mondale, Public Relations Advisor Jerry Rafshoon, and Deputy News Secretary Rex Gramun, Carter found them all concerned about his drop in popularity. The president decided to call for a week-long assessment of his presidency with his staff and trusted outside advisers. Carter accepted criticism that he seemed "bogged down in the details of administration" and "involved in too many things simultaneously," had "delegated too much authority to . . . Cabinet members," and was not following through with policy initiatives.[10]

According to Garthoff, the fact that Carter was beset by domestic political problems was not a factor in the Soviet decision to invade Afghanistan. Nor did the Soviets seem influenced by perceptions of Carter's indecisiveness in foreign policy and U.S. military weakness. They might have been concerned about a possible U.S. invasion of Iran in response to that country's taking of U.S. hostages. But Soviet plans for military intervention were made before Carter's reaction could have been factored into the equation. Instead, Garthoff reached the same conclusion as Dobrynin as to the main reason for Soviet military intervention: the Soviets saw their decision not "as an opportune option but as a security imperative; not as an opportunity for expansion but as a reluctant necessity to hold on; not as something they were free to do but as something they were regrettably bound to do. It was a decision forced by events, not an opportunity created by them."[11]

The Soviets were also probably not worried that their military intervention in Afghanistan would derail détente. They considered it a defensive move to protect their vital security interests and to stabilize the geopolitical balance of power. They had protested against U.S. military intervention in the Dominican Republic in 1965, and against the U.S. role in the overthrow of President Salvador Allende in Chile in 1973. But they did no more than this more because they accepted both actions as having taken place in America's backyard, as within its sphere of influence, and presumably as necessary for its security. Moscow at least tacitly had accepted the historic Monroe Doctrine. Similarly, the United States had protested against the Soviet invasion of Czechoslovakia in 1968 but did little else. Seemingly, Washington had accepted the new Brezhnev Doctrine. This held that the Soviet Union had the right to intervene militarily in any country where socialism was threatened by "counter-revolutionary forces."

Developing U.S.-Soviet Conflict in the late 1970s
Between 1976 and 1979, several Soviet political and military "advances" went unchecked by the U.S. despite continued warnings:

- *Cuban involvement in Angola as proxy for the Soviet Union.* First noted by U.S. intelligence in 1976, U.S. diplomatic protests were lodged with the Kremlin in 1976, 1977, and 1978, and U.S. Army forces were placed on alert in 1977. No forceful action to back the protests was ever undertaken.

* *Soviet export of the MIG 23/Flogger D ground attack aircraft to Cuba.* American intelligence confirmed the delivery in Cuba during the fall of 1978. The Carter administration stridently opposed the elevation of the Cuban military threat to the United States via official diplomatic channels and protested it in the United Nations. Congress decried it, and the media ensured that it was publicly condemned in the world press. Again, the United States undertook no overt actions to block their introduction into the Western Hemisphere.
* *Soviet Army brigade stationed in Cuba.* Soviet troops, probably stationed in Cuba since 1961 in conjunction with the construction of Soviet Short-Range Ballistic Missile launch pads, were "discovered" in 1979. The Carter administration publicly portrayed this as totally unacceptable, yet true to form took no action to force their withdrawal.

The Carter administration's response to Soviet advances in the Western Hemisphere was mirrored by other foreign policy problems in the Middle East:

* In August 1978, despite official U.S. policy not to meet with representatives of the Palestine Liberation Organization (PLO), Ambassador Young held an unofficial meeting with its representatives at a time when PLO terrorism threatened U.S. mediation efforts between Israel and Egypt. To Israel, the meeting signaled insincerity; to Egypt, uncertainty.
* The American Embassy in Teheran was overrun on November 4, 1979 by Islamic fundamentalist students loyal to the Ayatollah Khomeini. They seized U.S. citizens and other employees remaining in the embassy as hostages and held them for 444 days. This violation of U.S. sovereignty went unanswered for weeks as the administration wrestled over which course of action to follow. The impotence of the administration's actions was highlighted by a failed rescue attempt, which the Iranian press displayed to the international public with pictures of crashed helicopters and stories of a failed U.S. invasion.[12]

When the Soviets made their decision to intervene militarily in Afghanistan, they believed that the White House was already considering a more confrontational policy to make up for recent geopolitical setbacks.

President Carter needed to demonstrate stronger leadership in U.S. foreign policy to a variety of audiences: the voters whom he needed for re-election in 1980; the Soviets, whose threatening actions needed to be checked; NATO allies, who expected forceful leadership in the alliance; and the Egyptians and Israelis, who were counting on Carter's leadership in their pursuit of peaceful relations. Consequently, ratification of the Salt II treaty was in doubt; NATO was preparing to install missiles in Europe; and the White House was playing the "China card," that is, forming a closer association with the PRC by extending formal diplomatic recognition and most-favored-nation (MFN) trading status.

Countdown to the Decision

The Soviet invasion of Afghanistan in 1979 did not catch the Carter administration totally off-guard. Brzezinski had advised the president in March that he, Secretary of Defense Harold Brown, Secretary of State Cyrus Vance, and Deputy Secretary of State Warren Christopher were concerned "over the Soviets' creeping intervention in Afghanistan."[13] In May, Brzezinski told Carter: "The Soviets would be in a position, if they came to dominate Afghanistan, to promote a separate Baluchistan, which would give them access to the Indian Ocean while dismembering Pakistan and Iran. I also reminded the president of Russia's traditional push to the south."[14] In July, President Carter was warned that the Soviets would probably unseat Afghan Prime Minister Amin. This warning was made public to place pressure on the Soviet Union. In early September, the president directed Brzezinski and the National Security Council (NSC) to prepare contingency plans for a U.S. response in the event of a Soviet military invasion of Afghanistan.[15] Brzezinski explained to Carter his views on why the Soviets were becoming more assertive and why their aggression in the Third World, especially their use of Cuban proxy troops in Africa, needed to be linked with other U.S.-Soviet issues.[16]

Brzezinski's warnings went unheeded. Freeing U.S. hostages in Iran became the predominant problem for Carter. Nothing the administration did seemed to bring a suitable response from the Iranian government. President Carter soon became obsessed with the hostage crisis. "More than anything else," as he wrote later in his autobiography, "I wanted those American prisoners to be free."[17]

Carter's efforts to get the hostages released did not alleviate public anxiety. By December 1979, Carter was under pressure to declare his candidacy for reelection. The administration realized that something had to be done prior to the 1980 campaign to counter the perception of a weak and indecisive president.[18] The Soviet invasion of Afghanistan appeared to provide that opportunity.

The Soviets were surprised by what they considered Carter's overreaction and seeming obsession with their invasion of Afghanistan. Within weeks, Carter would be calling it "the greatest threat to peace since the Second World War."[19] The Afghan issue clearly dominated U.S.-Soviet relations. On December 28, after meeting with the NSC, Carter sent a message to Brezhnev demanding withdrawal of Soviet forces. In a press conference the same day, he stated that the invasion was "a grave threat to peace" and "a blatant violation of accepted international rules of behavior." According to Dobrynin, later that afternoon Carter talked with Brezhnev on the Afghanistan issue over the hot line.[20]

Carter met with his advisers between December 30 and January 4, 1980 to review forty proposed sanctions.[21] Of these, Carter selected seven:

1. Embargo of future grain sales;
2. Cancellation of all planned state visits and meetings;
3. Banishment of the Soviet fishing fleet from U.S. territorial waters;
4. Denial of international credits to the USSR;
5. Restriction of high-technology transfer;
6. Strengthening of ties with other countries fearful of Soviet aggression—namely the PRC; and
7. Boycott of the 1980 Summer Olympic Games in Moscow.

At a nationally televised press conference on January 4, Carter announced his request for the Senate to postpone debate on ratification of Salt II. He also stated that he would delay the opening of new Soviet and American consulates; cancel a number of exchange programs; and send U.S. military aid to Pakistan. In his address, the president hinted that he might call for a boycott of the 1980 Summer Olympics scheduled for Moscow. He maintained that the United States would "prefer not to withdraw," but that athletes and spectators might be endangered if there were "continued aggressive actions" by the Soviet Union. On January 5, the White House tried to get the United Nations to condemn the Soviet invasion. But the Soviets vetoed the Security Council condemnation resolution. On January 14, the General Assembly condemned the invasion. Finally, on January 20, President Carter announced that he had asked the U.S. Olympic team to boycott the Summer Olympics.

President Carter as Decision-Maker

Foreign Policy Context of Decision

President Carter's response to the Soviet invasion of Afghanistan was influenced by three views of international relations in the 1970s: bipolarity, multipolarity, and interdependence. According to Kenneth Waltz, world stability was enhanced by the relations between the two superpowers, the United States and USSR. Waltz claimed that "the size of the two great powers [gave] them some capacity for control and at the same time insulate[d] them with some comfort from the effect of other states."[22] A second view, multipolarity, was expressed by balance of power theorists such as Henry Kissinger. In their view, a multipolar world enhanced political stability. Third, Stephen Krasner and other interdependence theorists argued that increasing economic and political interdependence between nations would foster peaceful coexistence.

In attempting to achieve balance in his foreign policy, President Carter appointed to his administration advocates of the bipolar and interdependence schools. Their juxtaposition in foreign policymaking contributed to confused White House responses to the Afghanistan situation. Secretary Brown, best associated with the Waltzian school, was comfortable with the stability afforded by the bipolar world. Secretary Vance, deeply interested in nuclear disarmament, believed that acknowledging the bipolar balance of power would maximize U.S. flexibility in obtaining the SALT treaties. On the other hand, Brzezinski developed linkage to a fine art, playing on the theme of international interdependence. His idea was to link granting the Kremlin MFN trading status with its compliance with U.S. objectives in human rights and nonaggression.

This idea of linkage originated during the Nixon administration. It was first presented on May 10, 1973 in National Security Directive Memorandum (NSDM)-212. In this directive, Nixon established internal policy guidelines relating economic incentives to desired conduct by Eastern European countries. It sought "not only improved resolution of bilateral issues . . . but also 'satisfactory' political conduct on international issues in which the United States had particular interest."[23] The Nixon administration proceeded to push for MFN status for the USSR. However, these efforts were challenged in late 1972 and early 1973 when Senator Henry M. Jackson (D, Wash.) and Representative Charles Vanik (D, Ohio) attempted to amend the President's omnibus trade bill by refusing to grant credits and MFN to "nonmarket economies" that restricted free emigration of its citizens.

The Jackson-Vanik Amendment called for a link between U.S. foreign policy and Soviet domestic policy, focusing most specifically on emigration rights of Soviet Jews. But Nixon and Kissinger believed in the grand strategy of linkage to moderate Soviet foreign policy. They linked a whole array of foreign policy issues to create a framework for détente between the superpowers. Trade was an important dimension of this linkage. Kissinger noted in his memoirs that he and Senator Jackson were "committed to the same objective: increasing emigration (especially of Soviet Jews) from the Soviet Union. The dispute was over tactics. The administration doubted that overt pressure could succeed; Jackson insisted that no other method would work."[24]

The Jackson-Vanik Amendment temporarily held up passage of the trade bill. Instead, complex triangular negotiations developed between the Ford (post-Watergate) administration, conservative senators, and the Soviet government headed by Leonid Brezhnev. On January 3, 1975, a beleaguered President Ford reluctantly signed the trade bill that included the Jackson-Vanik Amendment.

Context of Decision within President Carter's National Security Strategy

U.S.-Soviet trade increased dramatically during the Carter administration. Responding to apparent improvement in Soviet human rights policy, U.S. trade restrictions were liberalized. In 1978, U.S.-Soviet trade reached an all-time high of 2.8 billion dollars. However, as the winter of 1978 approached, relations began to chill when the Soviets shipped MIG-23 attack aircraft (nuclear weapons system capable aircraft) to Cuba and signed treaties of friendship with North Vietnam, Ethiopia, and Afghanistan. Brzezinski urged Carter to take advantage of the "China card" by raising Soviet concern over a budding U.S. relationship with the PRC. Subsequently, President Carter and Chinese Communist Party Chairman Hua Guofeng announced on December 15, 1978 the establishment of full diplomatic relations between the two countries. They were made official on January 1, 1979.

While the Soviets expected the normalization of U.S. relations with the PRC, their neighbor but also long-time rival and potential enemy, the suddenness of the announcement caught them off-guard. The Soviets believed that the Carter administration did not know what its priorities were. In response, the Soviet Union stalled on SALT II talks, pulled back on some economic agreements, and began to reassess its relationship with the West. Brzezinski reasserted the MFN argument to get the Soviets moving again. If the Soviets wanted MFN trading status and technology transfer from the West, they had to withdraw immediately from Afghanistan. The cost would be the same if they wanted to host the 1980 Summer Olympics. The United States also reminded the Soviets that their continued suppression of human rights violated the Helsinki Accords they signed in August 1975, as well as other international agreements. Such linkage was clear to the Carter administration, but confusing to the Soviets.

Until the Soviet invasion of Afghanistan, the Carter administration had been sending mixed signals to the Soviets on détente. The president was receiving conflicting advice from his top foreign policy advisers. National Security Advisor Brzezinski favored a hard-line response based on the primacy of a geopolitical struggle with the Soviet Union. Secretary of Defense Brown, a conservative hard-liner, believed as did Brzezinski that the Soviet drive into Afghanistan was a continuation of Russia's historical drive south for access to warm water ports. Secretary of State Vance, on the other hand, advocated reliance on diplomatic responses and sought issues of prospective compromise with the Soviet Union. The main struggle for the president's ear was between Brzezinski and Vance.

By early January 1980, the ascendancy of Brzezinski's views started to become evident. This was indicated, for example, in Carter's January 4 speech to the nation. It became much clearer in the president's State of the Union Address on January 23 when he announced the Carter Doctrine: The U.S. would consider any Soviet attempt to commit aggression in the Persian Gulf a threat to its vital interests. This doctrine was in keeping with the president's belief that the Soviets had their eyes on Middle East oil when they invaded Afghanistan. It was also a triumph for the geostrategic views of Brzezinski. "For me," Brzezinski wrote in his memoirs, "it was a particularly gratifying moment because for more than a year I had been seeking within the U.S. government the adoption of such a policy."[25]

This policy divergence among Carter's key foreign policy advisers became public. The president's desire for open and public debate, coupled with the lack of centralized control over public statements of administration officials, led to contradictory policy statements that caused some confusion within the Kremlin leadership.

Brzezinski consistently stressed geopolitical motives for the Soviet invasion of Afghanistan. Vance, however, while agreeing with Brzezinski that a firm response to the Soviet action was necessary, stated that he was uncertain whether geopolitics or the desire to stabilize the situation in Afghanistan itself was the USSR's main goal.

For the first few months of 1980, while Brzezinski talked tough with the Soviets, Vance tried unsuccessfully to smooth things out with Dobrynin. He told the Soviet ambassador that he was consistently one of the few in the administration who sought to protect U.S.-Soviet relations against "all kinds of extremists, of whom there are quite a few in Washington." But Vance explained that the timing of the Afghanistan intervention was terrible because 1980 was an election year. Nevertheless, it was necessary "to avert a complete break in relations." Vance also advocated resuming talks on arms control, and stressed that "both our countries needed mutual understanding." Dobrynin concluded that "it was Vance who sought to prevent our relations from collapsing completely in the overheated atmosphere of the White House."[26] Carter's acceptance of Brzezinski's linkage approach accelerated the isolation of Vance from the foreign policy decision-making process. He finally resigned in April over the failed rescue attempt to free the hostages in Iran.[27]

Context of Decision within President's Relations with Allies
The U.S. call for a boycott of the Olympics went largely unheeded by its allies. In early January, several weeks before Carter announced the boycott, Deputy Secretary of State Christopher had felt out NATO allies on the possibility of a boycott. At the time, however, Christopher had orders to tell them that the United States was not then contemplating a boycott. Garthoff argued that most European allies did not believe Christopher was exercising genuine consultation and were irritated that Carter had already decided to take a unilateral initiative.[28]

The effectiveness of Carter's leadership was clearly undercut by the lack of unanimity among NATO allies. While West Germany supported the boycott (as did several other major countries, notably Japan and the PRC), Great Britain, France, Italy, and most other NATO countries attended the Olympics. NATO allies were willing to strongly condemn the Soviet invasion through the United Nations and to show diplomatic disapproval by absenting their ambassadors from Soviet National Day parades in Moscow (in 1980 and 1981), but not to endorse the far stiffer measures advocated by the United States. NATO countries believed détente was still operating favorably in Europe, so they were less willing than the United States to risk damage to its continuation. In addition, NATO countries did not consider it in their best interest to curtail trade with the Soviet Union. In fact, they saw U.S. trade restrictions as an opportunity to expand their own with the Soviet Union. As a result of all these factors, they refused to answer Carter's call for an Olympic boycott.

Carter's failure to make the case for linkage before the Soviet Union and the International Olympic Committee (IOC)
Although the invasion of Afghanistan surprised the Carter administration, the call for an Olympic boycott must have seemed equally surprising to the Kremlin. The United States argued that the Soviet invasion of Afghanistan was a human rights violation and a threat to Western oil supplies. Also, it believed that Soviet manipulation of the world press during the Olympics would attempt to justify an illegal invasion of a neighboring country. Therefore, the presence of U.S. Olympic athletes competing in Moscow would seem to accept Soviet actions that the West opposed.

Soviet leaders believed Washington's arguments were totally unjustified. From their vantage point, Afghanistan was essentially a local security action, not a threat to world peace or Western oil. It was designed to stabilize, admittedly on their own terms, an unstable neighbor and contribute to world peace, not to threaten Iran and Pakistan as Brzezinski claimed. The Kremlin was quick to point out that since Afghanistan did not control any approaches to vital Western oil, Brzezinski's claim that this was the actual target of the Red Army was pure nonsense. Regardless of who viewed the situation, or how it was viewed, there was little doubt by January 1980 that the U.S.-Soviet dispute was primarily about bipolar dominance. Carter had to demonstrate his leadership to achieve U.S. goals in the Western Hemisphere, especially in Nicaragua where the Sandinistas had just gained power; in the Middle East by encouraging implementation of the Camp David peace accords between Egypt and Israel; and in Iran by gaining freedom for the hostages. The administration's 1979 foreign policy track record seemed abysmal. Something had to be done.

The boycott announcement on January 20, 1980 led internationally to the drawing of a battle line between the United States and the IOC in gaining support from public opinion. President Carter's initial plan was to press the IOC to move the games to another site or host competing games in other boycotting countries. There was much argument about the pros and cons of this proposal. But the IOC refused to alter the site. Its decision, coupled with the logistical impracticality of relocating the games, which normally takes four-to-six years to plan and organize, resulted in the third option: U.S. boycott of the Olympic Games. By selecting the Olympic boycott, the Carter administration's decision would have to be accepted in both the international and domestic arenas. The boycott announcement precipitated a bitter domestic debate between Olympic athletes and their friends and the Carter administration.

Domestic Context of Decision

The Olympic boycott was initially recommended by Vice President Mondale. Secretary Vance objected to the idea on grounds that it would provoke a Soviet boycott of the Lake Placid (New York) Winter Olympic Games scheduled for February 1980 and would be unfair to the athletes. However, the hard-line arguments of Brzezinski and Brown prevailed with the president. They convinced him that the prestige gained by the Soviets in hosting the Olympic Games would be unacceptable to the United States after the Soviets invaded Afghanistan.

Decision Options

In a letter sent to the IOC on January 20, 1980, President Carter outlined five points supporting the U.S. boycott:

1. The Soviet invasion of Afghanistan posed a serious threat to world peace, endangering neighboring independent countries, and Western access to vital oil supplies.
2. The Soviet Union should not expect business as usual with the world while attacking small countries.
3. Soviet sports were an extension of the same government that attacked Afghanistan.
4. The Soviet government attached great importance to the Moscow Olympics.
5. Therefore, a boycott would send a signal that could not be hidden

from the Soviet people, that would "reverberate around the globe," and hopefully deter future aggression.[29]

It is interesting that this list omitted Soviet human rights violations which had been extensively publicized since the Helsinki Accords. This omission led to criticism of President Carter until it was rectified on January 28 by Deputy Secretary of State Christopher. He added the persecution of noted Soviet scientist and human rights advocate Andrei Sakharov (who was exiled to the closed city of Gorky hundreds of miles from his home in Moscow) to the list of complaints when he testified to the Senate Committee on Foreign Relations. This opened the way for the administration to add human rights violations to their public complaints against the Soviet Union.

Several of Carter's inner circle of advisers strongly objected to the range of options being considered in the U.S. response to the Soviet invasion of Afghanistan. Debates raged over the domestic impact of a grain embargo. Robert Strauss, chairman of the 1980 Carter-Mondale Reelection Committee, Jerry Rafshoon, Jody Powell, Pat Caddell, and Vice President Mondale all pointed out that a grain embargo announced ten days prior to the Iowa caucus could seriously damage Carter politically. Tim Kraft, the Carter-Mondale campaign manager in Iowa, argued that: "Ten days ago we were headed for a solid win in Iowa. . . . Then the president drops out of the debate and sticks it to the farmers. All bets are off."[30]

Carter realized the potential liabilities of a grain embargo, but his sense of presidential responsibility and leadership prevailed over pollsters and public relations advisers. Carter was concerned about his leadership in world affairs. He wondered aloud: "How am I going to lead the West and persuade our allies to impose sanctions against the Russians if we aren't willing to make some sacrifices ourselves."[31] He also refused to debate Senator Kennedy for fear that he would be perceived as a candidate rather than president. Instead, Carter pressed forward with the unpopular aspects of his policy response to the Soviets by trying to demonstrate strong world leadership.

The proposed Olympic boycott also stimulated lengthy domestic debate. Arguments against the boycott included three major categories:

1. It isn't fair to the athletes!
2. Lack of presence doesn't prove anything; winning does!
3. Sports and politics must be kept separate!

It isn't fair to the athletes!

This emotional argument was most popular among U.S. athletes who had prepared for a once-in-a-lifetime opportunity to compete in the Olympics. The most passionate spokesman for this argument was Alaska Senator Ted Stevens. On January 29, he spoke before the Senate Foreign Relations Committee which had convened to consider two resolutions supporting the U.S. boycott.[32] William F. Buckley, Jr., the conservative political pundit, initially argued against the boycott. He stated that the boycott was asking too much of the athletes and that it would accomplish little more than conscripting athletes as the "hit men of foreign policy."[33] The Olympic athletes' anger was vocal and bitter. "Frankly, I'm sick and tired of being someone's political pawn," snapped all-American marathoner Roy Kisin. "The people suggesting a U.S. boycott are taking a pretty self-righteous position. Most of them have absolutely nothing to lose."[34]

By combining the boycott with other sanctions, President Carter effectively circumvented these arguments. Buckley soon changed his view on the boycott to support the president, writing: "If we feel free to ask the farmers to make contingent sacrifices and also manufacturers and technicians and workers who produce refined computers designed to go to Russia, then we can ask the United States athletes to forgo the competition in Moscow."[35]

Lack of presence doesn't prove anything, winning does!

This argument appealed to nationalist pride and past history, *Newsweek*'s Allen J. Mayer quoted discus gold-medalist Al Oerter's blunt comment: "The only way to compete against Moscow is to stuff it down their throats in their own back yard."[36]

Proponents of this argument recalled Jesse Owens' 1936 victory in the Summer Olympic Games in Berlin, Germany. Owens, a black athlete, won three gold medals and set three world records. Adolf Hitler, obsessed with the myth of Aryan supremacy, refused to recognize Owens' stunning achievements because he believed they blemished Germany's world prestige.

Another favorite example was the 1968 Mexico City Summer Games, where on the victory platform black U.S. sprinters Tommie Smith and John Carlos raised their clenched fists in the Black Power salute during the playing of the U.S. national anthem. This remained an enduring symbol of defiance against racism in the United States.[37]

There were other examples of protests at the Olympic Games, including:

- 1948: The IOC, fearing an Arab boycott, did not invite Israel to participate in the games.
- 1956: The Netherlands, Spain, and Switzerland boycotted the Olympics, protesting the Soviet invasion of Hungary.
- 1976: African nations boycotted the Olympics because New Zealand, on friendly terms with South Africa, planned to participate.[38]
- 1976: Canada recognized the PRC, forcing the Republic of China (Taiwan) to withdraw.[39]

Perhaps because of its power, the argument that competing and winning is most important was avoided by those who favored the boycott. However, they questioned its relevance, especially if the boycott's objective was to pressure the Soviet Union to withdraw its forces from Afghanistan. U.S. participation in the 1936 Berlin Games probably had augmented Hitler's credibility, but the embarrassment of the Owens victory certainly did nothing to slow Hitler's plans for conquest. Additionally, it is doubtful that an Olympic boycott of the 1936 games would have significantly altered Hitler's aggressive plans.

Sports and Politics must be kept apart!
This argument, legalistic and emotional in tone, probably generated more debate than the other two combined. It can be broken down into three segments:

1. The Olympic Games are apolitical business dealings and therefore not a forum for politics.
2. The ideal of the Olympics is to provide apolitical competition, fostering peace, as in ancient Greece.
3. Historically, the United States had separated sports and politics. It should remain consistent with its past.

Lord Killanin, president of the IOC, responding to the U.S. Olympic Committee (USOC) request to move the Olympics, noted that his group's agreement was with the Moscow Organizing Committee and not with the Soviet government. In so doing, the IOC accepted a Kremlin organizational anomaly, which was merely a ruse to fuel the myth that Soviet athletes were amateurs. The IOC indicated that as long as there was a contract, the Olympics would be held in Moscow and nowhere else.[40]

Carter discounted the contractual nature of the Olympics. Instead, he argued that Soviet sports were merely an extension of the Soviet government.[41] Moreover, boycott proponents believed that the contract argument had been countered before it had been levied. Previous boycotts had politicized the Olympics.

Proponents of the Greek ideal of the Olympics included Robert Kane, president of the USOC. He argued that a U.S. boycott would be traitorous to Greek ideals of the Olympiad and might result in U.S. expulsion from Olympic participation. Kane indicated that in previous boycotts outside forces and not governments had been the cause.[42] Athletes also supported this argument. Weight-lifter Bob Giordano stated: "I don't believe the sports world is any place to voice political opinions. No one condones anything the Soviet Union is doing in Afghanistan, but it is not our realm."[43] Some academics also followed this line. Robert C. Tucker, a noted Soviet expert, argued that permitting politics to overshadow the Greek ideal would encourage the Soviets to exploit resentment in the Third World by claiming capitalist oppression. Georgetown University Sovietologist Dmitry Simes worried that the Soviets would use the boycott as evidence of Western interference in their domestic affairs. This would permit the Soviets to rationalize their domestic human rights policies in order to guarantee internal stability.[44]

Boycott supporters countered this argument. Essayist Roger Rosenblatt noted that the ancient idealism ascribed by Baron Pierre de Coubertin, founder of the modern Olympic movement, never existed. The ancient ideal was to win. Losers were killed. The ancient games served to compare strengths in preparation for war. Moreover, hundreds of years of inactivity failed to kill the Olympic movement.[45]

Historic U.S. separation of sports and politics was seldom challenged by the mainstream of American public opinion. This point ran through all arguments against the boycott, but was never directly debated. In sum, those who thought it wasn't fair to the athletes argued that the boycott turned them into political pawns; those who argued that a U.S. presence was all-important avoided the political nature of that prestige; and those who felt that sports and politics must be kept separate were adamant in their belief that they always had been.

Some columnists argued against the separation of sports and politics in order to highlight their own grievances. For example, Kevin Lynch argued that the United States should rob the Soviets of any propaganda advantage from the Games. By boycotting, the United States would deprive the controlled Soviet media of any possible benefits they might gain from comparing U.S. and Soviet athletes.[46] And Manning Marable stipulated that the traditional separation of politics and sports had been nothing but a ruse to keep blacks out of the spotlight. As a result, their accomplishments would not translate into any political gains for them.[47]

Others argued that the Soviet Union's failure to separate sports and politics justified Carter's actions. If anyone doubted the political ramifications the Soviets attached to hosting the Olympics, they removed it through their propaganda. The tie of politics to sports was evident when the Soviet Union first entered the Olympics in 1952. From the outset, the Soviet media linked the success of Soviet athletes to successful diplomacy and foreign trade. When Moscow was awarded the 1980 Summer Olympics, the Soviet press crowed that this meant world recognition of the correctness of Soviet foreign policy. Thus to the Soviets, hosting the Olympics was clearly an integral part of their political and international objectives.

Domestic arguments over Carter's proposed Olympic boycott continued from its announcement through the opening ceremonies in Moscow. Regardless of the poignancy of arguments from boycott opponents, American public opinion generally supported President Carter's decision. Although a January 1980 *Time* poll of forty-two U.S. Olympians revealed that thirty opposed the boycott, *Newsweek* polls of the American public during that same month and in April indicated a rise in support from 56% to 67%.[48] Most Americans believed that if U.S. farmers had to suffer from a grain embargo, Olympic athletes should not participate in the Moscow Summer Olympics.

Carter's Leadership Role in the Decision

Unlike his predecessors, Richard Nixon and Gerald Ford, Jimmy Carter was not an experienced Washington bureaucrat or politician. He had previously served as governor of Georgia. His views of world politics were more akin to relations between states in the federally structured United States than to the comparative anarchy of international politics. In his study of the Carter administration's foreign policy process, Professor Alexander Moens found that Carter structured his cabinet according to a multiple advocacy decision-making model, first suggested by Professor Alexander George.[49] Multiple advocacy suggests that the president is the ultimate arbiter with his advisers and cabinet after they advocate their respective policy positions. Because each adviser presents solutions from his viewpoint, a diversity of policy options should be generated. The model also calls for a custodian-manager position, a neutral individual advocating no policy, but one who balances advocated policies in presenting them to the president. George stated that multiple advocacy places the president in the optimal position to select the best policy.

George's decision-making model has three main benefits:

1. It provides adequate diagnosis of the issue.
2. It approaches the issue from all vantage points, with costs and benefits fully weighed, and options thoroughly vetted.
3. It allows the president to monitor the effects of his policy, to determine when intended objectives are not being met, and to implement serial incremental changes to correct the course of deviant policy.

After examining four cases of Carter's foreign policy,[50] Moens found three major faults in the administration's decision-making process. First, it did not provide the president with the promised comprehensive lists of policy alternatives. The Olympic boycott illustrated this problem. The policy options considered were not equally weighted by a neutral arbiter and given to the president for a final decision. Brzezinski was the initiator of policy options. In his role as the self-appointed administrator of the conference system, he prioritized the options to his liking. He asked the other participants to bring their options to the table consistent with the NSC list.

Moens identified a second problem of the multiple advocacy system in the Carter administration. This involved a lack of sufficient information and option processing.[51] In theory, the differing opinions of the few decision-makers in the Carter administration should have stimulated debate. However, under Brzezinski's strong leadership, the decision-makers came to a rapid consensus on just about everything, thus limiting the options available to President Carter. The Olympic boycott decision demonstrated this problem. The policy option selected by Carter was based on Brzezinski's recommendation rather than open debate. Carter was involved in making the final decision. He encouraged advice, often attended meetings, and read all policy papers. Yet, despite all this, real policy debate never materialized.

Moens also found that the position of custodian-manager quickly evaporated in the policy fray. Carter relied on Brzezinski, who advocated the NSC position. This quickly elevated him to the position of advocate *primus inter pares*. In contrast, Secretary Vance was losing influence in Carter's circle of advisers by the time of the Olympic boycott decision.

Another possible explanation for Carter's difficulties may lie in the structural shift that was occurring in the roles of the president. Richard Rose observed: "In retrospect, the problems of the Carter administration appear less a reflection on the man in the Oval Office and more as symptoms of a structural shift from the modern to a postmodern President." Rose argued that the "modern president" was automatically afforded prestige which could be wielded at will, by virtue of his position as president of the most powerful nation on earth. In the postmodern world, smaller due to technology and increased communications, the president must be able to work the public, the international arena, and the Washington machine.[52]

Consequences of Carter's Decision for the United States, and Other Countries Involved

The United States

When Carter announced that the U.S. Olympic team would boycott the Moscow games and that the U.S. would embargo the sale of wheat to the Soviet Union, he appealed to U.S. patriotism. Carter also considered his actions a response to a national emergency. Carter's justifications were needed to counteract the displeasure of American sports fans. His decision was not easy, but he believed that if the Midwestern farmers had to make a sacrifice, the U.S. Olympic team should be required to do the same thing.

Carter's subsequent decisions had catastrophic consequences for his 1980 reelection prospects. He passed up the opportunity to debate Senator Kennedy ten days prior to the Iowa caucus because he didn't want the allies to perceive him as a man "fighting for his political life." When Carter delayed entering the presidential campaign to deal with the Soviet invasion and the hostage crisis in Iran, these actions were perceived as inconsistent in response to world and domestic problems and they highlighted what people disliked most about Carter: his indecisiveness. The end result was Carter's loss to Ronald Reagan in the 1980 election.

The Soviet Union

Of the 114 eligible countries, over 60 boycotted the Moscow Olympic Games and an additional sixteen refused to participate in the opening and closing ceremonies. Journalists from outside the Soviet bloc complained that the absence of strong teams from countries such as the United States, Japan, West Germany, and the PRC downgraded the competition. The fear of U.S. correspondents that the absence of their reporting would hide Soviet censorship was unfounded. *Pravda*'s blatant alteration of Lord Killanin's answer to the U.S. request for relocation of the Olympics was publicized around the world, especially the Third World.[53] *Pravda* only partially reported Killanin's answer: "Moscow was awarded the Olympic Games in recognition of its big contribution to international sports." In reality, Killanin went on to finish this thought: "not for any political reasons." Thomas Hammond went so far as to say, "the punitive measure that probably hurt Soviet pride the most was Carter's campaign to boycott the Moscow Olympics."[54] Robert G. Kaiser, a *Washington Post* reporter, stated that the boycott was a "genuine punishment for Afghanistan."[55]

Some Soviet officials admitted the boycott hurt their country.[56] During the boycott, the USSR made overt moves to encourage Third World participation by offering free airlift, room and board to Latin American teams, free gear and coaching to African teams, and a free visit by the Bolshoi Ballet to Jordan. *Soviet Life* magazine showed happy Americans enjoying the Games.[57] No direct mention was made of any boycotting countries. Aiding the Soviet camouflage was the make-up of the boycotters. *Time* noted that although the boycotting countries accounted for 73% of the gold and 71% of all non-Soviet bloc medals won at the Montreal Olympics in 1976, those countries that did participate in Moscow had won 72% of the gold and 79% of the total medals awarded.[58]

While Carter's resoluteness on the boycott issue may have reaped short-term gains, they did not produce any long-term changes in the perception of his presidency. Nancy and Richard Newell noted the limited impact of the boycott, especially with the only limited participation of key NATO allies:

> The Olympic boycott was intended to be a symbolic act of solidarity against aggression. As an invader, the Soviet Union was to be treated as a pariah, not a host. The impact of the boycott was to be psychological with political implications. Such intangibles are nearly impossible to assess. Much of the effect was lost when most Western European teams did not participate.[59]

Afghanistan

None of Carter's actions had much influence on Soviet involvement in Afghanistan. Garthoff assessed Soviet policy immediately after the invasion by observing:

> There was never any possibility that the Carter administration's punitive sanctions would lead the Soviet leaders to withdraw from Afghanistan. While their decision to intervene had been a difficult one, once the action was taken the stakes changed completely; while the world political costs were higher than expected, a withdrawal would be even most costly.[60]

Dobrynin also points out that the Kremlin all the while considered its Afghanistan intervention an essentially local conflict for limited objectives, and thus not a threat to U.S. vital interests in the Gulf. Therefore, the explanation for Carter's overreaction, he concludes, "was just a pretext for the Carter administration to resume the arms race on a still greater scale, strengthen the American military positions in the Gulf, and launch an overall anti-Soviet offensive . . . [that] threatened to destroy the process of détente irreparably."[61] Whether Dobrynin is right is uncertain, but it is understandable how the Soviets could have drawn this conclusion.

The war in Afghanistan dragged on until a UN-mediated ceasefire in 1988. It ground to a halt when economic pressures and domestic opposition inside the Soviet Union, including resistance to the military draft, affected the political and military leadership. Internal opposition became possible with Gorbachev's policies of *glasnost* (openness) that facilitated the loosening of central control in the Soviet Union. Gorbachev eventually realized that the Soviet economy could not support the war and that no political gains could be won.[62]

The Soviet position in Afghanistan had also been weakened by CIA covert action, the influence of millions of dollars of U.S. economic and military aid to the Afghan rebels, and effective assistance from predominantly Muslim nations, notably Saudi Arabia, Egypt, and Pakistan. Especially important in helping end the war were CIA-supplied ground-to-air Stinger missiles that limited the effectiveness of Soviet air power, and thousands of mules that carried supplies from Pakistan. The United States, which saw Soviet war-making in Afghanistan as part of a global contest for influence in the Third World, aided a motley configuration of Islamic Afghan rebels (*mujahadeen*) who fought both for independence of their country and for its protection against the assault of godless communism.

Soviet forces finally withdrew completely by February 15, 1989. In December of that year, the newly elected Soviet Parliament condemned the Soviet invasion as having been made by a narrow clique led by Brezhnev and as having turned into a terrible tragedy for all concerned, especially the Afghans. It was estimated that more than a million Afghans had died in the ten years of war. Several million more were seriously wounded, and about 4 million were left in Pakistan and Iran where they had fled as refugees. In addition, the country had been devastated by the war and its economy left in virtual ruin. When the war ended, the Afghan leader Najibullah, installed by the Soviet Union in 1986, remained at the head of the Kabul government. But the *mujahadeen* refused to accept the cease-fire agreement as long as Najibullah remained in power. When the Najibullah-led Afghan communist government collapsed in 1992, the *mujahadeen* took power. But this did not end the fighting, which raged on among rival Muslim factions.

Conclusion

President Carter believed that a U.S.-led boycott of the 1980 Summer Olympic Games in Moscow was a morally compelling response to the Soviet invasion of Afghanistan. The American people, including the Olympic athletes themselves, were divided over his boycott decision. Some thought the international community should punish the Soviets for their invasion of Afghanistan by refusing to participate in the Olympics. Yet others believed that politics should not mix with the Olympics and that American Olympic athletes should not have to sacrifice themselves on the altar of the Cold War. President Carter's main foreign policy advisers were also divided over the boycott decision. National Security Advisor Brzezinski strongly supported the boycott, based on his perception that it appropriately countered Soviet aggression in Afghanistan. Other advisers, particularly Secretary of State Vance, believed that a boycott would further damage U.S.-Soviet relations and hurt the cause of peace.

The U.S. decision to boycott the Olympic Games must also be considered in terms of effectiveness. Brzezinski believed that the U.S. could influence Soviet foreign policy by linking Soviet strategic desires to U.S. wishes. The Soviet Union neither accepted nor understood this linkage. Moreover, the boycott neither seriously damaged Soviet prestige nor helped forge withdrawal of Soviet armed forces from Afghanistan. Instead, it caused disunity within the ranks of NATO; led to a decrease in emigration of Soviet Jews which was to last until Gorbachev's reforms in the late 1980s; resulted in the Senate's nonratification of SALT II; and paved the way for a downturn in U.S.-Soviet relations. Carter's boycott decision angered many domestic supporters, and—because it did not have a favorable impact—added to the impression of Carter's administration as being weak and inept. These problems may have contributed to Carter's reelection defeat by Ronald Reagan in 1980.

Questions for Discussion

1. How important is prestige in a country's perception of its national interest?

2. What purposes, if any, were served by boycotting the 1980 Summer Olympic Games held in Moscow?

3. Should states always keep Olympic Games and politics separate?

4. How did the conflict between Zbigniew Brzezinski and Cyrus Vance contribute to the poor functioning of the Carter administration's foreign policy decision-making process?

5. Under what conditions should presidents bring individuals with such diverging approaches as Vance and Brzezinski onto a foreign policy team?

6. What should statesmen learn from this case study?

7. Do you believe that the Soviet military intervention in Afghanistan was related to the Kremlin's attempt to gain a strategic toehold closer to the oil-rich Persian Gulf?

8. Was there anything the Carter administration could have done to have deterred the Soviet invasion of Afghanistan?

9. Would prior U.S. consultation with NATO allies have yielded more support for the boycott?

10. How much credence do you give to the charge by Ambassador Dobrynin that Carter's decision to boycott the Olympics was just a pretext to satisfy conservative proponents of a get-tougher policy with the Soviets?

Notes

1. Andrew Jackson Young, Jr., served as U.S. ambassador to the UN from 1977–79. He was controversial because of his attempts to make the United States more responsive to moral issues in foreign policy. An ordained minister, he ran the United Church of Christ voter education project from 1961 to 64 which brought him in close contact with Martin Luther King, Jr., and he served as executive director of the Southern Christian Leadership Conference from 1964–1970. Official State Department policy prohibited any communication by U.S. representatives with the Palestine Liberation Organization (PLO) as a sanction for its involvement in international terrorism. Young, however, violated this policy by holding an unofficial meeting with representatives of the PLO to discuss Middle East problems. When this became public, the resultant outcry forced his resignation as ambassador.

2. Jimmy Carter, *Keeping Faith: Memoirs of a President* (New York: Bantam Books, 1982), p. 20.

3. Extension of MFN status would have improved trading opportunities between the United States and USSR and eventually have benefited the economic interests of both countries. This action, however, would also have accorded status to a violator of human rights and been in conflict with Carter's moral-based foreign policy.

4. Zbigniew Brzezinski, *Power and Principle: Memoirs of the National Security Advisor, 1977–1981* (New York: Farrar, Strauss, & Giroux, 1983), pp. 433–37.

5. See Anatoly Dobrynin, *In Confidence* (New York: Times Books, 1995), p. 436.

6. Raymond Garthoff, *Détente and Confrontation: American-Soviet Relations* (Washington, D.C.: The Brookings Institution, 1985), pp. 899–914; Henry S. Bradsher, *Afghanistan and the Soviet Union* (Durham, N.C.: Duke University Press, 1983), p. 104; and Thomas T. Hammond, *Red Flag over Afghanistan* (Boulder, Colo.: Westview Press, 1984), pp. 123–24.

7. Richard C. Thornton, *The Carter Years* (New York: Paragon House, 1992), p. 456.

8. Dobrynin, pp. 441–42.

9. Carter, pp. 114–15.

10. Ibid., p. 117.

11. Garthoff, p. 925.

12. Carter, p. 491.

13. Brzezinski, p. 426.

14. Ibid., p. 475. Baluchistan refers to the arid mountainous region of southeast Iran and west Pakistan inhabited mainly by nomadic, Farsi-speaking Baluch nomads. It is bordered on the north by Afghanistan, on the West by Iran, on the east by the Pakistani states of Sind and Punjab, and the south by the Arabian Sea.

15. Brzezinski, p. 427.

16. Ibid., p. 428.

17. Carter, p. 4.

18. Ibid., pp. 554–71.

19. "Meet the Press," television news show, January 20, 1980.

20. Dobrynin, p. 445.

21. Brzezinski, pp. 433–37.

22. Kenneth N. Waltz, *Theories of International Politics* (New York: McGraw-Hill, 1979), p. 159. This theory is fleshed out in chapters 7–9.

23. Garthoff, p. 496.

24. Henry Kissinger, *Years of Upheaval* (Boston: Little, Brown, 1982), p. 254.

25. Brzezinski, p. 443.

26. Dobrynin, pp. 446–49.

27. Desert One, the rescue attempt of April 25 aimed at securing the liberty of the U.S. hostages from Teheran, is a prime example where Vance's moderation was not allowed to temper Brzezinski's and Brown's aggressiveness. While it would be presumptuous to blame the mission's failure on this, one must question whether the mission would have been undertaken at all had Vance had the opportunity to contribute to the decision-making process. Even Vance did not go so far as to say this, but the decision was deliberately made during his absence, and his resignation over the affair made a strong public statement about the strength of his feelings and the inability of Carter to harmonize positions of his advisers.

28. Garthoff, pp. 951–52.

29. Jimmy Carter, "Letter to the USOC," January 20, 1980," *Department of State Bulletin*, 80, (March 1980): 50–51; Brzezinski, pp. 427, 476; Carter, pp. 50–51.

30. Hamilton Jordan, *Crisis* (New York: G. P. Putnam's Sons, 1982), p. 101.

31. Ibid., p. 100.

32. Senate Committee on Foreign Relations, *1980 Summer Olympic Boycott: Hearings before the Committee on Foreign Relations*, 96th Congress, 2nd Session, January 28, 1980, pp. 2–4.

33. William F. Buckley, Jr., "Get Out," *National Review*, 24 February, 1980, 244–45.

34. Allen J. Mayer, "An Olympic Boycott," *Newsweek*, 28 January, 1980, 27.

35. Buckley, p. 245.

36. Mayer, p. 27.

37. Smith set a world record in the 200-meter sprint (19.8 seconds) and won the

gold medal. Carlos placed third. Both were expelled from the U.S. Olympic team for life because of their silent protest against racism.

38. Many African nations boycotted these games because New Zealand, which earlier that year had segregated its rugby team in preparation for a series of games in South Africa, was to participate. The African nations therefore boycotted to protest New Zealand's indirect support for apartheid.

39. This contentious issue demonstrates the political nature of the International Olympic movement.

40. Mayer, p. 28.

41. Carter, pp. 50–51.

42. Robert J. Kane, "Should U.S. Boycott Olympics? No, 'The Games should be kept free of politics as much as possible.' " U.S. News & World Report, 21 January, 1980, 27–28.

43. Mayer, p. 20.

44. Vance Morrow, "The Boycott That Might Save the Games," Time, 11 February, 1980, 72–75.

45. Roger Rosenblatt, "The Games: Winning without Medals," Time, 4 August, 1980, 67–68.

46. Kevin Lynch, "On the Left," National Review, 7 March, 1980, 265.

47. Manning Marable, "Black Olympians?" The Nation, 22 March, 1980, 326.

48. See David Alpern, "Carter's Gamesmanship," Newsweek, 21 April, 1980, 41–42.

49. Alexander Moens, Foreign Policy under Carter: Testing Multiple Advocacy Decision Making (Boulder, Colo.: Westview Press, 1990); Alexander George, "The Case for Multiple Advocacy in Making Foreign Policy," American Political Science Review, 66 (September 1972): 751–85.

50. SALT 11; the Ogaden War (In 1977, Somali troops invaded Ogaden in support of the Western Somali Liberation Front's demands for self-determination. Ethiopia recaptured the area with the aid of Soviet and Cuban forces in 1978); diplomatic recognition of the PRC; and the fall of the Shah of Iran.

51. Moens, p. 171.

52. Richard Rose, The Post Modern President, 2d ed. (Chatham, N.J.: Chatham House, 1991), p. 26.

53. "Olympic Pomp and Afghan Travail," U.S. News & World Report, 28 July, 1980, 8.

54. Hammond, pp. 123–24.

55. Robert G. Kaiser, Washington Post, January 10, 1980, p. A19; quoted in Hammond, p. 124.

56. "Soviet View: They're Threatening to boycott," U.S. News & World Report, 28 April, 1980, p. 7.

57. Soviet Life magazine was a propaganda publication, circulated in the United States, that reported on the official news from Moscow in English. In format, it was very similar to Life magazine. By agreement with the Soviet Union, the

United States published a magazine in the Soviet Union with comparable purpose and format.

58. "Guess Who's Coming to Moscow?" *Time,* 9 January, 1980, 66.

59. Nancy P. Newell and Richard S. Newell, *The Struggle for Afghanistan* (Ithaca, N.Y.: Cornell University Press, 1981). p. 193.

60. Garthoff, p. 991.

61. Dobrynin, p. 448.

62. See Robert G. Kaiser, *Why Gorbachev Happened* (New York: Touchstone, 1992), pp. 202–3, 259, 295.

Selected Bibliography

Anthony Arnold. *Afghanistan: The Soviet Invasion in Perspective.* Stanford, Calif.: Hoover Institution Press, 1981.

Henry S. Bradsher. *Afghanistan and the Soviet Union.* Durham, N.C.: Duke University Press, 1983.

Zbigniew Brzezinski. *Power and Principle: Memoirs of the National Security Advisor, 1977–1981.* New York: Farrar, Straus, & Giroux, 1983.

Jimmy Carter. *Keeping Faith: Memoirs of a President.* New York: Bantam Books, 1982.

Anatoly Dobrynin. *In Confidence.* New York: Times Books, 1995.

Raymond Garthoff. *Détente and Confrontation: American-Soviet Relations.* Washington, D.C.: The Brookings Institution, 1985.

Thomas T. Hammond. *Red Flag over Afghanistan: The Communist Coup, the Soviet Invasion, and the Consequences.* Boulder, Colo.: Westview, 1984.

Alexander Moens. *Foreign Policy under Carter: Testing Multiple Advocacy Decision-Making.* Boulder, Colo.: Westview, 1990.

Nancy P. Newell and Richard P. Newell. *The Struggle for Afghanistan.* Ithaca, N.Y.: Cornell University Press, 1981.

Richard Thornton. *The Carter Years.* New York: Paragon House, 1992.

Cyrus Vance. *Hard Choices: The Critical Years in America's Foreign Policy.* New York: Simon & Schuster, 1983.

8

President Reagan's Decision to Bomb Libya

Setting and Overview of Reagan's Decision

On the evening of April 14, 1986, President Reagan announced in a nationally televised address that air strikes had been carried out against "the headquarters, terrorist facilities, and military assets that support Muammar Qaddafi's subversive activities." The targets were Tripoli, Libya's capital, and Benghazi, the country's second largest city.

President Reagan blamed the Libyan leader for the April 5th bombing of a West Berlin discotheque which had killed an American soldier and a Turkish woman and had caused injuries to some 230 other people. "Today we have done what we had to do. If necessary, we shall do it again," he stated.[1]

An earlier White House statement asserted that there was "clear" evidence that Libya had been planning future attacks. The Reagan administration defined the military operation as an exercise of self-defense, and the discouragement of future terrorist acts.[2]

Besides retaliation and punishment for alleged involvement in terrorist activities against dissident Libyan exiles, U.S. civilian and military personnel, and civilian and military targets of other countries, the bombing raids were also generally understood to have had other goals. These included provoking dissension and a possible military revolt against Colonel Qaddafi. One of the targets was a military barracks in which he had one of his residences. This led to speculation that another aim was the physical elimination of the Libyan leader.

The Reagan administration proclaimed the air raids a success. However, serious questions were later raised. Colonel Qaddafi had survived the attack on his residential quarters although his baby daughter was killed and other family members were injured. In the eyes of critics, this cast Libya in the role of a victim. Moreover, one of the American planes, with its crew of two, was lost, possibly shot down by Libyan anti-aircraft defenses.

It was generally understood at the time that the sources of international terrorism lay in complex Middle East political conflicts. Some questioned whether the air raids would deter terrorism. In the late 1980s, international terrorism abated. However, perhaps the explanation for this change lies more in the movement toward settlement of some of the fundamental problems of the Middle East, particularly the fate of the Palestinians and the reestablishment of Lebanon as a viable state after years of civil war, than in Reagan's bombing of Libya.

President Reagan's Decision

ON APRIL 14, 1986, PRESIDENT REAGAN ORDERED UNITS OF THE U.S. ARMED FORCES, BASED IN EUROPE, TO CARRY OUT AIR RAIDS ON TARGETS IN LIBYA'S TWO LARGEST CITIES OF TRIPOLI AND BENGHAZI. DESCRIBED AS MILITARY AND INTELLIGENCE FACILITIES, THESE TARGETS INCLUDED LIBYAN LEADER COLONEL MUAMMAR QADDAFI'S HEADQUARTERS COMPOUND, WHICH ALSO SERVED AS ONE OF HIS RESIDENCES, AND SEVERAL MILITARY BASES AND INSTALLATIONS. THE BOMBING RAIDS WERE DESCRIBED AS A RETALIATION AGAINST LIBYAN-SPONSORED TERRORIST ATTACKS ON AMERICAN CIVILIANS AND PROPERTY.

President Reagan's decision was more controversial abroad than in the United States. Foreign critics as well as a few in the United States criticized the air raid on the following grounds:

1. Use of force in this instance risked provoking more violence and terrorist responses and therefore defeating the very purposes of the armed action.
2. The raid had caused the death of 37 Libyans and the wounding of nearly 100 others. There was also substantial damage to homes and other civilian property.

3. If, as the attack on Colonel Qaddafi's residence at night suggested, the aim was to kill the Libyan leader, this would be morally objectionable and contrary to U.S. law. The Reagan administration formally denied that killing Qaddafi was one of the aims of the air raids. Nevertheless, some officials stated that if he had been killed, it would not have been regrettable and would have been regarded as an indirect result of an otherwise justifiable operation. Such an act would have violated the ban on the assassination of foreign leaders contained in an executive order which was signed by President Gerald Ford and reaffirmed by President Jimmy Carter.
4. The raid placed those Arab leaders, such as President Hosni Mubarak of Egypt, who were close allies of the United States, in a difficult situation of being torn between having to express sympathy and support (whether genuine or feigned) for a fellow Arab leader and country and maintaining a posture of friendship with the United States.
5. Given the fact that evidence of Libyan involvement in terrorist attacks on U.S. citizens or assets was never clearly established on the grounds that this would compromise intelligence assets, questions were raised about the appropriateness and legality under international law of military actions against Libya on the basis of U.S. claims of the right to self-defense.
6. The exact nature of Libyan involvement in terrorism was never clearly established. Did it mean, for example, merely supporting political groups which used terrorist methods of their own choosing, or did it mean direct organization and control of terrorism by Libya for its own ends?

Background of the Decision

Historical Context

When President Ronald Reagan came into office in January 1981, relations between Libya and the United States were already bad. However, they got steadily worse as the Reagan administration chose to pursue a vigorous policy of asserting and defending U.S. interests, including the use of military force.

There were many interconnected causes of conflict between the United States and Libya. Some had to do with the character of Libya's leader, Colonel Muammar Qaddafi. Others stemmed from the ideological options and policies which the Qaddafi regime pursued in Africa and the Middle East.

Between 1951 when Libya became an independent state under the monarchical rule of Emir Muhammad Idris al-Sanussi (King Idris I) and the coup d'état of September 1969 that overthrew him, the country's domestic and foreign policies were basically conservative. Western interests, including a United States air base, were welcomed in the country. This political orientation was increasingly opposed by political groups in Libya which were oriented toward a republican, nationalist, and anti-imperialist political posture.

The 1969 coup was led by Colonel Qaddafi who subsequently became Libya's undisputed leader. The new regime abolished the monarchy, ousted British and U.S. military installations, including Wheelus Air Force base located outside the capital, Tripoli. Qaddafi also nationalized foreign-owned assets, most significantly the oil industry, which had become the basis of the country's modern economy but had remained under the domination of Western companies.

In foreign policy, Qaddafi aligned the country with militant Arab nationalism. He sought to unite all Arab lands, eliminate foreign economic and political domination, and support the political and military campaigns of the Palestinians and other Arabs against Israel. In the wider context of international politics, Qaddafi placed Libya in the forefront of Third World states which opposed the United States and other Western states on such issues as the structure of the international economy ("North-South" issues), the continuation of the apartheid regime in South Africa, Portuguese colonial rule in Africa (until 1975), and support for nationalist and Marxist anti-U.S. regimes and political movements in Latin America and the Caribbean.[3]

For a brief period, Qaddafi was seen in the United States and other Western circles as a Third World leader who might be on their side in the context of the Cold War. At the early stage, he was as hostile to the Communist countries, whose atheism he abhorred, as the Western colonial legacy in Libya and elsewhere. There are even reports that in this period, the CIA assisted the Qaddafi regime against his internal political enemies.[4]

Eventually, Qaddafi came to see a basic harmony of interests between Libya and the Soviet Union and its allies. In the United Nations and other international forums, Libya was generally among the most militant Third World states opposing the United States and its allies. Qaddafi's rhetoric was consistently belligerent and uncompromising.

The brief period of harmonious relations between the new Libyan regime and the United States was only an interlude to an inherently adversarial relationship. Shortly after the 1969 coup, the Nixon administration blocked the sale of twelve C-130 military cargo planes to Libya. The Ford and Carter administrations progressively extended arms, technology, and trade embargoes against Libya.[5]

By the late 1970s, the issue of terrorism was injected into U.S.-Libyan relations. In 1977, the Carter administration received reports about a Libyan-supported assassination plot against Herman Frederick Eilts, the American ambassador to Egypt. At that time, Egyptian President Anwar el-Sadat was working to shift the country's policies toward accommodation with Israel and closer relations with the United States. This effort was fiercely opposed by radical Arab nationalists and the Palestinians. Qaddafi denied the involvement of his country in the alleged plot.[6]

In 1979, the State Department put Libya on a list of countries which were judged to support acts of terrorism. The list included a number of other radical regimes which were in conflict with the United States, such as Syria and North Korea.

Following the destruction of the American embassy in Tripoli in December 1979 by demonstrators protesting U.S. policies toward the new Islamic regime in Iran, President Carter ordered the withdrawal of all embassy personnel from the country. In May 1980, members of the Libyan People's Bureau (embassy) in Washington were expelled on the grounds that they had been persecuting Libyan dissident students in the United States.

In August, it was announced that the U.S. Sixth Fleet would conduct naval exercises in the Gulf of Sidra which Libya had claimed as its territorial waters since 1973. The Gulf of Sidra is the country's deeply indented Mediterranean shore, which is 290 miles wide and has a depth of about 150 miles. No other country recognized the Libyan claim, but none had challenged it with military force either.

The generally accepted territorial limit for maritime states under international law was twelve nautical miles. This was codified under the Law of the Sea Convention of 1982. When the naval exercises got under way, the U.S. fleet was kept outside the disputed waters, thus avoiding a direct confrontation with Libya.

In the 1980s, Libya provided military and political support to dissidents who sought to overthrow a number of African regimes which were aligned with the United States and other Western governments. For example, Libya attempted to install a friendly regime in Chad, its southern neighbor. The United States, France, and other Western governments opposed Libyan efforts in Chad and elsewhere.

Qaddafi had become a bitter foe of President Sadat after Egypt signed the Camp David Accords in 1978. This hostility was dramatically demonstrated when his assassination in October 1981 was openly celebrated in Libya.

In March 1982, President Reagan banned the importation of crude oil and the export of a wide range of products to Libya. Up to that time, the United States had been buying about a third of Libya's crude oil. Reagan hoped that the ban would have a significant impact on the country's economy and presumably lead to changes in its revolutionary policies.

In 1983, the Reagan administration initiated limited military maneuvers to support friendly regimes which appeared to be threatened by Libya. In February, Sudanese President Numeiri claimed to have uncovered a Libyan plot to overthrow his government. U.S. surveillance aircraft were sent into Egypt for intelligence gathering over Libya, and an aircraft carrier steamed toward the Gulf of Sidra. Later in the year, there were similar military maneuvers in response to Libya's involvement in the prevailing civil strife in Chad.

U.S.-Libyan Relations and the Problem of International Terrorism

It is unlikely that the conflict between the United States and Libya over the Middle East or other international issues would have led to military confrontation between the two countries. What ultimately led to violent conflict was the connection between the policies of the Libyan government and the international terrorism which had intensified in the mid-1980s.

Terrorism can be defined as the use of violent means by political groups or governments to achieve political goals in a manner which does not discriminate between civilian and military targets.[7] Terrorist actions include highjacking aircraft and ships; placing bombs on airplanes; bombing embassies and other official premises; shooting government officials; assassinating political opponents; attacking passengers on ships and aircraft; and kidnapping and holding individuals for monetary or other kinds of ransom.

In the 1980s, several groups were involved in terrorist activities, including Palestinians, various Lebanese political groups, the Irish Republican Army (IRA), Basque nationalists in Spain; Sikh nationalists in India; anti-Sandinista "contra" guerrillas in Nicaragua; and various anarchists or Marxist groups in Italy, Germany, France, and elsewhere. By the mid-1980s, terrorism had become a major international problem.

Libya's connection with terrorism was closely related to Colonel Qaddafi's vehement opposition to Israel and its support by the United States. Qaddafi supported the most radical Palestinian nationalist movements, including the Popular Front for the Liberation of Palestine (PFLP). This group rejected any compromise settlement of the Arab-Israeli conflict that did not eliminate Israel and restore the pre-1947 Palestinian territorial boundaries. Since these anti-Israel groups used such terrorist means as planting bombs and aircraft highjacking, the United States held Colonel Qaddafi accountable. The Libyan government also organized the murder of its opponents abroad and did not deny responsibility for them.

Terrorist actions against American citizens escalated during Reagan's two terms of office. One of the most dramatic incidents was the suicide truck bombing of the Marine barracks in Beirut, Lebanon, which killed 241 troops on October 23, 1983. They had been sent as part of a "peacekeeping force" which ended up engaging in armed conflict with some of the contending groups in the Lebanese civil war.

Another incident occurred on June 14, 1985, when Lebanese Shiite guerrillas highjacked TWA airlines Flight 847 en route from Athens to Rome and forced it to fly to Beirut. The highjackers demanded the release of 766 Lebanese and Palestinians held in Israeli prisons in exchange for releasing the 153 passengers and crew, of whom 104 were American citizens. One American was killed at Beirut airport and the others were released in small groups over the next two weeks. The crisis ended when Israel agreed to release a number of the Lebanese and Palestinian prisoners. On June 30, the remaining hostages were released by the highjackers.

By mid-1985, international terrorism, particularly the targeting of Americans, had moved to the top of President Reagan's agenda. On July 8, he devoted most of a speech before the American Bar Association to international terrorism. Reagan was critical of a number of countries, including Libya, North Korea, Cuba, and Nicaragua, which he described as "a confederation of terrorist states" that had carried out "outright acts of war" against the United States.

He asserted that the United States had evidence linking Libyan agents or "surrogates" to at least twenty-five terrorist incidents which had occurred in 1984. President Reagan also stated that Egypt had aborted a Libyan-backed plot to bomb the U.S. embassy in Cairo. He issued an implicit warning about a possible military response by stating that under international law, "any state which is the victim of acts of war has the right to defend itself."[8]

Throughout 1985, terrorist violence increased. On October 7, the *Achille Lauro*, an Italian cruise ship, was highjacked by Palestinian commandos in Mediterranean waters near the Egyptian coast. They demanded the release of fifty Palestinians held in jail by Israel on charges of terrorism. Before they sought asylum in Egypt on October 9, the highjackers killed one of the passengers, a disabled American citizen, and threw his body overboard.

On December 27, there were simultaneous attacks by guerrilla commandos using guns and grenades on passengers waiting at check-in counters of the El Al Israeli airlines at the Rome and Vienna airports. Eighteen people were killed and over 100 were injured. The casualties included twenty Americans. Responsibility for the attacks was claimed by the "Abu Nidal Group" (named after the nom de guerre of Sabri al-Banna, its Palestinian leader). This was a dissident splinter faction from the Al Fatah, the dominant component of the Palestine Liberation Organization (PLO). According to a note found on one of the commandos killed in the suicide attack, the action was retaliation for an earlier Israeli bombardment of the PLO headquarters in Tunis, Tunisia.[9]

Between 1984 and 1985, several citizens from Western countries were kidnapped in Lebanon. They were held by groups which demanded the release of Lebanese or Palestinians imprisoned in Israel or Western Europe on charges of terrorism or related offenses. By the end of 1985, five Americans were among the hostages, including the CIA station chief in Beirut, who was later killed.

Data collected by U.S. intelligence showed that international terrorism had increased from a yearly average of 500 incidents between 1979–83 to 780 in 1985. Casualties from these incidents increased from 1,279 in 1984 (including 41 U.S. citizens killed or wounded) to 2,200 in 1985 (including 198 U.S. citizens killed or wounded).[10]

In January 1986, President Reagan received a report from Vice President Bush's Task Force on Combatting Terrorism. This group had been established during the June 1985 hostage crisis involving the highjacking of a TWA airliner. The Task Force concluded that international terrorism was a priority problem and recommended to President Reagan specific measures to deal with it. These included improved coordination, better intelligence gathering, more effective communications and law enforcement, and expanded cooperation with other countries in combatting terrorism.[11]

President Reagan subsequently designated the State Department as the lead agency to combat terrorism. State Department officials initiated intensified high-level discussions, cooperation, and technical training and assistance in anti-terrorism efforts with about fifty foreign governments. By the end of 1986, over 3,000 officials from civilian agencies of other governments had participated in the State Department's Anti-Terrorist Assistance Program.[12]

Economic and Military Measures Prior to the Air Raids

Following the Rome and Vienna airport attacks, the Reagan administration believed that strong action against terrorism was needed. Libya was identified as the most serious threat. A wide range of policy options was considered, including economic sanctions, limited military pressure, and a direct military attack of some kind.

On January 7, 1986, President Reagan issued Executive Order 12543 declaring that Libya "constituted a threat" to national security and foreign policy. He ordered measures which would end nearly all economic ties between the United States and Libya. All Libyan assets in the United States, estimated to be worth $2.5 billion, were frozen. All American citizens, an estimated 1,000–1,500 persons, were ordered to leave Libya. American businesses were instructed to wind up their activities and leave the country.

In a news conference held on the same day, President Reagan linked the December 27 airport attacks and other terrorist incidents to Colonel Qaddafi. He stated that the Libyan leader's involvement in terrorism was "well documented."[13]

The State Department accused Qaddafi of using terrorism as one of the primary instruments of his foreign policy. He was specifically accused of operating training camps for foreign dissident groups; providing instruction in the use of explosives, highjacking, and assassination; sponsoring commando and guerrilla activities; and abusing diplomatic privileges by storing arms and explosives in diplomatic establishments.[14]

The Reagan administration debated the degree and kind of pressure which was needed to deter Libya from engaging in terrorist activities. On January 12, Secretary of State George Shultz, in a television interview, stated that it was necessary to raise the cost to those who perpetrated terrorist acts by making them pay a price, "not just an economic price."[15] Three days later, Shultz emphasized his arguments for armed reprisals by suggesting that the United States should not wait for absolute proof of responsibility before carrying out military retaliation.[16]

A more cautious view was expressed by Secretary of Defense Caspar Weinberger. He criticized those who sought "instant gratification from some kind of bombing attack without being too worried about the details."[17]

The Reagan administration increased pressure on Qaddafi in March 1986 through limited military maneuvers. They were related to the long-standing dispute stemming from Libya's claims to territorial jurisdiction over the Gulf of Sidra. Colonel Qaddafi had declared the Gulf a "zone of death" and vowed to destroy any American ships that entered the area.

According to Edwin Meese, who was one of President Reagan's closest White House advisers and served as attorney general, after the president was informed of Libyan efforts to prevent U.S. vessels from operating in the Gulf of Sidra, Reagan let it be known that the United States would not be "buffaloed or bullied."[18] Orders were given to respond with offensive means if the Libyans interfered with U.S. vessels. On August 18, 1981 two Libyan planes were shot down by U.S. aircraft when they challenged the American military units.

In March 1986, about thirty U.S. warships led by three aircraft carriers and 250 planes conducted maneuvers in the Gulf of Sidra. After Libyan planes fired two missiles at U.S. reconnaissance planes, missing their targets, U.S. forces attacked Libyan patrol vessels and missile sites. Two Libyan missile boats and missile radar sites were destroyed and seventy-two Libyan servicemen were reported to have been killed. Qaddafi responded by calling on Arabs to retaliate against Americans, a threat interpreted by American officials as incitement to anti-American terrorist acts.[19]

The Reagan administration explained the military maneuvers in the Gulf of Sidra as a challenge to Libya's extended territorial claims beyond twelve miles. However, U.S. officials conceded that the basic aim was to provoke the Libyans into an act which would provide a pretext to punish them for their support of terrorism. The United States also hoped to incite a military revolt against Colonel Qaddafi, but this did not happen.[20]

The West European Connection

Although terrorist attacks often targeted American citizens and assets, they occurred mostly in the Middle East and Western Europe. Yet, somewhat paradoxically, under the Reagan administration, the United States was more vocal and sought more vigorous economic, military, and political sanctions against states deemed to sponsor or support terrorism.

In his January 7, 1986 statement announcing the economic sanctions against Libya, President Reagan had called upon the West European allies to follow suit. He sent Assistant Secretary of State John Whitehead to Europe to lobby for strong economic measures against Libya. Italy banned arms sales to Libya and took steps to prevent Italian companies from taking over businesses which would be abandoned by American interests. Otherwise, the response of other U.S. allies was "unsupportive."[21]

For several reasons, West European leaders were reluctant to follow the Reagan administration in taking strong measures against Libya. In the first place, they were not entirely convinced that Libyan policies were the principal causes of international terrorism. They also argued that fighting terrorism should involve addressing the political roots of this phenomenon. A good deal of terrorist activity in Europe and the Middle East involved Palestinians or Lebanese who were reacting to the effects of the 1982 Israeli invasion of their country. France, Italy, and Greece, in particular, supported the Palestinian quest for some form of statehood. Resolution of these issues was considered by many in Europe to be a more appropriate response to international terrorism than punitive economic and military measures against Libya.[22]

West European countries, especially France, Spain, Italy, West Germany, and Britain also had important economic links with Libya. Libya exported oil to Western Europe, which sold manufactured products and participated in lucrative development projects in Libya.

In 1984, Libya was France's fourth largest trading partner, importing about $753 million and exporting $233 million worth of goods. About 5 percent of French oil imports came from Libya. In 1986, there were an estimated 1,000 French citizens in Libya. Spain imported $969 million and exported to Libya $293 million worth of goods. Libya provided about 80 percent of Spain's natural gas.

Italy, the former colonial ruler (between 1911 and 1947) had the closest economic relations with Libya. It was that country's largest trading partner. Trade between the two countries was valued at $4 billion. Italy had ownership shares in Libyan oil wells, while Libya shared ownership in FIAT, Italy's largest industrial company. Libya owed Italy about $800 million in loans and other financial obligations. In 1986, about 15,000 Italians were employed in Libya.

West Germany was Libya's second largest trading partner. It imported some $2 billion from Libya and exported $885 million worth of goods. There were an estimated 1,500 West Germans in Libya. British trade with Libya was worth $800 million in 1985. An estimated five thousand British citizens were in Libya.[23]

West European governments were concerned about the security of their economic interests and the physical and economic welfare of the thousands of their citizens who might be harmed in case of economic or military sanctions against Libya. These considerations reinforced their reluctance to emulate the Reagan administration's militant posture toward Colonel Qaddafi.

Some European states, such as Britain, took a dim of view of the effectiveness of economic sanctions. They believed that economic sanctions could not succeed unless all countries supported them.

Despite these considerations, the West Europeans took some limited measures in response to the Reagan administration's appeals. At a meeting on January 28, 1986, European Community leaders decided to ban arms sales to countries which supported terrorism. They also declared that they would ensure that their citizens would not take advantage of the withdrawal of U.S. businesses from Libya.

By April, the Reagan administration believed that the West Europeans had not taken sufficient measures to deter or punish Qaddafi. Consequently, the momentum toward vigorous military action against Libya continued to build.

Countdown to the Decision

Early in 1986, President Reagan ordered the National Reconnaissance Office, a secret agency responsible for procurement and deployment of U.S. intelligence and spy satellites, to move a signals intelligence satellite from orbit over Poland to North Africa to monitor Libyan communications. Interception stations in England, Italy, and Cyprus were ordered to monitor and record all communications out of Libya.

On April 2, a bomb exploded on a TWA flight en route from Rome to Athens, killing four people, including three Americans. Nineteen other people were wounded. A previously unknown Arab group claimed the attack was in retaliation for U.S. military actions in the Gulf of Sidra. Colonel Qaddafi condemned the bombing. Reagan administration officials expressed doubt about Libyan involvement in the terrorist attack. At the same time, White House Press Secretary Larry Speakes stated that Libyan complicity could not be ruled out.[24]

On April 5, a bomb exploded at *La Belle,* a West Berlin discotheque frequented by Americans. One American soldier and a Turkish woman were killed and 230 others, including fifty Americans, were injured.The bomb exploded just before 8 p.m. (Washington time) on April 4 (April 5 in Germany). By the next day, the National Security Agency had intercepted, decoded, and translated a cable from the Libyan People's Bureau (embassy) in East Germany reportedly stating: "We have something planned that will make you happy."[25] Another intercepted message reportedly confirmed with satisfaction the fact of the bombing. These messages were dispatched to California where President Reagan was spending the Easter holiday. He made the decision to bomb Libya on the afternoon of April 5.[26]

In a televised news conference on April 9, President Reagan declared that the United States was prepared to act if evidence pointed directly to Libyan complicity in the discotheque bombing. He called the Libyan leader the "mad dog of the Middle East." Colonel Qaddafi denied any Libyan involvement and challenged President Reagan to produce evidence. He also threatened retaliation for any U.S. attack through worldwide assaults on U.S. targets.[27]

As tension between Libya and the United States mounted, Italian Prime Minister Bettino Craxi declared that President Reagan needed to offer "clearer" evidence of Libyan involvement in recent terrorist attacks if he wanted European support for action against Libya. Chancellor Helmut Kohl stated that West Germany had indications of Libyan involvement but opposed any military retaliation.[28]

The Reagan administration was still divided over the wisdom of a military attack on Libya. For example, Shultz, supported by White House Chief of Staff Donald Regan and National Security Advisor John Poindexter, argued for punitive air strikes. In contrast, Defense Secretary Weinberger was cautious and the Joint Chiefs of Staff were divided. Questions were raised about the deterrent effect of air strikes and the possible stormy reaction in the Middle East region, which was of vital interest for U.S. foreign policy.[29]

At this time, Vernon Walters, the U.S. ambassador to the United Nations, was sent on a mission to Western Europe to solicit support for impending action against Libya. He was successful only in Britain. Prime Minister Margaret Thatcher agreed to the use of British NATO bases as a staging ground for some of the planned air raids.

On April 14, President Reagan ordered the air attacks on Libya. A few hours before the raids, he met with congressional leaders to inform them about the decision.

President Reagan as Decision-Maker

Foreign Policy Context of Decision

President Reagan, like Eisenhower, Carter, and Clinton, came to Washington without any previous experience in the federal government. His only previous elected office was two terms as governor of California (1967 to 1975). By the time Reagan ran for governor he had completed the remarkable political transformation from a New Deal Democrat (who had campaigned on radio in 1948 for President Truman and "Democratic Senate stars of the future like Hubert H. Humphrey")[30] to a conservative Republican who had endorsed Senator Barry Goldwater's unsuccessful electoral challenge against President Lyndon Johnson in 1964. In 1976, Reagan unsuccessfully challenged President Gerald Ford for the Republican nomination at the party convention.

As governor, Reagan had gained some exposure to international affairs. On four occasions, President Nixon sent him and his wife Nancy abroad as "good will" representatives. On these trips, Reagan met eighteen heads of state in Europe and Asia.[31]

By the time he became president, Reagan had developed a set of clear, simple and strongly held views on foreign policy. His world view was Manichean: the world was divided between allies and adversaries; patriots and villains; loyal friends and untrustworthy enemies. The evil side was represented by the Soviet Union, other communist countries, and all those who supported, aligned themselves with, or sympathized with them.[32]

During the 1980 presidential campaign, Reagan argued that under President Carter, the "bad guys" had caught up with and moved ahead of the "good guys" in the contest for global hegemony. Reagan claimed that the Soviet military intervention in Afghanistan, the overthrow of the Shah's regime in Iran by the Ayatollah Khomeini's revolution, and the assumption of power by the Sandinista Front in Nicaragua—all occurring in 1979—were evidence of weak American leadership.

By the time he moved into the White House in January 1981, President Reagan's views on U.S. foreign policy could be summarized in six propositions:

1. The United States represented all that was good for the human race, and the rest of the world should try to emulate it in the political, economic, and social spheres.[33]

2. The underlying cause of Third World crises and tensions was Soviet influence, either direct or through local allies.
3. The United States should take opportunities to project and use power to enforce solutions. In addition, it should rid itself of the "Vietnam syndrome," which was reflected in the discrediting of the utility or legitimacy of the use of American military and political power.[34]
4. The United States should orient its policy in specific regions on an East-West axis to counter Soviet influence.
5. The United States should not seek collaboration with the Soviets in dealing with world trouble spots, but should act unilaterally to curb or minimize Soviet influence.
6. This tough approach would be an improvement over the "timid" and "ineffective" policies of the Carter presidency.[35]

Consequently, Reagan believed that the nation's pride and confidence had to be restored by resolute means against all opposition in both domestic and foreign policy.

Despite the bellicose tone he adopted toward the Soviet Union and other perceived enemies of the United States, President Reagan was pragmatic in the use of force. He would resort to direct military intervention only in situations where the United States had overwhelming military superiority, could anticipate no danger of defeat, or engage in direct battlefield confrontation with the Soviet Union.[36]

For example, even though his first secretary of state, Alexander Haig, had made some belligerent remarks to the effect that Cuba was "the source" of trouble in Central America, there was no evidence that anybody in the Reagan administration ever proposed invading that country. Neither did President Reagan seek to use direct military force in countries such as Nicaragua, Angola, or Afghanistan whose governments he strongly opposed. His foreign policies reflected the calculations of a leader whose mentality was "an extraordinary combination of the ideologue and the realist."[37]

The Reagan Doctrine

The Reagan Doctrine resulted from Reagan's conservative ideology, his view of the major crises and events of the 1970s, and his pragmatism. The Reagan Doctrine was designed to deal with perceived Soviet challenges in the Third World. It included the direct and indirect use of American resources to counter and overthrow regimes deemed hostile and aligned with or sponsored by the Soviet Union and Cuba.[38]

Qaddafi's revolutionary foreign policy orientation tended to align Libya with Soviet foreign policy goals. Given Reagan's worldview, this coincidence of Libyan and Soviet policies placed Qaddafi in the enemy's camp.

Shortly after coming into office, President Reagan intensified previous diplomatic, military, and economic pressure against Libya. In early 1981, following reports that Libyan "hit men" had been sent to the United States to hunt down anti-Qaddafi Libyan exiles, he ordered the U.S. embassy in Tripoli and the Libya People's Bureau in Washington to be closed. He also ordered that all Libyan visa applications be subjected to a mandatory security advisory opinion and advised American oil companies in Libya to reduce the number of their American employees.

In March 1982, the Reagan administration announced an embargo on Libyan oil and imposed an export license requirement for all American goods bound for Libya, except for food, medicine and medical supplies. It also called upon its West European allies to support the economic sanctions. In 1983, movements of Libyan diplomats accredited to the United Nations in New York were curtailed. In November 1985, the import of all Libyan oil products was banned. This was followed by economic sanctions in early 1986, imposed in response to the December 27, 1985 terrorist attacks at the Rome and Vienna airports where five Americans were killed.

Military pressure against Libya was applied through aerial and naval challenges in the Gulf of Sidra. This was part of Reagan's campaign to provoke the overthrow of the Qaddafi regime. The Reagan administration also supported anti-Qaddafi exiles and regimes such as those in Egypt, Sudan, and Chad which were hostile to Qaddafi. By early spring 1986, the ouster of Qaddafi had become "a virtual obsession" for the Reagan administration.[39] Although officially denied, one of the goals of the 1986 air raids appears to have been the physical elimination of Colonel Qaddafi.[40]

Meese related that with the 1986 air raids against Libya, Reagan intended to send a "loud and clear" message:

> no longer could Third World despots challenge the United States and depend on America's post-Vietnam guilt complex, or its uncertainty about its global role, to bind our hands. No longer would we act as a "pitiful, helpless giant," crippled by internal divisions or ideological confusion.[41]

The punitive application of the Reagan Doctrine against Libya demonstrated the pragmatic streak in Reagan's *modus operandi*. Qaddafi's Libya was a low-risk target in military and political terms. Its inexperienced military had failed to inflict any damage on U.S. naval and air units in previous clashes in the Gulf of Sidra. Politically, Qaddafi was surrounded by enemies in the North African region. His belligerent style and his reputed open use of terrorist methods against his opponents abroad as well as his general association with terrorism (sometimes exaggerated or distorted) made it difficult for most governments to come to Libya's defense.

Domestic Context of Decision

One of the factors which helped President Reagan's 1980 election was the plight of the fifty-two American hostages at the American embassy in Teheran, Iran. President Carter had failed to free them in an disastrous rescue mission. The Iranian hostage crisis had damaged President Carter. U.S. foreign policy appeared weak, incoherent, and incapable of protecting U.S. national interests abroad.

During the 1980 presidential campaign, Reagan pledged to restore America's self-confidence and pride. He argued that U.S. standing in the world had eroded over the previous decade. International terrorism, which threatened Americans, was a major problem. R. W. Apple of the *New York Times* observed that "One of the reasons he was elected in the first place, and one of the reasons his popularity has continued at a high level, is the belief of the American public that he would stand up to, would face down, the nation's enemies."[42] According to a New York Times/CBS news poll of April 1986, Americans considered terrorism the number one problem facing the nation.[43]

As the Reagan administration considered a military response to the West Berlin discotheque bombing, congressional leaders from both parties endorsed such action. Senator Richard Lugar (R, Indiana), the chairman of the Senate Foreign Relations Committee and Representative Matthew McHugh (D, N.Y.), a member of the House Select Committee on Intelligence, indicated support for military retaliation against Libya. However, Senator Lugar also called upon Secretary Shultz to consult with the Foreign Relations Committee concerning the impending military operations in conformity with the 1973 War Powers Resolution.[44]

Following the air raids, there were other expressions of public and congressional support. However, Senator Robert Byrd (D, W.V.) dissented. He argued that economic rather than military reprisals should have been used.

Some congressional leaders complained that they were not informed of the bombing raids until a few hours before they occurred.[45] Congressman Dante Fascell (D, Florida), chairman of the House Committee on Foreign Affairs, objected to what he regarded as the circumvention of the War Powers Resolution. He argued that the likelihood of hostilities stemming from the presence of U.S. military units in the Gulf of Sidra should have led President Reagan to consult with Congress.[46]

The air strikes against Libya were widely supported by U.S. public opinion. A New York Times/CBS poll taken shortly after the air raids showed that 77 percent approved of the military action. The poll also revealed widespread fears that the attack on Libya would lead to more international terrorism.[47]

Decision Options

During the last part of 1985, President Reagan ordered a review of the options for military action against Libya. The Defense Department drew up a plan for a massive seaborne attack. Because this was considered excessive, a decision was made to use an air strike.[48]

President Reagan was angered by the terrorist attacks at the Rome and Vienna airports in December 1985. This strengthened his conviction that a forceful response was needed. At the same time, he had to consider the likelihood that any military action against Libya would endanger the lives of the estimated 1,500 American citizens still living there.

Reagan also had difficulty deciding which targets to attack. For example, the Abu Nidal Group which had claimed responsibility for the attacks, was a "freelance" organization. Reagan stated: "I want to punish the right people. I don't want to lay waste the buildings of an area or a whole city and not know that we have hit the perpetrators."[49]

Nevertheless, one day after the airport attacks, an interagency group considered military action against Libya. Chaired by Donald Fortier, deputy assistant to the president for national security affairs, it included specialists from the Departments of Defense and State, the CIA, the White House, and other agencies.

Secretary Shultz argued for military action against Libya. He believed that the United States "seemed virtually paralyzed after terrorist attacks abroad."[50] As far as he was concerned, the link between Abu Nidal and Libya was clear. In contrast, Secretary Weinberger feared inflaming the Arab nations and creating problems for states which welcomed U.S. forces. He was also concerned about the potential loss of American and Libyan lives resulting from military actions against Libya. Consequently, Weinberger favored diplomatic and economic sanctions against Libya while Shultz argued for strong military measures.

On January 2, 1986, President Reagan received the military options for attacking Libyan military camps and bases. In determining a response, Reagan had to consider a number of domestic and foreign policy constraints.

First, there was the danger of American casualties which would have a negative impact in the United States. Second, West European allies had important economic interests which might be jeopardized by an American military strike against Libya. Third, Arab allies of the United States such as Egypt and Saudi Arabia would be put in the difficult position of either condoning a military attack on an Arab state or condemning the action. After taking these options into account, President Reagan decided on economic sanctions against Libya.

The April 5th discotheque bombing dramatically changed the administration's position. Now it seemed a more direct linkage could be established between Libya and terrorist actions against U.S. military personnel. However, several factors still weighed against U.S. military reprisals. U.S public opinion would react negatively to any substantial loss of American lives. There were American hostages in Lebanon who could fall victim to a likely frenzy of revenge in the Middle East. West Europeans remained opposed to military action as a solution to the problem of international terrorism. Moreover, they were not convinced of the Reagan administration's "evidence" about the nature and degree of Colonel Qaddafi's culpability in the discotheque bombing.

Libya's direct involvement in the West Berlin discotheque bombing remained unclear, in part because the Reagan administration's statements contained a degree of ambiguity. For example, shortly before the bombing of Libya, a "senior" administration official stated that there was "incontrovertible evidence" of Libyan involvement.[51] The next day, White House Chief of Staff Regan stated that the administration was "close to a final conclusion" about Libya's culpability in the bombing.[52] However, on April 12, other Reagan administration officials were quoted as stating that evidence implicating Libya was "strong but not conclusive."[53]

One day before the air raids, Deputy Assistant Secretary of State John Whitehead stated in a television interview that even more important than Qaddafi's involvement in the discotheque bombing was information the administration had about future Libyan plans for "literally dozens" of other terrorist actions around the world. It was those plans the administration had to foil in order to protect the lives of Americans "which are in danger." At the same time, Robert Oakley, ambassador-at-large for counter-terrorism at the State Department, stated that evidence linking Libya to the discotheque bombing was still being examined "because we want to make the best case possible."[54]

The Reagan administration refused to publish the transcripts of the intercepted messages between East Berlin and Tripoli, arguing that this might jeopardize its intelligence sources. This reticence led some critics to suggest that a neutral interpretation of the messages might not have provided the "smoking gun" that was required to justify the bombing of Libya.[55]

The administration also had a problem deciding which targets to attack. Economic facilities, including oil wells which provided the cash for Qaddafi's aggressive foreign policies, had to be excluded because of concern for the economic interests of West European allies.

Until April 14, when the final order for the air strikes was given, the Reagan administration considered the possibility that military action might be called off. This would have required European allies to take strong economic measures against Libya. In addition, Colonel Qaddafi would have had to formally renounce terrorism—in effect cry "Uncle!" None of these things happened.[56]

Reagan's Leadership Role in the Decision

One of the outstanding characteristics of President Reagan's leadership style was the tendency to delegate power to his trusted aides and subordinates. He would establish the broad policy goals and then allow cabinet and other officials to work out the details.[57] This type of leadership style has been attributed to Reagan's background as a Hollywood actor. Some critics argue that Reagan was often doing nothing much more than acting out roles and getting manipulated by others who were making the actual policies he propounded.[58]

President Reagan disagreed with this view of his leadership style. Instead, he explained his approach as follows: "The chief executive should set broad policy and general ground rules, tell people what he or she wants them to do, then let them do it. . . . As long as they are doing what you have in mind, don't interfere, but if somebody drops the ball, intervene and make a change."[59]

After the Vienna and Rome airport attacks in December 1985, President Reagan confronted a choice between economic sanctions and some form of unilateral military action against Libya. In January, he chose economic sanctions. By March, he had moved toward limited punitive military measures, which had the additional aim of provoking a coup against Colonel Qaddafi.

Meese argued that President Reagan was actively involved in all the decisions involving the bombing of Libya. After the discotheque bombing, "The president never hesitated. He gave the order for a swift and sure response. He directed Secretary Weinberger and the Joint Chiefs to come up with a very specific and highly focused plan to punish Qaddafi's terrorism."[60] Meese further claims that Reagan was even involved in the selection of targets for the April air raids:

> I vividly remember the Joint Chiefs of Staff assembled in the Oval Office, showing the President maps of Tripoli and getting his direction about targets. A great deal of care was taken in the planning, with the President insisting on precision bombing of military targets. In some cases, because these were close to civilians populations, they were excluded from the target plan at the President's command.[61]

Meese's views about avoiding civilian targets are in stark contrast to those of others who believed that the death of Colonel Qaddafi was one of the major aims of the air raids. In fact, there were civilian deaths, injuries, and property damage because the attacks included areas which were close to civilian housing.

Consequences of Reagan's Decision for the United States and Other Countries Involved

There was strong support in the United States for the president's actions. Colonel Qaddafi had already acquired the image of a villain and the decision to punish him was applauded. There was, however, some doubt about the impact of the bombing raids on curbing international terrorism.

The immediate results of the bombing raids on Libya were clearer than the long-term consequences. Within Libya, 37 people were killed and 93 wounded in the air raids. There was substantial damage to military and civilians installations, including the diplomatic premises of such Western countries as Italy, France, Finland, Austria, and Switzerland.

Outside the United States, the impact of the bombing raids was almost uniformly negative. Before the raids occurred, all West European allies, with the exception of Britain, were generally opposed to military action against Libya. France, Italy, and Spain refused to allow U.S. Air Force jets launched from British airfields to overfly their territories. This forced the U.S. planes to make a detour over the Atlantic Ocean, adding 1,200 nautical miles to their long trip to Libya.

The United Nations (through the secretary-general), the Non-Aligned Movement (a grouping of over 100 mainly African, Asian and Latin American states), and most of the West European allies condemned the bombing. Italy had tried to dissuade the United States from carrying out the attacks. The Belgian Foreign Minister declared: "We do not think the Sixth Fleet is the best way of fighting terrorism."[62]

Thousands of people demonstrated against the bombings in such Western European cities as London, Paris, Rome, and Bonn. Only British Prime Minister Thatcher supported the Reagan administration. She had earlier opposed the use of military force but changed her mind. Her support was widely regarded as a *quid pro quo* for earlier U.S. support during Britain's 1982 confrontation with Argentina over the Falklands.[63]

There were also acts of violence in protest against the air strikes. A U.S. embassy official in Khartoum, Sudan was shot and wounded. Subsequently, dependents of embassy personnel were evacuated. Two British and one American hostage, who were being held in Lebanon, were killed by their captors. Another Briton was seized and reportedly killed too.A fire bomb was thrown into the U.S. embassy compound in Tunis, Tunisia. In Central America, there was a bomb blast in front of the U.S. consulate in San Jose, Costa Rica. However, it was not clear whether this attack was a protest against the bombing of Libya or against U.S. policies in Central America.[64]

The air strikes also had a short-term negative impact on U.S.-Soviet relations. After lodging verbal protests, the Soviet Union declared that it had decided to put off a planned meeting between Foreign Minister Eduard Shevardnadze and Secretary Shultz. The meeting was to have discussed the planned summit meeting between President Reagan and Soviet leader Mikhail Gorbachev.

The bombing attack on Libya also affected U.S.-Arab relations. President Mubarak, a key supporter of American-sponsored peace plans for the Arab-Israeli conflict, found himself in an ambiguous and embarrassing position. Although Egyptian relations with Libya were bad in part because of Egypt's close relationship with the United States, Mubarak could not openly condone or support a military attack on a neighboring Arab state.

Even though West European allies were almost unanimous in their criticism of the air raids, they were spurred to take stronger measures against the Qaddafi regime. They clearly wanted to show that there were nonviolent means available to discourage Libya from involvement in terrorist activities.

A special meeting of foreign ministers of the European Community held on April 14, 1986—hours before the attack on Libya—identified Libya as "implicated in supporting terrorism" but did not impose any economic sanctions. It urged restraint "on all sides" and decided on a number of measures designed to restrict the activities of Libyan agents in Europe.[65] They included restrictions on movements of Libyan citizens and imposing stricter visa requirements on their entry. A week later, the foreign ministers met and decided to reduce Libyan diplomats and nondiplomatic personnel in their countries. They also banned Libyans expelled from one country from entering another, and required Libyan diplomats to get special permission to travel outside the cities where they were posted.

On April 25, it was announced that Attorney General Meese and a number of his European counterparts had reached a new agreement to share information about international terrorists. On April 30, the European Community announced the suspension of all sales of butter to Libya.[66]

Conclusion

Immediately after the launching of the air raids on Libya, President Reagan described the two goals of the operation: retaliation and punitive discouragement of future terrorist activities. On both counts, the achievements were dubious.

The bombings were reported to have shaken Colonel Qaddafi. And for the next two years, there were no reports of anti-U.S. terrorist activities involving Libya. However, on December 21, 1988, a Pan

American World Airways jet, Flight PA 103, was blown up over the Scottish village of Lockerbie, killing all 243 passengers and the crew. Most of them were American citizens.

On September 19, 1989, a French DC-10 airliner, UTA Flight 772 was blown up over the Sahara desert north of Chad, killing all the passengers and crew. The Reagan and Bush administrations blamed both terrorist attacks on Libya and Colonel Qaddafi. If, in fact, Libya was responsible, it was apparent that Qaddafi had not been deterred by the 1986 air raids. On the other hand, some disputed the extent of Libyan culpability in these subsequent airline bombings.[67]

In the early 1990s, the incidents of international terrorism declined dramatically. Significant changes took place in the international political system, including the disintegration of the Soviet Union and the Communist bloc in Eastern Europe; German unification; the beginning of a peace settlement between the Israelis and the Palestinians and some of the Arab states; and the end of apartheid in South Africa.

Britain, West Germany, and Italy, all of which were targets of domestic and international terrorism in the 1980s, took effective actions to curb such attacks. President Reagan was successful in encouraging West European governments to initiate more aggressive preventive police, intelligence, and other measures to curb terrorist acts. Consequently, some credit can be attributed to the U.S. air strikes as a way of focusing West European attention on the need to take stronger measures against international terrorism.

Several U.S. presidents, beginning with Nixon, were frustrated by the ability of Libya, an underdeveloped country of less than 4 million people, to thumb its nose at the United States. On various occasions, attempts were made to help bring about the downfall of its radical and eccentric leader. If the air raids were intended to bring about this result, they failed. Colonel Qaddafi remained in power for many years after the 1986 bombing raids.

From the perspective of American domestic politics, there is no doubt that the air strikes reinforced President Reagan's image as the man who restored America's global stature as a confident superpower. The air strikes also contributed to the reduction of the impact of the "Vietnam syndrome" on U.S. foreign policy. On the other hand, at the outset of the 1990 Gulf War (between the U.S.-led coalition and Iraq), the reluctance of many in Congress, the media and public opinion to place American troops "in harm's way" indicated that the syndrome had perhaps not entirely disappeared.

It is also ironic that President Reagan decided to bomb Libya to deter terrorism during the same time he and his advisers were secretly selling arms to Iran. The covert arms deals with Iran were intended to free American hostages held in Lebanon. Reagan and his advisers hoped Iranian "moderates" could influence Islamic fundamentalists to release the hostages. However, Reagan's decision to ship arms to Iran only led to more demands and the release of a very few hostages. The Iran-Contra Affair became President Reagan's greatest foreign policy fiasco.

Questions for Discussion

1. Was a military strike the best means to deter Libya's involvement in international terrorism?

2. Should President Reagan have heeded the appeals of the United States' Western European allies and used nonviolent economic and diplomatic means to deter Libya?

3. Did the Reagan administration make a convincing case about Qaddafi's responsibility for the West Berlin discotheque bombing?

4. If Colonel Qaddafi had been killed in the air raid on his residence, would that have been morally and political justifiable?

5. Why were American citizens and property so often the targets of international terrorism?

6. Why were Western European governments reluctant to take forceful measures against Libya prior to the bombing?

7. Would the death or overthrow of Qaddafi have reduced the level of international terrorism?

8. Why did most of the rest of the world condemn the U.S. bombing raids?

9. How would you rate the danger posed to the United States by international terrorism?

10. How should the current presidential administration handle international terrorism?

Notes

1. *Weekly Compilation of Presidential Documents*, 22.16. (1986): 491.
2. Ibid., 490.
3. Ronald B. St. John, "Terrorism and Libyan Foreign Policy, 1981–86," *The World Today*, 42.7 (July 1986): 111–15.
4. Geoff Simons, *Libya: The Struggle for Survival* (New York: St. Martin's Press, 1993), pp. 304–6.
5. Edward Schumacher, "The United States and Libya," *Foreign Affairs*, 65.2 (Winter 1986/87): 329–48.
6. Simons, p. 299.
7. Cf. "Terrorism consists of a series of acts intended to spread intimidation, panic, and destruction in a population. Those acts can be carried out by individuals and groups opposing a state, or acting on its behalf." Gianfranco Pasquito, "Terrorism," in Adam Kuper and Jessica Kuper (eds.) *The Social Science Encyclopedia* (London: Routledge & Kegan Paul, 1985), p. 851.
8. *Department of State Bulletin*, 85.2101 (August 1985): 7–10.
9. *New York Times*, December 29, 1985.
10. Robert Oakley, "International Terrorism," *Foreign Affairs*, 65.3 (1987): 613.
11. Ibid., 613–14.
12. Ibid., 614.
13. *Weekly Compilation of Presidential Documents*, 22.1 (1986): 21–22.
14. *New York Times*, January 9, 1986.
15. Ibid., January 13, 1986.
16. Ibid., January 16, 1986.
17. Ibid., January 17, 1986.
18. Edwin Meese III, *With Reagan: The Inside Story* (Washington, D.C.: Regnery Gateway, 1992), p. 201–2.
19. Ibid., 202–3.
20. Frederick Zilian, Jr., "The U.S. Raid on Libya—and Nato," *Orbis*, 30.3 (Fall 1986): 505–6.
21. Ibid., p. 504.
22. St. John, p. 114.
23. Zilian, pp. 512–20.
24. *Facts on File*, 46.2367 (April 4, 1986): 217
25. Seymour M. Hersh, "Target Qaddafi," in Richard J. Stillman II, *Public Administration: Concepts and Cases* (Boston: Houghton Mifflin Company, 1988), p. 427.
26. Ibid.

27. *New York Times*, April 10, 1986.

28. Ibid., April 12, 1986.

29. Ibid.

30. Lou Cannon, *Reagan* (New York: G. P. Putnam's Sons, 1982), p. 72.

31. Ronald Reagan, *An American Life* (New York: Simon & Schuster, 1990), pp. 186–88.

32. Hedrick Smith, Adam Clymer, Leonard Silk, Robert Lindsey, and Richard Burt, *Reagan the Man, the President* (New York: Macmillan, 1980), p. 97.

33. Wilbur Edel, *The Reagan Presidency* (New York: Hippocrene Books, 1992), p. 168.

34. Robert W. Tucker, "Reagan's Foreign Policy," *Foreign Affairs*, 68.1 (1989): 9.

35. Fred Halliday, "The Reagan Administration and the Middle East," in Morris H. Morley, (ed.), *Crisis and Confrontation: Ronald Reagan's Foreign Policy* (Totowa, N.J.: Rowman & Littlefield Publishers, 1988), p. 132.

36. Edel, p. 215.

37. Tucker, p. 12–13.

38. Halliday, pp. 150–54. For an interpretation with a different and more sympathetic emphasis, see Jean Kirkpatrick and Allan Gerson, "The Reagan Doctrine, Human Rights, and International Law," in Louis Henkin et al., *Right v. Might*, 2nd ed. (New York: Council on Foreign Relations, 1991), pp. 37–69.

39. Schumacher, p. 329.

40. See Hersh.

41. Meese, p. 204.

42. R. W. Apple, "Reagan Confronts an Intractable Qaddafi," *New York Times*, April 13, 1986, section 4, p. 1.

43. Ibid., April 12, 1986.

44. Ibid.

45. Ibid., April 15, 1986.

46. "War Powers, Libya, and State-Sponsored Terrorism," Hearings before the House Committee on Foreign Affairs, 99th Cong., 2d Sess. 2 (1986), cited in Louis Fisher, *Presidential War Power* (Lawrence, Kan.: University Press of Kansas, 1995), p. 144.

47. *New York Times*, April 17, 1986.

48. Christopher Andrews, *For the President's Eyes Only* (New York: Harper-Collins, 1995), pp. 482–83.

49. *New York Times*, April 12, 1986.

50. Ibid.

51. Ibid., April 11, 1986.

52. Ibid., April 12, 1986.

53. Ibid., April 13, 1986.

54. Ibid., April 14, 1986, p. A6.

55. See Simons, pp. 323–27.

56. *New York Times*, April 15, 1986.

57. Meese, pp. 14–26.
58. Edel, pp. 145–66.
59. Reagan, p. 161.
60. Meese, p. 203.
61. Ibid., p. 205.
62. *New York Times*, April 16, 1986.
63. Zilian, p. 513.
64. *New York Times*, April 16 & 17, 1986.
65. *Keesing's Contemporary Archives*, 32.6 (1986): 34456.
66. Zilian, pp. 499–500.
67. Simons, pp. 8–14, 30–69.

Selected Bibliography

Andrews, Christopher. *For the President's Eyes Only*. New York: Harper-Collins, 1995.

Cannon, Lou. *Reagan*. New York: G. P. Putnam's Sons, 1982.

Edel, Wilbur. *The Reagan Presidency*. New York: Hippocrene Books, 1992.

Meese, Edwin. *With Reagan: the Inside Story*. Washington, D.C.: Regnery Gateway, 1992.

Morley, Morris H. (ed.). *Crisis and Confrontation: Ronald Reagan's Foreign Policy*. Totowa, N.J.: Rowman & Littlefield Publishers, 1988.

Reagan, Ronald. *An American Life*. New York: Simon & Schuster, 1990.

Simons, Geoff. *Libya: The Struggle for Survival*. New York: St. Martin's Press, 1993.

Smith, Hedrick Adam Clymer, Leonard Silk, Robert Lindsey, and Richard Burt. *Reagan the Man: the President*. New York: Macmillan, 1980.

9

President Bush's Decision to End the Persian Gulf War at 100 Hours

Setting and Overview of Bush's Decision

On August 2, 1990, Iraq's armed forces attacked Kuwait. Kuwait fell within hours. The Emir (Muslim chieftain) of Kuwait, along with most of his family and entourage, fled to sanctuary in Saudi Arabia, where they sat out the war. Iraq's swift military action sent shockwaves throughout the Middle East. Neighboring countries, particularly Saudi Arabia and the United Arab Emirates, felt immediately vulnerable. In August, Iraq ignored a series of UN resolutions that condemned its invasion, demanded unconditional and immediate withdrawal, and imposed a trade embargo. At the same time, Iraq announced that it had annexed Kuwait, making it "Province 19."

The United States assumed responsibility and leadership for counteraction. President George Bush and Secretary of State James A. Baker III prepared the diplomatic path for the Security Council's adoption of Resolution 678 on November 29. This called for Iraq to withdraw from Kuwait by January 15, 1991 or face UN authorized military force. In the meantime, under UN auspices the United States organized and directed Operation Desert Shield. It put together the Gulf Coalition whereby states in the Middle East and elsewhere contributed soldiers as well as logistical, medical, and financial assistance. The United States itself placed about 450,000 troops in the region. This was the largest U.S. military operation since the Vietnam War. The main goal of Desert

273

Shield was to deter an Iraqi attack on Saudi Arabia. The United States believed that protection of the vast Saudi oil reserves was vital to the economy of the United States and the rest of the industrialized world.

When Iraq still refused to withdraw from Kuwait, pressure grew to respond militarily to Iraq's invasion. President Bush overcame significant domestic opposition as well as questionable constitutional authority to his use of military force. On January 12, he persuaded both houses of Congress to authorize him to use military force to drive Iraq from Kuwait. On January 16, Operation Desert Storm began. Air and cruise missile strikes punished Iraqi positions. Iraq's leader, Saddam Hussein, responded by launching SCUD missile attacks on Saudi Arabia and Israel. Appealing to the Palestinians, Saddam tried unsuccessfully to draw Israel into the war and to tie his invasion of Kuwait to the Arab-Israeli conflict. His call for negotiations to discuss both issues was ineffectual. The United States, fearing an unbearable strain upon Arab coalition members, managed to keep Israel out of the coalition and the war itself.

Coalition forces, led by General H. Norman Schwarzkopf, pounded Iraqi positions inside Kuwait and in Iraq. In addition, coalition strategy called for destruction of Iraq's military command and communications systems as well as the country's infrastructure. For weeks the coalition air force, using its uncontested superiority to full advantage, unmercifully struck both day and night. Civilian as well as military casualties were very high. Use of offensive "smart bombs" and defensive Patriot missiles, touted in extensive television coverage, impressed the American public. When Iraq refused to withdraw from Kuwait by a February 23 deadline, the ground war began the next day. By this time the American people were giving Bush overwhelming support.

After driving Iraq from Kuwait and destroying a large part of Iraq's vaunted Republican Guard, Bush unilaterally declared an end to the war after 100 hours. The president made this decision clearly and decisively. Yet controversy developed almost immediately. Kuwait was liberated, but a number of serious questions about achievement of the war's political goals remained.

President Bush's Decision

ON FEBRUARY 28, 1990, PRESIDENT BUSH DECIDED ON A UNILATERAL CESSATION OF HOSTILITIES. THIS ENDED THE PERSIAN GULF WAR 100 HOURS AFTER THE START OF THE GROUND WAR.

Bush's decision was controversial for several main reasons:

1. An unremorseful Saddam Hussein was left in power.
2. The elite Republican Guard was only partially destroyed.
3. Saddam proceeded to persecute the Kurds in the north of his country and Shiite Muslims in the south.
4. There was serious doubt over the destruction of Iraq's nuclear, biological, and chemical weapons capabilities as well as its stockpiles of SCUD missiles.
5. There was criticism that ending the war at precisely 100 hours was more of a public relations stunt than a sound military and political decision.
6. It was unlikely Iraq would have to pay for the destruction of oil wells in Kuwait as well as the environmental damage it wreaked during the war.
7. It was unclear whether General Schwarzkopf actually agreed with the decision.
8. The extent to which the war had brought peace and stability to the Gulf region was uncertain.

Background of the Decision

Historical Context

The Persian Gulf is an extremely important strategic body of water. More than half the world's oil reserves are located in the countries along its border. This oil is the main source of supply for the rest of the world. After World War II, the United States worked with Great Britain to control this vitally important natural resource. They would not allow any outside power, particularly the Soviet Union, to gain significant influence in the region and the power to impede the flow of oil to the West. To achieve this goal, the United States and Britain developed a "Northern Tier" strategy. They strengthened both the military defense capabilities and the internal security forces of such states as Turkey, Iran, and Iraq. In return, leaders of these countries guaranteed an uninterrupted flow of oil at a very reasonable price.

By the early 1970s, Britain was forced to pull back its military forces "East of Suez." This left the United States as the main Western power in the Persian Gulf area. After the 1973 Yom Kippur War, Saudi

Arabia led an Arab oil embargo against the West. When this eased, the United States adopted a "twin pillars" strategic policy in the Gulf. Washington relied on Iran and Saudi Arabia, the two largest oil producers in the region, to maintain stability and the flow of oil. But when the Shah of Iran was overthrown in 1979, and when later that year the Soviet union invaded Afghanistan, the United States relied on the new Carter Doctrine. This held that the United States would regard as a threat to its vital interests (i.e., oil) any Soviet aggression in the Persian Gulf. It also resulted in the establishment of a rapid deployment force intended to deter and defend against threats in the region.

The Iran-Iraq War

The Iran-Iraq conflict had deep historical, territorial, religious, and power political roots. Iraq, a predominantly Arab country, was a rival of Iran, which is mainly Persian. During the 1970s, Iran and Iraq quarreled over two main issues. First, each wanted to control the Shatt al-Arab waterway. This is the 120-mile confluence of the Tigris and Euphrates rivers that empties into the Gulf. And second, each supported minority factions seeking autonomy from central government rule in the other state. Iran supported the Kurds and Shiite Muslims in Iraq, whereas Iraq aided the Baluchis, Kurds, and Arabs in Iran. At that time, the United States backed the Shah's efforts to destabilize Iraq. After the Iraqi Revolution of 1958, U.S. influence in that country had diminished rapidly. Moreover, prospects for Iraq's becoming a client state of the Soviet Union had increased.

The Algiers treaty of 1975 temporarily resolved these disputes peacefully. Iran and Iraq, each seeking to avoid war, agreed on the boundary for the waterway and to refrain from aiding minority rebels in the other. The Shah even prevailed upon Saddam Hussein, who by this time was Iraq's leader of the Ba'ath (Arab Socialist Renaissance) Party and uncontested strongman, to deport the Ayatollah Khomeini from Iraq, where he had been living in exile since 1964.

When the Shah fled his country in 1979 after the revolution erupted, U.S. influence in Iran disappeared virtually overnight. When Iranians took Americans in the U.S. embassy as hostages, Khomeini denounced the United States as "the great Satan." In turn, he became Washington's number one enemy in the Middle East.

At first, Saddam thought that after its revolution Iran would focus on internal issues and leave the Gulf to himself. But soon Iran began bringing up old territorial claims and exhorting Shiites in the Gulf area to rebel against their rulers. The Ayatollah called for a revolution in the region that would unite all Muslims against Western infidels and their ruling Arab "stooges." Saudi Arabia and the Gulf states, armed and supported by the West, were alarmed. They looked for added military support and diplomatic aid from the United States. Furthermore, they looked to Iraq, with its long border with Iran, to contain the Iranian Revolution. Iraq also considered itself a bulwark of defense against Iran. So did the United States. Saddam decided to take the military offensive against Iran. On September 17, 1980, Iraq repudiated the 1975 treaty. A few days later, Iraqi forces invaded Iran.

During the ensuing war, the Reagan administration adopted an official policy of neutrality. Behind the scenes, however, it "tilted" toward Iraq. Basing its strategy on *realpolitik*, Washington sought to achieve a stable balance of power by bolstering Iraq. The main goal was to prevent Iran from becoming the dominant power in the Gulf and spreading its radical Islamic fundamentalism. A related goal was to reduce Iraq's dependence on the Soviet Union.

Washington's policymakers realized that supporting Iraq was a gamble, but they decided it would be too damaging to U.S. interests if Iraq lost the war. It was not that they were naive about Saddam. As Geoffrey Kemp, the Middle East section chief of the National Security Council (NSC) quipped: "We knew he was an S.O.B., but he was our S.O.B."[1] Simply put, compared to the Ayatollah Khomeini, Saddam seemed more appealing.

This "tilt" toward Iraq had several dimensions. First, in 1982 the State Department certified to Congress that it had removed Iraq from its list of states sponsoring terrorism. This was done despite evidence to the contrary. When off this list, Iraq became eligible for U.S. loan guarantees and trade benefits. From 1982 through July 25, 1990 (just before Iraq invaded Kuwait), the Agriculture Department's Commodity and Credit Corporation (CCC) extended Iraq about $1.9 billion in loan guarantees. Iraq thus was able to finance purchases of advanced weaponry and high-tech equipment (e.g., high-speed computers, high-frequency synthesizers, and sophisticated machine tools) that could be used for military or civilian purposes. Iraq used much of this dual-use technology for military projects and research programs.

In 1983, President Reagan's National Security Decision Directive (NSDD) authorized a "limited intelligence sharing program with Iraq." Consequently, the United States gave Iraq sensitive intelligence about Iran's military from satellites and U.S.-controlled Airborne Warning and

Control System (AWACS) planes based in Saudi Arabia. Furthermore, in 1983 the Reagan administration began urging its European allies to sell arms to Iraq, but not to Iran. At the same time, deeply concerned about Iraq's faltering military position and angered by Iran's suspected role in the bombing of U.S. Marine barracks in Lebanon, Reagan launched an arms embargo against Iran called "Operation Staunch."[2] This led the United States into an even closer relationship with Iraq.

The Iran-Iraq War ended when a UN-arranged cease-fire agreement was implemented on August 20, 1988. Between the end of this war and the time Saddam began to threaten Kuwait in 1990, Washington began paying less attention to the Persian Gulf region. The perceived threat from Iran diminished, especially after Ayatollah Khomeini died in 1989. There were also hopes that new Iranian leaders would focus more on domestic improvements than exporting revolution. Given these new developments, some lower-level U.S. Middle East advisers advocated a policy change. They argued that the balance of power situation had changed in the Gulf and Iraq was now the main threat in the region. Accordingly, they wanted the United States to end economic and military aid to Saddam.[3]

The new Bush administration, however, decided not to change Reagan's "tilt" toward Iraq. There was a hardened mind-set among top level Bush advisers that Iran was Washington's most dangerous enemy in the region. Nobody wanted to be accused of being "soft on Iran." Another factor was that these advisers did not believe Iraq would threaten the region. They thought Saddam would have his hands full with postwar domestic reconstruction efforts. Thus they did not believe he posed a serious threat to the Gulf and U.S. oil interests. In addition, by 1988 the United States was benefitting economically from its tilt toward Iraq. In 1981, before the tilt began, the United States imported no Iraqi oil. But by 1988, it had become a major buyer. Another point is that with the Cold War coming to an end, Bush began to focus his attention more on rapidly changing developments in Eastern Europe and the Soviet Union.[4]

On October 2, 1989, Bush issued the secret National Security Directive 26 (NSD 36). This held that the flow of Persian Gulf oil and the security of the moderate Gulf states were vital to U.S. national interests. To achieve this security, Washington sought to develop "normal relations" with Iraq. The idea, as Bush later maintained, was to bring Iraq into the "family of nations." The strategy was to use "economic and political incentives for Iraq to moderate its behavior, and to increase our influence with Iraq." Bush thus wanted Iraq to replace Iran as one of the "twin pillars" to secure U.S. interests in the Gulf.

In November 1989, Bush arranged for over one billion dollars in aid for Iraq. The Carter administration had pressured the Shah to moderate his repressive domestic policies. The Bush administration, however, made no such effort with Saddam. For example, Bush continued Reagan's policy of virtual silence on Saddam's human rights violations, particularly gassing the Kurds in 1988, and he ignored congressional calls for sanctions. Bush even authorized $1 billion in new CCC credit guarantees to Iraq for 1990.

When Saddam began threatening Kuwait in early 1990, U.S. policy continued despite recognition that it had some problems. Bush gambled that continuing aid to Iraq, reiterating U.S. friendship with the Iraqi people, and denying that the U.S. military presence in the Gulf threatened Iraq, together would restrain Saddam's potentially aggressive behavior in the Gulf.

After Iraq invaded Kuwait on August 2, 1990, the Bush administration still tried to justify its policy of support for Saddam. Though clearly a failure, the official line was that it had laudable intentions. Criticism that a tougher policy toward Saddam might have prevented the Gulf War was muted during the war itself, for it would have undermined Bush's leadership. Just how conciliatory Bush's policy was toward Saddam came out later.

Ambassador April Glaspie's Meeting with Saddam Hussein

On July 25, 1990, a highly controversial meeting took place in Baghdad between April C. Glaspie, U.S. ambassador to Iraq, and Saddam Hussein. According to an Iraqi transcript of the meeting, Glaspie said: "We [the United States] have no opinion on the Arab-Arab conflicts, like your border disagreement with Kuwait." In testimony before the Senate Foreign Relations Committee in March 1991, Glaspie gave a different version. She claimed that although she did tell Saddam the United States sought closer relations with Iraq, in no way did she say the United States would not react strongly to an Iraqi invasion of Kuwait. In fact, she expressed the State Department's concern that Iraqi soldiers were massing along the Kuwait border. According to Glaspie, Saddam then offered reassurances that Iraq would not invade.

The official U.S. record of this meeting seems to indicate Glaspie hardly took a firm stand against Saddam.[5] One thing that is certain is that Glaspie did not act on her own. Rather, she faithfully followed

State Department policy. Just the day before her meeting with Saddam, Glaspie had received a cable from Secretary of State Baker that said: "While we take no position on the border delineation raised by Iraq with respect to Kuwait, or on other bilateral disputes, Iraqi statements suggest an intention to resolve outstanding disagreements by the use of force, an approach which is contrary to U.N. charter principles." The State Department apparently had serious concerns about the possibility of an Iraqi invasion, but clearly these were not strong enough to act upon.[6]

The Alleged Cover-up of U.S. Aid to Iraq

President Bush never fully explained his conciliatory Iraq policy to the American people, especially with regard to details on U.S. economic and military assistance. Alan Friedman, an investigative journalist for the *Financial Times* of London, maintains that Bush was not honest with the American people. According to Friedman, after Iraq's invasion of Kuwait Bush engaged in "a systematic cover-up in order to avoid being embarrassed politically." The president did not want to have to explain this earlier support for Saddam. Friedman wrote how millions of American tax dollars had helped Saddam develop some of his most advanced weapons used in the Gulf War.[7] Countries around the world, especially Britain, also extensively supplied Saddam with similar aid. Afterwards, Prime Minister Margaret Thatcher's government had problems of its own "Iraq-gate."[8] Moreover, various governments in the Gulf, including Saudi Arabia and Kuwait, helped bankroll Iraq to stop Iran. In fact, governments and private businesses around the world tried to cash in on the war by selling arms and related material to Iraq. Some of this aid helped the development of Saddam's nuclear weapons program.[9] Clearly, all this aid gave Saddam both the where-withal to invade Kuwait and the impression he could do it with impunity.

Saddam Hussein's Invasion of Kuwait

Some background information on Iraq's ruling Ba'ath Party and Saddam Hussein himself is useful in understanding Iraq's invasion of Kuwait. Ba'athism developed in the 1930s as a mixture of pan Arabism, Islam, and Marxism. It also drew upon the experience of fascism in establishing and maintaining a highly repressive and efficient internal security apparatus. One of Ba'athism's cardinal tenets was strong opposition to Israel and the West. In time, two rival conflicting wings developed within the Ba'ath Party. One took power in Syria in 1963, and the other in Iraq in 1968.

Saddam became a member of the Ba'ath Party in the 1950s. He was vice president in 1979 when he took over leadership of Iraq from President Ahmak Hasan al-Bakr. Saddam was an extremely power-thirsty leader who dreamed of becoming another Saladin, the Moslem leader who drove Christian soldiers from Jerusalem in the twelfth century. He also sought to follow in the footsteps of Gamel Abdel Nasser, former president of Egypt, in becoming the leader of the Arab world. During the 1980s, while Saddam made war on Iran, he sought to win widespread Arab support. He appealed to Arab masses over the heads of their leaders in the Gulf states, Saudi Arabia, Egypt, and elsewhere. He considered these states vulnerable to his propaganda that focused on Israel's occupation of Arab land. Largely because of this theme, he won support of the Palestine Liberation Organization (PLO).

During the 1980s, Saddam built a strong power base inside Iraq. This was rooted not only in the Ba'ath Party, but also in his clan from his home town of Takrit. Interestingly, this was also the hometown of Saladin. Using extensive nepotism, Saddam made many of his relatives close personal aides and government officials. After having almost destroyed his country in the war with Iran, and after having brutalized the Kurds (even using chemical weapons after accusing them of subversion), Saddam still was not through with his adventurism. He soon turned his attention to neighboring Kuwait.

There were several main reasons for Iraq's invasion of Kuwait. The first was historical. Saddam disputed the legitimacy of the Iraq-Kuwait border. His claim had at least some validity. Before World War I, Kuwait and Iraq, like most other states in the Middle East, were part of the Ottoman Empire. After this empire's defeat, the victorious European allies, particularly Britain and France, drew new borders. Their main aim was satisfaction of their own commercial, political, and strategic interests, not the betterment of the people themselves.

In 1922, Sir Percy Cox, Britain's High Commissioner in the Gulf, simply took his red pencil and unilaterally drew the boundaries between Kuwait, Saudi Arabia, and Iraq. These borders intentionally separated Kuwait from Iraq, which restricted Baghdad's access to the Gulf. After the war, Britain created the state of Iraq which became a British mandate. Britain wanted to keep Iraq somewhat weak so it could be assured of maintaining land access to India, her prize colonial possession in Asia, and of controlling Iraq's suspected vast oil reserves.

The tiny sheikdom of Kuwait was established in the mid-eighteenth century when tribesmen agreed to support the As-Sabah family. They chose as their ruler Sheik Sabah Abd ar-Rahim, founder of the subsequent ruling dynasty. When neighboring rival Arab tribesmen cast eyes on Kuwait, the Sabah family sought protection from Britain. Britain was concerned about Turkish, Russian, and German interests in the sheikdom. In fact, the Germans and Turks considered Kuwait a possible terminus in their plans for a Berlin-Baghdad railroad. In 1899, Britain agreed to provide minimal protection for Kuwait as well as a subsidy to support the Sabah ruling family. In return, Kuwait promised to keep away other foreign powers. When World War I broke out, Britain recognized the independence of Kuwait and pledged more extensive protection. After the war, in the Treaty of Lausanne, Turkey gave up any residual claim to Kuwait.

Iraq didn't become formally independent until 1932, though British influence still predominated there. At that time, Iraq recognized the existing border with Kuwait. In 1961, Kuwait's status as a British protectorate ended. The international community recognized it as an independent state. Kuwait became a member of the UN and Arab League. The same year, Iraq's ruler Abdul Karim Qassim renewed Iraq's claim to Kuwait. He opposed Kuwait's membership in the UN and the Arab League. He also appointed the sheik of Kuwait as governor of the Iraqi province of Basra. The Iraqi leader massed troops on the Kuwaiti border to press the issue. Qassim backed off when Britain sent its own troops to Kuwait. When he was overthrown in 1963, the new ruling Ba'ath Party recognized the independence of Kuwait and accepted the Iraqi-Kuwaiti frontier. The specific border line, however, remained unsettled.

In 1990, Saddam again argued that Kuwait was part of Iraq. According to the Iraqi leader, therefore, the takeover of Kuwait was the beginning of the "reunification" of the Arab people. Other Arab leaders quivered. Indeed, if Kuwait were not a legitimate country, the legitimacy of others created by the British (including Saudi Arabia, Oman, Qatar, Bahrain, and the United Arab Emirates) was also in question.

The consensus of Western legal opinion is that Iraq had no legitimate historical claim to Kuwait.[10] The viewpoint in the Arab world, understandably, is much more sympathetic if not supportive of Iraq's position. This legal claim notwithstanding, Saddam had more important reasons for invading Kuwait. He claimed that Kuwait's "feudal" government conflicted with "progressive" Arab nationalism. He also pointed out that the boundary with Kuwait denied Iraq legitimate "strategic access" to the Gulf. Iraq, he argued, needed a port on the Persian Gulf which he believed should be within Iraq's sphere of influence. Saddam also laid claim to two strategically important Kuwaiti islands, Bubiyan and Warbah. At different times Iraq even sought to buy or lease these islands, but to no avail.[11] When Kuwait rejected Saddam's efforts in 1989 to secure these islands, he asserted that Kuwait had sided with his enemy Iran and thus should also be considered Iraq's enemy.

Saddam also charged that Kuwait, Saudi Arabia, and the United Arab Emirates were waging economic warfare against Iraq. The war against Iran had left Iraq with a huge debt of $80 billion as well as rampant inflation. Saddam believed that these states should have been grateful for Iraq's containment of revolutionary Iran and thus helped pay off its debt. Instead, they steadfastly refused.

In the opinion of some experts, such as Laurie Mylroie, the issue of oil was the most important factor in Saddam's invasion of Kuwait.[12] There were two main dimensions to the oil problem. One was that Saddam accused Kuwait of violating oil production quotas set by the Organization of Petroleum Exporting Countries (OPEC) by deliberately overproducing oil. This resulted in a glut on the world market and a depression of the price of oil. For every one dollar drop in the price of a barrel of oil, Saddam asserted, Iraq lost $1 billion. The second was that Iraq accused Kuwait of "slant drilling" in the Rumalian oil field. This field, which lies partially under Kuwait but mostly under Iraq, is roughly fifty miles long. Saddam believed that Kuwait illegally extracted oil from Iraqi land during the 1980s. He calculated that because of this Iraq had lost about $2.4 billion worth of oil. On August 1, 1990 Iraqi and Kuwaiti leaders met in Jiddah, Saudi Arabia to discuss their differences. These talks broke down after only two hours. Evidently, Saddam was bent on gaining by force what he could not win at the bargaining table. The next day, Iraqi forces invaded Kuwait.

Saddam's Miscalculations

Saddam thought he would achieve an easy, quick victory. In this he was right. Kuwait was greatly overmatched militarily and was easily conquered. On August 8, Saddam addressed his nation: "Thank God, we are now one people, one state that will be the pride of the Arabs." He then announced that Iraq had annexed Kuwait which it called "Province 19."

But Saddam seriously miscalculated regional and world reaction to his invasion. He greatly overestimated the degree of Arab approval. He believed that he would win widespread Arab support by linking his takeover of Kuwait to Israel's occupation of Arab lands, and, if war broke out, by drawing Israel into hostilities. His support from the Arab world was significantly more than from elsewhere. This indicated that Saddam had struck nerves that elicited some positive response. Few Arabs openly approved of his annexation of Kuwait. Yet many quietly objected to the U.S.-led coalition that they believed smacked of Western imperialism and whose major goal was maintaining the flow of cheap oil.[13]

Ultimately, official Arab support for Saddam was very limited. The PLO openly embraced Iraq's action for several reasons: there were no serious prospects for significant movement in peace talks with Israel; momentum from the *intifada* (uprising) against Israel that had begun in 1988 had slowed; the Soviet Union, its longstanding patron, was on the verge of collapse; and its leaders felt isolated in Tunisia. King Hussein of Jordan, with his large Palestinian population, leaned toward Saddam in a delicate display of support. Other Arab states like Sudan, Mauritania, Algeria, and Yemen offered varying degrees of assistance.

Twelve Arab countries, most notably Syria, Egypt, Saudi Arabia, and the Gulf States joined the anti-Saddam coalition.[14] Critical in this regard was U.S. success in keeping Israel out of the war. This was no easy task considering, among other provocations, repeated Iraqi SCUD missile attacks on Israeli cities. Moreover, Saddam surely did not anticipate that xenophobic Saudi Arabia, with its puritanical Wahabbi sect of Islam that so fears "contamination" by the West, would allow Western military forces on its soil and join in a U.S.-led coalition to drive him out of Kuwait. Evidently, he also did not expect the United States to risk a major military entanglement in the Gulf. He assumed that with memory of the 1983 massacre of U.S. Marines in Lebanon still fresh, the American public would be in no mood to risk another catastrophe. He also hoped that the "Vietnam syndrome" would prevail. That is, the United States would not place large numbers of soldiers in a far-off region of the world and commit itself to the possibility of a long, drawn-out war whose outcome would be far from certain. Saddam must have been shocked when the United States so quickly organized the UN coalition that furnished about 600,000 troops, medical and logistical support, and financial assistance.[15]

Saddam also assumed that his standing army, the fourth largest in the world (the U.S. then ranked seventh), would be a far better fighting force than it proved to be. He thought that with its battlefield experience in the war with Iran and its supply of advanced military technology, his army could at least hold its own against the coalition. He especially expected superior fighting by his highly trained elite Republican Guard. If the United States did fight, chances were that it would be (in the words of Mao Zedong) a "paper tiger." Saddam probably assumed the United States would "cut and run" when American soldiers started to return to the United States in body bags and the war dragged on. Moreover, Iraqi propaganda focused on Kuwait's utilization of its vast oil wealth that pampered the country's elite. Surely, Saddam thought, American public opinion would not support a war to restore to power the autocratic emir and the rest of his ruling family. To Saddam's dismay, President Bush won support at home and abroad by emphasizing the theme of Iraqi aggression and the threat of Saddam's takeover of Kuwait to the West's oil supplies.

Finally, it was not surprising that Saddam believed that the United States, as well as Saudi Arabia and the Gulf states, still expected Iraq to hold the line against the spread of Iran's radical Islam. After all, they had supplied him with substantial military and economic assistance for this purpose during the 1980s. In addition, he had interpreted Ambassador Glaspie's comments to mean the United States would not militarily intervene to block Iraq's invasion of Kuwait. At the most, Saddam probably assumed that his takeover of Kuwait would annoy his benefactors, that it would blow over, and that things would soon return to business as usual. He surely did not expect his Kuwait gambit to effect such a stunning reversal of U.S. policy.

Operation Desert Shield

President Bush was stunned by Iraq's invasion of Kuwait. He deemed it a personal betrayal. Critics of Bush's policy, such as Senator Al Gore (D, Tenn.), charged during the 1992 election campaign that Bush ignored numerous indications of a possible Iraqi attack that he should have anticipated. Worse still, he had armed Saddam and provided him with the military wherewithal to attack Kuwait. According to Gore, although Bush wanted the American people "to see him as the hero who put out a raging fire, he [was] the one who set the fire. He not only struck the match, he poured the gasoline on the flames. So give him credit for calling in the fire department, but understand who started the blaze."[16] Bush's defenders, such as Washington writer Milton Viorst, thought otherwise. "Bush was hardly wrong in feeling betrayed," Viorst argues. "He had tried to play fair with Hussein—though not to coddle him—and wound up being kicked in the teeth. He had earned the right to tell the voters that he had pursued a wise and honorable policy, and that it failed."[17]

Both before and after Iraq's invasion, Bush could have offered to serve as mediator in the Iraq-Kuwait dispute. Instead, he issued a number of directives designed to pressure Saddam to withdraw. These included freezing all Kuwaiti assets in the United States to prevent Saddam from using them; and reflective of the new friendly relationship between the United States and Soviet Union, Secretary of State Baker and Soviet Foreign Minister Edward Shevardnadze issued a joint statement condemning the invasion and calling for an Iraqi withdrawal.

Bush also worked hard to secure United Nations support for actions taken by the United States. On August 2, Resolution 660 of the Security Council condemned Iraq's invasion and demanded an immediate and unconditional withdrawal. On August 6, the Security Council passed Resolution 661 that imposed a near total embargo on Iraqi imports and exports, with the exceptions of some imports of food and medicine. On August 25, the Security Council passed Resolution 665, authorizing the use of force to prevent leaks in the embargo.

Iraq retaliated. On August 13, after having sealed its borders four days earlier, Baghdad announced that for the time being foreigners would not be allowed to leave Iraq or Kuwait. Although Saddam called foreigners inside Iraq "guests," they really were hostages. Soon Iraq began holding Westerners, especially American and British citizens, as "human shields." Saddam hoped these Westerners would keep the coalition from attacking targets inside Iraq and Kuwait. Iraq's actions backfired, for they only brought more scorn on Saddam and increased the resolve of the coalition. Recognizing his stratagem had failed, Saddam decided to release all foreign hostages on December 6. This was a week after the Security Council passed a resolution authorizing the use of military force after January 15 if Iraq had not withdrawn by then.

Simultaneous with his diplomatic moves after Iraq's invasion, President Bush began preparing for military action if needed. Bush had important diplomatic and strategic concerns. He saw Iraq's seizure of Kuwait as a test for his "new world order" in the post–Cold War period. As the world's remaining superpower, the United States would assume responsibility for leading a collective security arrangement under UN auspices. The United States also was worried about the implications of Iraq's control of Kuwait and potential aggression against other Gulf states, particularly Saudi Arabia with its vast oil deposits. Most of the

Saudi oil fields were in the east, and thus particularly vulnerable to nearby Iraqi troops.

King Fahd's approval of foreign troops on his soil was critical. Realizing the task ahead, on August 6 Bush dispatched Secretary of Defense Richard Cheney to Jiddah to convince the king of the imminent danger to his country and the need to station foreign troops there. The Saudis, fearful of pollution to their culture and religion, initially opposed this idea. But Cheney told Fahd that U.S. satellite intelligence indicated that Saddam was massing large numbers of troops on the Saudi border. After convincing Fahd that his country was in great peril, the king reluctantly agreed to accept American ground forces.

On August 7, Washington announced the sending of ground troops and jet fighters totaling 50,000 men and women. By September, the U.S.-led coalition had stationed about 100,000 troops in the Gulf. Deployment was justified under Article 51 of the UN Charter that provides for states to exercise their "inherent right of individual or collective self-defense." The next day, in a television address Bush announced that a line had "been drawn in the sand" to stop the aggression of Saddam Hussein. Bush also announced four major goals that justified the sending of troops:

1. Immediate, complete, and unconditional withdrawal of all Iraqi forces from Kuwait;
2. Restoration of Kuwait's legitimate government;
3. Preservation of the security and stability of Saudi Arabia and the Persian Gulf; and
4. Protection of the lives of American citizens in the Gulf area.

U.S. Public Opinion, Congress, and Desert Storm

Persuading King Fahd to accept U.S. troops on Saudi soil proved the key to the eventual success of the Gulf War. Without American troops in Saudi Arabia, Saddam might have knifed through that country, captured its oil wells, and thereby significantly altered the course of Middle East history. The massive troop build-up in Saudi Arabia was an excellent staging ground for Desert Storm, the war that drove Iraq from Kuwait.

Building a domestic consensus would not be easy. One of President Bush's toughest challenges was to convince the American public and Congress of the need to go to war against Saddam. To this end, he cast Saddam as one of history's most despicable leaders: Saddam was an international criminal who callously broke international law; he was another Hitler who suppressed and even killed his own people, who committed aggression against Kuwait, and who threatened the independence of his other neighbors; he was building a nuclear arsenal that would endanger world peace; and he endangered the world's oil supply. It was this last issue that at the same time proved most controversial and effective. Critics did not want to send U.S. troops to secure Saudi oil fields. They shouted "No blood for oil!" But supporters remembered the long gas lines caused by the 1973 oil embargo. More importantly, they feared potential job loss.

President Bush decided to build up U.S. forces in Saudi Arabia without waiting for congressional authorization to use military force. On November 8, he announced the sending of 200,000 more troops to Saudi Arabia. When Congress did not act then, Bush's decision became a *fait accompli*. Bush assumed that he had the right to use military force under UN Resolution 678 of November 29. This authorized the anti-Saddam coalition to use "all necessary means" against Iraq if it did not withdraw from Kuwait by January 15.

Bush also assumed he had the necessary authority to go to war under the Constitution. As commander-in-chief, the president stated he did not need congressional authorization. Congress was far from enthusiastic about engaging in war. Several key Senate leaders were reluctant to support military action. For example, in November 1990, Sam Nunn (D, Ga.), chairman of the Armed Services Committee, questioned whether the liberation of Kuwait was a vital issue. And Robert Dole (R, Kan.), Minority leader, said as late as December 30 that restoring the emir of Kuwait to power "wasn't worth one American life."

Bush waited until January 8, 1991 to formally ask for congressional approval. The president did not ask Congress for a declaration of war, yet he considered it politically prudent to seek congressional support. Events were moving swiftly. On January 12, 1990, with hostilities imminent, Congress approved war. At this point, Senator Dole supported Bush's position. The vote in the Senate (52 to 47) was closer than in the House (250 to 182). In the end, therefore, most legislators believed that Congress had to stand behind the president and U.S. troops.[18] On January 14, Bush signed the joint resolution authorizing him to use the force he needed.

Bush's use of military force in Desert Storm raised troubling constitutional questions regarding the primacy of presidential and congressional authority in war-making. The 1973 War Powers Resolution was intended to resolve the dilemma of divided authority. This resolution limited presidential commitment of American troops to hostilities without congressional authorization to 60 days, possibly to 90 days under special circumstances. Bush resolved this constitutional controversy unilaterally by making an executive agreement to deploy and eventually commit U.S. troops to battle. He was confident that he could win public backing for war.

Opinion polls conducted early in the crisis showed little public enthusiasm for the use of military force. By late November, support had built to about 59 percent. Still, though, the public preferred that Bush explore all avenues for peaceful resolution. They would support use of military force against Iraq only as a last resort. "Operation Desert Shield" became "Operation Desert Storm" on January 17, when coalition forces unleashed punishing air strikes against targets in Iraq and Kuwait. The war began two days after the deadline for Iraqi withdrawal imposed by the UN.

President Bush justified the use of force in an address to the American people. He stated that the twenty-eight states of the coalition had "exhausted all reasonable efforts to reach a peaceful resolution [with Saddam]. . . . Regrettably, we now believe that only force will make him leave Kuwait."[19] U.S. Ambassador Thomas R. Pickering stated the official goal of the coalition to the UN Security Council: "Although coalition forces are striking military and strategic targets in Iraq, our goal is not the destruction, occupation, or dismemberment of Iraq. It is the liberation of Kuwait."[20]

By this time American public opinion was strongly behind the president. It was not that Americans clamored for war. Rather, they supported it when it seemed inevitable. Professor John Mueller summed up public support for Bush's war-making:

Public opinion about starting a war against Iraq changed little during the debate over Gulf policy. Bush was able to pull off his war . . . not because he convinced a growing number of Americans of the wisdom of war, but because of his position as foreign policy leader, because he enjoyed . . . a fair amount of trust at the time with respect to this matter, and because of the anticipation that the war would resolve a pressing and important issue and would be comparatively quick and low in casualties. The opinion dynamic that probably helped him most, however, was a growing fatalism about war—as time went by, the public became increasingly convinced that war was inevitable. In that sense, the public was willing to be led to war: for many the attitude was, "Let's get it over with."[21]

Countdown to the Decision

Coalition forces, under the command of General Schwarzkopf, virtually destroyed Iraq's naval and air forces in the first few weeks of the war. Planes attacked Iraq's infrastructure, military command and communications system, and ground troops deployed in and around Kuwait. The coalition had overwhelming superiority in the air war. In a somewhat bizarre move, Saddam sent many of his planes to neighboring Iran, which remained neutral during the war. Saddam then tried a "scorched earth" policy by ordering his troops to destroy anything of value in Kuwait, such as desalinization plants. He also unleashed "environmental terrorism" by setting Kuwaiti oil fields on fire. It took almost two years after the war to cap these oil wells. At the same time, he launched repeated SCUD missile attacks against Saudi Arabia and Israel, hoping to draw the latter into the war. Saddam soon realized that if he could not win the war, he could make a coalition victory very costly.

At the end of January, President Bush stated that the coalition did not seek the destabilization of Iraq. Its main goal, he said, was expulsion of Iraq from Kuwait in accordance with UN Resolution 678. On February 15, Iraq offered to withdraw from Kuwait and relinquish its claim to the country. But Bush called this offer a "cruel hoax" because it contained a number of unacceptable conditions such as cancellation of all sanctions. The same day, Bush called for the Iraqi military and people to remove Saddam from power.[22] Dissident groups inside Iraq, particularly the Kurds and Shiites, interpreted this as a signal of U.S. support to revolt. But it was unclear how Bush wanted this to develop. A revolt might achieve one major goal, namely Saddam's ouster, but it might also work against another goal of maintaining a strong Iraq as a bulwark against Iran. Ideally, Bush probably hoped for a swift and simple change of power.

On February 18, Soviet President Mikhail Gorbachev proposed a peace plan. But Bush considered this unacceptable for it did not require Iraq to pay reparations. Moreover, the two-day pause between ceasefire and withdrawal would have allowed Saddam time to resupply his forces and avoid destruction of his armor and artillery. This would be the last official attempt to avoid a ground war.

The air war lasted forty-three days. Though tremendously successful, the White House believed it could achieve only so much. Bush realized a ground war would be necessary to finally defeat Saddam. He also realized time was of the essence. The ground war had to take place before March, when Ramadan, the Moslem holy month, began. In addition, if he waited too long, weather conditions would change and intense desert heat would become too oppressive for ground action. Schwarzkopf and his advisers devised a battle plan. The general realized the pressure of time to begin the ground war, but he wanted to wait until he was sure coalition forces were fully ready.

Schwarzkopf feared political expediency in Washington might prevail over military requirements. Moreover, he was angered by White House "hawks" who pressed for an early land war. In his book that came out after the war, Schwarzkopf criticized these "hawks" (presumably Brent Scowcroft, the national security adviser, and Robert M. Gates, former deputy national security adviser and later director of the Central Intelligence Agency) without identifying them.[23] "The increasing pressure to launch the ground war early was making me crazy," Schwarzkopf wrote. "There had to be a contingent of hawks in Washington who did not want to stop until we'd punished Saddam. We'd been bombing Iraq for more than a month, but that wasn't good enough. These were guys who had seen John Wayne in "The Green Berets," they'd seen "Rambo," they'd seen "Patton," and it was very easy for them to pound their desks and say: 'By God, we've got to go in there. . . . Gotta punish that son of a bitch!' Of course, none of them was going to get shot at."[24] Reportedly, Schwarzkopf also clashed with General Colin Powell, chairman of the Joint Chiefs of Staff (JCS), who also urged an early land war. They even engaged in a shouting march on the telephone. White House officials defended the speed-up of the ground war. Their concern was that the longer the war, the harder it would be to keep the coalition together. They worried how long Israel, continually pummeled by SCUD attacks, would stay out of the war. They also realized the fragility of the coalition that included twelve Arab states as well as the Soviet Union.

On February 22, Bush gave Saddam an ultimatum: withdraw unconditionally by noon on February 23 or face a ground assault. Bush said Saddam had to meet several requirements:

1. Complete withdrawal within one week.
2. Removal of all Iraqi forces from Kuwait City within forty-eight hours of the beginning of the withdrawal.
3. Release of all prisoners of war and third-country civilians within forty-eight hours.
4. Removal of booby traps and mines from oil facilities and other areas.[25]

Saddam steadfastly refused, denouncing Bush's demands as "shameful." Consequently, on February 24 coalition forces launched a massive ground offensive. Saddam announced that the "mother of all battles" had begun. Bush called this the "final phase" of the war. The next day, Saddam announced he would withdraw from Kuwait. But Bush, believing the Iraqi leader would not meet all the demands of his ultimatum, increase the ferocity of the coalition assault. On February 26, Iraq announced it would accept all the terms for cessation of hostilities. Both his army and his country had suffered tremendous losses. Many units were surrendering, and it was possible that if the war continued his whole army, including the Republican Guard, would collapse. Thus Saddam had virtually no alternative. On February 27, Bush announced that Iraqi forces had begun to retreat from Kuwait and that the nation had been liberated. With this major goal met, the president decided to end the war at 8 A.M. on February 28. This would be exactly 100 hours after the start of one of the most devastating ground wars in history.

President Bush as Decision-Maker

Foreign Policy Context of Decision

President Bush considered foreign policy his main expertise. In fact, his resumé in this area is very impressive. His experience included stints as U.S. ambassador to the UN (1971–73), head of the U.S. Liaison Office to the People's Republic of China (1974–75), and director of the Central Intelligence Agency (1976–77). Yet the defining experience in his life that shaped his policy toward Iraq was World War II, where he served as a Navy pilot.[26]

Bush considered the Persian Gulf war a "good" and "moral" war fought against the forces of evil. As the president put it in a December

1991 interview: "I've got it boiled down very clearly to good and evil. And it helps if you can be that clear in your own mind."[27] Bush compared Saddam's invasion of Kuwait to Hitler's invasion of Czechoslovakia. He also feared another "Munich" if the world did not force Saddam from Kuwait. Appeasement had led to World War II, so Bush had to resist Saddam's aggression by drawing a line in the desert sand. As one of Bush's advisers noted: "He is deathly afraid of appeasement. His generation had to fight a war over it, and he feels that if he blinks today, he will be leaving a real mess for the next generation to clean up. You have an aggressor and if you let him take over Kuwait, he will take over Saudi Arabia and become the paramount power in the Middle East."[28]

Bush acted on the basis of realpolitik. If Saddam's aggression against Kuwait had been left unchallenged, the whole balance of power in the Middle East would be upset—to the detriment of the security of Israel and key Arab states such as Saudi Arabia. Furthermore, Saddam's actions had threatened the world's oil supplies and consequently the security of the United States, Western European countries, and Japan that depended so heavily on an interrupted oil flow to fuel their economies.

Bush repeatedly referred to Saddam's human rights abuses cited by Amnesty International. He was distressed by the heavy toll of suffering and believed it was worth the sacrifice of battle to stop the abuses. Bush also considered military force a legitimate and effective instrument of foreign policy that he could use with the support of the American people. In his mind, he had already used force successfully to remove General Manuel Noriega from office in Panama in October 1989. As the public generally supported this action, there was reason to believe it would also support war against Saddam.

Finally, Bush was eager not to repeat mistakes made by the United States in the Vietnam War. In an interview with *U.S. News and World Report*, Bush referred to the lessons of Vietnam: "Never fight a war with hands tied behind your back. Never send a kid into a battle unless you're going to give him total support. Don't send a mission that is undermanned. Don't send them in where you tell commanding officers what they can't do."[29] Evidently, Bush had remained a supporter of U.S. goals in Vietnam. It was just its strategy and tactics that he thought were wrong.

Context of Decision within Bush's National Security Strategy
Not to be underestimated was Bush's vision for the post–Cold War world. He called for a "new world order." Yet a fundamental problem

was discerning exactly what he meant and how he planned to achieve his goal. The United States had become the world's only superpower and should act accordingly. But exactly what did this mean? To begin with, the United States sought and gained cooperation from the Soviet Union. Whether Saddam would have undertaken his aggression against Kuwait during the Cold War is problematical. Surely, the Soviet Union would have realized the inherent dangers of such a move and probably would have restrained Saddam. The end of the Cold War, however, brought new regional and world dynamics.

Bush believed that resistance to Iraq should be multilateral through the UN. This was both a philosophical and practical strategy. The president's experience in the UN undoubtedly was an important influence. He categorized his strategy for Desert Shield as "coercive diplomacy." This meant an explicit use of military force by the United States and its coalition partners to try to pressure Saddam to withdraw his occupying army from Kuwait. When this failed, Desert Storm became the new paradigm for the use of military force.

Context of Decision within President's Relations with Allies

Washington's major NATO allies, France, the Federal Republic of Germany, and Britain, all supported President Bush during Desert Shield and Desert Storm. French public opinion strongly favored forceful action against Saddam. But there were complications. France had been a major seller of arms to both Saudi Arabia and Iraq. Moreover, France's defense minister, Jean-Pierre Chevenement, who belonged to the French-Iraqi Friendship Society, strongly opposed contributing troops to the coalition. Finally in December the French government under President François Mitterand cooperated fully with Bush and sent troops to fight in the coalition. German support was less direct. The German public generally endorsed the war effort, but constitutional restrictions kept Germany from sending troops to the Gulf. The German government under Chancellor Helmut Kohl, however, provided significant logistical assistance.

In making his decision to end the war, the only ally that Bush had significant consultation with was Britain. Prime Minister Margaret Thatcher had always supported tough action by Bush and his predecessor, Ronald Reagan. In 1985, for example, she had strongly backed Reagan's bombing of Libya in an attempt to stop state-sponsored terrorism. In the summer of 1990, she had fully supported Bush's initiative for Desert Shield. When she resigned in late November, her strong presence was missing from subsequent U.S.-British relations. The new prime minister, John Major, continued Thatcher's commitment to Desert Shield, but he did not have the influence of the "Iron Lady" in Washington. Major's national security adviser, Sir Charles Powell, doubted the wisdom of ending the war so soon. British Foreign Secretary Douglas Hurd did offer some suggestions, such as ensuring that any cease-fire guarantee the release of all allied prisoners of war. He also cautioned about repeating the "Cossack factor": forced repatriation of Soviet prisoners after World War II to almost certain death.

Domestic Context of Decision

There was much public debate in the United States regarding the buildup of troops under Desert Shield and the fighting during Desert Storm. By the time the war began, the president had clearly won congressional support. When Bush decided to end the fighting, he did so with overwhelming public support. He thus felt confident to do so with minimal consultation with Congress and virtually no public debate.

On February 27, Bush talked with Scowcroft, Baker, and Hurd about the progress of the war and when to end it. The main issue was the future of Iraq and its postwar military capability and potential. Scowcroft stated he thought coalition forces had largely destroyed Iraq's capability to develop weapons of mass destruction (WMD). The United States realized Iraq still had stocks of chemical weapons, but it believed Iraq would not use them. It was after the war ended that U.S. intelligence learned that coalition forces had not destroyed significant numbers of Iraq's nuclear and biological weapons targets.[30]

Discussion then moved to the Oval Office. Bush said he liked how the war was going. He also was confident that the Republican Guard was being destroyed. The president, who had watched pictures of the violent war on television, expressed concern that if it continued in this devastating manner, he might be accused of slaughtering defenseless Iraqi soldiers. Soon Secretary Baker added that new information from the UN indicated that Iraq had agreed to Security Council demands.

Cheney and Powell then joined the meeting. Bush asked what the Pentagon needed to end the war. Cheney agreed with Powell that the goals of the war had almost been reached. As Cheney said: "We are basically there. It could be over by now or maybe by tomorrow." Bush then said he wanted to determine precisely when to end the war.

Cheney responded: "We'll talk to Norm." Powell was not sure how much destruction the coalition had wreaked on the Republican Guard, but like Bush, he was concerned about reports of the "Turkey Shoot" on the "Highway of Death" out of Kuwait. Powell said Schwarzkopf told him "we are at most twenty-four hours away. . . . We are in the home stretch. Today or tomorrow by close of business." Bush asked Hurd what British military commanders thought. Hurd replied that they too thought the war could end within a day or two.

Powell then stated that political considerations should also be considered in the ending of the war. Bush responded: "We do not want to lose anything now with charges of brutalization, but we are also very concerned with the issue of prisoners. The issue is how to find a clean end. This is not going to be like the battleship Missouri" (where Japan signed the surrender after World War II).

Baker supported the argument to end the war, stating: "We have done the job. We can stop. We have achieved our aims. We have gotten them out of Kuwait." But he expressed concern about Saddam's remaining in power and the future of the embargo. Bush agreed with Powell's recommendation to use the threat of air strikes to ensure Iraqi compliance with the cease-fire. The president noted that the people wanted an end to the war. "They are going to want to know we won and the kids can come home. We do not want to screw this up with a sloppy, muddled ending." Bush then asked Scowcroft to write a speech announcing the war was over. Public relations would govern the exact timing.

All Bush's key advisers (Baker, Scowcroft, Cheney, and Powell) agreed with his decision to end the war after 100 hours. Powell's subsequent justification is illustrative. In his autobiography published in September 1995, Powell scoffed at criticism that Bush bungled the Gulf War by stopping it before capturing Baghdad or finishing off Saddam Hussein. "What tends to be forgotten," Powell countered, "is that while the United States led the way, we were heading an *international coalition* carrying out a clearly defined UN mission. That mission was accomplished." Moreover, Powell noted, coalition members, particularly the Arab states, "never wanted Iraq invaded and dismembered."[31]

Other advisers, however, such as Paul D. Wolfowitz, undersecretary of defense, had reservations about Bush's decision. To begin with, Wolfowitz was troubled by the symbolism. He pointed out that a 100-hour war had an unhappy meaning for the Arab world, for after President Nasser of Egypt nationalized the Suez Canal in 1956, Britain, France, and Israel had launched a 100-hour war to regain control of the waterway. Pressure against this action by President Eisenhower was instrumental in their decision to stop military action. According to Wolfowitz, in the Arab mind the 100-hour war still smacked of Western and Israeli aggression. After Cheney discussed this objection with Scowcroft, the defense secretary asked Wolfowitz jokingly whether he would be happier with a 99-hour war. Evidently, the White House had not considered the point raised by Wolfowitz. Nor did it believe the American public would care.

Wolfowitz also questioned whether it was wise to announce a cessation of hostilities. In his view, the allies could stop their attacks without telling the world. A public announcement that the ground war was over, in his view, might reduce incentive inside Iraq to overthrow Saddam.

Inside the CIA, there was also no enthusiasm for Bush's decision to end the war at 100 hours. Lt. Col. Michael Tanksley, an Army officer who worked on the team of Iraq analyst Charles Allen, reportedly exclaimed in frustration: "One goddam day too soon." When Allen told CIA deputy director Richard Kerr about the decision, he seemingly knew nothing about it.

On the battlefield, there was also some second guessing of Bush's decision. For example, several Army division commanders, such as Maj. Gen. Barry McCaffrey, did not believe the war should end before the entire Republican Guard had been destroyed. They wanted to drive to the Basra canals to cut off the fleeing Iraqi soldiers. As Col. Paul Kern, McCaffrey's 2nd Brigade commander stated in exasperation: "You are prepared to go. You are ready to go, and you have a good plan. Everything is in your favor. And then you stop and say why?" He then added: "I knew that this would be a military decision that would be debated for years to come in terms of where we stopped. The sense was there: 'success but.' "

Dissent regarding the decision time to end the war also may have come from Schwarzkopf. The general believed he had two main military goals: liberation of Kuwait and destruction of the Republican Guard. He clearly accomplished the first, but not the second. Schwarzkopf realized the primacy of politics in war, but he was concerned that Republican Guard troops were still escaping. Ending the war so soon prevented their complete destruction.

Officially, the general supported Bush's decision. Privately, however, and in some cases obliquely in public references, Schwarzkopf raised some doubts about the wisdom of ending the war at 100 hours.

Note these remarks he made in a British television interview with David Frost:

> Frankly, my recommendation had been . . . continue the march. I mean, we had them in a rout and we could have continued to wreak great destruction upon them. We could have completely closed the doors and made it in fact a battle of annihilation. And the president made the decision that we should stop at a given time, at a given place, that did leave some escape routes open for them to get back out, and I think that was a very humane decision and a very courageous decision on his part also. Because it's one of those ones that historians are going to second-guess forever. . . . There were obviously a lot of people who escaped who wouldn't have escaped if the decision hadn't been made to stop where we were at that time. But again, I think that was a very courageous decision on the part of the president.[32]

Schwarzkopf later apologized to Bush for "a poor choice of words." In his autobiography, he wrote that he had agreed with Bush's decision: "[W]e'd kicked this guy's butt, leaving no doubt . . . that we'd won decisively, and we'd done it with very few casualties. Why not end it? Why get someone else killed tomorrow? That made up my mind." The general finally answered: " 'I don't have any problem with it.' "[33]

As the good soldier, Schwarzkopf maintained that his duty was to carry out orders from his commander-in-chief. Because of the delicate nature of this matter, how serious his misgivings were about Bush's decision may never be known with certainty. We do know, however, that the president considered several other options.

Decision Options

Bush had four main options besides ending the war at 100 hours:

1. Total destruction of the Republican Guard. Bush discounted this option, however, because of concerns that the world would be revulsed by continuation of a "Turkey Shoot" along "the Highway of Death."
2. A march to Baghdad and subjugation of Iraq. Some reporters, like A. M. Rosenthal from the *New York Times*, wrote in support of this option. How could the war end successfully, they argued, if Iraq re-

mained a threat. This was especially so if its capability for producing weapons of mass destruction was not completely destroyed.

Bush probably reviewed this option, although Schwarzkopf claims it was never considered. When the war ended, Schwarzkopf wrote, "there was not a single head of state, diplomat, Middle East expert, or military leader who, as far as I am aware, advocated continuing the war and seizing Baghdad." No Arab troops fought on Iraqi soil during Desert Storm. This meant it would have been left for the United States and Britain to capture the city and become occupying powers. This might have cost the lives of many U.S. soldiers. It also would have been an expensive burden unacceptable to the American taxpayer. Furthermore, it would have lent support to Saddam's characterization of the war as a conflict between the forces of the Arab world and Western imperialism. Finally, Schwarzkopf pointed out, conquering Iraq would have exceeded the UN's mandate that called for expulsion of Iraq from Kuwait.[34]

3. Removal of Saddam from power. Could the U.S. military have captured Saddam? Or killed him in battle? If so, would he have become a martyr? Surely, Saddam and his entourage were extremely difficult targets. As the United States found out in Panama when searching for General Noriega, dictators who want to hide are not easily located. Saddam moved often from hiding place to hiding place. Doubles posing as Saddam increased the problem of finding him. It would have been against the law for the United States to have officially tried to assassinate Saddam. But like the U.S. bombing raid on Libya in 1985, Washington would not have been unhappy if Saddam had been killed in similar action. What Bush did do, however, was call for the Iraqi military and people to overthrow Saddam. This call was to have tremendous negative repercussions after the war.

4. A Five-Day War. This had the advantage of historical one-upmanship: the coalition would have defeated Iraq in one day's less time than it took Israel to win the Six-Day War in 1967. Schwarzkopf wrote: "Powell chuckled. 'That has a nice ring to it. I'll pass it along.' "[35] Nothing more came of this idea, however.

The decision to end the war at 100 hours seemed to Bush and his advisers the best course of action. It seemed the best public relations gimmick. More importantly it satisfied the main UN goal of forcing Iraq to withdraw its occupation forces from Kuwait. Yet at the same time it left many loose ends, many of which would haunt the United States and Gulf region for years to come. Bush's decision called into question both his judgment and leadership throughout the crisis and its aftermath.

Bush's Leadership Role in the Decision

President Bush rightfully deserves credit for convincing King Fahd of the need to station foreign troops in his country. But perhaps his greatest accomplishment during the Gulf crisis was his organization and leadership of the UN coalition. It was somewhat easy to gain the support of NATO. Neither Thatcher, Mitterand, nor Kohl needed prodding. Gaining the cooperation of Gorbachev required some finesse. Although the Cold War had ended, the Soviet Union was in turmoil. Moreover, earlier it had supplied Iraq with sophisticated weapons and military advisers, some of whom repeatedly were still in Iraq at the time of the invasion of Kuwait.

Most difficult were Bush's efforts to win support of key Arab states such as Syria and Egypt. To do this, Bush had to convince these countries of Saddam's aggressive designs beyond Kuwait. He also had to make sure Israel would not join the coalition and would stay out of war should it develop. Much of the credit for the successful building of the coalition should be given to Secretary Baker. The coalition he forged with Arab states and the Soviet Union and without Israel was a remarkable achievement. He traveled to Damascus to convince President Hafez al-Assad that joining the coalition would help Syria break out of its diplomatic isolation, especially since it could no longer expect the Soviet Union to supply weapons. He promised President Mubarak that the United States would forgive billions of dollars of Egyptian debt. Perhaps Baker's one faux pas was when he publicly added his own practical goal for the buildup of U.S. forces. The "economic lifeline" of the West was at stake, he argued, and "to bring [the crisis] down to the average American citizen, . . . that means jobs."[36]

During the Gulf War, for the most part Bush successfully avoided the style of "micro-management" that had so hamstrung earlier presidents like Jimmy Carter. Instead, Bush focused on the big picture, or "high strategy." The president was clearly the person in full command of decision-making. He acted confidently and without equivocation. By being so decisive, he was able to shed "the Wimp factor" that had plagued him during the 1988 presidential election. This time, Bush always made it known where he stood. For example, when Saddam invaded Kuwait, he predicted confidently that this aggression "will not stand." Moreover, Bush openly vented his anger at Saddam for the invasion. He felt betrayed that Saddam had taken this step despite Washington's "tilt" toward Iraq during its war with Iran. Bush was especially perturbed that Iraqi forces had committed such atrocious human rights violations. Faced with this sudden turn of events, Bush did not shrink from the use of force.

Throughout the Gulf crisis, Bush exercised a collegial style of leadership.[37] Observers considered him a specialist in "interpersonal relations."[38] The president worked well with his "buddies," a small inner circle of close advisers that included Baker, Scowcroft, and Cheney. These advisers remained unified in support of the president and acted with a certain "like-mindedness." There were clear advantages to this unified approach to decision-making. Yet homogeneity, as *New York Times* columnist William Safire noted, resulted in the "absence of creative tension" and "original thinking."[39] There was no doubt, however, that it was the president who made the decisions. The State Department was generally out of the decision-making loop during the crisis. Bush tended not to seek advice from the department, whose secretary of state for Near Eastern affairs was John Kelly, an expert on Western Europe. Ambassador Glaspie, a well-trained expert of Arab affairs, was never asked for her advice after her controversial meeting with Saddam preceding his invasion of Kuwait.

Bush was receptive to diverse opinions, but he stuck fast to his own in decision-making. This was especially true in his relationship with Congress. As stated above, he was willing to take advice from Congress, but did not believe its consent was necessary.[40] Throughout the crisis, he consulted informally with members of Congress; used cabinet officials like former representative Cheney to act as liaison with his former colleagues and to testify before congressional committees; consistently explained his positions and actions; and sought support. He left no doubt, however, that the president was the chief decision-maker.

Although Bush downplayed the role of Congress (which wanted to rely more on sanctions against Iraq and return the country to the State Department's state-sponsoring terrorism list), he seemed very much attuned to the need for support of American public opinion. He was very much aware that one of the most important factors that hurt the White House during the Vietnam War was failure to win enough public support for its decisions. In contrast, Bush successfully cultivated public support during the Gulf crisis. The public was elated by what certainly looked like a dazzling military success.[41] But once the glow of victory in the desert began to fade, the public began to focus on the results of the war. Resounding success on the battlefield did not seem to be matched by postwar results.

Consequences of Bush's Decision for the United States and Other Countries Involved

Not long after the war ended, Bush's critics stepped up their attacks. They wanted to know, for example, whether it was wise for the United States to have "tilted" toward Iraq during its war with Iran, especially if this meant providing so much economic and military aid to Saddam. They also questioned the failure of the United States to deter Saddam's invasion of Kuwait, pointing especially to Ambassador Glaspie's controversial meeting with Saddam. The Bush administration was accused of sending mixed signals to Baghdad, which Saddam interpreted as a green light to attack. During Desert Shield, critics focused on the failure of "coercive diplomacy." Bush was accused especially of not letting economic sanctions run their course. Bush was also criticized for doing an end run around Congress and not abiding by the Constitution in sending troops to the Gulf. When Desert Storm began, opponents argued that a war fought primarily to secure oil supplies was hardly a just war. Critics also pointed to what they called "managed news" from the Pentagon. In their estimation, the Bush administration had kept the truth hidden about Iraqi civilian casualties and had given too effusive praise to pinpoint kills by "smart weapons." They especially pointed to misleading and even false reports of the successful destruction of SCUD missiles by Patriot anti-missiles. All this was added to criticism of Bush's decision to end the war at 100 hours.

On the other hand, Bush received high marks for his accomplishments during the entire crisis, as well as the decision to end the war. Bush was praised for the following accomplishments: understanding the dangerousness and ruthlessness of Saddam Hussein; standing firm against Iraqi aggression; protecting American national security—defined at least in terms of securing oil supplies; convincing King Fahd of the seriousness of Saddam's threat and the necessity of massing thousands of Western troops on Saudi soil; keeping Israel out of the war; working through the UN; putting together the UN coalition (especially influencing the Soviet Union and key Arab states to get aboard and prevailing upon Israel to stay out of the war); and keeping coalition casualties so low. Bush was also applauded for ending the war so early. Supporters were impressed by his demonstrated high regard for human life. They also approved of his view of realpolitik in the Gulf area. This meant, among other things, the president's decision not to occupy or try to destroy Iraq.

The key question left unanswered by Desert Storm is whether the war ended too soon at 100 hours. Opinion is mixed. We will now examine the main short and longer-term consequences of Bush's decision.

The United States

After the Gulf War, President Bush boasted that at last the United States had "kicked the Vietnam syndrome." No longer would the United States shrink from using military power abroad in defense of principle or vital national security interests.

Bush's main publicly stated goals of the war were to drive Iraqi forces from Kuwait, restore the Kuwait government, protect U.S. citizens, and to maintain the security and stability of Saudi Arabia and the Persian Gulf. These goals were achieved, although some of them (e.g., restoration to power of the autocratic emir of Kuwait) were questionable. Yet other central war goals, not publicly declared, were not satisfied. These included destruction of Iraq's vaunted Republican Guard, elimination of Iraq's capability to produce weapons of mass destruction, and removal from power of Saddam himself.

Many wondered why the coalition did not finish off the Republican Guard. "The gate is closed," General Schwarzkopf boasted publicly in Riyadh just before the war's end, but it was not. Because the trap was poorly designed and sprung too soon, almost two-thirds of Saddam's elite forces escaped back to Iraq. In addition, Bush had decided that humanitarian and political considerations should prevail over military objectives. At the time, he and his principal advisers believed that achievement of the administration's publicly stated goals was sufficient. In retrospect, of course, they were dead wrong. They also miscalculated about how much the coalition had destroyed Saddam's capacity to make weapons of mass destruction. The war had wiped out much of Saddam's conventional war-making capability, but what of his capability to produce and stock pile chemical and biological weapons? Equally important, what was left of Saddam's nuclear weapons development program? After the war, UN monitors inspected Iraq's weapons production sites. Iraq only reluctantly cooperated. To their dismay, they concluded that Iraq's nuclear and biological and chemical warfare capabilities were farther advanced than most outside experts had believed. There was still serious concern that Saddam maintained significant capability in these areas.

Perhaps the most important question was why Saddam was left in power. Israeli Prime Minister Yitzhak Shamir was shocked by this. Shamir said he and his cabinet ministers "almost fell off our chairs" when Bush ended the Gulf War before Saddam was toppled.[42]

In a television interview five years after the end of the Gulf War, President Bush stated that in retrospect the U.S.-led coalition "could have done more" to weaken and topple Saddam. With Saddam still in power, Bush said: "We all, the world assumed . . . that Saddam could not survive a humiliating defeat. I miscalculated." Although he doubted that he could have forced Saddam into a surrender ceremony "which would visibly increase his personal humiliation," he could have demanded a subordinate Iraqi official to appear at such a ceremony to show "they were throwing in the towel." At the time, though, Bush believed it was unclear whether Saddam's successor would have been any better. If the Ba'ath Party had installed a new leader, there still might not have been any significant change in postwar developments. If no strong leader had emerged, the Iraqi state might have weakened and possibly fallen apart. The United States feared destabilizing Iraq and presenting Iran with an opportunity to fill a power vacuum. This had been a major consideration of U.S. policy since the beginning of the Iran-Iraq War. Reportedly, advisers such as General Powell were "convinced that it would not be in the U.S. interest to have a totally defeated Iraq with no capability to defend itself."[43] Arab leaders, including King Fahd and President Assad, feared that destabilization of Iraq might lead to "Lebanonization," that is, turmoil and near destruction caused by warring factions within the country. The United States encouraged rebellions by the Kurds in the north and Shiites in the south, but they failed.

Iraq

When the Gulf War was over, Saddam still had the capability to ruthlessly suppress these rebellions. Not only did he have much of the Republican Guard at his disposal, he also could utilize armed helicopters. At the cease-fire negotiations, Iraq asked permission to use these weapons. General Schwarzkopf, trying not to be unnecessarily punitive, acquiesced—provided they were kept away from and did not threaten U.S. forces. At the time, Schwarzkopf had no idea what was behind Iraq's request. Later, of course, Schwarzkopf realized he had made a tragic mistake. Almost immediately, Saddam began to wage a new war against his own people. The U.S. Air Force flew many missions to drop supplies to the Kurds, who fled from Iraqi firepower over the mountains with mainly the clothes on their backs. Many Kurds died from the fighting. Many more were ravaged by hunger and disease. Once again, the world watched on television desperate people struggling for freedom from Saddam's brutality. The UN eventually established a no-fly zone to keep Iraqi forces out of Kurdish territory. This afforded the Kurds some protection, at least on a temporary basis. But many still felt betrayed. For after calling upon them to revolt against Saddam, the United States offered no real assistance.[44] Less visible to the outside world but no less horrible was Saddam's persistent suppression of Shiites. Among other things, Saddam drained the marshes where they lived, which was their lifeblood. Thus Saddam committed additional acts of environmental terrorism as well as human destruction.[45]

Desert Storm killed hundreds of thousands of Iraqis, many of them innocent civilians. Although the United States most likely did not target civilians—Saddam's claims to the contrary—their loss of life was an unavoidable result of war. After the war, the Iraqi people continued to suffer. Repeated air strikes had destroyed much of Iraq's infrastructure. In addition, the UN embargo had limited Iraq to importation of food and medical supplies. The UN agreed to let Iraq sell some oil to pay for these supplies if Saddam abided by certain conditions of distribution. But Saddam refused to accept any conditions on his freedom of action. He did circumvent the embargo by selling oil through Iran, but his people rarely benefited from these transactions. As could be expected, the embargo did not hurt Saddam. He never missed a meal, nor was he unable to find heating oil or gasoline. Instead there were thousands of unknown victims, especially the children and those needing medical attention.[46]

To a great extent, Saddam successfully portrayed the United States as the villain responsible for the severe shortages. He pointed to the United States as the main force working to maintain the UN embargo. The United States, in turn, stated repeatedly that Iraq had not completely met all conditions for removal of the embargo. Saddam finally gave up its claim to Kuwait. Yet Washington claimed that Saddam's capability to produce weapons of mass destruction, including nuclear weapons, was

not totally destroyed; that he still committed terrible human rights violations against his own people; and that he had not returned or accounted
for all Kuwaiti missing persons or prisoners of war.

Kuwait

Though many believed the Gulf War was fought at least partially to
"grow democracy" in the Middle East, no such result occurred in
Kuwait. The emir returned to power and once again, in essence, politics
was business as usual. To many Kuwaitis, several years after the war,
victory seemed hollow. Their country had recovered from the war's
physical destruction, but psychological and emotional scars remained.
One reason was that Baghdad continued to turn a deaf ear to Kuwait's
persistent demands to return several hundred missing Kuwaiti citizens.
The more fundamental problem, however, was that despite the fact
Kuwait had significantly beefed up its military, the country still remained vulnerable to another possible invasion from Iraq.

The Middle East

The Gulf War raised several questions of justice and morality. Two
stand out. The first was whether the United States fought a just war.
Supporters of the war claim it was just. They argue it was fought to defend a small country against being swallowed up by an aggressive
neighbor and to protect vital U.S. security interests. Opponents claim
the war was unjust because it was fought mainly to secure the supply of
cheap oil. The second was that Saddam committed both war crimes and
crimes against humanity before, during, and after the Gulf war. Yet he
was not removed from power or brought to justice. Saddam even
claimed a political victory. After all, he pointed out, he stayed in power
whereas Bush did not.

These questions aside, the Gulf War led to some significant developments in the Middle East. Strikingly, it exploded the myth of Arab
unity. Saddam wanted the world to believe he was fighting to realize a
single Arab nation. Instead, the war highlighted intra-Arab conflicts.
Saddam, after all, had called into question the legitimacy of states in the
Middle East created artificially by British imperialism. He had also
sharpened the focus on inequality between oil-rich and oil-poor states
in the region, as well as what oil revenues were being used for. In addition, the absence of democracy in Arab states was seen as a more seri-

ous, pressing problem. The war brought to the fore problems of democracy throughout the Middle East. In the short run, however, tensions and conflicts arising from this issue such as in Egypt led to even more autocratic rule. In the end, the U.S. taxpayer indirectly propped up President Mubarak's authoritarian rule by writing off Egypt's huge debts after the war. The influence of democracy certainly was not felt in Syria. Assad, who himself was a perpetrator of the most gross human violations against his own people as well as a sponsor of terrorism around the world, received his reward for participating in the coalition. The world tacitly accepted Syria's large military presence and political influence in Lebanon.[47]

Yet the war brought at least a semblance of stability to the region. Saudi Arabia benefited militarily from increased protection from the United States, and economically (an extra $80 billion over the first five years) from making up the shortfall of oil sales denied to Iraq. Perhaps the most important, potentially longlasting postwar development was that the Gulf War broke the log jam in the Arab-Israeli peace process. The PLO, which had supported Saddam, was left with no supporters. Its major non-Arab patron, the Soviet Union, collapsed in December 1991. And its Arab sponsors, notably Saudi Arabia and Kuwait, expelled Palestinians and cut off their aid. Israel, though still the strongest military power in the region, realized that the raining of Iraq's SCUD missiles on Tel Aviv and the continued threat of nonconventional warfare (chemical and biological weapons) left it more vulnerable than previously thought. Seeking a new conception of security, Israel soon made historic agreements first with the PLO and then with Jordan. Subsequently, Syria and Israel began peace talks. Fulfillment of the peace process still faced hard times, but the war had given it a major boost.

Conclusion

Few experts predicted the Gulf War would end so quickly with such few casualties suffered by coalition forces. Liberating Kuwait with an amazingly low loss of American lives played a major role in Bush's winning the backing of the American people for his decision. Almost no experts expected the war to end with only 155 U.S. military men and women killed, which represented 0.03 percent of the total U.S. force in the Gulf. Schwarzkopf said this was "almost miraculous, even though it will never be miraculous to the families of those people."[48]

Bush's decision to end the war at 100 hours will be debated for years to come. A unilateral declaration of an end to hostilities was certainly unusual. Also distinctive was the fact there was no military occupation of Iraq and no required change of Iraqi leadership. Bush will be praised for the stunning victory of Desert Storm; for his humaneness in not slaughtering fleeing, defenseless Iraqi troops; for fulfillment of the major UN goal of liberating Kuwait; for his decisive and effective leadership at home and the anti-Saddam coalition abroad; and for protection of vital U.S. oil interests. Yet he will be criticized for ending the war too soon; for leaving Saddam in power and much of his war machine intact; for not destroying the Republican Guard; and for urging the Kurds and Shiites to topple the Iraqi dictator without giving them the necessary support.

In an address to a joint session of Congress on March 6, 1991, President Bush envisioned a new world order which, in the words of Winston Churchill, "the principles of justice and fair play . . . protect the weak against the strong." Bush then called for "a world where the United Nations, freed from Cold War stalemate, is poised to fulfill the historic vision of its founders. A world in which freedom and respect for human rights find a home among all nations."

The Gulf War was fought in defense of the principle that the UN would not allow borders to change by aggression. At least in the Middle East, this principle received added credence. But Bush's rhetoric notwithstanding, the Gulf War seemed to reaffirm the old order in the region marked by the flow of cheap oil to the West and the shoring up of feudal Arab regimes. The world must wait to see whether President Bush's publicly proclaimed vision of a new world order will prevail in the Middle East. Time will also tell how significant in this regard was his decision to end the war at 100 hours. In the words of General Schwarzkopf, we will "probably never know if one or two days would have made much difference."

Questions for Discussion

1. Do you agree with Bush's decision to "tilt" toward Iraq in its war with Iran?

2. Did Saddam have any valid reason to invade Kuwait?

3. Did Bush give "coercive diplomacy" enough of a chance before embarking on Desert Storm?

4. Should Bush have continued the war until the Republican Guard was completely destroyed, even if this meant killing defenseless soldiers in a "turkey shoot?"

5. Should Bush have insisted on Saddam's removal from power before ending the war?

6. Was it wise for Bush to call for an uprising of the Iraqi military and people to overthrow Saddam without lending U.S. support?

7. Did the United States fight a just war in the Gulf?

8. How important was it for the United States to "kick the Vietnam syndrome"?

9. Should Bush have stopped the war without further attempts to destroy Iraq's capability to produce weapons of mass destruction, including nuclear weapons?

10. Middle East expert Jere Bacharach says Operation Desert Storm will stand in history as "an unresolved war" because it left so many fundamental problems unsettled. Do you agree?

Notes

1. Quoted by Judith Miller and Laurie Mylroie, *Saddam Hussein and the Crisis in the Gulf* (New York: Times Books, 1990), p. 143.
2. In 1985–86, the U.S. arms-for-hostages deal with Iran clearly conflicted with the embargo.
3. There were several internal papers written by members of the State Department's policy planning staff that urged a reconsideration of U.S. policy toward Iraq. See, for example, "Containing Iraq," written by Richard Herrmann and Stephen Grummon; and the paper written in September 1988 for president-elect Bush by Zalmay Khalilzad. For details, see Don Oberdorfer, "Missed Signals in the Middle East," *Washington Post Magazine*, March 17, 1991, pp. 19–41; and Elaine Sciolino and Michael Wines, *New York Times*, June 27, 1992. Cited by Alexander L. George, *Bridging the Gap: Theory and Practice in Foreign Policy* (Washington, D.C.: United States Institute of Peace Press, 1993), p. 33n1. See also Bruce W. Jentleson, *With Friends Like These: Reagan, Bush, and Saddam, 1982–1990* (New York: Norton, 1994), pp. 90–91.
4. George, pp. 34–35.
5. In her cable to Washington after the meeting (leaked partially to the press), entitled "Saddam's Message of Friendship for President Bush," Glaspie de-

scribed Saddam in reassuring words as "cordial, reasonable, and even warm." For further comments on this cable, see Jentleson, pp. 170–71.

6. For a complete U.S. transcript of Glaspie's meeting with Saddam Hussein, see Micah L. Sifry and Christopher Cert (eds.), *The Gulf War Reader* (New York: Times Books, 1991), pp. 122–33. For a detailed review of U.S. policy toward Iraq leading up to the Gulf War, see Michael H. Gordon, "Pentagon Objected to a Message Bush Sent Iraq Before Its Invasion," *New York Times*, October 25, 1992.

7. Alan Friedman, *Spider's Web: The Secret History of How the White House Illegally Armed Iraq* (New York: Bantam Books, 1994). For a good case study of U.S. arms sales to Iraq, see Christopher M. Jones, "American Prewar Technology Sales To Iraq: A Bureaucratic Politics Explanation," in Eugene R. Wittkopf (ed.), *The Domestic Sources of American Foreign Policy*, 2nd ed. (New York: St. Martin's Press, 1994), pp. 279–96.

8. See Richard Norton-Taylor, "Shots in the Dark," *Guardian Weekly*, December 19, 1993, pp. 10–11. Norton-Taylor argues that the British government "was concerned above all about public opprobrium at a time when the true nature of Saddam's regime . . . [was] being exposed in the media." See also William Miller, " 'Arms-for-Iraq Affair' Threatens Tory Government," *Boston Globe*, March 6, 1994.

9. On Western aid for Iraq's nuclear weapons program, see Stephen J. Hedges and Peter Cary with Douglas Pasternak and David Bowermaster, "Desert Drama: Inside Saddam Hussein's Nuclear Nightmare," *U.S. News & World Report*, 25 November, 1991, 36–42; and Henry M. Rowan, "Left Holding the Bag in Iraq," *New York Times*, October 24, 1992. For a complete list of the countries that sold weapons and advanced technology to Iraq to help its nuclear and missile programs before the Persian Gulf War (as compiled by the Wisconsin Project on Nuclear Arms Control), see Douglas Jehl, "Who Armed Iraq? Answers the West Didn't Want to Hear," *New York Times*, July 18, 1993.

10. See Christopher Greenwood, "Iraq's Invasion of Kuwait: Some Legal Issues," *The World Today*, 47 March 1991, 39–42.; and Joe Stork and Ann M. Lesch, "Why War?" *Middle East Report*, November-December 1990: 11–17.

11. See Martin Staniland, *Getting to No: The Diplomacy of the Gulf Conflict, August 2, 1990 – January 15, 1991, Part 1: Background to the Conflict*, Institute for the Study of Diplomacy, Pew Case Studies Center, Georgetown University, Washington, D.C., pp. 2–4.

12. Laurie Mylroie, "Why Saddam Hussein Invaded Kuwait," *Orbis*, 37 (Winter 1993): 123–34.

13. See Mohammed Sid-Ahmed, "The Gulf Crisis and the New World Order," *Middle East Report*, January-February 1991, pp. 16–17; and Shibley Telhami, "Arab Public Opinion and the Gulf War," in Stanley A. Renshon (ed.), *The Political Psychology of the Gulf War* (Pittsburgh: University of Pittsburgh Press, 1994), pp. 183–98.

14. The other Arab countries that joined the coalition were Bahrain, Djibouti, Kuwait, Lebanon, Morocco, Oman, Qatar, Somalia, and the United Arab Emirates.

15. For a complete listing of contributions to the multinational coalition, see *The Middle East*, 8th ed. (Washington, D.C.: Congressional Quarterly, 1994), p. 113.

16. Elaine Sciolino, "Gore Says Bush's Efforts to Befriend Iraqi Leader Led to Gulf War," *New York Times*, September 30, 1992.

17. Milton Viorst, "Blaming Bush Unfairly for the Persian Gulf War: His Policy with Saddam Hussein was Right," *The Washington Post National Weekly Edition*, November 2–8, 1992, p. 25.

18. For a good discussion of the issue of the Constitution's war powers, see Michael J. Glennon, "The Gulf War and the Constitution," *Foreign Affairs*, 70 (Spring 1991): 84–101.

19. *The Stars and Stripes*, Commemorative Edition, "Bush: 'The World Could Wait No Longer,' " January 18, 1991, p. 6.

20. "U.S. Says Only Iraq Can Stop War Now," ibid., p. 9.

21. John Mueller, "American Public Opinion and the Gulf War," in *The Political Psychology of the Gulf War*, p. 206.

22. *The Stars and Stripes*, "Iraq Offers to Withdraw; Bush Calls It 'Cruel Hoax,' " pp. 60–61.

23. Speculation that these men were the "hawks" involved was made by Michael Gordon, "Schwarzkopf Says Hawks Pressed for Early Land War," *New York Times*, September 20, 1992.

24. H. Norman Schwarzkopf, *It Doesn't Take a Hero* (New York: Linda Grey / Bantam Books, 1992), p. 443.

25. *The Stars and Stripes*, "High Noon for Iraq," February 23, 1991, pp. 67–68.

26. For an excellent discussion of Bush's foreign policy principles that led to his actions in the Gulf War, see Stephen J. Wayne, "President Bush Goes to War: A Psychological Interpretation from a Distance," in Stanley A. Renshon (ed.), *The Political Psychology of the Gulf War*, pp. 29–48.

27. Quoted by Kenneth T. Walsh, "Commander in Chief," *U.S. News and World Report*, December 31 – January 7, 1990–91, p. 24.

28. Ibid., p. 25.

29. Ibid., p. 24.

30. See Michael R. Gordon and General Bernard E. Trainor, *The Generals' War* (Boston: Little, Brown and Co., 1995), p. 414. Most of the material for the remaining discussion of events leading to Bush's decision to end the war and its aftermath is taken from this book, pp. 413–32. Additional details are found in Schwarzkopf's *It Doesn't Take a Hero*, pp. 468–72.

31. Colin Powell, *My American Journey* (New York: Random House, 1995), pp. 326–27.

32. Quoted in Roger Cohen and Claude Gatti, *In the Eye of the Storm: The Life of*

General H. Norman Schwarzkopf (New York: Farrar, Strauss, & Giroux, 1991), pp. 288–89.

33. Schwarzkopf, *It Doesn't Take a Hero*, pp. 469–70.

34. Ibid., p. 497.

35. Ibid., p. 469.

36. For a detailed discussion of Baker's role in the Gulf crisis, see David Hoffman, "James Baker's Determination To Put the New World in Order," *The Washington Post National Weekly Edition,* August 24–30, 1992, p. 31.

37. For a good analysis of Bush's decision-making style, see Stanley Renshon, "Good Judgment, and the Lack Thereof, in the Gulf War," in Renshon, *The Political Psychology of the Gulf War*, pp. 67–105.

38. See James David Barber, *Presidential Character*, 4th ed. (Englewood Cliffs, N.J.: Prentice Hall, 1992), p. 6; and Bob Woodward, *The Commanders* (New York: Simon & Schuster, 1991), p. 302.

39. See Jentleson, p. 236.

40. See Brigitte Lebens Nacos, "Presidential Leadership during the Persian Gulf Conflict," *Presidential Studies Quarterly*, 24 (Summer 1994): 543–61.

41. For an excellent discussion of Bush's leadership during the Gulf War, see Cecil V. Crabb and Kevin V. Mulcahy, "George Bush's Management Style and Operation Desert Storm," in Richard W. Waterman (ed.,), *The Presidency Reconsidered* (Itasca, Ill.: F. E. Peacock, 1993), pp. 275–92.

42. "Shamir: Israel Was Stunned by Failure to Topple Saddam," *Jewish Advocate* (Boston), January 20–26, 1995.

43. Woodward, p. 374.

44. Tony Horwitz, "After Heeding Calls to Turn on Saddam, Shiites Feel Betrayed," *Wall Street Journal*, December 26, 1991.

45. "Iraqis Are Said to Wage War on Marsh Arabs," *New York Times*, October 19, 1993.

46. Barbara Nimuri Aziz, "Iraqi Embargo's Unknown Victims," ibid., May 30, 1995; and Jamal Halaby, "Lonely Iraq Grows Hungrier," *Rochester Democrat and Chronicle*, January 16, 1996.

47. See Tareq Y. Ismael and Jacqueline A. Ismael, "The Effects of the Gulf War on Arab Politics," *The Persian Gulf: Political and Economic Issues* (Washington, D.C.: The Middle East Institute, 1991), pp. 24–26; Michael C. Hudson, "After the Gulf War: Prospects for Democratization in the Arab World," *The Middle East Journal*, 45 (Summer 1991): 407–26.

48. Although U.S. casualties during the war were minimal, thousands died or suffered after the war. Some died from a "friendly fire" incident. As of summer 1995, at least 2,500 veterans had died from assorted other causes. In addition, more than 70,000 had reported unexplained, persistent illness that they insisted was caused by toxic battlefields. See Thomas D. Williams, "Doctors Find Common Trait among Ill Gulf War Veterans," *Hartford Courant*, July 2, 1995.

Selected Bibliography

Cohen, Roger and Claude Gatti. *In the Eye of the Storm: The Life of General H. Norman Schwarzkopf.* New York: Farrar, Strauss, & Giroux, 1991.

Friedman, Alan. *Spider's Web: The Secret History of How the White House Illegally Armed Iraq.* New York: Bantam Books, 1994.

George, Alexander. *Bridging the Gap: Theory and Practice in Foreign Policy.* Washington, D.C.: The United States Institute of Peace, 1993.

Gordon, Michael R. and Bernard E. Trainor. *The Generals' War.* Boston: Little, Brown and Co., 1995.

Jentleson, Bruce W. *With Friends Like These: Reagan, Bush, and Saddam, 1982–1990.* New York: W. W. Norton, 1994.

Miller, Judith and Laurie Mylroie. *Saddam Hussein and the Crisis in the Gulf.* New York: Times Books, 1990.

Reshon, Stanley A. (ed.). *The Political Psychology of the Gulf War.* Pittsburgh: University of Pittsburgh Press, 1994.

Schwarzkopf, H. Norman. *It Doesn't Take a Hero.* New York: Linda Grey / Bantam Books, 1992.

Sifry, Micha L. and Christopher Cert. (eds.). *The Gulf War Reader.* New York: Times Books, 1991.

Woodward, Bob. *The Commanders.* New York: Simon & Schuster, 1991.

10

President Clinton's Decision to Use Military Force to Restore President Aristide to Office in Haiti

Setting and Overview of Clinton's Decision

Jean-Bertrand Aristide, a Catholic priest, was elected president of Haiti on December 16, 1990. In what was hailed as Haiti's first free election, Aristide won about two-thirds of the popular vote. Most Haitians exulted in prospects for the dawn of democracy. One of the most important results of the election was a drastic reduction in the number of Haitians who sought asylum in the United States. The refugee problem, which intensified in the 1970s and 1980s under continued severe repression by the Haitian government, seemed to end virtually overnight. But when a military coup ousted Aristide on September 30, 1991, new waves of distressed Haitians headed toward U.S. shores.

The Bush administration, like Reagan's, considered most of these boat people ineligible for asylum because they were determined to have fled for economic rather than political reasons. When their numbers swelled into the tens of thousands, Bush began sending many to the U.S. Guantanamo Naval Base in Cuba for screening. Then when Guantanamo became inundated with Haitians, Bush determined there would be no more screening. In May 1992, he announced his policy of summary repatriation. Presidential candidate Bill Clinton pledged to

315

reverse Bush's "inhumane" policy. Instead, just before taking office President-elect Clinton reversed himself and continued the Bush policy.

Once in office, President Clinton faced the bedeviling problem of President Aristide's restoration to power. Officially, Clinton maintained that he wanted to expedite his restoration. In fact, however, Clinton pursued this goal with less than full enthusiasm. The president tried a blend of pressures against the *de facto* Haitian government led by General Raoul Cedras that proved weak and ineffective: stopping aid; setting up trade embargoes called for by the Organization of American States (OAS) and the United Nations (UN); undertaking a number of diplomatic gambits; and imposing a variety of sanctions.

In October 1993, Clinton sent several hundred U.S. military engineers to Haiti on the *USS Harlan County*. Their mission, in accordance with the Governor's Island agreement the previous July, was to help pave the way for Aristide's return to power by October 15. Demonstrations by an armed mob of Haitians at Port-au-Prince Harbor forced the ship to turn away before even docking. Clinton responded by stating that the United States might have to intervene militarily to force Haiti's military rulers to step down.

By the spring and summer of 1994, faced with increased pressure from domestic critics of his Haitian policy, Clinton decided to use military force if necessary to restore Aristide. In September, a U.S. invasion force was poised to invade Haiti. In a final, desperate attempt to avoid bloodshed, Clinton dispatched a negotiating team to Haiti led by former President Jimmy Carter. The agreement that Carter arranged for the Haitian military leaders to step down seemed to turn an admittedly failed Clinton policy into success. Aristide returned to Haiti peacefully on October 15, 1994. Many serious economic, political, and social problems remained, but there was a ray of optimism for Haiti's future.

President Clinton's Decision

ON SEPTEMBER 15, 1994, PRESIDENT CLINTON STATED IN AN NATION-WIDE TELEVISED ADDRESS THAT HE WAS PREPARED TO USE MILITARY FORCE TO INVADE HAITI IF THE MILITARY DICTATORS OF THAT COUNTRY WOULD NOT STEP DOWN. U.S. TROOPS WOULD BE SENT UNDER THE UN SECURITY COUNCIL RESOLUTION OF JULY 31. THE GOAL WAS TO RESTORE PRESIDENT ARISTIDE WHO HAD BEEN OUSTED BY A COUP IN SEPTEMBER 1991. A LAST MINUTE DIPLOMATIC AGREEMENT WITH THE MILITARY

JUNTA, NEGOTIATED BY FORMER PRESIDENT JIMMY CARTER, FORMER
CHAIRMAN OF THE JOINT CHIEFS OF STAFF COLIN POWELL, AND SENA-
TOR SAM NUNN, PRECLUDED A BLOODY U.S. INVASION. ON SEPTEMBER
19, U.S. TROOPS ENTERED HAITI. THIS ACTION PERMITTED ARISTIDE TO
RETURN TO POWER PEACEFULLY ON OCTOBER 15, 1994.

Clinton's decision to restore Aristide to power by military force if
necessary was controversial for these reasons:

1. The Central Intelligence Agency and a number of influential congressmen opposed the restoration of Aristide, whom they considered left-wing and anti-American.
2. Business feared that Aristide's socialist populism would hurt their
   interests.
3. Critics charged an invasion was unwarranted because U.S. vital interests were not at stake.
4. Skeptics claimed an invasion would invoke memories of a previous
   invasion of Haiti in 1915 when U.S. troops stayed as an occupying
   force until 1934.
5. Detractors argued that an invasion would be a sour reminder of
   other more recent U.S. invasions such as in the Dominican Republic
   (1965) and Grenada (1983).
6. Some feared a botched invasion would weaken President Clinton's
   credibility in the world as a strong leader.

Background for the Decision

Historical Context

Over 500 years ago, when Europeans encountered the New World,
Haiti was a jewel of the Caribbean. It seemed blessed by Mother Nature. Surrounded by blue ocean waters, it had abundant coffee and fruit
trees, rich fertile soil, and an inviting tropical climate. Today, this pris-
tine Haiti can be found only in history books. Sorrowfully, the country
has been ravaged by deforestation, devastated by the depletion and
squandering of its natural resources, racked by desperate poverty, bur-
dened by political oppression, and weakened by the lowest life ex-
pectancy and literacy rate in the Western Hemisphere.

In 1804, when former slave Toussaint L'Ouverture led a successful revolt of black slaves against French rule, Haiti became the second country in the hemisphere to win independence from European colonialism. Fearing the bloody revolution's potentially adverse effect on southern slavery, the United States reacted in a hostile way. It isolated Haiti and did not extend diplomatic recognition until 1862, during the Civil War. Haiti's economy floundered, and the country stumbled through numerous revolutions, coups, upheavals, and crises.

On July 28, 1915, U.S. Marines invaded Haiti. They were ordered to eliminate "a public nuisance on our doorstep." President Wilson's official reason was humanitarian. In the wake of a massacre of political prisoners, he wanted to protect American and Haitian lives. Wilson also wanted to stabilize the country that had gone through seven presidents in seven years, to thwart any attempts by Germany to seize the country, and at the same time to protect U.S. interests in the newly opened Panama Canal. U.S. occupation did not end until 1934. During this period, in effect Haiti became a U.S. protectorate. Though the U.S. built roads and hospitals and imposed relative political stability, it also left a bitter legacy of imperialism. The Haitian economy, previously dominated by French and German interests, became almost totally dependent on the United States. In addition, just as it had done in Nicaragua and the Dominican Republic, the United States played a major role in creating the army in Haiti. Known then as "the Haitian Guard," these soldiers behaved like an occupying army. They helped the Marines chase down rebel peasants ("Cacos") and routinely acted as a repressive domestic political force. U.S. intervention thus led to a succession of puppet dictatorships. Corruption, repression, and chaos ensued.[1]

In 1957, François (Papa Doc) Duvalier rose to power. Though Duvalier officially won the popular vote, his election victory was marred by cheating, intimidation, and other "irregularities." In 1964, Duvalier designated himself President-for-life. Until his death in 1971, he ruled by coercion and terror, especially through the Tonton Macoutes (in Creole, "Uncle Knapsack," a bogeyman who searches for bad children and kidnaps them in his bag). This secret police organization served as Duvalier's private security force. It was comprised largely of illiterate peasants, former soldiers, and a motley assortment of criminals and mercenaries. They were trained as brutal, paramilitary thugs who intimidated and terrorized people and were responsible for many of the most reprehensible deeds of the government, such as organizing the "disappearance" of political opponents. When Papa Doc died in 1971, he arranged for his son Jean-Claude (Baby Doc) to carry on the Duvalier rule. Though Baby Doc eventually took some half-hearted steps to improve human rights—largely to appease President Carter and obtain U.S. aid—he mainly followed in his father's dictatorial footsteps.

Baby Doc, like his father, was to be President-for-life. But in 1986, he was overthrown by a popular revolt and driven into exile. After a succession of military regimes, in December 1990 the Haitians elected Father Jean-Bertrand Aristide by about a two-thirds majority. The poor Haitian masses were jubilant, for Aristide promised deliverance from their suffering. But Aristide's rule lasted only nine months. On September 30, 1991 he was ousted by a military coup and forced into exile in the United States. The stream of refugees that had virtually stopped after Aristide's election started up again almost immediately after the coup.

Haitian Boat People

President Kennedy, disgusted at the outrages of Papa Doc's rule, pressured the dictator to reform. In fact, in 1961 Kennedy even considered support for an invasion of Haiti by exiles to overthrow Duvalier. Haiti staved off any such action when it helped the United States by voting to expel Cuba from the OAS and reportedly made its harbors and airfields available to the United States during the Cuban missile crisis. But in 1963, when the Haitian military forcefully took over the Dominican embassy in Port-au-Prince, Kennedy suspended economic and military aid and evacuated all American citizens from Haiti.

In September 1963, during this tumultuous period, the first Haitian boat people arrived in southern Florida. The Immigration and Naturalization Service (INS) denied their request for political asylum and returned them to Haiti.[2] There would be no more boat people for another ten years. Under the Nixon administration, as under Johnson's, considerations of the Cold War dominated U.S. policy toward Haiti. In 1969, Nixon arranged economic aid through the Inter-American Development Bank and International Monetary Fund. Then when Baby Doc took power in 1971, Nixon resumed direct aid—mainly through the U.S. Agency for International Development.

At the same time, Washington made it harder for Haitians to immigrate legally to the United States. INS policy considered most Haitian applicants as a potential economic burden. It also smacked of racism, as Washington feared a political backlash from admitting large numbers of black immigrants. This restrictive immigration policy led to an increase of boat people. As more and more Haitians arrived in Florida, often aided by smugglers, pressure on Washington to stop the flow increased. The INS feared that a liberal policy toward Haitian immigration might trigger similar outpourings of refugees from elsewhere in the Caribbean. As a a result, it denied most requests by Haitians for asylum. Soon though, the United States welcomed thousands of Cuban refugees.

The Double Standard toward Cuban and Haitian Refugees

The U.S. had consistently criticized communist regimes for restricting emigration and pressured tham to liberalize their emigration policies. In turn, the United States was especially receptive to immigrants from communist states. Because of Washington's strong anti-communist posture, it was assumed that someone fleeing a communist country qualified for refugee status. On the other hand, Washington was almost hostile to refugees and asylum-seekers from noncommunist authoritarian regimes, especially those deemed friendly to the U.S.[3] Such was the case with Haiti.

On March 15, President Carter signed the Refugee Act of 1980.[4] One of its goals was to eliminate the legal bias in adjudication claims toward those fleeing communist regimes. In practice, however, little changed. Carter had arranged with Fidel Castro for large numbers of Cubans to go to the United States. On April 19, 1980, the boatlift from Mariel Harbor in Cuba (known as the Mariel boatlift) began. Within months approximately 125,000 Cubans arrived by boat in southern Florida. Many had a background of mental illness or violent crime. In fact, there were some indications that Castro saw this boatlift as an opportunity to empty his mental institutions and prisons. At the same time, a few thousand Haitian boat people arrived in Florida.

The disparity of treatment between Cuban and Haitian arrivals was striking. Cubans were welcomed as political refugees and in some cases even given cash gifts by U.S. officials, but Haitians generally were rejected as economic migrants and held in jails. There were also charges of racism. About ten percent of the Cuban refugees were black, compared to almost all of the Haitians. One disgruntled Haitian boat person denied asylum in the United States expressed his dismay in this blunt way: "We have suffered just as much as the Cubans have. We just want to be treated the same way they are. Are we less human than the Cubans?"

Advocates of the Haitian boat people rallied in support. They staged marches in major cities such as Miami, Washington, and New

York.[5] They also sponsored hunger strikes, undertook letter-writing campaigns, and arranged for meetings with members of Congress and White House officials. The congressional Black Caucus was especially active. Soon the Senate Judiciary Committee held hearings on the Cuban-Haitian situation. Some minor policy changes did result. Yet though Carter did ease restrictions against the Haitians and many were admitted into the U.S., he did not recognize Haitians as refugees. Soon Castro stopped the exodus of Cubans.[6] But Haitian boat people continued to come in sizable numbers.

Many Americans, especially in Florida, strongly opposed the Mariel boatlift. They were upset over the cost of absorbing such large numbers of refugees in such a short time. But they could not overcome the lobbying of the strongly anti-communist Cuban-American community. Haitians suffered the backlash.

During the 1980 presidential campaign, Republican Party leaders in Florida called for restrictions of Haitian immigration. A few months after Ronald Reagan took office, the INS, which until then generally released Haitians who had fled to the United States, began to step up detention. When Krome North, the main detention center for Haitian boat people outside of Miami became overcrowded, additional centers were set up in various places around the country including Lake Placid, New York; Brooklyn, New York; Morgantown, West Virginia; Lexington, Kentucky; Big Springs, Texas; and Fort Allen, Puerto Rico.

President Reagan decided to shrug off strong public opposition to this detention policy. When the president sent Ernest Preeg as ambassador to Haiti in the spring of 1981, he was told his highest priority was to stop the flow of Haitians to the United States. On September 23, 1981 President Reagan made an agreement with Baby Doc to interdict ships suspected of carrying Haitian migrants, interrogate the passengers, and send back those without U.S. entry documents or who were unable to make a convincing case for asylum. Haiti was the only country with which the United States had such an agreement. Reagan's executive order of September 29 stated that the Haitian boat people had become "a serious national problem detrimental to the interests of the United States."

The 1981 agreement called for the Haitian government to crack down on the brisk smuggling trade in human cargo. It also was to refrain from persecution of returnees. U.S. political officers from the U.S. embassy would check out their treatment by interviewing individuals with an interpreter. Not surprisingly, no case of persecution was ever discovered. Private individuals, however, learned of many serious ones.

Restriction of the flow of Haitians to the U.S. was remarkably successful. From the start of the interdiction program until the September 1991 coup that ousted President Aristide, the U.S. Coast Guard repatriated 22,716 Haitians. Twenty-eight were permitted to enter the United States to pursue asylum claims.[7] After the coup, U.S. ships continued to interdict Haitian boat people and screen them for asylum. When large numbers rendered this procedure unworkable, the Bush administration brought boat people to the U.S. Naval Base in Guantanamo Bay, Cuba.

By February 1992, Washington decided this outlet was no longer acceptable. A complicating problem arose when some Haitians at Guantanamo were found to have AIDS or to be HIV positive. Bush then established an in-country processing program (ICP) to screen refugees. Finally on May 24, Bush issued an executive order that the U.S. Coast Guard would interdict Haitian boats and return passengers directly to Haiti without asylum screening. Bush merely assumed that most Haitian boat people were economic migrants. Moreover, he justified his new policy on humanitarian grounds, a traditional ideal of U.S. foreign policy. It was deemed necessary to protect Haitians from losing their lives in a perilous 600-mile journey to the United States made in rickety boats through shark-infested waters. Paradoxically, the United States had criticized Britain earlier for forcibly repatriating Vietnamese refugees from Hong Kong, where they had fled in desperation.

Clinton's Policy toward Haitian Refugees

During the 1992 presidential campaign, Bill Clinton scolded President Bush for maintaining a "cruel policy of returning Haitian refugees to a brutal dictatorship without an asylum hearing." If elected, he pledged to change this ostensibly unfair and illegal policy. Clinton stated on the stump, for example: "If I were President, I would—in the absence of clear and compelling evidence that they weren't political refugees—give them temporary asylum until we restored the elected government of Haiti."

Just weeks after Clinton won the election, he was already mindful of the domestic political pitfalls of fulfilling his campaign pledge. Reportedly, Clinton aides were advising him not to repeat the mistake of the Mariel boatlift made by President Carter. Clinton, then governor of Arkansas, had to handle riots by about 20,000 of these Cubans who had been transported to a relocation center at Fort Chafee. Governor Clinton, who had invited the Marielitos, remembered well that these riots contributed to his failed reelection bid.[8]

President-elect Clinton faced the prospect of a flood of Haitians clamoring to enter the United States. He had just lost Florida's twenty-five big electoral votes to Bush, so he was wary of alienating that state's political constituency, especially its leaders. On January 11, a Florida newspaper printed a major story highlighting that state's worry over Haitian immigration. Reporter John Glisch wrote this summation of the situation: "Many fear that tens of thousands of refugees could sail for Miami around Inauguration Day, Jan. 20, because of President-elect Bill Clinton's pledge to give Haitians a fair hearing for political asylum in the United States." He noted that Clinton's campaign pledge had made him "something of a savior in Haiti. Since then, there has been a flurry of boat building on the Haitian coast and a boom in the smuggling of Haitians into South Florida."[9] At the same time, Florida Governor Lawton Childs was complaining bitterly about the financial burden of handling large-scale immigration. Because of the political influence of the big Cuban community in south Florida with its strong opposition to Castro's Communism, neither Childs nor Clinton at that time seriously considered banning Cuban immigration. Because Haitians had no equivalent political clout, it was easier to prohibit their immigration.

During the election campaign, besides maintaining that he would not return Haitians without a fair hearing to determine whether they were refugees, Clinton called for tightening of the economic embargo placed on Haiti by the OAS; blocking oil shipments; and increasing U.S. pressure to restore Aristide to office in Haiti.

After his election, Clinton started "clarifying" his position. In reality, this meant backtracking. Soon, he maintained he opposed a "mass migration." And finally, on January 14 he reversed himself completely when he announced he would continue Bush's policy of summary repatriation of Haitian boat people. That morning, in a taped Voice of America (VOA) radio broadcast to Haiti (translated into Creole for direct dissemination to Haitian broadcasters), Clinton stated: "Those who leave Haiti by boat for the United States will be intercepted and returned to Haiti by the U.S. Coast Guard. Leaving by boat is not the route to freedom." Clinton's remarks followed a radio address on January 11 by Aristide who appealed directly to Haitians to support Clinton's decision and remain in Haiti. Aristide reluctantly supported Clinton's new policy because he believed that with Clinton's help he would be restored to power in a matter of weeks.

Countdown to the Decision

In March 1993, President Clinton met with Aristide and pledged that the United States would contribute its "fair portion" of a $1 billion aid program for Haiti. Clinton also named Lawrence A. Pezullo, former ambassador to Nicaragua at the time the Sandinistas assumed power, as special adviser on Haiti. Clinton then tried a "carrot-and-stick" strategy to restore Aristide. In June, Clinton imposed additional sanctions on Haitian leaders. He also tried diplomacy.

The United States actually arranged to restore Aristide through the Governor's Island Accord of July 3, 1993. According to this agreement, the Haitian military rulers would resign by October 15 and Aristide would go back to Haiti on October 30. In return, Aristide reluctantly promised amnesty for the coup leaders. In addition, the United States would lead an international effort to train the Haitian military. But almost immediately after the accord, the Haitian military increased its repression and violence. Especially heinous was the assassination on the street of Aristide supporter Antoine Izmery on September 12. This incident told people that "you cannot hide behind a priest's vestments and not even a church offers a safe refuge."[10]

The most embarrassing episode for the United States occurred on October 12. Clinton had dispatched to Haiti a few hundred military engineers to start rebuilding the country's devastated economic infrastructure. When they arrived in Port-au-Prince Harbor on the USS Harlan County, they were met by a mob of about 100 Haitians brandishing machetes and waving guns in the air. This demonstration was presumably organized by the Haitian military junta. Under orders from Secretary of Defense Les Aspin, the ship turned away and sailed with its tail down toward the Guantanamo Naval Base.

This incident became a symbol of failure for U.S. policy toward Haiti. A very weak Haitian military (7,000 strong, with no air force and no fighting ships) had forced the most powerful country in the world to back off. Clinton scrambled to recoup his losses. One week later, the president ordered an infantry company to go on standby alert at Guantanamo. He also dispatched six destroyers to patrol waters off Haiti to enforce the oil and arms embargo imposed by the UN Security Council.

The president reported the deployment of U.S. Navy ships to Congress in a letter on October 20. In this letter, Clinton maintained that his action was "consistent with the War Powers Resolution"; that U.S. forces would "remain prepared to protect U.S. citizens in Haiti, and act in cooperation with the U.S. Coast Guard" to support the interdiction of Haitian migrants; that "the United States strongly suppports the Governor's Island Agreement and restoration of democracy in Haiti"; and that actions to deploy U.S. ships "are consistent with United States goals and interests and constitute crucial support for the world community's strategy to overcome the persistent refusal of Haitian military and police authorities to fulfill their commitments under the Governor's Island Agreement."

Congress debated limiting Clinton's authority to send troops to Haiti unless specifically authorized by statute. The Senate approved (by a vote of 98 to 2) an amendment that appropriated funds would not be spent for U.S. military operations in Haiti without its advanced approval. Two exceptions would be protecting U.S. citizens who faced "imminent danger" and safeguarding U.S. national security that required immediate action.

What was at stake in Haiti seemed far larger than Haiti itself. If a military junta with impunity could overthrow a democratically elected president on the U.S. doorstep, what message did this send around the world? President Clinton continually maintained that one of his major foreign policy goals was to enlarge democracy. If he could not do this in nearby Haiti, where else could he succeed? It seemed that the Haitian military understood U.S. domestic politics quite well. Just weeks before the USS Harlan County incident, American television viewers had watched several bodies of U.S. servicemen killed in Somalia being dragged through the streets of Mogadishu. The junta leaders anticipated correctly that Clinton would not risk further loss of lives of U.S. soldiers. Their success emboldened them to continue thumbing their noses at the United States and to ignore the Governor's Island Accord.

On December 14, John Shattuck, assistant secretary of state for human rights and humanitarian affairs, called for a review of U.S. Haitian policy. There was something wrong, he intimated, when since the September 1991 coup over 40,000 Haitians had fled by boat toward the United States and only a very few had been accepted for asylum.[11] Indeed, Clinton's forced repatriation policy was causing increased embarrassment for his administration. So bad was the situation that national security adviser Anthony Lake privately called it "a dark stain" on the administration. In public, however, administration officials defended the policy, claiming the United States was working hard to restore Aristide. Critics, though, like the Rev. Richard Ryscavage, executive director of the Migration and Refugee Service of the United States Catholic Conference, charged that Clinton's policy was "no better, and in some ways worse, than it was under the Bush Administration."[12]

Clinton's Haiti policy began to change in early spring 1994. On May 8, after a six-week policy review, Clinton stated he would reverse his Haiti policy which admittedly was not working. He announced that on June 16, U.S. officials would start interviewing Haitian boat people on the high seas to see whether they qualified for asylum. Many critics had been demanding a change in U.S. policy of summary repatriation. Some political observers charged that Clinton was bowing to pressures of the congressional Black Caucus, whose votes he needed for passage of his domestic programs on health care, welfare, and crime. Especially influential, perhaps, was Randall Robinson, black executive director of TransAfrica Forum, a research and lobbying group. Robinson fasted for twenty-seven days to force a change in Clinton's policy.[13]

Clinton also replaced Pezullo, his point man on Haiti, with black Democrat William H. Gray III, president of the United Negro College Fund and former chair of the congressional Black Caucus. By doing this, he tried to defuse charges that his policy toward Haitian boat people was racist. The president had already been stung by Aristide's criticism. At a Washington news conference on April 20, the exiled Haitian leader vehemently condemned Clinton's Haiti policy as "a cynical joke," "racist," and "really a way to say we don't care." Aristide added that Clinton had not shown the "political will" to make tough decisions to restore him to power. Clinton's advisers, such as Lake, Pezullo, and Deputy Secretary of State Strobe Talbott tried unsuccessfully to placate Aristide.[14] Earlier, the White House had urged Aristide to share power with the Haitian military and other political enemies. When Aristide steadfastly refused to bend, some members of the administration called him obstinate and a troublemaker. As one State Department official remarked: "I think that what Aristide is calculating, his agenda if you will, is to keep torpedoing every kind of agenda that brings national reconciliation. That leads you to the only, the ultimate, consequence of where he takes you, which is military intervention."[15]

Clinton's most significant annnouncement on May 8 was that he would not rule out the use of force to remove the Haitian military junta.

The House of Representatives then debated several amendments to limit Clinton's military options in Haiti. On May 24, a "sense of Congress" amendment was approved by a vote of 223 to 201 stipulating "that the United States should not undertake any military action against the mainland of Haiti unless the President first certifies to Congress that clear and present danger to citizens of the United States or United States interests requires such action." But this amendment was removed in a separate vote on June 9. Then on June 29, the Senate rejected an amendment stating that funds could not be used for any U.S. military operation in Haiti unless authorized in advance by Congress.

Between these two congressional votes on the use of force, Clinton widened U.S. sanctions against the military dictatorship. On June 12, he ordered cessation of most private financial dealings between Haiti and the United States and banned commercial air travel between the two countries (effective June 25); and on June 21, he froze the U.S. assets of Haitians living in Haiti. On July 11, the Haitian military junta ordered the OAS/UN human rights monitoring mission to leave. They left two days later. On July 5, Clinton again changed his refugee policy: those Haitian boat people whom U.S. officials determined faced persecution would be sent to "safe havens" in the area, such as Panama.

On July 31, the Clinton administration facilitated adoption of a UN Security Council resolution "inviting" all states, especially those in the region of Haiti, to use "all necessary means" to remove the military dictatorship. In response, on August 3 the Senate approved by a vote of 100 to 0 a "sense of the Senate amendment that the UN resolution did not authorize deployment of U.S. armed forces in Haiti under the Constitution or the War Powers Resolution." At a news conference on August 3, Clinton denied he needed congressional approval to invade Haiti.[16] On August 26, the president reportedly agreed to an invasion plan that the military had been preparing for months. Then on August 31, Talbott and Deputy Defense Secretary John Deutch stated that the United States would send troops to Haiti either to furnish security for Aristide's return or, if necessary, to force the military junta to leave office. By this time, Haiti clearly had moved from the backburner to a boiling issue for the Clinton administration.

Consequently, despite strong congressional and popular opposition to an invasion (according to polls, 73% disapproved), on September 15 President Clinton stated in a nationally televised speech that he was prepared to use military force to invade Haiti under the UN Security Council resolution of July 31. U.S. troops could lead a multilateral force "to carry out the will of the United Nations." Addressing the military junta directly, Clinton declared: "Your time is up. Leave now, or we will force you from power."

President Clinton as Decision-Maker

Foreign Policy Context of Decision

When U.S. presidents during the Cold War utilized military force, wisely and effectively or not, they generally did so within the grand strategy of containment. Clinton was the first post–World War II president with no military service. More importantly, he was the first to take office in the post–Cold War world. This called for a new U.S. foreign policy vision and strategy.

No new strategy was in place when President-elect Clinton made his stunning reversal of his campaign pledge regarding Haitian boat people. The decision was made in December 1992 and early January 1993 when Clinton and his transition team advisers were struggling to find their way in foreign policy. Clinton was focusing on fulfilling his principal campaign pledge to "grow the economy" and provide jobs for a recession-laden America. His decision to continue the Bush policy, therefore, was seen basically as an ad hoc, reactive move.

When Clinton took office, he still had no strategy. In his inaugural address that focused on domestic issues, the new president gave only a faint hint of a major foreign policy goal: advance the cause of democracy. But how and when to do this? How would Haiti relate to this goal?

Clinton's basic foreign policy principles, goals, and strategy began to be defined publicly only in the fall of 1993. On September 27, 1993 Clinton made a major foreign policy address before the UN. The president declared: "Many people ask whether the United States plans to retreat or remain active in the world. Let me answer that question as clearly and plainly as I can. The United States plans to remain engaged and to lead." But Clinton's tone was somewhat defensive. It indicated a less than enthusiastic inclination to intervene except in places of high national interest that had both a good chance of success and a viable exit point. Haiti did not seem to meet these requirements.

In comments made to reporters in his White House office on October 30, 1993, Lake provided an additional framework for understanding Clinton's policy toward Haiti. As regards Somalia and Haiti, "countries that are ripping themselves apart," Lake argued that the United States would lose sight of the larger strategic issues if it focused on such secondary issues. He said that with "the drama of crises like Somalia, or the difficulty of issues like Bosnia, or the immediacy of an issue like Haiti, . . . we are trying to remind Americans . . . that the most fundamental questions are what happens to areas of greatest strategic importance to us like Russia." Lake then categorized Clinton's foreign policy as "pragmatic neo-Wilsonian." He intimated that Clinton would not rely purely on balance of power like President Nixon, or on excessive moralism like President Carter. Instead, in places like Haiti Clinton would find something in between.[17]

Domestic Context of Decision

Pressure exerted by the congressional Black Caucus and TransAfrica was pivotal in forcing the Clinton administration to make Haiti a very high priority and to restore Aristide to power. Pressure from these groups on Clinton became so intense that by the spring of 1994 it had overcome the impact of two other major factors:

1. The influence of opponents of Aristide who tried to discredit him as an unstable, anti-American, undemocratic left-wing ideologue and demagogue unworthy of U.S. support; and
2. Biased media coverage of Haiti that failed to place the overthrow of Aristide in fair historical perspective, especially regarding the role played by the United States historically in Haiti and Aristide's hopes and goals for the Haitian masses.

The influence of Aristide's opponents

The Haitian military leaders who overthrew Aristide relied on supporters of the Duvaliers to keep themselves in power. They also counted on anti-Aristide forces in the United States and elsewhere. Who were Haiti's military leaders, and why did they feel so confident in defying the wishes of the international community?

Lieutenant General Raoul Cedras, Brigadier General Phillipe Biamby, and Lieutenant Colonel Michel François all came from notable pro-Duvalier families. Cedras was the son of a Duvalierist mayor of Jeremie. A mulatto, he was accepted into the mostly black (noir) class of Haiti's military academy that Baby Doc reopened in 1971—only for children of Tonton Macoutes or staunch Duvalier supporters. As president, Aristide had actually promoted Cedras when his troops provided security for his election. Cedras then turned against Aristide and played a key role in the coup that ousted him. Cedras became commander-in-chief of the army and the new political strong man.

After the coup, Cedras made his friend Biamby his chief of staff. Biamby had been expelled from the army because of his role in a failed coup attempt in 1988 against military dictator General Prosper Avril. Cedras and Biamby supposedly worked well together in planning and carrying out terror. Reportedly, Biamby had been involved in several political assassinations. In addition, he had helped organize several violent, heavily armed extreme right-wing political groups such as the innocuously named Front for Advancement and Progress of Haiti (FRAPH, which in French means "to beat"). FRAPH was the largest and most important organization for paramilitary gunmen called attachés. It was led by Emmanuel Constant, the son of an army commander under Papa Doc. Some of its members were children of the Tonton Macoutes. Though they told foreign journalists they were not Duvalierists, they told Haitian journalists that they welcomed pro-Duvalierists as members.[18] Other members openly proclaimed their support for Duvalierism and publicly paraded around and about some of the same business as their infamous predecessors.[19]

François played a major role in the 1991 coup. He was the son of a member of Papa Doc's presidential guard. Like many other Latin American military leaders (e.g., General Manuel Noriega, imprisoned in the United States on a drug charge after the U.S. invasion of Panama; and Roberto D'Abuisson, the leader of right-wing death squads in El Salvador during the 1980s), François had been trained at the School of Americas in Fort Benning, Georgia. Supposedly, this program not only provided expert U.S. military training, but also inculcated respect for democratic ideals.[20] At the time of the coup, as a former member of the Presidential Guard under Biamby, François headed the Cafeteria, a downtown Port-au-Prince police station. François then became national chief of police. Soon, he personally controlled about 1,500 soldiers and another 1,500 attachés.

These, then, were the Haitian leaders who ousted Aristide, were terrorizing the Haitian people, and were defying the wishes of the international community to restore Aristide. President Clinton publicly expressed his determination to restore Aristide to power, but his efforts lacked enthusiasm.

Aristide, to say the least, was a very controversial figure. When elected president as leader of his political party called Lavalas (flood-tide), most Haitians rejoiced. But the Bush administration was hardly exuberant.[21] As Haitian expert Amy Wilentz observed:

> The United States never wanted Aristide—a wildly popular leftist priest and rote denouncer of Yankee imperialism—to become president of Haiti. The Bush administration worried that his ability to rouse the rabble might be turned against industry and Haiti's elite, and his discourse as president, although more moderate than it had been, did nothing to alleviate those fears. . . . [Yet], in spite of its concerns, the administration rightly, and gracefully, accepted Aristide's victory at the polls.[22]

Aristide's background helps explain why first Bush and then Clinton gave him such lukewarm support. In fact, by May 1994 Bush was publicly arguing that the United States should no longer support the restoration of Aristide to power.

Aristide was born in 1954 into a religious Roman Catholic family. It was no surprise, therefore, that he decided to join the priesthood. In 1982 he entered the Salesian Order. After Baby Doc was driven from office in 1986, Aristide delivered blistering sermons against Haiti's traditional ruling elite. Excoriating the Catholic Church hierarchy, rich businessmen, and political dictators for oppressing the masses, Aristide called for the overthrow of the entire system. He criticized the Haitian government as "Duvalierism without Duvalier," and described Haiti as "a prison" where "men with the spirit of beasts have turned it into a killing ground, a concentration camp." In this prison, he argued, the rules were: "Never ask for more than what the prison warden considers your share; . . . remain in your cell. Though it is crowded and stinking and full of human refuse, remain there, and do not complain. . . . Do not organize; . . . accept your plight silently." And finally, he added angrily and sarcastically: "Never try to escape, for escape means a certain return to this prison, and worse cruelty, worse torture. If you dare to escape in our little boat, the corrections officers from the cold country to the north will capture you and send you back to eke out your days within the confines of your eternal prison, which is Haiti."[23] Aristide made especially vitriolic attacks against the Catholic "bourgeois" Church. He complained that there were "false saints . . . [who] are full of importance yet insignificant, and they are keeping the poor down, they are stepping on the poor."[24]

The Haitian government responded by trying to suppress and even kill Aristide. So many times did Aristide escape the authorities and possible death that he became known as "Mister Miracles," which added to his charisma with the masses.[25]

The Catholic Church reacted on December 15, 1988 by expelling Aristide from the Salesian Order. Though Aristide remained a priest, he was barred from publicly performing his priestly duties. Distressed by the poverty and political repression of his countrymen, Aristide became the leader of Haiti's Ti L'egliz (Little Church) and a proud proponent of the radical wing of liberation theology. This not only mixed Christianity with Marxism, which the Vatican deemed unacceptable, but it also preached—through hundreds of ecclesiastical base communities in local parishes—the possible use of violence to overthrow the existing political, economic, and social system supported by the Catholic Church hierarchy. The Salesian Order claimed that it ousted Aristide because of his "exaltation of class struggle" that conflicted with official Vatican opposition to liberation theology. The Haitian bishops were dismayed at Aristide's attempts to "destabilize" the Catholic Church. Thus they and the Vatican opposed his quest for the presidency, and were outwardly dismayed by his election.

Aristide's stature in the eyes of the Church diminished further when soon after his election, mobs burned down the Catholic Cathedral in Port-au-Prince, stripped the Vatican's representative to his underpants, and beat his assistant. The Vatican maintained that this was Aristide's way of venting his anger at the Church for expelling him and stripping him of his public duties.[26] Subsequently, the Vatican refused to name an ambassador. When it appointed one after Aristide was overthrown, the Vatican had the dubious distinction of being the only government in the world to extend official diplomatic recognition to the military junta.[27]

This act angered those who interpreted recognition as giving "a diplomatic blessing to a political order whose violence against the poor violates every tenet of Catholic social teaching." Moreover, critics were enraged that the Vatican remained silent in face of ongoing brutality by the Haitian government against innocent civilians. Some even charged that the Vatican itself, with its "top-down monarchical style, which stoutly resists all efforts for accountability, dialogue and democracy in the life of the church, is less than enthusiastic about the concept and reality of democracy" in the secular political realm. Thus, critics concluded, those who sought to restore Aristide to power should hardly have looked for support from the Vatican. "The Vatican record in Haiti does not suggest an institution suited to neutral brokering, let alone the promotion of justice or democracy," critics held. Instead, the Haitian military junta saw the Vatican as an ally.[28]

The Vatican and Haitian bishops were not the only opponents of Aristide. Voodoo priests also feared that Aristide, with his liberation theology, would marginalize their importance and diminish their influence. Aristide also upset Haitian army officers because in his sermons he identified those who brutalized the people. The wealthy elite in Haiti also loathed Aristide because he charged they had become rich and fat at the expense of the masses.[29] The American embassy in Haiti also scorned Aristide because he argued that U.S. businesses had exploited the masses by keeping them in terribly low-paying jobs.

Thus there were people in the United States, both inside and outside government, who worked hard to block Aristide's return to Haiti. The Central Intelligence Agency spearheaded efforts to keep Aristide away. The CIA had long-time links to Haitian governments, stemming from the days when Papa Doc gave himself life-time tenure in office. Although, as mentioned earlier, the United States at first opposed this ruthless dictator and tried to oust him from office, his staunch anti-communism bailed him out. This counted for a lot in Washington, especially during the early years of Castro's rule. The United States went on to fund, supply, and train the Haitian military.

Soon after Papa Doc's death in 1971, the CIA created the Haitian intelligence service. One major reason the CIA wanted to keep Aristide from the presidency was that it wanted to maintain its sources of information. Despite the CIA's rather close connections in Haiti, its intelligence record was poor. For example, the CIA did not foresee the violence that occurred after the 1987 election and the 1991 coup. Reportedly, a crucial source of information for the CIA was none other than Cedras, who understandably continued to supply the CIA with information critical of Aristide.

CIA analysts, however, did correctly predict that the Haitian military would block Aristide's return to Haiti. This was scheduled for October 1993, in accordance with the Governor's Island Accord the United States made with the Haitian military leaders on July 3 of that year. The CIA, however, worked to prevent Aristide's return. Its senior Latin American analyst Brian Latell, who had traveled to Port-au-Prince in July 1992, told members of Congress that he "saw no evidence of oppressive rule" in Haiti. He then concluded: "I do not wish to minimize the role the military plays in intimidating and occasionally terrorizing real and suspected opponents," but "there is no systematic or frequent lethal violence aimed at civilians." This conclusion sharply differed from a 1992 State Department report that held: "Haitians suffered frequent human rights abuses throughout 1992, including extra-judicial killings by security forces, disappearances, beatings, and other mistreatment of detainees and prisoners, arbitrary arrests and detention and executive interference in the judicial process."[30]

In the Clinton administration, the CIA still was in the forefront of a disinformation campaign to smear and stir up opposition to Aristide. One thing it did was issue a "psychological profile" that raised questions about Aristide's emotional stability and mental state. Reportedly, too, opponents of Aristide circulated a document in Congress that detailed Aristide's presumed instability. Among other problems, in the 1980s Aristide was supposed to have been under a physician's care for depression in Canada. This document, according to CNN News, was based on unsubstantiated leaks from Aristide's political enemies in Haiti. Some administration officials doubted its authenticity and finally called it an outright forgery.[31] Yet others, notably Latell, stood by its major conclusion and testified as such to the Senate Select Committee on Intelligence.

Given this background of the CIA's work with right-wing elements in Haiti, it was not surprising to read the accusation in the October 24, 1994 issue of *The Nation* that the CIA had actually helped Constant establish an organization that grew into FRAPH. Reportedly, FRAPH was to "balance the Aristide movement" and do "intelligence" against it. On October 5, a front-page headline in Haiti's influential *Le Nouvelliste* newspaper asked: "Are the American Embassy and FRAPH strolling hand-in-hand?"[32] Given the long, sordid history of U.S.-Haitian relations, Haitians were understandably cynical about actual U.S. goals. Such covert CIA operations, if true, were diametrically opposed to President Clinton's public support of Aristide.

Accusations of biased media coverage of Haiti

Aristide's name had also been tarnished by charges that he condoned and even urged violence by mobs against his political opponents. This included "Pére Lebrun", or "necklacing," which meant burning a tire around a person's neck. Critics point in particular to one inflammatory speech Aristide gave in September 1991 as evidence that he condoned and even urged mob lynchings. In this speech, Aristide supposedly incited his crowd of listeners to give the enemy "what he deserves." He then referred several times to "Pére Lebrun" as "a beautiful instrument" with a "good smell" and a "nice firm bed" that the masses should use to fight oppression. Suggesting that the crowd should resort to violence when legal measures failed, Aristide remarked: "Your tool is in your hands! Your instrument is in your hands."[33]

The media often focused on any signs or evidence of mob violence allegedly instigated by Aristide. One reporter wrote from Port-au-Prince in the *Washington Post*: "Mobs heeded his word in several instances; I saw harrowing photographs here depicting the charred remains of men who had been burned alive." Arguing that Aristide's return would not be in the best interest of the Haitian people, she concluded: "What is required is a policy aimed at advancing the interest of the Haitian people rather than one that promotes Aristide."[34]

Such articles call into question the impact of U.S. media coverage of Haiti in general on U.S. policy toward Haiti. The Boston Media Action (BMA) analyzed 415 articles on Haiti from the *New York Times*, *Washington Post*, *Boston Globe*, and *Miami Herald* in the weeks following the September 1991 coup. It found that these four leading newspapers spotlighted alleged human rights abuses of the Aristide government more than those of the military junta.

The BMA report also found that these newspapers failed to bring out the important negative historical role played by the United States in Haiti. There was little mention, for example, of the impact of occupation of Haiti by U.S. Marines in 1915–34. Nor was there much discussion of Washington's support for the Duvaliers, its establishment of the Haitian intelligence service, and its founding and training of the Haitian military. Such coverage, it concluded, perpetuated the "myth that violence is endemic to Haiti" and that there was little or nothing Washington could do to change a country mired in poverty and engulfed by violence and terror.

The BMA report also concluded: "Press coverage [of Haiti] was so out of line with the thinking of those who presumably have the most crucial perspective—the Haitian people—and it so ignores the role of the U.S. in the history of Haiti that its bias can only appear as systematic." Although the report does not make direct accusations of intentional media bias, its main point is tremendously important. Most Americans have not studied Haiti and know little of Haitian history. In history textbooks used in U.S. schools, there is virtually nothing written on Haiti, except perhaps a brief note of its liberation from France by

Toussaint L'Ouverture and maybe a statement on the repressive rule by the Duvaliers. What Americans know about Haiti, especially its most recent history, they learn mainly through the media. The media thus has an awesome responsibility to cover important issues fully and fairly. According to the BMA report, it failed in the case of Haiti.[35]

To what extent President Clinton was influenced by the CIA's charges of Aristide's emotional and mental stability and biased media coverage is uncertain. The CIA's role in Haiti raises several questions that relate to Clinton's decision to forcibly repatriate Haitian boat people. First, to what extent was Clinton a virtual prisoner of past CIA policies? A young President Kennedy, inexperienced in foreign policy, went along with recommendations for the Bay of Pigs invasion made by the Eisenhower administration, with disastrous consequences. Did a young President Clinton, also very green in the foreign policy arena, feel it was best or just safer for U.S. national security not to rock the CIA boat? Second, how independent a role did the CIA play under Reagan and Bush, and how much did this continue under Clinton? Third, to what extent may Clinton have been influenced by right-wing anti-communist ideologues held over from the Reagan-Bush years? Did their distress over Aristide's liberation theology and almost visceral anti-Americanism have much of an impact on Clinton? And fourth, to what extent may Clinton have been influenced to cover up CIA activity in Haiti as part of a wider Reagan-Bush cover-up of atrocities committed by right-wing death squads in El Salvador and the arming of Saddam Hussein in the 1980s?

Clinton's decision may also have been influenced by FBI charges in late 1992 that Aristide ordered the murder of Roger Lafontant, the hated interior minister under Papa Doc. Lafontant had been in prison for leading a failed coup attempt in January 1991.[36] Coming when they did, these charges surely did not improve Aristide's reputation with Clinton. The media also highlighted charges against Aristide for human rights violations and resorting to violence against the Haitian people. To the American public, Aristide hardly seemed like a Jeffersonian democrat.

Biased media coverage may have influenced presidential decision-making. Articles that focused on Aristide's alleged instigation of mob violence, buttressed by unproven charges by the CIA and FBI, led some U.S. lawmakers to denounce Aristide. In a spirited debate on October 20, 1993, for example, several senators cited Aristide's speech of September 1991 and referred to CIA charges of emotional instability.

Jesse Helms (R, N.C.) even went so far as to label Aristide a "psychopath" who did not hesitate to violate human rights.

As consummate politicians, American presidents both follow and lead public opinion. But if the public has distorted and inadequate knowledge of an issue, the foundation of representative democracy is weakened. The nature of media bias made it easier for Clinton to garner public support for his decision to summarily repatriate Haitian boat people. At the least, this bias diminished the possible growth of public opposition to his decision. Perhaps too, as a newly elected president inexperienced in foreign affairs, Clinton thought it best to maintain policy continuity.

Decision Options

Before deciding on military intervention to restore Aristide to power in Haiti, Clinton weighed various options.[37] Some advisers suggested that he urge the UN to follow the Cambodia model in Haiti. This meant sending a big peacekeeping force there to prepare for a restoration of democracy. Others doubted that the UN would undertake another mission of such magnitude and complexity, especially with the almost certain opposition of the Haitian military government. Instead, they urged paving the way for the return to democracy by adding a somewhat larger UN force to the eighteen observers from the OAS who were already on site.[38]

Clinton also considered working closely with former Argentine Foreign Minister Dante Caputo, UN Secretary General Boutros Boutros-Ghali's personal representative in Haiti. Clinton thought that the time was not right to work with Caputo. He had no real power or authority, given his charge merely to report back to the UN General Assembly whose recommendations are merely advisory. Perhaps Clinton would work with the UN envoy some time in the future, but he needed to adopt a policy on boat people right away.

Clinton rejected the idea of tightening the embargo and other sanctions or plugging their leaks, which were considerable. He was struck by the harmful effects sanctions had on innocent Haitian civilians. Clinton also debated whether to lift sanctions against the Haitian government. Perhaps he could do this once the process of trying to restore democracy shifted into higher gear. He decided to accept the prevailing argument that the Haitian military government would deem lifting sanctions a move of weakness. At the same time, he opted for moderate sanctions. Yet these sanctions would continue to leak, enrich the Haitian military through sale of contraband items such as fuel, allow U.S. businesses to keep assembly plant production going for exports, and hurt the poorest Haitian people the most.

Clinton weighed allowing Haitians to receive temporary protected status in the United States. But his aides reminded him that "temporary" had almost always meant "permanent." Once achieving permanent status, moreover, they would win the right to sponsor admission of relatives. This would result in "chain migration." Clinton surely was also aware that by giving Haitians temporary protected status, he could be opening the floodgates for thousands more from countries in Central America, such as El Salvador and Guatemala, who could start flocking to U.S. shores on his watch.

Clinton considered taking more Haitians onto Guantanamo, with the possibility of establishing a "temporary safe haven" site there. Supporters of this option, mainly groups outside the administration such as the Washington-based U.S. Committee for Refugees, insisted that Guantanamo could easily accommodate thousands more Haitian refugees and urged the U.S. government to build additional weather-safe shelters. Opponents of this idea, however, argued persuasively that the United States could not satisfactorily handle significantly larger numbers on the base.

Clinton could have pushed for third party asylum,[39] at least on a temporary basis. The most likely possibilities included the Dominican Republic, the Bahamas, Jamaica, Belize, Venezuela, Suriname, Honduras, and Panama. But these countries had their own problems of severe unemployment and opposed being pressured to serve as "dumping grounds" for desperately poor Haitians. Furthermore, most Haitians preferred to come to the United States. The third party option, then, was not considered realistic. As mentioned above, in July 1994 Clinton did finally allow some fleeing Haitians to go to Panama, where they received temporary protected status. But this policy shift in itself was too little too late.

By the spring and early summer of 1994, all Clinton's attempts to get the Haitian military leaders to step down and allow the restoration of Aristide to power had failed. What remained was the option of U.S. military intervention. President Reagan had invaded Grenada in 1983, ostensibly to protect American lives threatened by political instability on the island. President Bush had intervened in 1989 in Panama under Operation Just Cause that led to the overthrow, capture, and imprisonment of General Noriega. The official reason for this invasion was to protect lives of American citizens and to stop drug trafficking.

Clinton could have used either Reagan's or Bush's rationale to intervene militarily in Haiti. Yet in the case of Haiti there were some important differences: there was the bitter memory of U.S. military occupation from 1915 to 1934; there was the more recent recollection of Johnson's invasion of the Dominican Republic in 1965—ostensibly to ensure political stability but in reality to stop the threat of communism there (by preventing the return to office of the democratically elected Juan Bosch); and there were doubts about an easy exit strategy. Clinton also could have followed Bush's example in Somalia. With Operation Restore Hope, U.S. forces were sent in under UN auspices mainly to prevent further starvation of innocent Somalis and to establish some stable political and legal order in a country plagued by chaos and gang warfare. Clinton could also have intervened in Haiti using Bush's argument in Iraq to save the Kurds. Bush acted, among other reasons, to prevent Saddam Hussein from engaging in further mass violations of human rights against his own people. But Washington only temporarily helped the Kurds. Saddam remained in power and no end to his political oppression was in sight.

From the time Clinton made his decision to continue Bush's Haiti policy until May 1994, when he announced an end to the policy of repatriation of Haitian refugees without asylum hearings, the president had faced calls both against and for U.S. military force in Haiti. Arguments abounded concerning the possible use of unilateral U.S. military intervention, regional intervention through the OAS, or international intervention through the UN. Most of the debate focused on the advisability of unilateral U.S. military force.

Observers such as Thomas Carothers of the Carnegie Endowment for International Peace argued that of all the options on Haiti, invading was the worst. He maintained, *inter alia*, that the United States had "no interest at stake in Haiti so compelling as to warrant unilateral military action," that U.S. military intervention would violate international law, and that it "would set a dangerous example for other regions where our strategic interests are greater."[40] Congressional opposition was led by the powerful Senate Minority Leader Bob Dole (R, Kansas), who called the possible use of U.S. military force in Haiti a "big, big mistake."

Supporters of an invasion of Haiti included *New York Times* reporter William Safire, who argued for "a Bay of Pigs that succeeds." In short, Safire advocated U.S. training of Haitian refugees to go to Haiti to overthrow the military. Unlike the Bay of Pigs fiasco where the CIA secretly trained Cuban operatives, Safire argued, the United States should widely publicize the Haitian military enterprise. Moreover, it would have a much better chance of success because unlike the admiration of many Cubans for Castro, presumably most of the Haitian people were hostile to the ruling military junta.[41] Congress also joined the debate over the use of military force. In April 1994 Representative David Obie (D, Wis.) called openly for a U.S. invasion. Representative Charles Rangel (D, N.Y.) of the congressional Black Caucus and others also publicly supported U.S. military intervention. Then in May, Senator John Kerry (D, Mass.), a member of the Foreign Relations Committee, argued that if aggressive diplomacy and increased sanctions did not force out the Haitian military leaders, "we must be willing to seek international approval to use military force."[42]

Author Elizabeth Drew, a respected observer of Washington politics, maintains that the Clinton administration from the outset was split over the use of military force in trouble spots around the globe such as Bosnia, Somalia, and Haiti. According to Drew, General Colin Powell, chairman of the Joint Chiefs of Staff, was hesitant to use force; national security adviser Lake and deputy security adviser Samuel R. (Sandy) Berger strongly supported forceful action; and Secretary of State Warren Christopher leaned more toward the position of Pentagon leaders. They were reluctant to urge military intervention because they believed that Lake and Berger lacked sufficient foreign policy experience that involved the use of military force.[43]

When Clinton changed his Haiti policy in May 1994, he said he would not rule out the military force option. Father Aristide, though frustrated because he had not returned to Haiti, at first did not openly support the use of U.S. military force. He claimed that the Haitian constitution barred him from requesting foreign intervention. In addition, the OAS and neighboring countries like the Dominican Republic were against intervention. (In August, countries in the region changed their minds.) France also resisted invasion. Foreign Minister Alain Juppé, who met with Clinton at the White House on May 12, said France would take part in a UN force in Haiti after democracy was restored, but would "certainly not" join an intervention to oust the military junta.[44] At the same time, Zbigniew Brzezinski, President Carter's national security adviser, predicted that the United States would militarily intervene in Haiti. Brzezinski maintained that the decision would be a "hard call" for Clinton, but it would be determined largely by domestic political pressures.[45] Brzezinski was on the mark. The only question seemed to be the timing of an invasion and working out its practical details.[46]

Clinton's Leadership Role in the Decision

Lack of foreign policy experience

Experience in foreign affairs helps but is not a *sine qua non* for successful presidential decision-making. This was a controversial subject in the 1988 presidential election when Bush derided Michael Dukakis for his lack of foreign policy experience. Dukakis gamely fought back, even riding in a tank for a campaign advertisement of dubious value. Bush, in an unsuccessful run for the Republican presidential nomination in 1980, had also criticized Ronald Reagan on the same grounds, stating: "We cannot take a chance on another president who has absolutely no experience in foreign affairs."

The noted historian Arthur Schlesinger, Jr., writing in defense of the Dukakis candidacy, argued that "the most effective" presidents in foreign policy in the twentieth century, specifically Theodore Roosevelt, Woodrow Wilson, and Franklin D. Roosevelt, were state governors. Schlesinger then refuted two widely held propositions about the indispensability of foreign policy experience: "foreign policy is so arcane that only long involvement in its making and execution can equip a person to handle the sacred mysteries, and . . . past involvement provides a guarantee of superior wisdom in analysis and decision." He then argued against both propositions. "Anyone with political judgment, intellectual curiosity, a retentive memory, a disciplined temperament and sense of the way history runs," he maintained, "can grasp the dynamics of foreign policy quickly enough." As for the second proposition, he argued that "people with 'experience' in foreign affairs can make dreadful misjudgments. . . . The last thing the United States needs is a set of officials whose foreign policy 'experience' lies in applauding, ratifying and extending error." Schlesinger then concluded: "Experience has its value, but not when it sanctifies our perceptions of yesterday, and blinds us to the dangers and hopes of tomorrow."[47]

Schlesinger used some persuasive arguments. Indeed, some of the biggest mistakes in U.S. foreign policy have been made by "experts." It was our "best and brightest," for example, who pushed the United States deeper and deeper into the Vietnam War.[48] Moreover, it was our experts on Latin America who helped develop and shape U.S. support for various dictatorial regimes in Haiti, as well as other countries in nearby Central America such as El Salvador and Nicaragua. Though rightly claiming credit for his leadership role in the Persian Gulf War, Bush suffered from several major blunders in his own foreign policy. These included failing to follow up his Gulf victory, which allowed Saddam Hussein to rebuild his army and systematically destroy Shiite Muslims in southern Iraq, linking U.S. policy toward Mikhail Gorbachev and preservation of the Soviet Union, and insisting on summarily returning Haitian refugees.

Bush's mistakes were so egregious that Clinton even scored some foreign policy points of his own during the presidential campaign, especially in its latter stages. They were made by a president whose resumé was packed with foreign policy experience. Presumably then, one could argue they were caused more by errors of judgment or faulty government intelligence than by his lack of foreign policy knowledge, focus, or strategy. It is on the latter grounds that criticism was levelled against Clinton.

Clinton's role on the Haiti "team"

Clinton's inexperience in foreign affairs, coupled with his determination to be the "domestic policy president," led him to rely very heavily on his advisers—especially at the outset. It was they who in early 1993 convinced him to renege on his campaign pledges and continue Bush's policy toward Haiti, and one year later, to use military force to restore Aristide to power.

By late December 1992, Clinton transition team members reportedly informed advocates for Haitians seeking to flee to the United States that the president-elect would stick to his campaign pledge of allowing a fair asylum hearing.[49] The team on Haiti was led by J. Brian Atwood. He worked closely with Bernard W. Aronson, a holdover from the Bush administration who was still serving as assistant secretary of state for Inter-American affairs, having replaced Elliott Abrams. Aronson, like Henry "Scoop" Jackson, was a Democrat who was liberal on domestic policy but fiercely anti-communist and conservative in foreign policy. A former speech writer for Jimmy Carter, Bush had appointed him to shore up the bipartisan image of his foreign policy team. Aronson had strongly opposed the Sandinistas in Nicaragua, and reportedly had even raised funds for the Contras.[50] He soon became Bush's point man on Haiti. Clinton had asked Aronson to stay on in his job because he knew Lake and Berger from the time they worked together during the Carter administration. Reportedly, Clinton's transition team relied heavily on Aronson's (and most likely Bush's) views on Haiti.[51]

One senior administration official told the media that in early January 1993 Clinton called Haiti "our first foreign policy crisis." On January 5, Clinton presided over a four-hour session in Little Rock, Arkansas. This official said Clinton expressed concern for the fate of Haitians fleeing their country by boat, commenting: "There was a prospect during the transition of a real human disaster if all the ships had launched, and a lot of people had drowned."[52]

Pezzullo, Clinton's main adviser on Haiti, resigned in the spring of 1994 when he became identified with a failed U.S. Haitian policy. But many people blamed Clinton. They criticized him for not taking charge of the Haiti problem, relying instead on deputies to formulate and carry out U.S. policy. Moreover, Clinton's diplomacy seemed based more on improvisation, desperation, and luck than on good strategy. Moreover, critics charged the president's Haiti policy was marked by striking failures: lack of clear vision or strategy; placement of Haiti on the foreign policy backburner with the unrealistic hope that its problems would resolve themselves or fade away; irresoluteness and indecisiveness (especially regarding refugees, sanctions, the use of force, and the return of Aristide); inadequate articulation of clear goals to Congress and the American people and inability to enlist the support of both; and overall weak leadership.

The Carter Mission to Haiti

In spring 1994, Clinton assumed a greater leadership role when he took the initiative to change his Haitian refugee policy. When he decided to use military force to restore Aristide, events moved swiftly to a climax. On September 17, Clinton dispatched a mediation team to Haiti to make an eleventh-hour attempt to peacefully resolve the crisis. It was headed by former President Jimmy Carter and also included General Powell and Senator Sam Nunn. Carter, who had earned a reputation as a peacemaker in Panama, Ethiopia, and North Korea, had been urging Clinton to let him undertake a peace mission to Haiti. He reminded Clinton that he had gotten to know General Cedras when he went to Haiti to monitor the December 1990 election. Clinton told Powell the former president sometimes was "a wild card." He then added: "But I took a chance on him in North Korea, and that didn't turn out too badly." Powell asserts that Clinton's chief concern was that if Carter went to Haiti, "the next thing you know, I'm expected to call off the invasion because he's negotiating a deal." The Carter team realized an invasion was imminent, but they hoped it could happen peacefully. Powell maintains that Clinton leaned toward approving the Carter mission, but only if it "stuck to negotiating how, not if, our troops would go ashore."[53]

Clinton's top foreign policy advisers reportedly were split over the wisdom of the Carter mission. Secretary of State Christopher, despite public protestations to the contrary, opposed the mission and was kept out of the policy loop. National security adviser Lake and Deputy Secretary of State Talbott initially expressed strong reservations, but soon supported the president's position. With only minutes left to make up his mind, Clinton met in the Oval Office with Vice President Al Gore, who strongly supported the mission, Leon Panetta, his chief of staff, and Lake. Clinton then gave the final OK. It was Lake's task to consult with Secretary of Defense William Perry, Chairman of the Joint Chiefs of Staff Gen. John M. D. Shalakashvili, and Talbott on ways for a peaceful resolution of the crisis.[54]

The Carter team left for Haiti on September 17. All during negotiations there, it was "in constant touch with President Clinton."[55] On September 18, with U.S. parachutists already airborne, the U.S. negotiators succeeded in averting a bloody invasion. They signed an agreement with eighty-one-year-old Emile Jonassaint, just appointed president by the Haitian military junta. It called for the resignation of the military leadership by October 15; legislative amnesty for the military (the stipulation that stirred the most controversy both in Haiti and the United States); the restoration of Aristide; an end to UN imposed sanctions against Haiti; the holding of free and democratic elections; and uncontested entry of U.S. forces.[56]

Carter's mission brought about a successful dénouement to the Haiti crisis. Powell praised Clinton "for taking a politically risky eleventh-hour gamble."[57] Almost overnight, it seemed, Clinton's policy toward Haiti had changed from failure to success. Once again the president had become "the comeback kid."

Operation Restore Democracy began on September 19 when approximately 20,000 U.S. troops landed in Haiti to prepare for Aristide's return. For several difficult weeks U.S. forces, working with the Haitian army and security forces, reduced the level of violence in the country and finally forced the military rulers into exile. On October 15, Father Aristide flew to Haiti on a U.S. plane and triumphantly returned to his homeland. He called for reconciliation and an end to violence. One short journey was over, but the long march to democracy had just begun.

Consequences of Clinton's Decision for the United States and Haiti

The United States

Restoring Aristide to power peacefully in Haiti earned Clinton high marks at home and abroad. His image as a world leader, tarnished by policy failures in Haiti and other world trouble spots such as Bosnia and Somalia, was shined up appreciably. Yet serious U.S.-Haitian issues remained. Among the most important were providing economic aid to Haiti; planting and growing democracy; inculcating respect for human rights; resolving the problem of Haitian refugees (both those who had already fled Haiti and those contemplating flight); and stopping the drug traffic.[58] U.S. troops established a relatively safe and secure environment in Haiti. They also paved the way for U.S. economic assistance. Early optimism led to a flurry of international aid activities.

Haiti

When Aristide returned to Haiti, the country still faced a host of daunting economic, political, and social problems. Economically, Haiti had to start to rebuild virtually from scratch. Its infrastructure was devastated; its per capita income had plunged to about $250 a year (the lowest in the hemisphere); more than two-thirds of the population was jobless; and there was widespread malnourishment and starvation. The country thus needed large doses of outside aid and investment to restart her economic engines.[59]

Although Haiti received pledges of aid from the European Union, the World Bank, and the Inter-American Development Bank, it had to rely mostly on the United States. Washington made Haiti its highest per capita recipient of foreign aid.[60] According to Mark Schneider, assistant administrator for Latin America and the Caribbean for AID and Clinton's chief adviser on economic aid for Haiti, by the year 2000 the United States wanted to cut drastically the number of Haitians who lived in extreme poverty. Aristide himself said that an important first step was for Haitians to move from "abject poverty to misery with dignity."

Haiti undertook a privatization program designed to sell shares in large state-owned enterprises such as flour and cement companies, utilities, telecommunications, and shipping to both domestic and foreign buyers. But many Haitians were wary of succumbing to a new form of dependency on foreigners.[61] Domestic economic reform was also a top priority. Simply stated, the rich had to pay more and a long legacy of government corruption had to end. Haiti had received large amounts of U.S. economic aid previously, but much of it was siphoned off by the government and its supporters and never reached the masses. It remained to be seen how well Haiti could end corruption and handle foreign assistance.

Politically, Aristide also had his hands full. One key question was what to do about supporters of the Haitian military regime who had terrorized the masses and committed all sorts of horrific crimes. Aristide insisted that the coup leaders who overthrew him had to be punished. International human rights groups estimated the coup-related death toll at 180 to 500, but Aristide cited the figure of over 1,000.[62] Supporters of punishment believed that there could be no real peace without justice. But when Aristide returned to Haiti, an open question was whether he would try to bring to justice Haitian military leaders who, in accordance with the Carter deal, had gone into exile.

A related question was what to do about political opposition. Every democracy must encourage legitimate political choices for its voters. But many members and supporters of FRAPH, it was alleged, had committed crimes against the people. Moreover, in what American officials claim was an embarrassing but innocent bureaucratic error, FRAPH's leader Constant evidently was allowed to slip into the United States on a tourist visa on Christmas eve of 1994. Earlier in December, he had ignored a summons to testify at a Haitian government hearing about FRAPH's role in brutal crimes against supporters of Aristide. Although U.S. officials claimed they would try to revoke his visa and deport him, at first they could not find him. Understandably, many Haitians looked upon this situation with a great deal of skepticism.[63] Constant finally was arrested on May 10, 1995. He was jailed in Maryland, where he awaited extradition. In June, 1996, the U.S. set Constant free, causing a torrent of protest from human rights groups in the U.S. and Haiti.

Aristide insisted that Haiti must move toward conciliation. Facing a dilemma similar to President Nelson Mandela's in South Africa, Aristide had to decide the optimum blend of punishment for past misdeeds and amnesty for future reconciliation. He was determined that there would be no reprisals by his government. Yet Haiti still had to build a political as well as economic infrastructure. In Thomas Jefferson's words, Haiti needed an "enlightened citizenry." The Haitian people would also have to gain experience in meaningful political campaigning, voting, and the like, and to establish a rule of law.

Preliminary elections were held on June 25, 1995, with Aristide supporters winning easily. Then on December 17, René Préval, the Lavalas candidate, whom Aristide backed, was elected president. He took office on February 7, 1996, in a notably peaceful transfer of power. Though the elections were chaotic and fell far short of acceptable standards of mature democracies, at least they were a start. It was widely recognized that democracy could not be transplanted from the United States; nor could it grow overnight. Patience and hard work would be needed if Haiti were to make a successful transition from dictatorship to democracy. Safety and security for the Haitian people were also necessary for the transition. Terror and violence as a way of life would have to stop. This was no small task, and there were bound to be setbacks. In the spring of 1995, for example, there was great consternation when a political opponent of Aristide was shot down in broad daylight on a busy street in downtown Port-au-Prince. No suspects were arrested. There were even accusations that Aristide supporters were involved. This killing clearly was a major blow to hopes for building democracy in Haiti.[64]

President Clinton visited Haiti on March 31. His trip, the first by an American president since Franklin D. Roosevelt went in 1934 to mark the end of U.S. occupation, was a triumph. At a ceremony at the National Palace, Presidents Clinton and Aristide complimented each other effusively. Clinton called Aristide a man of "tremendous courage" whose "strength in the face of great challenge reflects the unbreakable will of the Haitian people." Aristide, in turn, thanked Clinton for forging "a tunnel of hope through a mountain of suffering" and led the crowd in a responsive chant offering Clinton "the warmth of the light of a welcome never before seen."[65]

In his speech, Clinton stated that in April responsibility for the security of Haiti would shift from American troops to a UN peacekeeping force. A smaller number of U.S. troops (about 2,400) would begin work with a UN force that numbered about 7,000. U.S. troops had been training Haitian soldiers mainly for routine civilian police work. In general, they had done a very creditable job in preparing for Aristide's return to Haiti and helping the country get started in solving its most serious problems. When Aristide returned, he started to dismantle the army which historically was used by the government as an instrument of oppression against the people. There was no doubt that for democracy to survive in Haiti old-fashioned militarism had to go.[66] Many believed Haiti did not need an army for national defense. They thought it should follow the example of Costa Rica, which had no standing army and relied on a civilian police force to keep law and order. In February 1995, Aristide adopted the Costa Rica model. He eliminated the armed forces and started training a civilian police force. This force was a distinct improvement over the past, but reportedly some officers still were engaging in brutality.

Socially, Haiti also faced a hard road ahead. One of Aristide's highest priorities was improving the lot of women and changing the way they were viewed. At a three-day conference held in January 1995, Haitian women heard lectures on the role of women in Haitian history, on human rights, and on AIDS. Helped by nongovernmental organizations (NGOs), women worked to organize especially to help their families. A particularly important goal was to institute a credit bank for women.[67]

As regards education, a major campaign had to be undertaken to improve Haiti's literacy rate of barely 25 percent. Haiti also had to rebuild higher education. Many of the country's academics and intellectuals who had fled Haiti to escape persecution returned to join their beleaguered colleagues who had stayed. Some had returned when Aristide was elected, but after the coup only a minority was left. The rest were either killed or fled again. Although the need to improve higher education was a lower priority than primary and secondary education, significant improvement on all levels was necessary. Most Haitian children were not attending school, in many cases because there were not enough teachers. Thus teacher training alone was a formidable task. Universities would also have to train those people capable of conceptualizing and implementing reforms. As Suze Mathieu, an American-educated anthropologist who was dean of students at Quisqueya University concluded: "We need competent people who can rethink this society. We need a whole new vision, and a university is in a position to help produce this."[68]

Haitians also faced the problem of reconciling the gulf of hostility between its tiny light-skinned elite who control most of the country's wealth and the predominantly poor black masses. There is virtually no middle class. Under Aristide, the elite feared loss of their wealth, status, and personal safety. As one Haitian put it, "people were afraid to even drive the street in their vehicles. If you had a Mercedes, you left it at home." This is why much of the elite supported the coup that drove Aristide into exile. It wasn't that they necessarily endorsed the thuggery and brutality of the military.[69] A year after Aristide's return to Haiti, he was still despised by many of the country's elite. But because he reached out to business leaders for help in jump-starting the economy, he had won the support of some who now believed he was "not the radical priest we knew before."[70] Thus as regards social transformation, perhaps Haiti would learn from the South Africa experience, or perhaps these two countries would learn from each other.

The future of Haiti's boat people also remained. As noted earlier, on May 2, 1995 the United States officially changed its thirty-five-year-old special policy toward Cuban refugees. Those at Guantanamo (about 20,000) were admitted into the United States in a last-time special arrangement. In future, any Cubans who fled to Guantanamo or Florida would be summarily repatriated. Back in Cuba, they would be eligible to apply for a limited number of yearly immigrant slots. The door to the United States for Haitians at Guantanamo, housed separately from the Cubans, remained virtually shut. The Clinton administration argued that the Haitian situation was different because Haiti had become a democracy. By May 1995, the Clinton administration had forcibly repatriated about 6,000 Haitians from Guantanamo. Only about 500 returned voluntarily. Those left were about 240 unaccompanied children. A few were allowed into the United States as hardship cases, but most remained in limbo, neither wanting to return to Haiti nor able to enter the United States.[71]

A further problem was that no new policy toward Haitian refugees was instituted after the 1981 U.S.-Haiti accord on boat people was scrapped. Under Reagan, Bush, and Clinton, the United States had categorized most Haitians trying to flee to the United States as economic migrants rather than political refugees. After Aristide's return, Washington was hard pressed to explain why there were virtually no attempts to escape the country—despite the continuation of terrible poverty. The United States preferred a new repatriation agreement. The Haitian government's position was that if the United States did not want Haitian refugees, it had to make sure it delivered the promised aid money. Haiti also wanted U.S. assistance in defraying the high costs of returnees, including those from other countries like the Dominican Republic. About 25,000 Haitians had fled there from 1991 to 1994.

By the end of 1995, the problem of "boat people" arose again. The U.S. Coast Guard began returning hundreds a week to Haiti. Returnees echoed continued despair, claiming they had left because of "la misère," that is, no work and no food.[72] Whatever the resolution of these deep problems, one thing was clear. Ultimately, responsibility of solving them remained with the Haitian people themselves.

Conclusion

When Clinton decided to reverse his campaign pledge on Haitian refugees, he maintained publicly that he would press hard for Aristide's return. His actual goal, determined largely by domestic political considerations, was stemming the tide of Haitian refugees. The boat people became a political football in U.S. politics. The debate focused on what the best policy was to keep the refugees out of the United States rather than on what was best for the Haitians.

One dilemma for Clinton was that he and his advisers doubted Aristide's democratic credentials. They were apprehensive over the consequences of his liberation theology and anti-Americanism. Clinton believed that in the short run Aristide's return to Haiti probably would curtail the refugee flow. But he feared the priest's return would anger his opponents, particularly the elite and military. This might set off yet another cycle of violence, retribution, and instability, resulting in an even larger flood of refugees.

Unable to resolve this dilemma, Clinton hedged. He only halfheartedly tried to return Aristide to power. Moreover, other aspects of Clinton's policy contradicted his professed goal of returning Aristide. Those few who dared venture into U.S. processing centers in Haiti found it very hard to prove they were political refugees. Improving the in-country processing program, therefore, in effect meant downplaying the oppressiveness and desperation of the Haitian political solution. This, in turn, made Aristide's return to power less likely. Though Clinton's instincts were democratic, he reluctantly opted, in effect, to continue Bush's policy toward Haiti rather than take bold initiatives. Clinton hoped that Haiti would remain a backwater problem that would resolve itself without a significant increase in refugees admitted to the United States, without U.S. military intervention, and with minimum damage to the presidency and U.S. national security.

When Clinton announced a change in his Haiti policy in May 1994, he admitted failure. What had gone wrong? In short, the president had operated in an ad hoc manner because he lacked a clear vision or strategy. Furthermore, he was indecisive regarding treatment of the boat people, imposition of sanctions, and the use of force to return Aristide.

Why, then, in August 1994 did President Clinton decide to send U.S. troops into Haiti when such action was so strongly opposed by Congress and the American public? Perhaps he wanted to appear more decisive. Or maybe at this point he believed military intervention was his only option. In any event, Clinton decided to dispatch the troops. They arrived in Haiti not as invaders but as peacekeepers. They would handle the transition from military rule to democracy according to the agreement brokered by President Carter's mediation team with Haiti's military dictatorship.

Questions for Discussion

1. Should the United States accept all applicants for asylum? If not, what criteria for acceptance should be used?

2. Why was there a double standard in U.S. treatment of applications by Haitians and Cubans for asylum? Do you agree with this disparity of treatment?

3. How important was Florida's domestic politics in determining Clinton's reversal of his campaign pledge toward Haitian boat people?

4. Why did the Central Intelligence Agency oppose the restoration of Aristide to power?

5. Why was the Vatican so distrustful of Aristide?

6. Were vital U.S. national interests at stake in Clinton's decision to invade Haiti?

7. Would you have supported forceful U.S. military intervention to restore Aristide to office?

8. Do you think that the recommendation of *New York Times* columnist William Safire that the United States should launch "A Bay of Pigs that succeeds" was sound?

9. To what extent was Clinton's decision to use military force to restore Aristide determined by U.S. domestic politics?

10. How good are the prospects for Haitian democracy?

Notes

1. See Jean-Claude Bajeux, "An Embarrassing Presence" (trans. by David Jacobson), *The New York Review of Books*, 3 November, 1994, 37–40. Bajeux became director of the Ecumenical Center for Human Rights in Port-au-Prince, Haiti. After being forced to flee Haiti in 1993 because of his antigovernment activities, he went back after Aristide's return. For a less critical analysis, see Richard A. Best, Jr., "The U.S. Occupation of Haiti, 1915–1934," A Congressional Research Service (CRS) Report for Congress, May 26, 1994.
2. U.S. Congress, House Committee on the Judiciary, Subcommittee on Immigration, Citizenship, and International Law, "Haitian Emigration," 94th Cong., 2d sess., committee print, 1976. Cited by Alex Stepick, "Unintended Consequences: Rejecting Haitian Boat People and Destabilizing Duvalier," in Christopher Mitchell (ed.,), *Western Hemisphere Immigration and United States Foreign Policy* (University Park: Pennsylvania State University Press, 1992), p. 131.
3. On this double standard, see, for example, G. Loescher and J. Scanlan, *Calculated Kindness: Refugees and America's Half-Open Door* (New York: The Free Press, 1986); and V. Nanda (ed.), *Refugee Law and Policy: International and U.S. Responses* (New York: Greenwood Press, 1989).
4. This act provides guidelines for the admission of those seeking refugee and asylum status. The United States adopted the UN Protocol Relating to the Status of Refugees which stipulates that "a refugee is a person who is unwilling or unable to return to his country of habitual residence because of a well-founded fear of persecution on account of race, religion, nationality, membership in a particular social group, or political opinion." In general, there is no significant distinction between refugee and asylum status. As of 1990, Congress may also provide Temporary Protected Status (TPS) for persons deemed deserving of entry into the United States because they are fleeing potentially dangerous situations but who do not fall under the usual categories of refugee or asylee. A person granted asylum, refugee, or TPS status is protected against forced return to a country of persecution (*refoulement*).
5. For details of this campaign of support, see Stepick, p. 140n.
6. Automatic U.S. acceptance of Cubans as refugees ended abruptly in August 1994. During the summer, thousands of Cubans, desperate to flee their country

for economic and political reasons, took to the high seas on home-made rafts and headed toward Miami. Caught off guard by this sudden surge of boat people, and pressured by Governor Lawton Childs of Florida to stop the flow because of its high economic cost, Clinton reversed traditional U.S. policy. He ordered the Coast Guard to interdict Cuban boat people and send them to Guantanamo. On May 2, 1995, Washington concluded an agreement with Havana to return most of them to Cuba. There they could apply to enter the United States along with others who wanted to leave. The agreement, which provided for an immigration ceiling of 20,000 per year, evoked strong opposition within the American-Cuban community.

7. See L. Guttentag and L. Daugard, "United States Treatment of Haitian Refugees: The Domestic Response and International Law," American Civil Liberties Union, *International Civil Liberties Report*, June 1993, p. 10. Cited in "No Port in a Storm," Americas Watch, National Coalition for Haitian Refugees, and Jesuit Refugee Service/USA (September 1993), p. 6.

8. See Richard Estrada, "Clinton had no choice on Haitians," *Dallas Morning News*, January 8, 1993.

9. John Glisch, "South Florida Braces for Haitian Time Bomb; Many Fear That after Clinton Becomes President, an Exodus of Haitian Refugees Will Rival the Mariel Boat Lift of 1980," *Orlando Sentinel Tribune*, January 11, 1993.

10. Larry Rohter, "Liberal Wing of Haiti's Catholic Church Resists Military," *New York Times*, July 24, 1994.

11. "U.S. Aide to Seek New Policy on Fleeing Haitians," ibid., December 15, 1993.

12. Steven A. Holmes, "Pressure Builds Over Return of Boat People to Haiti," ibid., December 17, 1993.

13. Gwen Ifill, "President Names Black Democrat as Haitian Envoy," ibid., May 8, 1994.

14. Steven Greenhouse, "Aristide Condemns Clinton's Haiti Policy as Racist," ibid., April 22, 1994.

15. Quoted in Catherine S. Manegold, "Jean-Bertrand Aristide," *The New York Times Magazine*, May, 1994, 40.

16. For details on Clinton's relationship with Congress regarding authorization of U.S. troops in Haiti, see Louis Fisher, *Presidential War Power* (Lawrence: University Press of Kansas, 1995), pp. 154–57.

17. Thomas Friedman, "Clinton's Foreign Policy: Top Advisor Speaks Up," *New York Times*, October 31, 1993.

18. Gary Pierre-Pierre, "Terror of Duvalier Years is Haunting Haiti Again," ibid., October 18, 1993.

19. See Douglas Farah, "Duvalierists Prominent in Haiti Struggle," *The Washington Post*, October 24, 1993; and Larry Rohter, "Haiti's Attachés: Deadly Heirs to the Tonton Macoutes," *New York Times*, October 4, 1994.

20. Strong criticism of the School of the Americas had been voiced in Congress since 1993. Representative Joseph P. Kennedy II (D, Mass.), one of its strongest

opponents, called the school a Cold War relic that either should shut down or change its mission. See Eric Schmitt, "School for Assassins, or Aid to Latin Democracy?" *New York Times*, April 3, 1995.

21. Many in the Bush administration actually had pulled for the election of Marc Bazin, a former World Bank economist, who came in second. They felt Bazin would have been much easier to work with than Aristide. The Haitian masses obviously thought otherwise.

22. Amy Wilentz, "Deep Voodoo," *The New Republic*, 9 March, 1992, 20. Wilentz is the author of *The Rainy Season: Haiti Since Duvalier* (New York: Simon & Schuster, 1989).

23. Jean-Bertrand Aristide, "A Letter to my Brothers and Sisters," *In the Parish of the Poor* (Maryknoll, N.Y.: Orbis, 1993), pp. 33–34.

24. "Walking in the Light of Christ," ibid., p. 75.

25. See Anthony P. Maingot, "Haiti and Aristide: The Legacy of History," *Current History*, 91 (February 1992): 66.

26. Alan Cowell, "Aristide Has Long Posed Problem for Vatican," *New York Times*, October 29, 1993.

27. For an analysis of the historical role of the Catholic Church in Haiti, see Anne Greene, *The Catholic Church in Haiti: Political and Social Change* (East Lansing: Michigan State University Press, 1993).

28. See Maureen Fiedler and Rev. William R. Callahan, "Church Complicity," *The Boston Globe*, December 19, 1993. Fiedler and Callahan are co-coordinators of Catholics Speak Out in Washington.

29. See Rick Bragg, "Haiti's Light-Skinned Elite: The Tiny Minority behind Aristide's Ouster," *New York Times*, August 28, 1994.

30. See Stephen Engelberg, Howard French, and Tim Weiner, "CIA Formed Haitian Unit, Later Tied To Narcotics Trade," ibid., November 14, 1993.

31. "U.S. Rejects Report on Aristide," ibid., October 31, 1993.

32. See John Kifner, "Haitians Ask If U.S. Had Tie to Attachés," ibid., October 6, 1994. In an interview with "60 Minutes" on December 3, 1995, Constant claimed he was a paid informer for the CIA, starting shortly after the coup that overthrew Aristide. According to Constant, the CIA station chief in Haiti, with whom he met regularly, gave him a code name "Gamal," a sophisticated walkie-talkie, and $700 a month in cash. See Tim Weiner, "Haitian Ex-Paramilitary Leader Confirms CIA Relationship," ibid., December 3, 1995.

33. Pamela Constable, "Haiti: A Nation in Despair, a Policy Adrift," *Current History*, 93 (March 1994): 111.

34. Lally Weymouth, "Haiti vs. Aristide," *The Washington Post*, December 18, 1992.

35. See *Human Rights in Haiti: A Study of (Lives in the) Balance*, Haiti Communications Project, Cambridge, Mass., 1992.

36. See Jack Anderson and Michael Binstein, "FBI Probe May Involve Aristide," *The Washington Post*, December 17, 1992

37. An options paper on Haiti was prepared for Clinton by former Representative Steven Solarz, who visited Haiti in late 1992. He presented it to Clinton in December.

38. John M. Goshko, "Clinton Urged to Signal Strong Intentions on Haiti," *The Washington Post*, December 20, 1992.

39. U.S. policy generally followed the internationally accepted position that voluntary repatriation is most desirable for asylum seekers, that acceptance into the "country of first asylum" is the second best option, and that resettlement in a third country is the last satisfactory solution.

40. Thomas Carothers, "The Making of a Fiasco," *New York Times*, May 12, 1994. For another strong argument against U.S. military intervention in Haiti and other world trouble spots, see David Fromkin, "Don't Send in the Marines," *New York Times Magazine*, 27 February, 1994, 36–37.

41. William Safire, "For a Haitian Legion," *New York Times*, May 9, 1994.

42. John Kerry, "Make Haiti's Thugs Tremble," ibid., May 16, 1994.

43. Elizabeth Drew, *On the Edge: The Clinton Presidency* (New York: Simon & Schuster, 1994), pp. 333–34.

44. Douglas Jehl, "Paris Opposes Using Force," *New York Times*, May 13, 1994.

45. John Dillin, "Zbigniew Brzezinski Prediction: US Will Intervene in Haiti Mess," *Christian Science Monitor*, May 6, 1994.

46. Eric Schmitt, "U.S. Pessimistic about Avoiding Invasion of Haiti," *New York Times*, September 4, 1994.

47. Arthur Schlesinger, Jr., "In Foreign Policy, Experience Counts Not," *Wall Street Journal*, August 26, 1988.

48. See David Halberstam, *The Best and the Brightest* (New York: Vintage, 1972).

49. See Dick Kirschten, "Haitian Headache," *The National Journal*, March 13, 1993.

50. See John Lichfield, "Bush to Nominate Hard-liner to Control Latin American Policy," *The Independent* (London), February 2, 1989.

51. Ibid.

52. Ibid.

53. Colin Powell, *My American Journey* (New York: Random House, 1995), p. 598.

54. See Elaine Sciolino (with the reporting assistance of John H. Cashman, Jr., Steven Greenhouse, and Douglas Jehl), "On the Brink of War, a Tense Battle of Wills," *New York Times*, September 20, 1994; and John Kiffner, "2 Key Advisors in a Bitter Duel On U.S. Policy," ibid., September 23, 1994.

55. Powell, p. 600.

56. For the complete text of this agreement, see Maureen Taft-Morales, "Haiti: Efforts to Restore President Aristide, 1991–1994," CRS Report for Congress, May 11, 1995, p. 11.

57. Powell, p. 602.

58. See Maureen Taft-Morales, "Haiti After President Aristide's Return: Concerns of the 104th Congress," CRS Issue Brief, June 6, 1995.

59. See John Kifner, " 'Nothing to Build On': Haiti Starting at Zero," *New York Times,* December 4, 1994.

60. For details, see Larry Nowels, "Haiti's Economic Recovery Program and U.S. Aid: A Fact Sheet," CRS Report for Congress, January 9, 1995.

61. See Amy Kaslow, "Haiti's Future Depends on United States Help to Grow the Economy," *Christian Science Monitor,* March 31, 1995. By the end of 1995, when Haiti's privatization program lagged, the United States threatened to cut off economic aid.

62. See Howard French, "Haiti's Ousted Chief Insists Coup Leaders Must Be Punished," *New York Times,* November 16, 1994.

63. See Larry Rohter, "Mystery of the Missing Haitian Bully," ibid., February 14, 1995.

64. See Eric Schmitt, "Haitian Officials May have Plotted to Kill Opponent," ibid., March 30, 1995; and John Kifner, "Haiti Murder Investigation: Avenues with Few Answers," ibid., April 11, 1995.

65. Larry Rohter, "Clinton, in Haiti, Marks the Withdrawal of G.I.s," ibid., April 1, 1995.

66. For a good discussion on the future of the Haitian military, see Kern Delince, "Haiti Needs No Army," ibid., November 8, 1994. Delince is a Haitian who worked as a librarian for twenty years in Brooklyn, New York, and who has written (in French) two books on Haiti's military and one on the country's political system.

67. See Kathie Kiarreich, "For Women in Haiti, a Fresh Start," *Christian Science Monitor,* April 19, 1995.

68. See Claudia Kolker, "Haiti's Universities Face Struggle to Rebuild Their Nation and Themselves," *The Chronicle of Higher Education,* November 9, 1994, pp. A40–42.

69. Rick Bragg, "Haiti's Light-Skinned Elite: The Tiny Minority Behind Aristide's Ouster," *New York Times,* August 28, 1994.

70. Julia Preston, "Age of Aristide: Haiti Calmed After a Year," ibid., September 20, 1995.

71. See Mireya Navarro, "Many Haitian Children View Camps' Limbo as Permanent," ibid., May 1, 1995.

72. Larry Rohter, "Tensions Build Again in Haiti," ibid., November 30, 1995; and Paul J. Smith, "Why Haitians Are Fleeing Their Homeland," *Christian Science Monitor,* February 16, 1996.

Selected Bibliography

Aristide, Jean-Bertrand. *In the Parish of the Poor.* Maryknoll, N.Y.: Orbis, 1993.

Best, Richard A., Jr. "The U.S. Occupation of Haiti, 1915–1934." A Congressional Research Service Report for Congress, May 26, 1994.

Ferguson, James. *Papa Doc, Baby Doc: Haiti and the Duvaliers*. Cambridge, Mass.: Basil Blackwell, 1987.

Greene, Anne. *The Catholic Church in Haiti: Political and Social Change*. East Lansing: Michigan State University Press, 1993.

Haiti Communications Project. *Human Rights in Haiti: A Study of (Lives in the) Balance*. Cambridge, Mass.: Haiti Communications Project, 1992.

North American Congress on Latin America (eds.). *Haiti*. Boston: South End Press, 1995.

Nowels, Larry. "Haiti's Economic Recovery Program and U.S. Aid: A Fact Sheet." A Congressional Research Report for Congress, January 9, 1995.

Stepick, Alex. "Unintended Consequences: Rejecting Haitian Boat People and Destabilizing Duvalier." In Christopher Mitchell (ed.) *Western Hemisphere Immigration and U.S. Foreign Policy*. University Park: Pennsylvania State University Press, 1992.

Taft-Morales, Maureen. "Haiti: Efforts to Restore Aristide, 1991–1994." A Congressional Research Service Report for Congress, May 11, 1995.

———. "Haiti after President Aristide's Return: Concerns of the 104th Congress." A Congressional Research Service Brief, June 6, 1995.

Amy Wilentz. *The Rainy Season since Duvalier*. New York: Simon & Schuster, 1989.

Appendix A

Case Study Structure for Analyzing Controversial Presidential Foreign Policy Decisions

As discussed in the Introduction, we have developed a framework for presenting the case studies of controversial presidential foreign policy decisions. We show below two outline versions for our approach. The first may be adapted for a comprehensive study of controversial decisions. This version could be used by instructors in developing their own cases or by more advanced undergraduate and graduate students. The second version is a shorter approach that may be adapted for undergraduates writing term papers on a case.

Comprehensive Outline for Class Studies

I. Introduction
   Setting and Synopsis of Decision
   The President's Decision
   Controversial Aspects of Decision

II. Decision Background
   Historical Background
   Countdown to Decision

III. The President as Decision-Maker
   Foreign Policy Context, including foreign policy principles, world view, national security strategy, relations with allies.
   Domestic Context of Decision
   Options Considered and Rejected

Justification for Decision
President's Leadership Role in Decision

IV. Outcome of Decision
Short-term and Long-term Consequences for United States
Short-term and Long-term Consequences for Other Countries
Involved

V. Conclusion

Shorter Outline for Case Studies

I. Setting and Synopsis of Decision

II. The President's Decision

III. Historical Background to Decision (including Countdown to Decision)

IV. The President as Decision-Maker
Options Considered and Rejected
Goals of Decision and Justification
President's Leadership Role in Decision

V. Outcome of Decision for the United States

VI. Conclusion

Appendix B

Suggested Topics for Additional Controversial Presidential Foreign Policy Decisions

President Truman
Dropping Atomic Bombs on Hiroshima and Nagasaki
Launching the Berlin Airlift
Removing General Douglas MacArthur during the Korean War
Recognition of the State of Israel
Developing the Hydrogen Bomb

President Eisenhower
Removing President Arbenz from Power in Guatemala
Removing Premier Mossadegh from Power in Iran
Refusing to Intervene Militarily to Aid France at the Battle of Dien Bien
Phu in Indo-China
Initiating the Doctrine of "Massive Retaliation"
Supporting Military Intervention in Lebanon

President Kennedy
Acquiescing to the Building of the Berlin Wall
Instituting a Quarantine during Cuban Missile Crisis
Sending U.S. Military Advisers to Vietnam
Supporting the Neutralization of Laos
Signing the Limited Nuclear Test Ban Treaty with the Soviet Union

President Johnson
Supporting Military Intervention in the Dominican Republic
Asking Congress to Approve the Gulf of Tonkin Resolution
Approving the Bombing of North Vietnam

President Nixon
Visiting the People's Republic of China

Signing the Anti-Ballistic Missile Treaty with the USSR
Putting U.S. Forces on Worldwide Alert during the Yom Kippur War in the Middle East
Supporting Pakistan in the India-Pakistan War
Overthrowing Allende in Chile

President Ford
Freeing American Troops Captured during the Mayaguez Incident
Signing the Helsinki Accords
Signing the Trade Bill that Included the Jackson-Vanik Amendment

President Carter
Approving Diplomatic Recognition of People's Republic of China
Granting Most-Favored-Nation Status to People's Republic of China
Accepting the Deposed Shah of Iran into the United States
Negotiating the Camp David Accords with Egypt and Israel
Signing the Panama Canal Treaties
Advocating the Neutron Bomb

President Reagan
Supporting the Invasion of Grenada
Approving the Dispatch of AWACS Planes to Saudi Arabia
Supporting the Contras in Nicaragua
Supporting the Strategic Defense Initiative
Undertaking Constructive Engagement with South Africa

President Bush
Supporting the Invasion of Panama
Renewing Most-Favored-Nation Status to People's Republic of China After Tiananmen Square Massacre
Ordering Summary Return of Haitian Boat People
Restricting Loan Guarantees for Israel
Opposing Independence for Ukraine

President Clinton
Renewing Most-Favored-Nation Status for People's Republic of China
Sending U.S. Troops to Somalia
Lifting Trade Embargo against Vietnam
Supporting the North American Free Trade Agreement
Providing Loan Guarantees for Mexico
Sending U.S. Troops to Implement the Dayton Peace Agreement on Bosnia

Appendix C

Student Evaluation of Controversial Presidential Foreign Policy Decisions

Introduction

As discussed in the Introduction, students should find it useful to conduct in-depth evaluations of the ten case studies of controversial foreign policy decisions made by presidents. We offer below a two-part evaluation procedure that can be used for class discussion of the cases. We encourage you to copy the evaluation procedure and apply it to our cases and others involving controversial presidential foreign policy decisions.

STUDENT ANALYSIS OF CASE STUDY

Each case in chapters 1 to 10 of this book represents a controversial presidential decision in U.S. foreign policy. Experts disagree over the degree of controversy, the success of the president in achieving goals, the short-term and long-term consequences, and the effectiveness of presidential leadership.

We are asking you to evaluate and explain each of the decisions and then to answer several free response questions. When possible, give specific examples to support your evaluation. You may utilize other readings (assigned or unassigned) as needed or desired.

Part One deals with your ratings of agreement or disagreement in response to five statements concerning the president's decision. Part Two includes your responses to three additional questions about the president's decision.

Part One
Evaluation Issues

Name of Case _____

Your Name _____

Please evaluate each of the five statements regarding the president's decision by circling one of the five choices and then providing your reasons.

Statement One: The president's decision was controversial in terms of domestic politics. Consider, for example, the role of public opinion, the media, interest groups, and Congress.

Evaluation Score:

Strongly Agree	Somewhat Agree	Somewhat Disagree	Strongly Disagree	Unsure
1	2	3	4	5

Reasons:

Statement Two: The president's decision was controversial within the circle of presidential advisers.

Evaluation Score:

Strongly Agree	Somewhat Agree	Somewhat Disagree	Strongly Disagree	Unsure
1	2	3	4	5

Reasons:

Statement Three: The president was successful in achieving the major goals of his decision. In your explanation, identify what you consider to be the president's two most important goals.

Evaluation Score:

Strongly Agree	Somewhat Agree	Somewhat Disagree	Strongly Disagree	Unsure
1	2	3	4	5

Goal 1: _____

Reasons:

Goal 2: _____

Reasons:

Statement Four: The president exercised effective leadership in the decision. In your explanation, evaluate the president's leadership style, including flexibility, compassion, desire to please, decisiveness, ability to make hard choices, open-mindedness, experience, and pragmatism.

Evaluation Score:

Strongly Agree	Somewhat Agree	Somewhat Disagree	Strongly Disagree	Unsure
1	2	3	4	5

Reasons:

Statement Five: History will judge the decision favorably. In your explanation, consider, for example, the impact of the decision on U.S. foreign policy, how it affected the president's performance in office, and the consequences of the decision on other presidents facing similar problems or controversies.

Evaluation Score:

Strongly Agree	Somewhat Agree	Somewhat Disagree	Strongly Disagree	Unsure
1	2	3	4	5

Reasons:

PART TWO
FREE RESPONSE QUESTIONS

Name of Case _____

Your Name _____

1. What decision would you have made in response to the controversial foreign policy problem? Consider that you were aware of the same issues as the president who had to deal with them. If you would have made the same decision, state your reasons. If you would have made a different decision, state it briefly and give your reasons.

2. What lessons do you believe the president learned or should have learned from his decision?

3. What lessons did you learn from the president's decision, including the decision-making process if applicable?

Index